October 1999, New Trier News
Age 17

A BOND LIKE NONE OTHER: SPORTS

My relationship with my grandfather is a good one. We get along very well, and love talking. However, if we're not talking about sports, we're disagreeing about something else. If someone said the word "funny," I would answer "Jerry Seinfeld" while my granddad would say "Jack Benny." If someone said music, he would say "Frank Sinatra," while I said "The Beatles."

While I looked at these disagreements, I noticed that there is one thing that seems to tie the generations together: sports.

There are always generational arguments about whose movies are more entertaining, or whose music sounds better. My grandfather likes his music, and I like mine, and you will never see him in Blockbuster saying, "Hmmm, Dave Matthews Band. This looks good; maybe I'll buy it."

However, you will definitely see him watch athletes of our generation, like Griffey Jr., or Favre, or Tiger, and say, "Wow, those guys are good."

Someone growing up in the 1930's may think that Lefty Grove was the greatest pitcher of all time, and someone growing up in the 1960's may think that Sandy Koufax was the greatest pitcher of all time, and someone growing up in the 1990's may think that Roger Clemens in the greatest pitcher of all time.

Even with those different opinions, you could sit those three men down at any ballpark in any year, and they'd watch the game and have a great time. If you put them together in a movie theater during any year, two of them would probably hate it while the other thought that it was great. This goes for any sport.

Different-aged football fans can all get together and watch football, and they'll all be happy. Sports, though always changing, can bring together generations like no other activity.

This is not to say that only professional sports do this. College sports do it as well.

But even more than college sports is the force that high school sports has. Almost anyone, no matter where he grew up, will remember watching some sort of high school sports team. Both my dad and I went to high school football games, and both of us experienced the feeling of rooting for kids that we know, who represent a school that you attend. No matter how much the games change, the camaraderie of other fans and the excitement of beating a rival school will always be constant.

My dad played tennis for Mather High in Chicago, and even though he has no connection to the school today, he always likes to look in the paper and see how their tennis team is doing. It has also made him more interested in high school tennis in Illinois. He'll read the paper on a Sunday before I get up, and tell me how New Trier did on Saturday.

I go to the school, and I don't even follow the sports as closely as he does. He, like all other former high school athletes, can relate to what high school athletes experience. Even as the game changes, former athletes can still see what their children's teams are doing, and they can compare that to what they were doing, and vice-versa.

High schoolers now can talk to their parents, and realize that the relationship that they have with high school sports is closely related to the one that their parents had.

Generations come, and generations go, and so does music, movies, books, and clothes. All of those change, and all of those help separate us from our parents, and our parents from their parents. However, as much as sports change, it stays the same. Sports can always tie together the class of '69 with the class of '99.

Sports can make a bad grandson-granddad conversation good. Sports can be viewed by present day high schoolers as a fun Friday night, and by former high schoolers as the fun they used to have.

So go to a ballgame with your dad, and relish in the fact that, from Namath to Elway, Mantle to McGwire, sports keep the generation gap close — but not too close. After all, the differences make for good discussions.

WHY WE ROOT

(VOL. 1)

MAD OBSESSIONS OF A CHICAGO SPORTS FAN

JACK M SILVERSTEIN

Keylog Media LLC
Chicago

Why We Root (Vol. 1): Mad Obsessions of a Chicago Sports Fan

Published in the United States by Keylog Media, LLC, Chicago.

Copyright © 2024 by Jack M Silverstein

All rights reserved. Neither this book, nor any parts within it may be sold or reproduced in any form or by any electronic or mechanical means, including information storage and retrieval systems, without permission in writing from the author. The only exception is by a reviewer, who may quote short excerpts in a review.

Cover photo and design copyright © by Benjamin Schwartz.

Library of Congress Control Number: 2023936422

ISBN (paperback): 9781662939419
eISBN: 9781662939426

For Rose. Forever.

"Sports are like the reward of a functioning society."

— Washington Nationals pitcher Sean Doolittle, July 2020

CONTENTS

Introducing, A Fan   1

Part I: Sunday Rivals

   Barry Sanders once beat the Bears so badly
on Thanksgiving, I felt nothing but awe   13
   With apologies to Tony   15
   On the eve of the 2010 NFC championship game   19
   The 2012 Bears need a rescue   21
   Lovie's Bears reach the end of the road   22
   We need to talk about the Lions   24
   How I grew to hate, then pity, the Vikings   27
   Let's beat the Pack and clinch this damn division   32
   Tyji Armstrong, a mother's love, and
the meaning of sports   35

Part II: The Real First Championship

   Learning the Hard Way:
Overcoming the Bad Boy Pistons   43

Part III: Tall Tales

   First and Ten Northwestern!
The tale of the 1995 Rose Bowl Wildcats   51
   Michael Jordan's Flu Game, 20 years later   62
   Illinois's Arizona comeback to reach the Final Four   68
   Devin Hester's magical rookie year   75
   The Joakim Noah Celtics steal   80
   On Kerry Wood's retirement and the promise of 20 Ks   85
   The Nate Robinson Game   86
   The night the Blackhawks won the Cup but I got mugged   88
   Bobby Douglass and Justin Fields: Running men   92
   Burn on, big river, burn on   99

Part IV: The Old Ballgame

From the '93 Sox to the '98 Cubs: A sports conversion	107
My parents, Ron Santo, and my one true glove	111
A punch and a lunch: Barrett, Pierzynski and Herm's	122
The 2008 Cubs are on the ropes	127
All hail the Chicago Blue Sox!	130
A Cub to the last: a salute to Ron Santo	133
People will come, Jack. People will most definitely come.	135

Part V: The Bulls Are Back

The Bulls are back! A trip to the United Center	144
The Other Side: Gilbert Arenas Kills the Bulls	155
To the 2005 Chicago Bulls: A Thank You Note	160
Goodbye to the Memory Maker	165

Part VI: There's a timeout! (Where?) On the field

Goodbye dear friend: a love letter to Soldier Field	171
Bears-Eagles: The final game at Old Soldier Field	175
The Bryan Robinson Game: Our salute to Walter Payton	178
She's seen a century: Reflections on Bears football on Virginia McCaskey's 100th birthday	184

Part VII: Curse?

My Cubs column the morning of the Bartman Game	193

Part VIII: Heartbreak

The Bartman story, in three horrible parts	197
The Bears lose Super Bowl XLI	208
The 2008 Cubs get swept out of the playoffs	211
The Bears lose the 2010 NFC championship game	215
An ode to the 2011 ChicagoNow softball team	220
Down goes Derrick!	223
The premature pain of the double doink	224

Part IX: Lost in the Wilderness

They shoot baseball teams, don't they?	231

Part X: Two Saviors

A salute to rookie Derrick Rose	243
The Cutler trade	245
Passing is fun!	249
The Dragic dunk	252
Final thoughts on a team with a shot	254
The Bulls' living nightmare	256
For 1. (Derrick Rose suffers another knee injury)	257
D-Rose beats the Cavs	259
The Jimmy Clausen Game	263
Untitled (Bulls trade Derrick Rose)	267
6 questions about #6	269

Part XI: One Savior

The tale of Scottie Pippen and the 1994 Bulls	275

Part XII: So I Creep

Sports and the good life in sunny California	287

Part XIII: The Blackhawks Are Back

Thoughts and memories on a sport with no teeth	295
Life's a beach when your team is up	298
Corey Crawford watches Brent Seabrook end the Red Wings	301
Why we need the Blackhawks dogs	302

Part XIV: For A Winner

Give my best to Steve Goodman	307

Part XV: With New Eyes

One year later: a look back at Super Bowl XLI	313
One year later: a look back at the 2005 White Sox	318
How LeBron made me feel The MJ Pain	321
Final thoughts on fan interference and the 2003 Cubs	324
My most painful Bears memory – Super Bowl XLI	331
Bulls fans need new nostalgia	336
The Walkoff: a love story	340

Part XVI: The Fan Favorite
    Thomas Jones: pain, power, pride   365

Part XVII: Climbing the Mountain
    Take that Brett! Breaking the Favre curse   379
    The White Sox to the World Series!   391
    Robbie Gould beats the Seahawks   400
    The Cubs to the World Series!   403
    Untitled (a public plea on the eve of Game 6 of the 2016 World Series)   412

Part XVIII: The Battery
    "It's like a frickin' unsolved mystery." Mark Prior and Paul Bako reflect on the Bartman inning, 10 years later   419

Part XIX: Victory!
    Michael Jordan's last shot   435
    The White Sox win the World Series   440
    The Bears beat the Saints in the NFC championship   445
    Why we root.   452
    My favorite team of 2013: The ChicagoNow Dirt Angels   457
    We are the champions. The Cubs are the champions.   461

Her First Championship   **469**

About This Book   **475**

About the Author   **477**

Dedications   **479**

Acknowledgements   **481**

INTRODUCING, A FAN

INTRODUCING, A FAN

"Who do we like?" the boy asked his father.

"The guys in the dark shirts," the father answered.

"Oh. Who are they?"

"The Bears."

"Who's that guy?"

"That's Walter Payton."

"Who are those other guys?"

"The Lions."

"What's… who was it?"

"Walter Payton."

"Why did he stop running?"

"Because he scored a touchdown."

"Oh…"

"A touchdown is when someone runs with the ball into the endzone."

"Oh…"

"That big rectangle."

"OOOOOOhhhhhhh."

"What else do you want to know?"

Everything, as it turned out. My life's arc is intertwined with my sports fandom. Tell me a year and I'll tell you the game. It starts with family. My parents, my brother, my grandparents. The suspension of decorum to scream during an MJ dunk or curse on a Bears fumble. The way we changed the rules to accommodate these games. Nothing was more important than school. Nothing said "rules" like school. You only missed school when you were sick.

And then one day, you missed school because your father and Papa took you and your brother to a Cubs game.

Or you stayed up past your bedtime because the Bears were on Monday Night Football.

Or Aunt Gail bought you a single headphone cord that laced up my sleeve so that I could covertly listen to Game 1 of the '97 Bulls-Bullets series during my mother's best friend's adult Bat Mitzvah.

"Keep the earpiece in the palm of your hand," Gail explained. "When you're listening, just put your hand on your ear, like you're resting your head. When someone needs to talk to you, cup your hand and then put your hand in your pocket."

Family time wasn't only sports time, but sports time was always family time.

******

When I was coming up, the *Chicago Tribune* sports section was different from the other sections of the paper. Across the top was a thin blue stripe. The morning routine was as simple as it was thrilling. Get the paper. Flip till you see the blue.

In these pages I found the answers. The legends. The numbers. I found my education and my instructors. Sam Smith. Melissa Isaacson. Fred Mitchell. Bob Verdi. Jerome Holzman. In the *Sun-Times*, Lacy Banks, Carol Slezak — and later, my mentor Rick Telander.

We called it "The Sports." Not the sports page. The Sports. "Not now, I'm reading the sports." I read the sports every morning at breakfast. I saved big papers. Folded them. Placed them in a drawer. Championships. Drafts. Injuries. Retirements. Sammy's 300th home run. Gracie's 2000th hit. Phil's 500th win.

In the summer of '95, we moved from Evanston to Wilmette. A new school for the final year of middle school. Off to the unknown. Evanston's chief rival. Enemy territory. I loved to play sports — football, basketball, baseball — but *knowing* sports was my secret weapon. The 8th graders in Mr. Jacobson's home room would quiz me. First the big stuff. News of the day. MJ's career PPG. Walter's career rushing total. Rodman's rebounds the night before. Anything they could confirm in the sports.

Then they pivoted to the minutiae. Assist totals for Utah's backup center. The "others receiving votes" in college football's AP poll. Anything else they could confirm in the sports.

And then, validation.

"I can't believe you know that!"

******

For many children, sports fandom is their entrée into the adult world. School vs. work isn't a shared experience, and toys vs. tools aren't a shared experience. But suddenly, we all have sports. The first conversations I had with adults who were not my family nor my teachers or counselors were at restaurants, talking sports.

Vienna spots were key. My first was Mustard's Last Stand in Evanston, just next to Dyche Stadium. The men behind the grill: Keith and Steve. And always in the back corner at the final stool along the counter was Jerry, the owner, who would sit quietly reading the paper, eating, and discussing the events of the day with any customers who wanted to talk. When I was growing up, the walls featured images of MJ, Dawson, Gracie, Black Jack, Bobby Hull, Minnie Minoso, Scottie, Luis Aparicio, Johnny Lujack, the

1991-92 Blackhawks team photo, Steve Cauthen, Pat Fitzgerald, Bob Christian, Darnell Autry, the Wheaties Box dedicated to the 1995 Northwestern football team, and a plethora of Wildcat sports pictures, male and female. Conversations with Keith were to the point. A hello, and then straight into it.

"So," Keith might say, starting my bacon double-cheese, "Bears getting back to the playoffs this year?"

Keith Woods and I started talking when I was in grade school and continued talking for two decades until his death in 2013. I wasn't alone. Keith had two-decade-long conversations with practically everyone in Evanston and Wilmette. He was the first adult who took me seriously on my own terms without any responsibility to do so.

Sports radio did too. I was a Scorehead, calling in on overnights, sharing the vast, silent camaraderie of callers waiting on hold. We were out there, all of us, in our homes, in our cars, ready to tell Tommy "T-Dub" "Big Partner" Williams or Les "The Grobber" Grobstein how we felt about the Bears, the Bulls, baseball.

"Big Partner," I would say, "I know it's crazy to say this as Sox fans, but I'm excited that we landed Albert Belle." And you'd make your point, and ideally get a bit of back-and-forth with Tommy, who would eventually wish you a great night and move on to the next caller.

And you'd get to school the next day and get called out in the hallway by friends and classmates, exalting you, cheering, "I heard you on The Score last night!"

******

We had two superheroes, and they balanced well. Michael Jordan was the global icon. Walter Payton was the national hero. They were also both local legends, and everyone living between Gary and

INTRODUCING, A FAN

Milwaukee, between 1975 and 1998, has a story about intersecting with one or the other or both.

My stories were with MJ. I was eye-to-eye with the man twice. The first was early in the '90-'91 season outside of Chicago Stadium when my brother won a contest to shoot hoops at halftime of a Bulls game. My mother and I bumped into him pregame, outside of a VIP entrance where we were going to the parking lot to get Bulls cards for players to sign, and he was coming into the game. Despite a light but steady rain, MJ and I each stopped when we saw the other person. I looked up. He looked down.

I said, "You're Michael Jordan."

He said, "I am."

I then asked him to "Stay right here, I have some cards for you to sign," and ran toward the car, without keys, only stopping when my mother howled my name. I turned around. MJ was standing next to her, both looking at me in the rain. Jordan hadn't moved.

"Get back here," she said. "That's not how this works." I walked back while she took a pen and piece of scrap paper out of her purse, handed it to him and said "Thank you very much." He signed, and I said "Thank you!" and then, "You're going to win the championship this year."

"I think so!" he cheered. In agreement, we carried on our separate ways.

******

23 was the fantasy. 34 was the soul. We wanted to Be Like Mike, but we wanted to Run With Walter. Stride for stride with him. Air and Sweetness set the template for my childhood. Fandom would be fun!

And for a while, it was.

From my family's arrival in Evanston in 1984 until my high school graduation in 2000, the '85 Bears and the Bulls dynasty were the dual suns of our Chicago sports solar system. Our evolving rotation of moons included five baseball playoff teams, the Hawks in the '92 Cup and, for me and my friends, Northwestern's Rose Bowl.

The year we arrived, Walter ran the city, Ryno was NL MVP and the Bulls drafted Jordan. We had the Super Bowl Shufflin' Bears with Samurai, Dent, Danimal, Mongo, McMahon, Fencik, Otis, Wilber, the Fridge, Double D, Speedy Willie and an offensive line so beloved that they had their own poster, backups included.

On the Northside, 1989 brought another NL MVP with Andre Dawson, the NL Rookie of the Year Jerome Walton, and a pair of Cubs NL Cy Young winners past — Rick Sutcliffe '84 — and future: Greg Maddux, '92.

On the Southside, 1993 saw Frank Thomas win the first Sox MVP since Dick Allen, Jack McDowell the first Sox Cy since LaMarr Hoyt, and the club's second postseason since the '59 World Series. We had the Big Hurt, Black Jack, Rockin' Robin, Ozzie, Rock Raines, One Dog, Joey Cora, Alex Fernandez, Roberto Hernandez, Ellis Burks, and the man himself, Bo Jackson.

At the Old Barn, the Hawks of Belfour, Roenick, Chelios, Larmer and others reached the Stanley Cup Finals for the first time since 1973, while the Bulls became the city's first back-to-back champ since the '40/'41 Bears, and the first champ to clinch a title in Chicago since my father's beloved '63 Bears.

Scottie Pippen became a defensive juggernaut and all-around ace. Frank Thomas became arguably the greatest Chicago baseball player ever. Dennis Rodman became a cultural icon. Kerry Wood struck out 20 Astros. The Bulls won their 6th championship on MJ's "last shot" on June 14, 1998, and on the very next day, Sammy Sosa drilled three home runs in a 6-5 Cubs win over Milwaukee, part of Sosa's record-breaking June (20 home runs) and NL MVP season: 66 home runs, 158 RBI, .308 average, the best player on the first Cubs playoff team since 1989.

Sammy went on to delight Cubs fans and the baseball-loving world through his monster 2001 (.328, 64 HR, 160 RBI), ultimately giving way to the pitching-fueled 2003 Cubs of Woody and Prior.

Yes, while Chicago sports fans hold a legacy of trauma, the truth is that I grew up in the absolute perfect time to become a diehard Chicago fan. Even in our darkest hour – MJ retired! – we found light in the tunnel — "I'm back."

Yet there is another truth: Michael and Scottie papered over a lot of pain. The 21st century brought 20th century droughts. Thirty-nine years without a championship for the Hawks. Eighty-three years for the Sox. Ninety-two for the Cubs. Hell, even 15 years for the Bears, nipping at the heels of the franchise's then-longest streak without a championship. We entered the new century needing to resolve all of that.

That hunt — that is what this book is about. In this collection of columns and essays from 2003 to 2023, you'll see my quest to stop the bleeding. Lovie's Bears. The new Baby Bulls. How in 2003, I believed with all my sports-loving heart that we would at last slay the longest dragon. I didn't blink when we lost Game 5. I didn't break stride when a fan's hands broke our hearts. I entered Game 7 of the 2003 NLCS primed for a celebration. I walked out hollow.

In the parking lot I remember a guy in a Cubs jersey crying while his girlfriend consoled him. He didn't look up and I didn't slow down. My phone rang. It was my mom. She tried to give me solace. It was a nice gesture. Then my dad got on, and he listened patiently as I went on and on about how much it sucked and how I really thought we were going to win.

I stopped, and waited for him to respond, waited for him to comfort me in some way. He chuckled a bit, and I could sense his smirk on the other end.

"Just wait till it gets *bad*."

PART I:
SUNDAY RIVALS

Nov. 22, 2018, Windy City Gridiron
   Age 37

BARRY SANDERS ONCE BEAT THE BEARS SO BADLY ON THANKSGIVING, I FELT NOTHING BUT AWE

I wake in the night with cold sweats, whimpering, wondering, waiting for the fear to subside:

Could Barry Sanders somehow come back?

Stop it, I tell myself. That is silly. Barry Sanders is 50 years old. He has now been retired for twice as many years as he played for the Lions. Go back to sleep, sir. Number 20 roams no more.

Thank goodness.

Yes, today is Thanksgiving and the Bears are going to Detroit to play the Lions for the latest chapter in this storied history. Our first Thanksgiving game was in 1934. Our most recent, 2014. But the height of the turkey day rivalry came in the 1990s, when we linked up for four games between 1991 and 1999, losing three of four, including 1997.

Oh, 1997.

You might remember that day, Bears fans.

You definitely remember that day, Lions fans.

That was the day we were the turkey and Barry David Sanders was everything else. Cooked us. Carved us. Ate us. And bounced. Chef, host and house guest all at once.

The date was Nov. 27, 1997, and we were struggling. Mightily. We were 2-10, which was a nice upswing after starting 0-7. The Lions, meanwhile, were 6-6 and in the midst of one of those will-they-or-won't-they Wayne Fontes playoff years, an annual tradition at the Silverdome in the 90s.

Our Thanksgiving battle started well enough: we led 17-3 in the 2nd quarter behind some rockstar passing and catching from Erik Kramer and Ricky Proehl. Barry had two yards on five carries.

And then, disaster.

Sanders ripped off a 15-yard run and caught a 12-yard pass to launch Detroit's first touchdown drive. We hit a field goal to go up 20-10 — our final points of the game. Sanders closed the 1st half with a 40-yard touchdown run to pull the Lions to 20-17, and opened the 2nd half with four straight runs for 27 yards, leading to a Jason Hanson field goal to tie the game at 20.

Detroit took the lead on Scott Mitchell's 2nd TD pass of the game, and after the Lions forced and recovered a Kramer fumble, Sanders bagged runs of 25, 20, 19 and 15 yards, with the 25-yard and 15-yard runs going for touchdowns.

The Lions scored twice more on non-Barry plays and went home that day with a 55-20 win.

I was stunned.

And battered.

And frankly, in awe.

There is more to rivalry than bitter hatred. As much as I can't stand Lions fans right now, with their brash silliness and unearned swagger, I will never ever ever not like Barry Sanders. This man used to basically show up in my living room twice a year, beat my ass, and have me thanking him for the pleasure.

PART I: SUNDAY RIVALS

As a sports fan, I take my greatness where I can get it. Yes, it's preferred when it comes from my teams, but I know that on a long enough timeline that just ain't always possible. Now and again, I accept that any uplift in my sports viewing experience will be delivered by my opponent, so long as I can harness my ability to accept the beating as part of a sports fan's life.

When the giver of that beating is someone I can't stand, or the circumstances of the beating disrupt my team's consequential positivity — I'm looking at you, Bears-Packers Week 1 — I can't enjoy those, and in fact feel worse *because* I can't enjoy them. Like, objectively, I know what Aaron Rodgers did to us in Week 1 was nothing short of magic. But the pain outweighed everything else.

Barry Sanders, on the other hand, was always a joy to watch even when he was making my team look like children. Part of that is because the Lions are inherently not a threat (which makes their #WeOwnTheBears nonsense so aggravating) (like, y'all, you went 0-16 once. Sit down). But part of it is that Barry was just pure magic on the field and pure class off it that you couldn't help but smile even when he filleted you.

We were going nowhere in 1997. On Thanksgiving that year, Barry Sanders was going anywhere but. He's not coming back to haunt me. I wouldn't be angry if he did.

Oct. 6, 2009, ReadJack.com
    Age 27

WITH APOLOGIES TO TONY

Brett Favre is kinda like a father who left Mom and got a new girlfriend, only to leave her and come back to screw Mom's sister.

—Tony the Packers Fan, August 18, 2009

******

When I arrived at the bar, a tall, big-shouldered, dark-goateed man was standing outside in a green Aaron Rodgers jersey. It was Tony the Packers Fan: he was smoking a cigarette and taking a phone call.

…but really he was taking one more moment to compose himself before starting his bartending shift. Because just a few moments earlier, his Green Bay Packers had received the opening kickoff from the neighboring Minnesota Vikings. And while Aaron Rodgers was playing ball in *his* Aaron Rodgers jersey, a man in a fresh, purple FAVRE 4 was standing on the Minnesota sideline. It was Brett Favre, the Greatest Packer of Them All. And very soon, the man who Lambeau Leaped his way into the hearts of old Wisconsin would be using his mighty right arm to oppose Tony, Tony's Packers, and Packers fans everywhere in the cheese-eatin' world.

When Favre signed with the Vikes, I knew Tony was in trouble. We hardly spoke at season's start — highly unusual during Bears-Packers week — though I now realize that he and many other Pack fans were looking only to one game: Week 4, Green Bay at Minnesota, the day Number 4 would face the green and gold.

He emailed me at the start of this week:

> *gonna be really hard to root against him. no offense to the rivalry, but this game feels bigger than any recent bears packers game. who do you want to win?*

I shuddered when I saw that question. It didn't feel like a challenge, or basic curiosity, or even a simple sports conversation starter. Instead, it felt like an emotionally battered child questioning his divorced father in an effort to provide himself with reassurance that all is not lost in the world:

"Do you still love us? Do you still love Mom? Who do you want to win?"

PART I: SUNDAY RIVALS

I went inside and greeted our friends Ben and Ben.

"He's a wreck," I said, motioning to Tony, who was now behind the bar.

"Hasn't said much since we've been here," said Ben.

"Hasn't said much all week," Ben said.

Rodgers led the Pack to the Minnesota 24 after the opening kick, but the Vikings killed him for a sack and lost fumble to end the drive. The bar was a confused mix of Vikings fans, Packers fans, Favre supporters, Favre bashers, and curious onlookers, and the game's first big play provoked a roar from some and a groan from others.

Meanwhile, Tony was twisting off tops to a few Miller Lites. He did not appear to see the Rodgers fumble.

Nor did he make much noise a few minutes later when Favre went play action to his right from the one-yard line, faded back to the right hash at the ten, and then fired a ball all the way across the field to Visanthe Shiancoe in the left corner of the endzone.

And nary a peep was heard from our man Tony when, on the ensuing drive, Rodgers made a Luckman-esque jump-pass to rookie receiver Jermichael Finley, who eluded one defender and dragged another into the rectangle for the game-tying score.

In fact, Tony did not make a single game-based reaction until early in the second quarter on a fourth-and-three, when a Rodgers pass to Donald Driver was batted into the air and plucked safe by a diving Greg Jennings for the first down. A quick "woo!" and a slap of the bar was all we got. Then he was back to work.

At our table, we were pulling for the Vikings. It was simple enough: if the Packers won, the Bears would be locked into a three-way tie for first place. If the Vikings won, we would be a game up on Green Bay, and the Vikes would be talk of the town: undefeated at 4-0 and stuffed full of the cheer that accompanies a MNF win against a division rival in a showcase game of Great Significance.

And since we all figure the Vikings will fade in late November anyhow, better to have them burn out following a 4-0 start punched full of 'We won Favre v. Packers I' enthusiasm. To quote Tuco Benedicto Pacifico Juan Maria Ramirez: "I like 4-0 football teams like you. When they fall, they make more noise."

So we were go-go Vikings all the way around. Except there was poor Tony, tending bar with a burned out I'll-get-through-this look in his eyes.

"I know we said Minnesota, since it's better for the Bears," Ben said, "but I might switch. I'm feeling kind of bad for him."

"What?? Bad?! This is football!" said Ben. "Don't feel bad for him!"

Tony's quiet courage continued as the Vikings built a 30-to-14 lead behind a crippling pass rush and a wonderfully Favrian performance: 24-31, 271 yards, 3 TD, no picks, and a 135.3 rating, the 13th time in his career that he has posted a passer rating of at least 135. (In that span, incidentally, Bears quarterbacks have accomplished that feat three times.)

Each time Favre hit a receiver with a score, pumped his fist in a throwing motion out of excitement, leapt to chest bump a teammate in celebration, charged to make a block on a reverse, or ran on or off the field, Ben said: "Great. He only has so many of those left in that arm. Each one he uses up is one more he doesn't have against us."

And when the final horn sounded and the Vikings were the victors, Tony shook our hands one by one as we stepped out into the night, shaking his head and saying, "Next time. Next time."

PART I: SUNDAY RIVALS

Jan. 17, 2011, The Sports Blog Network
Age 29

ONE GAME TO RULE THEM ALL

Then it's war! Then it's war! Gather the forces! Round up the horses! It's war!
— Rufus T. Firefly

******

Steelers-Ravens was Armageddon, and Patriots-Jets was Spy Gate and Foot Gate and power-yaps between Antonio Cromartie and Tom Brady, but the NFC Championship needs no metaphors or pageantry, because it is Bears-Packers, and that is enough.

For the second time in 90 years, the Chicago Bears and Green Bay Packers will meet in the postseason. Last time it was a divisional tiebreaker to determine the other spot in the NFL Championship. (The Bears won 33-14, and captured the 1941 title a week later with a 37-9 win over the Giants.)

This time, it is the NFC Championship Game and a slot in Super Bowl XLV.

The Packers' last NFC title game was January 2008, with hopes dashed in overtime when Brett Favre, coming off a surprise Last Dance season, threw a limp pass to Giants' defender Corey Webster at Lambeau Field, setting up New York's game-winning field goal. Their last Super Bowl appearance was the John Elway helicopter game, their last Super Bowl victory a year earlier.

The Bears, of course, have not been to the playoffs since the 2006 season, when they bested the New Orleans Saints 39-14 at Soldier Field to advance to their first Super Bowl since 1985, which is, still, their last championship.

There's a lot riding on this game for each team, but nothing as great as the ultimate notch in smack-talk rights. Perhaps we fans hold those notches a bit more dear…

…but so what? Let the players focus on schemes and film and What We've Got To Handle This Week, Men, To Get To Where We're Trying To Go. Bears-Packers is for the fans, (and the players who know better), and next Sunday's game will be, regardless of outcome, among the greatest sports fan experiences of my career.

It's a game we've imagined our entire lives. Every season the Bears were NFC contenders, we Bears fans thought: "You know what would be great? If the Packers could pick their game up, get playoff-ready, and ride with us to the NFC Championship." I'd imagine that, when the Packers were ritualistically cremating us from 1994 to 1998, Pack fans thought the same.

"Yo Ric, Luke," I might say, "wouldn't that be something? Bears-Packers for all the NFC marbles?"

"Sure," Ric would say, "but we'd have to do it at Soldier Field."

"Oh of *course*," I would say while Luke nodded furiously, "of course it would be at Soldier Field."

And wouldn't you know it? It's at Soldier Field! The dream is alive! If we win, we are victors in The Greatest Bears-Packers Game That Ever Was. Beating the Lakers in 1991 was not nearly as important as beating the Pistons, and I'll bet when Red Sox fans daydream about 2004, their minds jump to the Yankees series, to Dave Roberts and David Ortiz and Curt Schilling and the rest of them, with the Cardinals a mere trace.

Losing to Seattle would have been brutal, losing to Atlanta no fun at all. But losing to Green Bay, while leaving us sad and anguished, comes with a full week of Bears-Packers celebration and memory recall. Believe me: by kickoff time Sunday, you will have heard stories about every relevant Bears-Packers game from Papa Bear to Charles

PART I: SUNDAY RIVALS

Martin. And you won't be bored. You won't be bogged. Each nugget will add to your anticipation. Each discussion will enrich your enthusiasm.

And when the kicker's foot strikes the ball to launch the game into existence, there will be no doubt: This is the championship. This is why we watch. This is why we root.

This, praise Sweetness, is why we love our Bears.

Dec. 17, 2012
Age 31

THE BEARS NEED A RESCUE

My heart hurts. The Bears hurt my heart.

Late Saturday night, three friends including G the Vikings Fan cornered me at a party and asked how worried I was on a 1 to 10 scale about the Packers. I thought deeply and said "about a 6."

They were shocked, but I explained. "Consider me a firefighter charging into a burning house. Flames have been raging since long before I even arrived. The scene is bleak.

"But I'm a professional. A 20-year veteran. I'm not going to storm a house while lamenting, 'Good God, I'm running into a death trap!' I'm going to assess the danger, plot my options, think positively, and attack."

"And if Rodgers scores on the first drive?" G asked.

"Well, once you step into the house, you're in the house. If the roof collapses and the heat is building and there's an 80-year-old stranded in an upstairs bedroom and you're calling for backup and no one can hear you, yeah, a 6 becomes a 9 pretty fast."

Still, early in the second quarter the Bears led 7-0 and looked as if they would rescue the 80-year-old and contain the blaze.

But the structural damage was significant. Soon enough, the Pack were in the endzone. Then a falling chandelier pins your partner's legs, Cutler throws a hideous interception with about 90 seconds left in the half, and Green Bay scores again.

When you get to the door, the 80-year-old is unresponsive. You chop through the wood, and by the time you place your hands on the man, the Packers have scored again and you're trying to remember the last time the Bears erased a 14-point deficit against Green Bay, and you're back in the depths of the Favre era and still haven't thought of a game.

The Bears score six more points, but there is never true HOPE. They drag the man out of the house, get him on the front lawn, and begin administering CPR, and though the man is coughing and groaning, the house has collapsed and the ambulance is late and you're just hoping the old man can hang on.

Dec. 31, 2012
  Age 31

BEARS REACH THE END OF THE ROAD

Shortly before the Vikings-Packers game, G the Vikings Fan looked at me sullenly. I had helped gather a large group of NFC North fans from all four walks of life, and following the Bears' defeat of Detroit, Minnesota's game against Green Bay was now a Vikings must-win.

"This might have been a bad idea," G said about the prospect of watching the Vikings lose while surrounded by Bears, Packers, and Lions fans. "If this goes bad, I might have to bounce."

I understood his concern — nobody wants to lose without empathy — but early in the first quarter, the Vikings were up 10-0 and it was not G who was greeted with a harsh reality, but me: I miscalculated my ability to root for the Packers. It was a foul, unnatural act that could no longer be tolerated. For the second half, I would leave our chances to fate, and the Packers be damned.

Unfortunately, on this afternoon, Fate employed Adrian Peterson. The great Minnesota tailback racked up 199 rushing yards and a touchdown; his final run was a 26-yarder that left him nine yards shy of breaking Eric Dickerson's single-season rushing record but that, more importantly, set up the Vikings for a game-winning field goal. Vikings 37, Packers 34.

That means the Bears will spend the postseason in the same place as the rest of us, at home, on a sofa, wondering how we ever reached a point where cheering for the Packers was an appropriate course of action. In a season that reached spectacular highs, the final mood is one of regret, failure, and doom.

We will go no further. We will play no more. Congrats to G and the rest of you Vikings fans out there. Sincerely, you earned it.

As for us, a season that at times strained the bond between Bears players and Bears fans ends with the two groups in total agreement: if we're rooting for the Packers in Week 17, something has gone terribly wrong. The poles have shifted. The Earth is not safe. Perhaps the Mayans were right after all.

Sep. 30, 2016, Windy City Gridiron
    Age 34

WE NEED TO TALK ABOUT THE LIONS

Back in September 2013, I interviewed fans of every NFC North team to learn the degree to which they were scared of every other NFC North team. At the time, the Bears were 3-0 in Year 1 of Trestman and three days away from playing the 2-1 Lions.

Not only was our record better, but we were riding a three-game winning streak over Detroit, with a 13-3 record in our last 16 games. That was our record in the Super Bowl season. Take your feeling of domination and control from 2006 — that's how we felt about the Lions before Week 4 of 2013.

Therefore, among my questions for those fans was this:

> When was the last time you felt the Lions held an unquestionable emotional advantage over your team? How long did that feeling last?

"Have they ever?" said Matt Clapp, AKA @TheBearNecess, epitomizing the tone of the responses. Our own Lester Wiltfong responded "Never." Two of the other Bears fans acknowledged Detroit's postseason appearance in 2011, a season with one of Detroit's only three wins over the Bears between 2005 and 2012.

Tony the Packers Fan ("I cannot remember a time when I've had that feeling.") and G the Vikings Fan ("Never. The Lions were bullied as a child, thus the complex they've developed as adults.") exhibited more confidence, while the one Lions fan was shaky:

2011 early in the season. Detroit was so fired up about this team. "Restore the roar" and all that. We had some great comeback victories and made the playoffs. It was a good time. Of course, this was immediately followed by prolonged and extreme disappointment.

We have to remember that the Lions' cosmic ineptitude was vaster than the 0-16 season. When we beat them in Week 13 of 2010, we dropped them to 2-10 on the season and an obscene 5-47 since their surprising 6-2 start in 2007. That 5-47, 0-16 losing juggernaut is the team in our hearts and minds when even today we look at a Bears schedule with friends prior to the season and start projecting wins:

"Texans, on the road. Could be tough. Depends on Watt I guess but let's conservatively put that down for a loss. Philly, Week 2. Should be good. Home against the rookie. Dallas on the road. Romo. Okay, let's just say that we will beat at least one of the Texas teams. That's 2-1. Lions. (This is where friends flash at each other a dismissive eye shimmy.) In Indy — ummmmmm... that can be a win. Jags yes. Pack. (This is where friends flash a panicked side face.) Vikes are tough. Okay, 5-3 at the bye. That'll work."

Notice how we chalked up an obvious win against the Lions, a Reece-staring-down-the-original-Terminator loss against Green Bay, and a splash-of-cold-water Vikings loss. Yet since 2010, our last trip to the playoffs, through today, here are the wins for the NFC North:

- Bears: 37 regular season wins, 0 playoff wins, 0 postseason appearances
- Vikings: 39 regular, 0 playoff, 2 postseasons, 1 division title
- Lions: 40 regular, 0 playoff, 2 postseasons
- Packers: 58 regular, 3 playoff, 5 postseasons, 4 division titles

Furthermore, let's return to that Week 4 matchup in 2013. I tweeted my confidence pregame:

"Okay, time to roll. Bears 31, Lions 10. Cutler's due for a 300-yard game. Hasn't had one since the 2012 opener. He gets it today. Bear Down!"

We lost 40-32. We've lost five straight more since then.

That's six straight losses. We have not defeated the Lions since the 2012 season finale, AKA Lovie Smith's Final Ride.

If that does not seem like a long time, remember that when Brett Favre hung a 10-game winning streak on us in the 1990s, by the end of win #6, Green Bay was on their way to a championship and we'd been thoroughly terrorized.

And if I may quote the *Shawshank* district attorney, while you think about that, think about this. With 16 games a season, the emotions a team stirs in a fan mean less than other sports (greater chance of significant deviation from expectations) but are more consuming. You sit in your feelings for an opponent for a full week — from four days before the game to two days after it.

That's why I think Bears fans have not faced up to our new reality.

We are the Lions.

Not historically, no. In that respect we're still the Bears.

But in terms of recent history, looking for the team that every other team in the division sees on the schedule before delivering the dismissive eye shimmy, we're that team right now. We are the NFC North's dismissive eye-shimmy team.

That's why this game is so important. The combination of an 0-4 start to a season + our first 0-4 start in 16 years + a seventh straight loss to the Lions could be the final Jenga piece that crumbles the Bears Fan John Fox Confidence Tower. His Windy City Gridiron approval rating has dropped steadily since the end of last season. He closed out 2015 at 94%. We're down to 42% now, and the hot seat looms.

The Lions must be dealt with swiftly. We must return them to their rightful place in our psyche's mud room. We must reset our dynamic in a post-Megatron world. We must send them scampering back to Detroit with my long-awaited 31-10 smackdown. They must never again forget they are the Lions.

Oct. 4, 2017, Windy City Gridiron
    Age 35

HOW I GREW TO HATE, THEN PITY, THE VIKINGS

I couldn't have been more than seven years old when a Vikings fan poured beer on me. This was at Soldier Field in either 1988 or 1989. An ass-kicking had occurred. In Week 3, 1988, we lost at home to the Vikings 31-7. In Week 2, 1989, we beat the Vikings at home 38-7.

After one of those two games, as my parents and brother left the stands, an either empowered or embarrassed Vikings fan in the seats above our exit let loose an either angry or anguished Viking cry and dumped beer on a group of Bears fans who were leaving. I was in the path of the pour. A scuffle ensued. My parents used the fracas as a chance to hustle the boys (me and my two-years-younger brother) out of the stadium.

My troubles continued in the parking lot. We had to pass a Vikings RV surrounded by purple-clad, beer-soaked Vikings fans. I found myself eyeing them all with suspicion. I wondered if they knew the pourer, and if they did, if they would support him in his efforts against us.

They picked up on my malice and sneered at me, a boy of either six or seven.

That was that for me and Vikings fans. I already hated Packers fans, but that was duty. This was personal. This was direct aggression toward my well-being. This was the sort of animus that would make a literal Viking duel a literal Bear all the way to the afterlife.

My Packers beef extended back to 1921. It was bigger than me. My Vikings beef, though — that was all me. I wasn't mad about Fran Tarkenton beating us in '61, or thinking about McMahon's rousing comeback in '85. My anger toward the Vikings started specifically with the team's fans and manifested itself in teeth-gritting fury toward Denny Green, Anthony and Cris Carter, Terry Allen, Warren Moon, Chris Doleman, John Randle, Robert Smith, Jake Reed, and the rest of the jerks.

Yet it was hard to watch the 1998 NFC championship game and not have my heart break just a little for those fans. I secretly loved the '98 Vikings, simply because they were so damn entertaining. Their offense was the most beautiful I'd ever seen. I was a Randall Cunningham fan from the Eagles days (mostly from Tecmo Super Bowl), and when his two-season comeback started in 1997 and then came to rip-roaring life in 1998, I was all in.

I was also a Randy Moss fan at Marshall after I saw him score his famous touchdown against Army. I wanted Moss on the Bears real bad, and was devastated when we didn't draft him. I always wanted to see Randall in a Bears uniform, and I always loved Denny Green. The '98 Vikings were special, and I wanted nothing more than to see what would have surely been one of the greatest Super Bowls ever when those Vikings met the defending-champion Broncos in Super Bowl XXXIII.

The Falcons stopped that with help from Gary Anderson, and a piece of me shuddered for the pain of my purple rivals.

Then came Daunte Culpepper, who I also liked in college. And then came the 2000 NFC title game, and a possible Super Bowl XXXV between the Vikings and the Raiders.

And then came 41-0.

When Brett Favre came to Minnesota, my empathy was with Tony the Packers Fan as he watched his beloved Brett suit up in purple. Yet I still kind of dug those 2009 Vikings, and the way Favre turned back the clock once more.

So there was something rather horrific about seeing Favre turn the clock back even further to his early league-leading interception days, tossing the Vikings out of a possible NFC-winning field goal against the Saints.

Yet my Vikings schadenfreude ran deep, and I took sickening glee in a video of Vikings fans losing their mind as their team blew the game.

That was the last year the Vikings were dominant. It's also the year I met Rob Watson.

Rob is a Minneapolis-native and loyal Vikings fan. Our friend group is two Bears fans, one Cowboys fan, and Rob, whom we all contact whenever anything goes awry with the Vikes. By the time we met, I was in my late 20s. I knew the history of the Vikings. I knew the four Super Bowl losses and the subsequent run of agonizing NFC championship game losses, starting in the late 1970s.

Yet I couldn't fully feel their pain until I saw it through Rob. As late as 2012, in fact, I wrote some of my harshest words ever about the Vikings and their fans:

> There is one thing on this Earth that Bears fans and Packers fans agree on, and that is their dislike for the Minnesota Vikings.

> They tend to be feckless beasts, and their fans are no better. They are a dome team masquerading as cold-weather warriors. They are rarely terrible and sometimes excellent, yet their most famous moments involve successful teams decaying at the seams right when victory seemed most assured. (See: 1999 and 2001 NFC championship games.)
>
> I mention this because while there were a lot of downsides to Sunday's 28-10 Bears win, the upside was they pounded the Vikings into the dirt like the chumps they've always been.

That story ran in *RedEye*. Rob read it as soon as it went live online. He texted me his complaints immediately after. I then wrote another column, apologizing:

> The text arrived about 30 minutes after my column went live on redeyechicago.com. It was my buddy G, a Vikings fan. He was not happy.
>
> "I want you to know I take personal offense to your column," he wrote. "You went too far."
>
> We'd been smack-talking all day both privately and on Twitter, and perhaps I was still channeling that mindset when I wrote my postgame column about my dislike of the Vikings. I'd imagine my disrespect of the Vikings wasn't what bothered him, though, but rather my disrespect of Vikings fans.
>
> Ripping the team is one thing, but taking shots at fans is another. He's right: I went too far.

It was in that column that, for the first time ever, I publicly acknowledged the Vikings' collective pain:

> I feel sorry for Vikings fans, probably more so than Cubs fans. We at least have Wrigley Field, beautiful summer afternoons, day drinking and a national myth to cushion our sadness. Vikings fans have gruesome winters, lukewarm summers and a football team that leaves scars on every generation of fans without so much as a championship or even a championship surrogate.

I followed that up with a classic "sorry not sorry." ("Am I wrong in calling them 'feckless beasts' as fans (not as people)? Not one bit. Their history has mutated them beyond recognition.") But for me, the floodgates were open. Even two weeks later when I opened a column writing that "There's something about the Vikings that, I don't know, just makes me want to puke." — I still felt bad for them.

Even after Rob and I led a group of football fans to watch the 2012 season finale of Bears vs. Lions and Vikings vs. Packers that ended with the Vikings knocking the Bears out of the playoffs, and even though our faces looked like this:

...I still felt bad for them.

And you know what? I still do.

The Vikings don't get nearly enough credit for their tragic history. I'd put them neck-and-neck with the Bills and Cardinals for the saddest NFL franchise, though at least older Bills fans recall with great pride the back-to-back AFL championships in 1965 and 1966.

Older Lions fans have the 1957 championship. Older Browns fans have the 1964 championship, as well as the title days of the 1950s. A Cards fan has to go way back to the 1947 Chicago Cardinals for that team's most recent championship.

But the types of losses the Vikings have incurred for every generation of Vikings fan combined with the lack of understanding of their pain makes Vikings fandom a trial I dare not undertake.

In 2013, I decided to immortalize the pain of Vikings fandom via Rob's memories. I asked him for a ranked list of his worst Vikings memories. This is a man who was born *after* the Vikings lost the last of their four Super Bowls, mind you.

Think about Rob's list. Listen to his voice. And when the Vikings come to Soldier Field this Monday night, just know Mitchell Trubisky's debut isn't our only reason to rejoice.

Dec. 14, 2018, Windy City Gridiron
    Age 37

LET'S BEAT THE PACK AND CLINCH THIS DAMN DIVISION

Robert says every time I write one of these we lose.

"No iconic wins against the Dolphins"? None once more. "Our last chance to beat Tom Brady"? Stopped at the 1. "The Lions are arrogant punks who keep beating us, and hot damn it's enough already"? Got that one right at least, but The Prophecy sunk no sooner than I put fingertip to keyboard.

Well I'm back at it and I surely don't care. You know why? Because this Bears team fills me with confidence. The purest kind. The kind that comes without internal backlash that then makes me jittery because my confidence feels too high.

This confidence builds on itself. This confidence is making me confident. And it is making me say one thing to myself this week and one thing only:

Let's beat the Pack and clinch this damn division.

The last time we had a "Holy moly we're actually really good now" season was 2005, and at that time in my life I leaned toward the Steady Progression mindset, whereby as a fan I wanted to feel the full arc of a team's rise. I wanted the "Oh wow we're here!" season AND the "WE ARE THE GREATEST" season and then I wanted the "Let's defend this thing" season and maybe even the "We must recapture our glory" season.

But pining for delayed success is a fool's nostalgia, as I rightly learned that year. Since then, I've been an all-in-when-the-time-is-upon-us fan.

The time is upon us.

The levels of success in this 2018 season have snuck up on me. I thought we would be good, but I didn't know we'd be this good. Even when we got Mack (and let's all say it again and again: WE GOT MACK!!) I don't think I truly knew that we were going to be in a position this early to wrap the division.

Part of that is because of the struggles of the Vikings, Packers and Lions. But part of that is us. Here's how I described it in our Cold Takes column this week:

This season has continued to just creep along, as we moved from "Thank goodness the Fox era is over" to "Yeah Nagy seems cool" to "We could compete for the 6th playoff spot!" to "WE GOT MACK" to "Oh damn, we're pretty good" to "Yeah but there will be growing pains" to "Oh damn, we've got an outside shot at the division crown" to "HEY LOS ANGELES HOW YOU LIKE DEM APPLES!"

It feels like every week brings a new level of consciousness for Bears fans about what this team is and what it can be, and all of that growth has coalesced into this moment right here, right now, where we can suddenly put something real next to those feelings. We can win the division now for the first time since 2010. That's not hypothetical but mathematical, and it's happening this week. Man I love this team.

It might not feel like it (or perhaps it does), but we are in the midst of our second longest postseason drought in franchise history. Seven seasons without making the playoffs. The longest drought was the 13 seasons from 1964 (the year after we won the NFL championship) to 1976 (Year 2 of Walter).

But of course in 1964 all we had was one championship game for a postseason, meaning only two teams made the playoffs. By '76, the NFL and AFL had merged and we now had a more proper postseason, though that was still only four teams per conference.

In the 16-game schedule (since '78) and/or in the wild card era (since 1990), the run from 2011 to the present is our longest playoff drought. We haven't even had a whiff of the postseason since the doomed conclusion of 2013.

The last time we clinched the division was Dec. 20, 2010, in Minnesota to play the Vikings, a 40-14 whupping that included Devin Hester breaking Brian Mitchell's combined KR/PR touchdowns record and Corey Wootton ending Brett Favre's career.

That's how long ago we were last in the playoffs: Brett Favre was on the field.

Brian Urlacher was too. They're both in the Hall of Fame now.

Football heroes of 2010 have been immortalized in bronze more recently than we've made the playoffs.

I know I've said this before and not always been successful, but again, I don't really care: this ends now. It ends with us finishing the job that we started Week 1 on the Packers. It ends with us breaking 12's spell on us. It ends with cheers at Soldier Field, with the most exuberant Club Dub that's ever been Dubbed.

It ends with hats.

It ends Sunday.

This division is ours.

Let's go out and take it.

Sep. 27, 2018, Windy City Gridiron
  Age 36

TYJI ARMSTRONG, A MOTHER'S LOVE, AND THE MEANING OF SPORTS

As a sellout crowd at Soldier Field cheered the Bears against the Buccaneers on September 26, 1993, one seat in the northeast corner remained empty. A ticket was purchased for section 26, row 19, seat 38, but no one sat there. The seat was draped only with a wreath of Bird of Paradise flowers.

The display was in memory of Annie Armstrong, the mother of Buccaneers tight end Tyji Armstrong, who had suffered a fatal heart attack there one year earlier, October 18, 1992, and died later that day. She was in town from Michigan with family to watch her son.

After that, every time Armstrong played at Soldier Field, he purchased the ticket for that seat, along with the other eight next to it for the Armstrong clan there that day. As NFC Central rivals, the Bucs and Bears played twice a year. Indeed, Armstrong bought that seat and laid out flowers in 1993, 1994 and 1995. He did it again in 1996 with the Cowboys and in 1998 with the Rams.

And indeed, at some point in each TV broadcast, or at least for those Bears-Bucs games, the announcers discussed Armstrong and his mother. They showed the empty seat. They showed the flowers.

"When we left (Chicago last year), I was thinking, 'I've got to come back every year,'" Armstrong said in September of 1993, leading up to his first game back at Soldier Field after his mother's passing. "I try not to think about it. I just hope I don't freak out."

In the midst of an NFL game, there were not a lot of reasons to put the camera on Armstrong. The 6'4, 260-pound tight end caught only 16 passes his first two years combined, grabbed 22 in his third year and 15 for the remainder of his NFL career. He spent his time in Tampa as TE2. He scored three NFL touchdowns, one per season from 1992 to 1994. He made more news for fines and fights than catches and highlights.

That anonymity made his story more striking. If he was a star, he would be discussed at length for any number of plays, to which the announcers would at some point add his mother's story as a veritable footnote.

Instead, the broadcast would halt and the cameras would find him and the announcers would tell the story of October 18, 1992.

This was a family reunion for the 1992 3rd round pick, his mother and other family members coming in from Michigan to see Tyji play. Before the game, he spoke and laughed with his mother. She had raised him, and he'd always been closer with her than his father.

"He was there financially, but from a father-son standpoint, he was never there for me," Armstrong told the *Tampa Bay Times* in August of '93. "Basically, I grew up in a one-parent family."

With his father's death before the 1992 draft, and with only four half-siblings, Armstrong called his mother "the only family I considered I had."

Just after halftime of that '92 Bears-Bucs game, the 51-year-old Mrs. Armstrong clutched her chest. Paramedics arrived, and word made it down from the stands to Buccaneers head coach Sam Wyche, who then had the task of telling this 22-year-old rookie that his mother was being rushed to an ambulance. Upon receiving word in the third quarter, Armstrong changed out of his uniform and followed the team doctor through the tunnels of Soldier Field just in time to see his unconscious mother loaded into an ambulance.

He rode with her to Mercy Hospital at 2525 N. Michigan Avenue. She was pronounced dead there at 2:53 p.m.

As a rabid, middle school-aged Bears fan, I always took note of these moments when announcers told Armstrong's story. They were jarringly different than the general tone of any typical televised sports game. Which is not to say that the pall of daily life didn't seep into broadcasts. In the unending thirst for sports human interest stories, that was actually fairly common.

This could be anything from announcers discussing the impact that the Yugoslav Wars had on Vlade Divac to Brian Urlacher or Brett Favre playing after the passing of a parent to a team recovering from the untimely death of a teammate.

And yet, all of these instances were framed in an athletic context. "How will a grieving Urlacher rebound against the Saints following his mother's death?" "Can you believe Favre threw four TDs the night after his dad died?" "The Comets are rallying around memories of their fallen teammate Kim Perrot." And so on.

The Armstrong story was different. It had no athletic connection. It was a human story, first and last. And it was present. Immediate. Active. The empty seat. The flowers. With every Bears-Bucs game of that era, the stands of Soldier Field bore the mark of Annie Armstrong's life and death. Those games carried both the specter of mortality and the spirit of eternity. Pain and love. Heartbreak and hope.

This was made more memorable by the otherwise colorless Bears-Bucs games of the era. From the '83 season to the first game of '96, the Bears and Buccaneers met 27 times. The Bears won 23. We swept the series every year from '83 to '88, winning 12 straight games. After Tampa swept us in our flukey-bad 1989 campaign, we ripped off runs of four- and five-straight wins against the ever-doomed Buccaneers.

The scores were lopsided too. We held Tampa under 10 points nine times, and held them at or below two touchdowns another nine times. We dropped 40 on them thrice. The day Annie Armstrong died, the Bears won 31-14. The day her son placed that wreath on that seat for the first time, the Bears won 47-17.

There would be so much more to discuss other than Armstrong if he played for a strong team of the era — the 49ers, Giants, Washington — or if he played for a deeper rival, like the Packers.

Instead, the one-sided nature of the bi-annual meetings made the flowers on the late Mrs. Armstrong's seat a reprieve from both the series' banality and the sport's brutality. I of course watched nearly every Bears game with my family when I was growing up. Suddenly, once per season, the sport I loved brought me a message of true life-and-death perspective. Even at that age, I was aware enough to empathize with the pain of this man I'd never met who played for a team for which I did not root.

And I was grateful for the perspective borne of that reprieve, a newfound understanding of why we root and what matters most.

"She wasn't conscious when I got to her under the stands," Armstrong said in the 1993 *Tampa Bay Times* interview. "But thank God we talked before the game. We laughed and joked. We were really tight. I really don't know if she knew I was there (in the ambulance), but I knew she would want me to keep going on no matter what."

This Sunday, the Bears host the Buccaneers for only the fifth time since the league expanded to 32 teams in 2002 and re-aligned the divisions, sending the Bucs to the newly formed NFC South and free of our twice-a-year bond. I don't know if Tyji Armstrong will be watching this game. I know he'll be thinking of his mother. That makes two of us.

PART II:
THE REAL FIRST CHAMPIONSHIP

March 2005, *"Bear Down and Get Some Runs"*
Age 23

LEARNING THE HARD WAY: OVERCOMING THE BAD BOY PISTONS

Michael Jordan and I came to Illinois together.

All we'd known was the East Coast, starting in Brooklyn, where we were both born, 18 years apart. Michael Jeffrey Jordan spent his childhood and college days in North Carolina, arriving at UNC in 1981, the year I was born. In 1982, while my family was living in an apartment in Brooklyn's Little Italy neighborhood, Jordan broke on the national scene, knocking out the Georgetown Hoyas for the national championship courtesy of his first in a career's worth of famous game-winners.

In 1983 we moved to Connecticut where my brother Michael Jeffrey Silverstein was born, a name he would unofficially change after the first Bulls championship to "Michael Jeffrey Jordan Silverstein," eventually ending up with the same nickname as our idol: MJ.

And in June of 1984, the Chicago Bulls drafted NCAA Player of the Year Michael Jordan with the 3rd overall pick, the same year that the Silverstein family returned to our Midwest roots with a move to Evanston, ending my parents' 12-year post-college East Coast run.

As a three-year-old with Chicago fandom rich in the blood, I could not have asked for a better time to move back. While doomed as apocalyptic by the great Orwell, 1984 was the beginning of a golden era in Chicago sports. The Cubs won the division that summer, going to the postseason for the first time since 1945. The Bears dominated in the fall and reached the NFC championship game, setting the table for their legendary 1985 run.

Of course, the city's most significant move of 1984 was the Bulls drafting Jordan. All told, my upbringing as a Chicago sports fan was fortuitous, and then some. I was born into a golden era, seeing all of the following before my 18th birthday:

1. The NFL's greatest team ever: the '85 Bears
2. Three Cubs playoff teams, including our first since 1945
3. One all-time great White Sox playoff team
4. The Hawks in the '92 Stanley Cup
5. One of the greatest Cinderella seasons ever with my beloved 1995 Northwestern Wildcats shocking the world to reach the Rose Bowl
6. 6 rings.

I was also blessed to watch Hall of Famers galore (Jordan, Payton, Scottie, Frank, Sammy, Chelios, Samurai, Hampton, Dent, Maddux, Rodman), and enough award-winning seasons — MVPs in two sports, DPOY in two sports, Rookie of the Year in three sports, along with three Cy Young awards and two Vezina Trophies — to last a lifetime.

Funny, then, that what stands out is the losing.

What stands out are the Detroit Pistons.

Even as a youth, I knew what was happening. Three straight years, we battled Detroit in the playoffs. Three straight years, we left bruised and beaten. I felt that pain. The Pistons were men. The Bulls were boys. The Pistons were evil but strong. The Bulls were good but weak. Exacerbating the bitterness was our childhood friendship with Aaron Wightman, Pistons fan, whose family was from Michigan. He was an incredibly nice kid who never once rubbed it in our noses, yet we all knew he had something over us. My friends and I would come together to watch the Bulls and Pistons battle, and at the end of it all Aaron, never a bragger, was smiling while we were silent. It was understood that no matter what happened with the Bears and Lions, Blackhawks and Red Wings, Cubs, White Sox, and Tigers, and no matter what happened when we played our own games at the school yard or in our backyards, nothing else mattered but this: Aaron rooted for the Pistons, we rooted for the Bulls, the Pistons dominated the Bulls, and there was nothing we could do about it.

It got to a point where it wasn't even about basketball anymore. In my mind, Bill Laimbeer was not a basketball player. He didn't even seem human. He was a supervillain, the Devil himself, a life force of pure evil sent to this planet to destroy our heroes, the Chicago Bulls. There were two supervillains in my childhood (and I say this with zero hyperbole): Saddam Hussein and Bill Laimbeer.

And frankly, I was much more terrified of Laimbeer. We had an entire army dedicated to stopping Saddam. Who was going to stop Laimbeer? Dave Corzine? Brad Sellers? A pre-goggles Horace Grant? Additionally, Saddam lived in Iraq. When you're nine, who the hell knows where Iraq is? On the other hand, as far as I knew, Laimbeer could make the drive west on 94 at any moment and, in about four hours, be here *in person* to terrorize us.

The Bulls were Batman and Superman, but unlike Lex Luthor or the Joker, Laimbeer and the Pistons held the upper hand against the forces of good. Imagine if Rocky had fought Apollo in all five movies and lost every time. Slowly, the emotional triumph and moral victory of the first film would be sucked out of the series until all that was left was the Italian Stallion bloodied in his corner, alone, crying, and coming back for more. He may have Adrian's love, he may have Mickey's guidance, but he'll never beat Apollo, his most hated enemy.

How long could we do this? How long could we reach the same point, challenged by the same team, and fail? We are optimists in this city — you have to be, if you plan on having any sort of longevity as a fan — but we carry a heavy heart. I was only in third grade at the time, an age when Anything Is Possible because you've got All The Time In The World, and even I felt it strongly: If we couldn't do it in 1991, we couldn't do it at all.

The Bulls must have had the same sense of urgency. With a conference-high 61 wins, home court advantage and the maturation of Jordan's "supporting cast," we were finally the favorites against the Pistons.

Still, I have to admit, I was nervous. By 1991 I had experienced much hardship with this Bulls team. I knew Chicago's history. I knew about the '69 Cubs and the Black Sox and I had watched as the Bears of the '80s fell to pieces. But then the series started, and everything changed. The Pistons tried all of their regular tricks, but nothing worked. They knocked us down, we got back up. You could feel the trends changing. As a fan, you could really feel it. When the series started we still had that nagging thought in the back of our minds: "*Please don't let them burn us again.*"

But they didn't. The Bulls stayed tough, and after winning the first two games at home, we finally felt that victory would happen. The momentum grew in school and the city, our confidence building both in our teams and in ourselves. It really felt like we, as sports fans, were growing stronger, and when we beat Detroit in Game 3 at the Palace, we knew the series was ours. Like the older brother who realizes his younger brother has surpassed him and his tricks are no longer effective, the Pistons came apart like children, and the Bulls came together as all great teams do.

Every Bulls fan has a favorite game or moment, the one that stands out from all the others. For me, along with The Charles Smith Game, The MJ & Pippen Show doesn't get any sweeter than Game 4 at the Palace, Memorial Day 1991. By the time that game rolled around, we knew it would be a sweep. It wasn't just that we were going to finally beat Detroit. We were going to break them down in a way they never imagined. At that point, letting them win even one game would have been a letdown.

We knew we were going to the Finals… there wasn't a question about that. But nobody talked at school about who we wanted to play in the Finals. We talked about Detroit. We had to show them how far we had come, so there was no doubt in their minds which team was better. They had to learn not just that we were more talented, but stronger, mentally and physically. They had to learn that they could not push us around any more, that no matter what they did or what they tried, they were not going to beat us because *we would not let them.*

I've never felt as connected to a community due to a sports team as I felt at the end of that game. I wasn't just watching in front of my TV with my family and friends. I was watching with every other Bulls fan alive. As we watched Isiah and his teammates walk off the court with time remaining, I knew I was thinking and feeling exactly what every other Bulls fan was thinking and feeling: *"WE did it. We finally did it."* When Detroit walked off the court early, it wasn't simply a show of bad sportsmanship, nor was it, as they claim, a chance for them to go off as champions with their own fans applauding. It was simply the natural reaction of a team that was totally and utterly defeated.

Deep down, they knew their time had passed. They could feel it. They saw then that what had separated our two teams in years past was not skill, but toughness, intelligence, experience, desire. Now that we could withstand and fight through whatever physical challenges they may have presented, we were on even ground, and once that happened they were no match.

I remember looking over at Aaron — we always watched these games together — and the look on his face exposed the sentiment of the Pistons and all of their fans:

We will never beat the Bulls again.

Me and MJ in the early 1990s, peak first three-peat

PART III:
TALL TALES

Sep. 2005, "Bear Down and Get Some Runs"
  Age 23

FIRST AND TEN NORTHWESTERN! THE TALE OF THE 1995 ROSE BOWL WILDCATS

What always made Northwestern football special was the access.

The stadium was left open during the week, and my friends and I would go there and play pick-up games on the turf. Sometimes we would just walk there after school and hang out on the benches, enjoying the feeling of being in the stadium of our favorite local team. When we couldn't go to the games, we could listen to the loud speaker from our houses while we played our own game of tackle or two-hand touch.

I rarely had actual tickets, but a lot of my friends did, and on game days we could usually get two of us in on one ticket, or on one stub during the second half. Failing that, we could always get onto the field afterwards. We could even get near the locker room, since we knew the tunnel at Dyche Stadium that the players used. Dyche was like having a friend with a huge backyard; we hung out there as much as we could.

One of my all-time favorite sports memories came in the fall of 1993 when the Cats were hosting Boston College. Northwestern trailed 21-14 late when Len Williams hit Lee Gissendaner with what seemed to be the tying score. Instead of kicking the extra point, the Cats went for two, and won 22-21. We didn't have tickets, watching instead from just outside of the gate on the east side of the north endzone. When the clock hit zero and the Wildcats won, they opened the gate and let us charge the field. People were going nuts; this was the same B.C. team that would go on to beat Notre Dame a week after the

Fightin' Irish would hand the eventual national champion Florida State Seminoles their only loss of the season.

Fans covered the field like children on candy. Fans were scaling the goalposts, and somebody lifted me up to climb too. A police officer made me get down but I did not care — the scene was awesome. Just a flood of fans going wild after our beloved Northwestern football team had come through with a huge win against a legit program.

My two friends and I left the field and went through the tunnel to the laundry room where the players would drop off their jerseys. We high-fived each one as they came through the hallway, and to our surprise we weren't the only visitors there. Former Northwestern running back, and then-Bears fullback, Bob Christian was in the house. He told us that B.C. alumnus and then-Bears receiver Tom Waddle, my favorite Bear of all-time, was at the game and had just left.

Even missing out on Waddle wasn't enough to ruin the moment. Bob Christian turned out to be one of the real nice guys in sports, and he was a Wildcat/Bear, which was an outstanding combo. Still, most of our focus was centered entirely on the thrill of the victory.

We left and walked down Central Street. Everybody — *everybody* — everybody was in a festive mood. That game was the first time that I ever saw the Cats get pub in *Sports Illustrated*. Granted it was a blip in the "Inside College Football" section in the back, but still. This is *Sports Illustrated*! The magazine that usually runs stories on Michael and Montana had a story on our Northwestern Wildcats. Amazing.

Later in the week we were back at Dyche, running around the stadium as we always did. Someone had drawn white footprints on the turf, tracking the exact route that Gissendaner ran on the final touchdown. Donny Burba and I took our ball and traded off jobs, one of us lining up as Williams and the other as Gissendaner, running the route exactly as it was drawn on the field, and then celebrating the touchdown, and then switching so that the other person would get

PART III: TALL TALES 53

to experience the thrill of the score. We did this for hours that day. It was all we talked about in school...

Since we were all so used to watching school upon school come into Evanston and trample our Cats, we soaked up every little bit of victory we could find. Especially the Boston College game, which felt like the Rose Bowl. It was wonderful.

And for a while, it was all we had.

******

The first indelible image of the glorious 1995 Rose Bowl season comes from the first game of the year. We were at Josh's house, watching the Cats battle Notre Dame in South Bend. Northwestern had played great football and led the Irish 17-9 late in the fourth. Notre Dame scored a touchdown and went for two and the tie, and here was our first miracle. Notre Dame's quarterback Ron Powlus dropped back to throw, slipped, and his knee hit the turf. And it took a second or two for the significance of that to sink in, but when it did... *Oh my God! He slipped! He slipped! His knee touched! I think we just beat Notre Dame.*

Is that possible?

I don't remember what happened after that. I don't remember if Notre Dame went for an onside kick. I don't remember if the Cats were able to kneel the ball down or if they had to pick up a first. I just don't remember. That image of Powlus slipping as he went back to pass: that I will never forget.

Had it really happened? Had we really defeated the Notre Dame Fightin' Irish, in South Bend no less? NU had a bye week after the Notre Dame game, which gave everybody two weeks to enjoy the glow of that victory. The following week we hosted Miami of Ohio, and after taking a 28-7 lead into the fourth, the Wildcats blew a pair of punt snaps and ended up losing 30-28. *Ah,* we thought. *That's Northwestern football.* We were upset, but we Understood. Week 3 had the Cats running over Air Force 30-6, and Week 4 had us beating Indiana 31-7. We were 3-1, with one huge upset win, one awful heartbreaking loss, and two big wins over weak teams at home.

What was this team? They looked good, better than most people thought they would be. The Cats had gained notoriety after beating the Irish, even gaining the number 25 ranking in the AP poll. They lost that ranking after the loss to Miami, and that big question was born.

It seemed as if they had some stars — I still remember *Sports Illustrated*'s one sentence preview of the Cats, something to the effect of: "Their best player is punter Paul Burton" — with sophomore tailback Darnell Autry, junior linebacker Pat Fitzgerald, and freshman receiver D'Wayne Bates. They had a great rushing attack, a steady quarterback with great leadership and a decent arm in Steve Schnur, and a terrific defense... but still: what were they?

We found out on October 7th.

That was the day the Wildcats traveled to Ann Arbor and beat Michigan.

******

One of the thrills of going to Northwestern games was the chance to see the Big Ten's best. No offense to NU, but when guys like Tyrone Wheatley or Desmond Howard came to town, it felt as if we were seeing, well, *real* players. Not that we didn't love our Wildcats. We did completely. But we had no illusions as to the level of talent at Michigan, Wisconsin, and Ohio State compared to the talent in Evanston. Their guys were headed to the NFL. Couldn't say that for many pre-'95 Cats.

The Wolverines were undefeated heading into our game, and in front of a national television audience the Wildcats let everybody know that they were the team that beat Notre Dame, not the one that lost to Miami of Ohio. When Northwestern took a lead into the lockerroom at halftime, my friends and I ran over to Mustards for a quick burger/dog pick up.

Keith, Steve, and Jerry the owner were there with a small TV on the counter to watch the game. We were all buzzing with excitement, and though it was understood that our orders were going to be in and out with much less than the usual conversation, we were all sharing this experience of our beloved Wildcats being a half of football away from beating the mighty Michigan Wolverines.

Sure enough, the Cats held on, knocking off Michigan 19-13. This time we believed it. This time we knew it was true. *Oh my God! We just beat Michigan! WE JUST BEAT MICHIGAN! WE JUST FUCKING BEAT MICHIGAN!!!*

The Michigan win moved us up to number 14 in the AP poll. Now we were in the thick of the college football big wigs. Barring a complete demolition, it was unlikely that we would lose our ranking after just one week. Instead it was a 27-17 win over the Golden Gophers in Minnesota. Darnell Autry continued his wonderful season with three touchdowns, and the Cats rallied from 14-3 to win their fourth in a row, spoiling Minnesota's homecoming in the process.

The following week was our homecoming, Wisconsin coming to Evanston. This was Important And Revealing Win Number Three, as the Wildcats trashed Wisconsin 35-zip. Now we were catching on, and the "first-time-sinces" were piling up.

The Wisconsin game was the first sell-out at Dyche since 1983 and the first shutout since 1986, a shutout they secured by stuffing the Badgers on a goal line stand at the end of the game. The win gave the Cats their first winning season since 1971, and made them bowl-eligible for the first time since the 1949 Rose Bowl. When the AP polls came out that week, the Cats were ranked eighth in the country, cracking the top ten for the first time since 1963 and giving them 1,000 points in the poll for the first time since 1959.

4-0 in the Big Ten, 6-1 overall, eighth in the AP.

We were catching on.

✶✶✶✶✶✶

October 28th: Another homecoming game, another comeback. The Cats trailed 14-3 and then scored two second-half touchdowns in Champaign to beat the Illini, with Darnell scoring the game-winning TD late in the fourth. The Cats were now sixth in the AP, and mighty Penn State was coming to town.

This was a big one, with ABC in the house to broadcast the game. ABC. This isn't cable we're talking about. ESPN is a huge deal, but there's something about being on a basic network where anyone with a television can find you. This was November, two days before my birthday, and the Cats were 7-1 and riding a six-game winning streak. This was the game where we would get our opportunity to show every football fan in America what this team was all about. Schnur and Autry and Bates and Musso and Hartl and fifth-year senior center Rob Johnson. Fitzgerald and Chris Martin and Ismaeli and Dailey and Rice and Collier and Rodney Ray. Sam Valenzisi and Brian Gowins, and yes, Paul Burton. Gary Barnett. The Northwestern Wildcats.

And they delivered. On national television.

Northwestern 21, Penn State 10. Our first-ever win over the Nittany Lions, and the first time that any school — ANY school, ever — beat Notre Dame, Michigan, and Penn State in the same season. The Cats were now guaranteed a January 1st bowl game, back in the days when that meant something.

The piece-de-resistance: Darnell Autry on the cover of *Sports Illustrated*.

The same *Sports Illustrated* that usually had Michael or Montana on their cover put Darnell Autry on it, the running back for, that's right, our very own, home grown, one and only Northwestern Wildcats.

PART III: TALL TALES   57

I nearly cried when I saw that cover. Especially the headline.

"DARNELL AUTRY LEADS POWERFUL NORTHWESTERN PAST PENN STATE."

It was the "powerful" that got me. It was such a wonderful adjective, one I hadn't yet heard. I'd heard "upstart," "surprise," "charismatic," "charming," "Cinderella," "gritty," "tough," and even "ferocious," but never "powerful." Powerful. Powerful. The POWERFUL Northwestern Wildcats. It was a word of such authority, and it came from *Sports Illustrated* of all places. It felt *legitimate*.

Now we were waiting for the collapse. The *Sports Illustrated* cover curse. But no: instead of a letdown, Northwestern beat Iowa 31-20, their first win over the Hawkeyes since 1973. This game had a sad side note: Pat Fitzgerald broke his leg and was knocked out for the remainder of the season. Still, the Cats were now 9-1 and 6-0 in the Big Ten. We were tied with Ohio State for first place in the conference, and were now eyeing the coveted Rose Bowl, back when *that* meant something.

We did not play Ohio State that season, and due to the Buckeyes' perfect overall record they held the tiebreaker against us for the Rose Bowl berth. Still, a bowl game was a bowl game, and like the team kept saying: "Somewhere warm on January 1st."

There was only one game left: November 18th in West Lafayette against Purdue. The Wildcats were looking to close out their perfect Big Ten season with a win, and once again the team showed that they were indeed a powerful group. Senior corner Chris Martin returned a pick 76 yards for a score, Steve Schnur hit Bates for a 72-yard touchdown, Darnell dominated with 226 yards on the ground, and the Cats took it to the Boilers 23-8.

We had won the Big Ten, a perfect 8-0 record in the conference, our first Big Ten title since 1936. The only thing left to do was watch the November 25th game between Michigan and Ohio State. If the Wolverines won, the Cats were headed to the Rose Bowl.

You have to remember: the excitement for this team all around Chicagoland was nearly unprecedented. It was an exciting team with an exciting story — no doubt about that. But there wasn't much else happening at the time. The only game in town that rivaled Northwestern were the Bulls, who were starting their first full season with MJ since 1992-93 and their first with Dennis Rodman. Everyone knew that the Bulls would be playing through June while Northwestern was done on January 1st. The Bears were following up a surprising 1994 playoff run with a mediocre 1995, the Cubs and Sox had sloshed through the strike-shortened 1995 season, and the Blackhawks were no longer the power they were in the early 1990s.

We were in a lull, and then along came this Little Engine That Could football team. They played hard, they played well, they ran the ball, they played intimidating defense (third in the country in points allowed), and they smiled a lot while doing it. What's not to love?

Finally, two days after Thanksgiving: Michigan-Ohio State. What a day. Except for possibly the bitter Notre Dame fans — and, obviously, Buckeye fans — we had the entire country rooting for Michigan. ABC ran a live feed from Evanston to show Coach Barnett and the NU players watching the game. I was in Evanston too that day, watching at Sven's house with the Staffords and many friends.

And wouldn't you know it? The Wolverines took it to the Buckeyes, defended their home field, and sent Ohio State packing, 31-23. Northwestern erupted. We erupted. The Cats were going to the Rose Bowl.

NORTHWESTERN IS GOING TO THE ROSE BOWL!
NORTHWESTERN IS GOING TO THE ROSE BOWL!
NORTHWESTERN IS GOING TO THE ROSE BOWL!
NORTHWESTERN IS GOING TO THE FUCKING ROSE BOWL!

******

The Rose Bowl.

PART III: TALL TALES   59

In Pasadena.

The Granddaddy of Them All.

This is the game where the best team in the Big Ten meets the best in the Pac 10. Teams play every year in those two conferences, hoping for a shot at this game. Major schools in other major conferences get to go to any other bowl they want, but not the Rose Bowl. The biggest game in college football was by reservation only, and this year, Northwestern's name was on the list.

Our opponent: the USC Trojans, the team that *Sports Illustrated* placed on its cover for its college football preview. Northwestern vs. USC. Now it was official. Nearly everybody in America knew something about the Wildcats. They were the biggest story in sports. Not just in college football or football or Evanston or Chicago or Illinois or the Midwest or college football. All of sports.

They spent the entire month of December as near superstars. They were ranked third in the nation, trailing only Nebraska and Florida, the two schools that would play for the national championship. Darnell Autry was invited to the Heisman ceremony in New York, where he placed fourth in the voting. *A Wildcat fourth in the Heisman voting? Are you kidding me???!!!* The Cats made it to a Wheaties box, the true sign of American sports royalty. Injured stars Sam Valenzisi and Pat Fitzgerald were named All-Americans. Darnell and Gary Barnett were on the cover of TV Guide. The team did a turn on Leno. You couldn't walk around the North Shore that winter break without seeing somebody in their purple.

At Mustard's one day in December, I saw a car in the parking lot with what had to be a brand new vanity plate: "BEAT USC."

When it was finally gametime, USC and superstar receiver Keyshawn Johnson were three-point favorites over Northwestern. And that was fine. I was in awe of the scene itself. The crowd was filled with so much purple you'd think somebody had dumped a vat of grape jelly over the stands. I remember being so thrilled just to see NORTHWESTERN in big bold letters in the endzone, a big purple endzone. I remember Darnell being sick for that game with the flu, but still getting his 100 yards as he had in every game that year. I remember the Trojans taking a big lead on us — Brian Musso fumbling and someone on USC scooping it up and running it back for a TD — and a feeling of "Well, it's been fun" settling into Ric's basement, where we watched the game.

I remember the glorious comeback, the Cats taking a 32-31 lead in the fourth quarter, and then having the ball with that lead.

And sadly, I remember the Trojans turning it around with a touchdown and a field goal to ice the game by a final score of 41-32.

We fought hard, and we lost.

So it goes.

That was the first game I'd ever cried after watching.

That was the first loss that ever filled me with pride and joy.

The next day, still in winter break, there was a feeling around Evanston. Everywhere you went, people had the same look on their faces. A tired, satisfied, happy look. We'd gone on a great journey together that took us farther than we'd ever expected, and we were all grateful for the ride.

I remember going into Mustards shortly there after. There had always been Northwestern stuff up on the walls. I remember a poster from the early 90's promoting the season, with autographs from the five players pictured including Williams and Gissendaner and Patrick Wright. There's a framed picture up to this day of Bob Christian with a handwritten note thanking Mustards for their great service and double cheeseburgers. There are team pictures of men's basketball and women's volleyball. There are pictures of softball players and swimmers. These pictures always came directly from the school, but now they were being joined with a *Sports Illustrated* cover, a TV Guide cover, a flattened Wheaties box.

And now, after the Rose Bowl, the front page of the *Sun-Times* was hanging behind the counter over the buns. The headline was perfect: A SCORE YOU'LL FORGET; A YEAR YOU'LL REMEMBER.

So true.

******

The following winter, my family traveled to Israel with a group from our synagogue. Remarkably, the Cats had followed up their Rose Bowl performance with a 9-2, 7-1 season, losing only to Wake Forest and Penn State. This earned them a split Big Ten title, with Autry and Fitzgerald having great seasons once more. This time it was Ohio State that went to the Rose Bowl while we went down to Orlando to play Peyton Manning and the Tennessee Volunteers in the Citrus Bowl. "*Somewhere warm on January 1st. Somewhere warm on January 1st.*"

It was late December, and we were looking at a temple that had once survived a cannon blast. I was wearing a Tommy Nevin's Pub t-shirt, and as I walked outside an older man who we did not know looked at my shirt.

"Tommy Nevin's? From Evanston?"

He was originally from Evanston, but had lived in Jerusalem for ten years. I told him that I was with my synagogue, and he told me a bit about life in Israel, and as we were talking one of the fathers in our synagogue group walked by, wearing his "1995 Northwestern Wildcats Rose Bowl" sweatshirt.

The man I was talking to saw the shirt, and did the biggest double take you've ever seen. His eyes bugged out of his face and he blurted out: "Oh my God! Northwestern went to the Rose Bowl???!!!!"

Still one of the best stories of all-time.

June 8, 2017, 16 Wins a Ring
    Age 35

A LOOK BACK AT MICHAEL JORDAN'S FLU GAME, 20 YEARS LATER

If you want to fully understand Michael Jordan's "Flu Game," you first have to understand one of Michael Jordan's greatest statistics: 357.

It's a stat that is rarely discussed. The number most associated with MJ, besides 23, is 6. As in "6 rings." Once upon a time, MJ's career was defined by a melange of numbers. People thought about 63 and 69. They pictured him in 9 and 45. They were astounded by 7, and later 10, for his scoring titles. They grimaced at .202 and glowed with pride over 72–10.

Now, it's 6. The only number of consequence. The one MJ chased more than any other. The one to which he drunkenly crooned after reaching it in 1998. He started counting after the first championship, flashing victorious fingers. Two in 1992. Three in '93. Four in '96. Five in '97. Six in '98.

No number in NBA history serves as more of a mic drop in current hoops debates than MJ's 6. The figure may be augmented in different ways, like "6–0" (his Finals record) or "6 for 6" (his Finals MVPs). But, unquestionably, 6 is the number. He likes it like that.

I like it too. I also like 357.

To me, that's Mike's hidden gem. And really, it's 357/358. That's MJ's run of Bulls games played after baseball, from March 19, 1995 ("I'm back.") to June 14, 1998 ("The Last Shot").

PART III: TALL TALES

Three-hundred fifty-seven out of three-hundred fifty-eight games, from age 32 to age 35. That's 263 of 263 regular season games, three of three All-Star games, 68 of 68 postseason games, and 23 of 24 preseason games.

The Flu Game was game number 245 — his 245th consecutive NBA game since returning from baseball.

That game, which was 20 years ago June 11, is now an archetype. Any player faced with illness in a big game is said to be experiencing his own "Flu Game." The backlash against current players over missing games to rest is a direct result of our feeling that Michael Jordan never rested.

"Hell," we say, "remember the Flu Game?"

Part of why we remember is that it solidified what we already knew: Jordan was a winner and a man who never quit. From his post-baseball return to Game 6 of the 1998 Finals, his teams went 283–74, a winning percentage equal to a 65-win NBA season. He led the East to wins in all three All-Star games. His Bulls swept their three first-round series, won all three second-round series in five games, and played in a Game 7 only once.

He dominated individually, too. In his three post-baseball seasons, Jordan went three for three on scoring titles, three for three on championships, three for three on Finals MVPs, two for three on MVPs, and two for three on All-Star MVPs.

I mean damn, in the one All-Star Game from '96 to '98 where Jordan didn't win MVP, he notched the game's first-ever triple-double.

Even in the 1995 playoffs, a supposedly "rusty" Jordan averaged 31.5 points per game, second only to eventual Finals MVP Hakeem Olajuwon's 33.0. In those playoffs, Jordan was sixth in PER, second in usage, fifth in plus/minus, and ninth in VORP. He also had the postseason's highest-scoring game, with 48 in the opener against Charlotte.

To put it lightly, from 1995 to 1998, Michael Jordan was a machine. And not just in games. Teammate Jud Buechler recalls times when Phil Jackson would let MJ take it easy in practice the day after a late game, focusing instead on scrimmages with the rest of the roster, only to have Jordan demand to tap in. Practice or game, the NBA Finals or a Wednesday against Vancouver, Jordan suited up.

"The guy amazed me—he never took a night off," Buechler told Sam Smith for Smith's 2014 Jordan oral history *There Is No Next*. "I think a lot of these guys now say, 'Hey, I'm a little banged up, this game doesn't really mean anything. They don't need me tonight. Let these other guys go.' He never did that. He's the star and he's playing the most minutes. ... It was a sense of 'the Bulls are coming to town and Michael Jordan's coming to town' and he knew that that place was going to be sold out. It's like, 'I'm gonna entertain these people. They're coming to see me.'"

Now, an argument can be made that Jordan's first retirement was the rest he needed to complete 357/358. While I acknowledge that minor league baseball (and the expectations on Jordan within it) cannot match the physical intensity of an NBA season (and the expectations on Jordan within *that*), I will note that in 1994, Jordan led the Birmingham Barons in games played (127) and was second in plate appearances with 497, followed by another 123 at bats in the Arizona Fall League, which closed out his one full year off the hardwood.

In 1994, Jordan was the only member of the Barons over the age of 25 to play 100 games. He was 31.

The man had a motor, and then some. He played and he won, no matter the circumstances. That's why 20 years later, the Flu Game sits at the heart of "6." It epitomizes our Jordan experience. That he could do anything. That he was indestructible.

June 11, 1997. The Delta Center. The night a legend became a myth. The night Jordan's mind hit the manual override on his body.

PART III: TALL TALES

"Let's just say, if I had to go through it again, I'd miss it. That's how sick I was," Jordan told *SLAM* magazine during the 1997 offseason. "I jeopardized my health, more so than I should have. And true, we won a championship ... but hindsight tells me I must have been a fool, and I don't think I'd do it again if I had to."

He couldn't think that way while curled in a ball on the floor of a hotel room in Park City, Utah, suffering from food poisoning and wondering why oh why he'd eaten that pizza. Tip-off for Game 5 was about 15 hours away. After taking a 2–0 lead at home, the Bulls dropped Games 3 and 4 to the Jazz. They'd faced a 2–2 tie in the Finals only once, five years earlier against Portland. They hadn't lost three straight non-preseason games with Jordan since starting 0–3 in 1991.

Jordan was old. He knew that. Before the season, he told Spike Lee that the Bulls' collective age meant no one should assume they would win "automatically." Their advantage was not athleticism. They succeeded because of talent, intelligence, experience, structure and resilience. Their edge was the ability to overcome mental and physical challenges, meaning Jordan simply had to power through what would be a grueling 18 hours or so, from waking up sick in the hotel, until the end of Game 5.

That's where it started—the hotel room. According to reporting before the game from Ahmad Rashad and Marv Albert, Jordan woke up at 3:30 in the morning with "flu-like symptoms" including a stomachache and a headache. He vomited all night. He stayed in bed all day. He didn't eat. He didn't practice. He missed the pregame shoot-around. Until he came to the court just before the jump ball, he stayed in a dark room in the stadium "trying to get some rest," he told Ahmad, while still vomiting.

"You get the idea he's having difficulty just standing up," Albert noted in the game's final minute.

"I really feel horrible," Jordan told Rashad before the game, about which Ahmad astutely reported: "And in his history, in games when he has either been hurt or sick, it's been bad news for the opponent."

Bingo. Jordan scored a game-high 38 points in 44 minutes, playing more minutes than any Utah player and fewer only to Pippen's 45. What enhanced the power of his performance was the transparency of his exhaustion. Jordan went full steam between the lines, and then during timeouts would sag on the bench with an icepack on his neck or head. He took it easy in the first and third quarters (with four and then two points) and played big in the second and fourth quarters (with 17 and then 15 points).

In one famous sequence, he picked off Stockton's pass, eluded Bryon Russell by dribbling behind his back and crossing back over to start the break, tossed a pass to a streaking Pippen, and then followed Pippen's missed layup with a rebound and a dunk.

Then he landed, and his body seemed to power down like a cell phone that was on 1 percent battery for the final 20 minutes of a phone call. Hang up the phone, and it dies on the spot.

That was Jordan that night. His physical state was such that at halftime, Bulls trainer Chip Schaefer told Ahmad: "He's exhausted, totally dehydrated, and a little bit out of it."

Still, the game would not be remembered as arguably Mike's masterpiece if he wasn't able to close the deal. With 45 seconds remaining in the 4th quarter, he tied the game with a free throw, missed the second free throw but got his own rebound, and then in the same possession, drilled a tie-breaking three with 25 seconds to play.

"He looks like he's a boxer just hanging on along the ropes," Albert said after the shot.

The Jazz got a dunk with 15 seconds left to pull within one, and then botched the closing sequence, as Malone—with five fouls—declined

PART III: TALL TALES 67

to foul Pippen. The Bulls passed their way down the court and got a dunk of their own, going back up by three with 6.2 seconds left.

And this is the origin of the defining image of the Jordan-Pippen relationship: Jordan slumping into Pippen's arms as the two men walked off the court. That image endures both because of what it says about the Jordan-Pippen partnership and because the sight of MJ's physical dependence was the final confirmation of the severity of his illness. That image finalized for the public the degree of difficulty Jordan faced, and thus how much he'd overcome.

The Jazz split a pair of free throws to end the game, with the Bulls winning 90–88. Two days later, Jordan hit Steve Kerr for a Finals-winning assist, capturing ring №5. Michael's next Bulls game was the 1997–98 preseason opener, which he played without Pippen (who had foot surgery four days before the preseason started) and Rodman (who didn't re-sign until the final two preseason games).

Jordan kept playing. He played the first three preseason games in the U.S., then led the Bulls in the two-game McDonald's Championship in Paris. Back in the states for a pair of games against the 76ers, Michael finally missed his first and only game since returning from baseball, sitting out the sixth preseason game of 1997–98 after having surgery on both feet to remove ingrown toenails.

He was supposed to rest until the regular season started, but the team's next preseason game was in Chapel Hill, home of Michael's alma mater UNC and, well, Mike didn't want to let anyone down.

He played that game and the final two, then started the regular season while Pippen recovered from his surgery. Jordan led the Bulls to a 24–11 record without Pip, played 13 more games with Pippen until the All-Star break, won the All-Star MVP, played 33 consecutive games to finish the regular season, won his 10th scoring title and fifth MVP, and then played 21 playoff games at a team-high 41.5 minutes while scoring 32.4 points per game.

At long last, in Game 6 of the 1998 NBA Finals and game number 357 out of 358, a 35-year-old Michael Jordan played a game-high 44 minutes and scored 45 of his team's 87 points, including his famous game-winner. He clinched ring No. 6 in a performance nearly as improbable as the Flu Game.

In the 1980s, Jordan's above-the-rim majesty was viewed nearly as sorcery. "Come fly with me," the video tape invited, but we couldn't. No one could, because only Jordan could make the impossible seem routine. He had—the people exclaimed—mastered gravity.

I never would have thought it was possible at the time, but today, we remember the Flu Game with more reverence than the day he scored 63. Larry Bird called it "God disguised as Michael Jordan." An apt description. That 63-point game felt like witnessing the power of a god. The Flu Game felt like witnessing the power of a man.

March 26, 2005, *"Bear Down and Get Some Runs"*
      Age 23

STORMING BACK: THE TALE OF ILLINOIS'S ARIZONA COMEBACK TO REACH THE FINAL FOUR

I'm trying to remember the last time I felt this good as a sports fan, and lemme say, it's a struggle. The Illini have just erased a fifteen point deficit to defeat the Arizona Wildcats in overtime and advance to the Final Four, and I'm so excited that I cannot even feel the bump on my knee I got when I banged it on the glass coffee table in front of me while bouncing during Illinois' comeback. It'll probably bruise by tomorrow, but GODDAMN-is-this-exciting!

PART III: TALL TALES

As far as the "as excited as" comparison, the best I can do is a comparison of opposite emotions: my current level of happiness against my level of sadness after the Cubs lost Game 7 to the Marlins. And honestly, at this very moment, I'm not sure what my answer would be.

I've always said that victory is sweeter after you've tasted defeat, and today's game was a perfect example of that. My girlfriend and I arrived in San Jose last night to stay at her parents' good friends' house, and we left this morning to go down to Monterey Bay and the 17 Mile Drive. We went down to Fisherman's Wharf in Monterey, and then to the beach. The scenery was beautiful — I sat on a rock at the beach and wrote some poetry — and we enjoyed Monterey, a nice little seaside town, as well as the 17 Mile Drive, a long and winding road, so to speak, through a forest and past the golf course. Nana pretty much demanded that I go and enjoy the beautiful sights, and so I did, calling her from there to say hello, and we're driving around, and we're driving around, and we're driving around, and then all of a sudden...

"Babe! It's 4:00!"

"Yeah?"

"Illini go on at 4:15!"

And with that we're off, speeding back to San Jose while cursing the radio for not having a good enough feed. We get back to the house, and by the time I figure out how to use their TV... *and* by the time I find CBS, the Illini are up two at halftime. I grab the two-liter bottle of Coke that they have in the fridge, grab a glass and throw three ice cubes in it, and stake out my position on a couch of a family I've known for less than 24 hours.

As the second half begins, Arizona seems to be playing with a bit more purpose than are the Illini, and yet Illinois stays with them. Back-to-back threes by Ivan Radenovic and Salim Stoudamire put the Wildcats up six 47-41, but a James Augustine dunk ties it up at 49. Channing Frye's layup puts Arizona up three, but Augustine's free throw cuts it to two. Jawann McClellan's dunk makes it 62-57, but Deron Williams' free throw cuts it to four. Then Hassan Adams gets a layup, and Mustafa Shakur hits a three, and Frye hits a three, and they're down twelve with under six to go...

"This isn't good," I say to no one in particular. "This isn't good."

Out of the corner of my eye I see the father, Alf, walk in and sit down on the other couch.

"How's it going?"

"Hey not good we're down can't talk now sorry."

"Oh. OK."

He sits quietly as I fall to pieces. After a full season of lackadaisically watching the Illini, a team that embodies everything I love about team sports, only now am I fully involved in this team and it dawns on me that I may have run out of chances to embrace them. This is a great team, and to have it end like this... it can't. We can't have another team go down like this, without a chance to show what they're about on the biggest stage. Here, in Chicago, at the former Rosemont Horizon, on Ray Meyer Court, the Illini are about to lose without a fight in front of a sea of heartbroken orange.

Dee dribbles right side and stumbles, losing the ball out of bounds, and the crowd is shocked. Stoudamire drives the lane and gets a block foul on Augustine, and then calmly hits both free throws.

"Come on Illini! Dig in here! Come on guys!"

But it continues, and when McClellan drives and is fouled by Roger Powell, Jr., I see a look of desperation in Powell's eyes as if the senior has seen the end of his career. You can see the determination in the faces of the Arizona players, like they know they have Illinois for the kill and all they have to do is finish them off. The Arizona lead is fifteen, 75-60, with 4:02 to play. Certainly enough time for a comeback — I watched

PART III: TALL TALES

Reggie Miller score eight points in 8.9 seconds to beat the Knicks in the playoffs in '95, and I watched Duke erase a ten point Maryland lead with under a minute to go in 2001 — but something has to be done — NOW.

As I'm thinking this, Deron squares up and hits a three, and the lead is down to twelve. I clap my hands, but Alf is not impressed.

"Well, they're still far behind."

"Yeah, but you gotta get *something* going."

"Well, I know what *I'm* gonna get going," and with that he heads into the bathroom.

McClellan goes back to the line and gets two more, but the next time down the floor the Illini kick it to Luther Head, who calmly nails a three of his own, and it's down to eleven points with under three to go.

"Yes! Here we go! Now keep it going guys!"

Just like that, the game is changed. It is still eleven points, but you can tell that Illinois understands exactly what they need to do to win and exactly how they are going to do it, and like they've done all season, it starts with defense. While Arizona is busy fantasizing about cutting down the nets, Illinois turns on the 'd' and begins attacking the ball with relentless fury, knocking down Arizona passes and turning them into fast break baskets. Dee gets a bucket to cut the lead to nine, Luther gets a dunk to cut it to seven. After another McClellan free throw, Deron hits a jumper to cut the lead to six, and after two free throws from Shakur, the game sits at 80-72 with a minute to play. But the tide has turned and the momentum has swung, and I know that Illinois has one more push in them. I feel it.

"Alright now! Come on! One more push!"

"What's that?" Alf asks, as he walks out of the bathroom and takes a seat back on the couch.

"NO!" I yell in protest. "I'm sorry, I didn't mean to yell, but you have to go back into the bathroom. We're coming back, and we've got it to eight, and I would hate it if we sat down to dinner in a few minutes and I was pissed off at you for ruining this game. So if you wouldn't mind…"

"Nope. I've got a friend just like you. I totally understand." And with that he casually walks back into the bathroom.

Now it is serious, and the Illini and the crowd at DePaul know that it is their game to win or lose. Luther comes down and hits a three, cutting the lead to five. Illinois forces another steal, and with the gym shaking and the fans going nuts, they kick it to Dee on the break and his layup gets it to three.

"Yes! Oh hell yes! We got this game! We got it!" We got it. I know this now, and the crowd knows it, and everybody is going bezerk. Arizona takes a full timeout, and as the Wildcats slink over to their bench, the Illini run to theirs and are greeted by their teammates who embrace them with high fives, chest bumps, and hugs. I'm jumping up and down with the fans at the Allstate, and on the way down on one jump I clock my knee on the glass coffee table.

"Yes! Yes! Ahhh! Ow! Oh, son of a bitch!"

"Baby," I hear from the other room, "you alright?"

"Fine! Yes! It's down to three points! Three points!"

"What was that bang?" a voice asks from the bathroom.

"I hit my knee on your table," I yell back.

"How's the table?"

"Fine. Don't worry."

"Is the game over yet?"

PART III: TALL TALES

"Nope."

"Okie doke. I'll be in here then."

"Yeah." I say flatly, waiting for play to resume. It does, and after a stop by the Illini they get the ball over to Deron, who dribbles at the top of the key, steps around a screen, and then let's fly on a three pointer. "There it is!" I yell in anticipation. It drops right through, *nothing but net*, and with that we've come all the way back. 80-80, half a minute left, and I smile, because it is obvious: this is now my team.

Illinois snuffs out Arizona's last shot of regulation, and as we head into overtime, the Illini clearly have the momentum. Deron hits another three to get things going, but Arizona responds with two Channing Frye buckets. Roger Powell gets a layup to put the Illini back up one, and then Deron hits yet another triple, and Luther's layup off of another forced turnover runs the Illini lead to 90-84. The Allstate Arena is about to erupt…

…but this is a strong-willed Arizona team, and led by Hassan Adams the Wildcats storm back. Adams gets a layup and a foul, and completes the three point play. Deron misses a pair of shots on Illinois' next possession, and then Adams gets the ball back and gets another bucket. 90-89, Illinois timeout.

"Alright, big possession now, just get two."

The Illini bring the ball up, swing it around, and look for the open shot.

"Two points now. Two points."

The clock ticks down, and the fans at the Allstate come to a fevered pitch.

"Two points. Two points."

25, 24, 23, and Luther Head pulls up for a jumper and misses. Rebound Arizona. Timeout.

"Damnit!"

As Arizona sets up their play, everybody in the gym knows where the ball is going: Arizona sharpshooting senior Salim Stoudamire. The guy has had a miserable night shooting the ball—nine points on 2 of 13—but every shooter has slumps. There's no doubt that he will have a shot to win the game. This is the guy who has led Arizona all season, the All-American who just two days earlier had confidently beaten Oklahoma State with a jumper as time wound down. If Illinois was going to the Final Four, they would need one last defensive stop, and they would need to stop Salim Stoudamire.

The ball comes in to Adams, and he takes it to the top of the key. Deron stays on him, and I watch Stoudamire on the near side, waiting for him to make his move as the clock runs down.

"Oh man, they're not gonna get it!" I say to myself as I watch it unfold. Stoudamire finally runs towards Adams, but our defense is too tight. Suddenly desperation sinks in for Arizona, as they realize their designed play is broken and all they will get is a panicked shot, and the Illini clamp down and the clock ticks away and the fans prepare to leap right out of the building, and all Stoudamire can do is watch as Adams' three-point heave falls harmlessly to the floor. Game over.

"Yes! Yes! Hell yes! Ahhh ha ha ha! Oh my god! Yes!" Finding no one else in the house anywhere near as excited as me, I call my dad and just start yelling as soon as he picks up.

"Wow! Wasn't that exciting?" he asks.

But I'm yelling too loud, hardly able to complete a sentence. Illinois is going to the Final Four, and I am going with them.

Aug. 11, 2016, Windy City Gridiron
Age 34

A SALUTE TO DEVIN HESTER'S MAGICAL ROOKIE YEAR

Every touchdown started with a pause.

When I close my eyes and picture him, that's what I see. Before the burst, before the high step, I see Devin Hester's pause. Typically this was the slightest of pivots to change direction, a Neo-dodging-bullets approach to returning kicks.

That was the pause on the Super Bowl return, when on the 16-yardline he pushed off the turf with his right foot, changed direction, slowed, pushed with his left foot, changed direction again, and then entered his sprint.

Other times the pause was a nearly imperceptible shift of balance as he sized up his route to the end zone and dusted confused defenders like Road Runner.

On the field goal return against the Giants, the pause was a bluff, a con, that devil-may-care smirk Paul Newman dropped in movies before he ate all the eggs or set down four of a kind.
No matter the circumstance, the pause belied the calculation. It masked the speed to come.

As I embark on this journey to re-live the masterful 2006 season, the name that immediately pops to mind is Devin Hester. When I think of the defense, I actually think of the 2005 team first, probably because the offense was plodding and the special teams were serviceable. I think I have more defensive memories from '05 than '06 — the Carolina sack-attack game, back-bending blitz mania on Brett Favre, the pick-sixes from Peanut and Nate and Mike Brown, Urlacher tossing Mike Vick around Soldier Field like the Cincinnati Zoo ape and that intrepid toddler.

To me, Hester epitomizes the difference between the '06 team and the '05 team: flashy brilliance mixed with popular appeal. An adrenaline shot to our heart that was the dagger in theirs.

Hester scored seven times in the 2006 season, yet it felt like he did it every week, didn't it? It's weird: Hester's brilliance is historicized on YouTube for future generations to behold, and yet the acts for which he is most famous (his touchdowns) cannot be properly appreciated without everything that happened around them.

After all, a five-year-old Bears fan in 2006 is an in-his-prime Bears fan of 15 in 2016. And this young fan can watch every Hester return touchdown again and again, from the season opener in Green Bay to his one-and-only with Atlanta.

Yet if you only know Hester from the touchdowns, you don't really KNOW Hester. Because the Hester experience is not just about the touchdowns. It's about the suspense. The anticipation of the ball in his hands. The way folks stopped grilling and set down the paper and came in from the kitchen and told the person on the phone to "hang on one sec because Hester's back deep."

The Hester experience was about the pause.

And you can't get that strictly on YouTube.

During training camp of 2013, I did a series of interviews asking Bears players for their "Welcome to the NFL moment." This was open to their interpretation — answers ranged from seeing their jersey hanging in their locker for the first time (Tillman) to lining up on the practice field (Forte) to getting fake released after being late to a meeting (Nate Collins).

Hester's moment, he started, was "the first game of my rookie year."

To which I immediately thought, *Of course, the touchdown against Green Bay. His first NFL score. Makes sense.*

PART III: TALL TALES

Nope.

"The welcome moment was when the jets flew over my head," Hester told me. "It was a new feeling. It's what the NFL is all about. A real football player will tell you that those jets mean something. I don't know what it is. It gives you chills from your pinky toenail to the last hair on your head. When those jets fly over your head, you know it's football time."

THAT'S how I felt watching Devin Hester line up to return a kick: like the jets were flying over my head.

Watching Hester return kicks in 2006 and 2007 was like watching Sammy Sosa hit home runs in 1998 and 1999: every time up felt like another was coming. And just as Sosa's 63 home runs in '99 can't touch his 66 home runs in '98 because of the playoff implications in the latter, so too did Hester's brilliance sometimes feel empty in 2007 compared to the game-winningness of his mad dashes in '06.

I'll give you an example.

The first time Hester felt like a legend was the Super Bowl. We're talking legend in the old-timey sense, when explorers would come ashore after months at sea and the folks on land would greet them, saying, "Word of your deeds has traveled far and wide!"

But the first time he felt like a Hall of Famer — like someone who could carry us to great heights all on his own, like someone about whom I would one day tell my children — was eight weeks earlier against the Rams.

That Monday night, December 11, 2006, the Bears arrived in St. Louis as the NFC's best team. At 10-2, we had clinched the division and were in a three-way tie for the best record in the league. Our offense, though sagging, was still the best it had been under Lovie Smith. Our defense, of course, was masterful.

And we had the league's new favorite weapon. Number 23. Devin Hester.

One week earlier, Hester scored his fourth return touchdown of the year, a 45-yard punt return at Soldier Field versus the Vikings.

"The wind was picking up and it was a bad situation, and he pooched the ball and (it) kind of hit on the field and kind of rolled," Hester said after the game. "I had enough time to pick it up and run, and kind of gave a right jab and brought it back around to the left, and my teammates picked up their guys and I got into the end zone."

That game, instead of just returning punts as he'd done all year, the Bears finally let Hester return kicks. He'd returned three in 11 weeks and returned three against Minnesota. (I am still stunned it took that long.)

Against the Rams he returned four kicks for 225 yards and two touchdowns; the first one set a new NFL record for special teams touchdowns in a season (5), and the second set a new NFL record for non-offensive touchdowns in a season (6).

"Let's see what he can do with a kickoff?" announcer Tony Kornheiser asked rhetorically after Hester ran a first-quarter kick back 94 yards for what the broadcast noted was his record-tying fifth return touchdown in a season. "How'd you like what you just saw?"

That TD gave the Bears a 7-6 lead. In the fourth quarter, with the team up 35-20, Hester struck again.

96 yards. Touchdown.

After both returns, Kornheiser argued for Hester as rookie of the year.

"Who's had more of an impact on the league this year than this guy?" Kornheiser said after the second touchdown. "He's saved the Bears in games. He's the x-factor for the Bears. He's scary every time he gets his hands on the ball. Do you penalize him? It's sort of like baseball, where you say 'I don't want to make a DH the MVP.' Do you penalize a guy because he's essentially a returner? Or do you say, 'He's the rookie who's had the most impact'?"

In that minute of announcing, Kornheiser summed up the now ten-year debate about Hester's Hall of Fame credentials. Is he out because he's "only a returner"? Or is he in because he's the greatest returner who has ever played?

To me that's a no-brainer. The only reason Hester is not considered a first-ballot HOFer is the Hall's bias against special teams.

But we'll leave that discussion for another day. For now, just close your eyes and picture that blur of a 23 streaking across your screen. Or, should you have been lucky enough to attend a game in which Hester scored, picture him soaring through your field of vision.

After we beat the Rams, the *Tribune*'s Fred Mitchell wrote about Hester's explosion onto the national scene and the impact he was having on opposing coaches. Hester's perspective on the treatment he would receive from kickers was prescient:

"This is the NFL and teams are not going to bow down to just one player," Hester said. "I think throughout the rest of the season they are going to continue to kick to me."

Sure enough, Hester had a great all-around return game the next week against Tampa Bay, was decent in the finale against the Packers, and was brilliant in the divisional playoff game vs. Seattle, where a 66-yard punt return touchdown (that would have given the Bears a 4th-quarter lead) was nullified by an illegal block.

Then of course he had the Super Bowl return.

And 2007.

And 2010.

And 2011.

And 2013.

And you get the idea.

Last month, the Falcons released Hester on the heels of toe surgery. He is 33. He is unemployed. He is one of the greatest athletes I have ever seen.

I still see him when I close my eyes. That pivot. That pause.

And then poof — he's gone.

May 1, 2009, ReadJack.com
  Age 27

WRITING IT RIGHT: JOAKIM NOAH AND GAME 6 OF THE 2009 BULLS-CELTICS SERIES

In the fabulously direct words of Bluto Blutarsky:

Ho-lee SHI-TTT!

(I mean, seriously, is there any other way to begin this column?)

And speaking of beginnings, where to? To Ray Allen dropping 51 on a postseason record-tying nine treys? To Captain Kirk showing a never-before-seen rage, balling his fists and squaring up against the suddenly Laimbeerian Rondo? To Johnny Fishsticks flashing an "I'm dropping 40 tonight" grin after hitting his third three of the game's first six minutes? To Allen and Eddie House each knocking down deuces that would have been game-tying triples had their toes

PART III: TALL TALES 81

been back *just a touch*? To Brad Miller redeeming his Game 5 layup/free-throw brick tandem by scoring the team's final five of regulation and last two points of the second *and* third overtimes? To Boston's entire starting frontcourt fouling out, and Ben Gordon as well? To Joakim Noah high-fiving every first-row fan after the game's wild conclusion? To Salmons hitting a layup that bounced off the *bottom* of the rim before trickling *up*? To the Bulls blowing a 12-point lead in the 4th, followed by Boston blowing an eight-point lead…in the 4th? To Allen's game-tying trey at the end of the second OT? To the Bulls' failure to even get a shot off with 7.6 seconds remaining following that Allen three-pointer? To Derrick Rose's game (almost) securing block on Rondo?

Yeah…that was all great.

But in telling the story of Game 6, in capturing the collective incredibleness of these first six games, there is only one starting point: Noah's improbably coordinated steal, drive, and dunk (and foul shot) that broke the 123-123 tie with 35 seconds to play.

Just before Noah's steal, I was actually getting bored. Crazy, I know, particularly in light of that thick paragraph above. But when you've already watched 322 minutes of playoff basketball over six games and you're in the midst of a 7th overtime period… when you've already seen a rookie point guard post a 36-11 in his playoff debut, a pair of UConn guards in a 72-point shoot out, and a non-flagrant foul call leading to an air-balled layup and a pair of missed freebies… well, when you've seen all *that*, even the most remarkable of occurrences can seem dull and predictable.

The fourth quarter? Up to snuff, for a while: the Bulls' 12-point and then 10-point lead vanishing in the midst of Boston's unfathomable 18-0 run, followed by the boys in white and red storming back from down eight to tie. But since we were already wondering if another overtime was in the cards, and since we reached that overtime by both Pierce and Gordon missing game-winning jumpers… well, it seemed a might forced, a basketball deux ex machina for the ages.

We experience sports like a story. The better the storytelling, the better the experience. And with overtime preserved only through both Pierce and Gordon missing, the sports screenwriting down the stretch was getting sloppy. That carelessness continued at the end of the first OT, with Pierce missing another potential game-winner, and then once more with the fabled Triple Overtime Playoff Game in reach, the sharpshooter Allen stroking a three to tie followed by the worst of plot contrivances: the Bulls failing to even hoist a game-winning attempt, the extra session ending with Miller and Salmons scrambling unsuccessfully for the ball like Rocky trying to wrangle the chicken.

They always say "you couldn't have written it any better."

Well this time, you couldn't have written it any worse.

Overtimes aren't fun just because they are overtimes. They're fun because of the drama. As I watched at Northside Bar and Grill, my favorite burger and beer joint in the neighborhood, that drama was dying.

At least we've got a crowd, I kept thinking. Earlier this month, I'd headed to Northside to see the Bulls beat the Sixers. It was a crucial, end-of-the-season game. To my surprise, mine were the only eyes on the screen. Now the place was packed, the whole joint rocking and rolling with every shot.

Much of the crowd had seemingly just come from work. Collared shirts, slacks, and briefcases abounded. Still, these guys were ready to root. One dude even brought a red SCOTTIE PIPPEN jersey with him, hanging it on the wall ledge next to his table, grabbing at it for good luck throughout the game. When the commercial break between overtimes two and three was ending, dude to my left suddenly snapped into a New Seriousness, snatching the jersey off the wall and putting it on over his blue pinstriped button-down.

I looked at the TV just before tip-off. It had been a physical series, but holy hell... are Salmons and Pierce elbowing each other *before*

PART III: TALL TALES   83

the tip? They surely were, and the crowd at Northside was just as amped — on either side of the TV I was eyeing, the Blackhawks were battling in Game 1 of their series, while the Cubs were playing the Marlins at Wrigley. They may as well have been televising *Heidi*.

There we all were — Salmons, Rose, and Hinrich; Pierce, Allen, and Rondo; the UC crowd; the gang at Northside; all of us locked in to this overtime-crazed best-of-seven with a tie game at 118.

A jumper from Rose. Bulls up two. A three-point play from Big Baby. Celts up one. Another jumper from Rose. Bulls back up, followed by the Captain splitting a pair from the line and the Jesus knocking down a deuce to tie it once more. The clock under two minutes now. The teams trading possessions. Nuhtin' for us, nuhtin' for them. Timeout Bulls. Minute-fifteen. Waiting. Waiting. Rolled up sleeves all around at Northside, the billiards game at a halt, the wait staff no longer waiting, the dude in PIPPEN 33 bouncing, the city of Chicago holding its breath, all of us standing. And then…

A Rose miss with 56 seconds left, Rondo with the board, the new Little Irritant bringing it up. Over to Big Baby — under 50 seconds now — and then Davis a handoff to Pierce coming around a screen to his left, Northside hopping. Pierce a step ahead of his man Salmons as he drives to the free throw line, and then spotting Scalabrine in the corner open for three. Pierce firing a pass, but Noah has hustled over and shoots his long fingers in front of Pierce's ill-fated throw.

Now Noah is running, and here's where things got crazy. Had it been Rose on the break, we'd've all been amped, waiting for the layup. But now, with big, goofy Joakim on the move and his ponytail swinging, I found myself in the throes of, like, eight separate emotions. I wanted Noah to score, but because it was Noah and not Rose or Gordon or Hinrich or Salmons or Anthony freaking Roberson, the excitement of an otherwise gimme-fast break was mitigated by the tension of Noah possibly dribbling off his foot or tumbling over or getting his layup blocked from behind. There was the amazing thrill of watching Noah outrun Pierce, but since he had Salmons trailing, a part of me was hoping that Noah would dump it off to his more fleet-footed teammate.

Now the mystery was building as to whether or not Noah would dish. And of course there was the innate comedy involved — had this been the first quarter of a November game rather than the third overtime of Game 6, the UC would have been in cheerful stitches as ol' Noah lumbered down the floor, something like the basketball version of Keith Traylor's interception in 2001.

But Noah did not pass, and he did not trip, and just as we were finally convinced that things would work out with a hard Pierce foul and a pair of Noah free throws, the basketball player basketball fans love to hate rose up and threw down a spectacular fast break dunk, the only exclamation point this game truly deserved.

"He got it! He got it! Holy shit! Noah got it!" The United Center was shaking. Noah was screaming. Northside was jumping. Pierce was disgusted (and gone, with his sixth foul). I looked at the baseball game, where I was surprised to notice that the Cubs were now tied in the top of the tenth. Not that anyone was watching. Certainly not PIPPEN, who was scooting around the bar and high-fiving every fan in sight. "The steal and the drive and the dunk!" he shouted to me. "Just like Pippen! Just like Pippen!" Noah knocked down the free throw and the Bulls led by three.

Naturally, things weren't over. We still had House's toe-tipping two-pointer, a pair of free throws from Miller, a Rondo bucket, Kirk's bricked layup with Rondo's possible goal-tend, Rose's game-saving block, Rose's game-resurrecting missed free throws, and Rondo's desperation three.

But so what? Joakim Noah streaking down the court, his hair behind him and the dunk ahead. I know a perfect ending when I see one.

May 20, 2012
Age 30

ON KERRY WOOD'S RETIREMENT AND THE PROMISE OF 20 KS

A row of K's.

That was the indelible image of Kerry Wood's career masterpiece. Not batter upon Houston batter whiffing another diving slider, but the front row of bleacher fans on May 6, 1998 each hoisting a colored K placard, the line of K's growing until each new strikeout was a challenge from Wood to the bleachers: I've got another. Do you?

The answer was 'yes,' but the challenge was reversed from then on, Cubs fans wondering if Woody had another masterpiece in him, and that answer was 'not really.'

Oh, there was Game 1 of the 2003 NLDS, where Wood added a game-changing RBI double to his 11 strikeouts on the mound. And he did pitch three more 10-K one-hitters.

Still, he never produced a sequence of truly dominant starts, never figured into the Cy Young discussion, and never led the Cubs to a World Series.

And sure, you can say that about every Cubs starter since 1945's Hank Wyse. Yet you wouldn't, because failing to make the World Series is an assumed trait of post-WWII northsiders.

Not for Kerry Wood. His dominance on that drizzly Wednesday afternoon made Cubs fans feel like future World Series champs. 20 K's was, surely, a preview of greatness to come. Instead, it was the greatest he would ever be.

And so what? No player in my lifetime ever felt more *committed* to this dreary franchise's hopeless quest for a trophy, and if the promise of '20 K' went unfulfilled, what else is new? These are the Cubs, where baseball dreams go to die. If he'd struck out 10 Astros instead of 20, would we have expected less? I suppose so. Would we be happier? I doubt it.

As it turned out, May 6, 1998 was a peak, not a promise. And because we were in it together from his first strikeout to his last, we felt his pain and he felt ours. He won't be a Hall of Famer, and his jersey probably won't be retired. But you can say one thing about Kerry Wood: he was a Cub. He was a Cub.

April 29, 2013
  Age 31

THE NATE ROBINSON GAME

Now THAT's what I call a playoff game!

And to think, it all started with a missed dunk.

Not just any missed dunk – this was a two-handed missed dunk by a wide-open Brooklyn Net.

And not just any Brooklyn Net, but former Bull C.J. Watson, the man whose foolish pass at the end of last season's Game 6 loss to Philadelphia put a cap on the Bulls' nightmare 2012 postseason.

And now here was Watson, elevating for the surest of NBA points, his team up 14 with 3:15 to play, and the ball fluttered off the rim. "Holy hell!" I shouted to my friends at The Anthem on Division Street. "Have you ever seen a guy brick an uncontested *two-handed* dunk?"

They shook their heads, all of us befuddled by what we'd witnessed, but that was nothing compared to what came next: a 14-0 run led by Nate "Ben Gordon" Robinson, who ripped off 12 straight points on a chaotic mix of off-kilter jumpers and down-the-pipe foul shots.

When the horn sounded on regulation and the ballgame headed to overtime, I texted my buddies Bryan Crawford and Chris Cason, two Bulls beat reporters at the United Center, and asked them to "describe the stadium right now in three words."

- Bryan: "Crazy as fuck"
- Chris: "Absolutely fucking crazy"

Well put, gents. What followed was an epic battle of attrition, one that announcer Steve Kerr dubbed "an instant classic" – and that was merely after the FIRST overtime. That period ended with Robinson and Brooklyn's Joe Johnson draining frantic jumpers in the final two seconds, Robinson's shot a leaner that can best be described as "off-balance," "unexpected," and "straight to the heart."

Despite fouling out, Robinson was the game's hero, scoring 29 of his game-high 34 points after the end of the 3rd quarter. His performance epitomized the team's effort – his shots weren't always pretty, but they almost always went in.

That, as Sean Connery once said, is the Chicago way: hard fought, hard earned, and one win away from the Miami Heat.

Go Bulls? Fucking A.

June 25, 2013
   Age 31

THE NIGHT THE BLACKHAWKS WON THE CUP BUT I GOT MUGGED

On the night the Blackhawks scored two goals in 17 seconds to win the 2013 Stanley Cup, I experienced my first mugging, about 30 feet away from my apartment.

All things considered, that wasn't the worst part of my night.

After all, as armed robberies go, this one was as non-confrontational as they get. Not to mention that I am a terrible candidate for a robbery target: this gentleman's entire score was a 3G Droid with a faulty camera, $5 in cash, and one debit card that accesses the checking account of a journalist. You're better off robbing a pizza delivery driver.

No, the night's low point came a few hours before the robbery, when I failed to see the game-tying and series-winning goals.

Earlier in the day, I'd headed to O'Hare with my friend Rob to see him off on his return flight to San Francisco. But the flight was delayed two and a half hours, so we kicked it in the Hilton hotel bar until his departure. I watched the first period at the bar and then took the Blue Line back to Wicker Park.

When I got back to the neighborhood, the game was in the second intermission. Rather than going to a bar, I went home to finish some work that was derailed by the delayed flight. Since I don't have cable, I figured I would just watch the game on a bootleg web feed and then head right back to the neighborhood if the Hawks won.

PART III: TALL TALES

But the web feed was choppy, so I kept an eye on the score on espn.com as I did my work.

After Game 1, I figured this series would go the distance. And when Milan Lucic scored to give the Bruins a 2-1 lead, my seven-game series intuition seemed accurate. I kept refreshing the browser: 2-1 Bruins, seven minutes left ... 2-1 Bruins, six minutes left ... 2-1 Bruins, four minutes left ... 2-1 Bruins, two minutes left ... "Well," I thought to myself, "that's gonna do it." I hit refresh again: 3-2 Blackhawks, 40 seconds left ...

"Holy shit!"

Now, if there is an upside to missing one of the greatest moments in Chicago sports history, it's that it proves just how NON-bandwagon I truly am. I would never miss an analogous moment for the Bulls or Bears. While I have always rooted for the Blackhawks, they have never been my team because hockey has never been my sport. I took a certain amount of pride in that distinction.

In retrospect, that was probably just the shock talking: I was downright dumbfounded in having missed one of the seminal moments in Chicago sports history. I snapped myself free of my philosophical daze, grabbed my wallet, my phone and my keys and darted out the door. Already the sounds of chaos were building: cheers booming out of homes, fireworks exploding, cars honking. "I missed it!" I kept thinking. "How the hell did I miss it? And what even happened??"

People were pouring out of the bars. I staggered over to the 6 Corners Sports Bar on North Avenue and stood outside the windows with a pack of police officers and civilians, all of us watching the Hawks celebrate on the Boston ice. 6 Corners was blasting "We Are the Champions," and fans were chanting "M-V-P!" for Patrick Kane, who was accepting the Conn Smythe trophy.

I was flabbergasted. I stepped into the parking lot across the street from Santullo's and called my girl. "I missed it!" I shouted to her in disbelief. I got a text from my dad: "No Game 7 like you thought, but it was all worth it. How about that game?" I called my folks and told them the bad news.

As we talked, I saw a friend, the rapper Que Billah, walking up North Avenue. "I missed it!" I said to him as we shook hands.

"I did too!" he said, equally shocked. "I was in the car on some whole other shit, heading to the studio. All of a sudden I heard people cheering. I figured, 'Oh, I guess the Hawks won.' Then I drove a bit more, and bam, more cheering! I was like, 'Damn, why are they cheering again?'"

He was heading into 6 Corners, and I joined him for a drink. On TV were helicopter shots of the madness in Wrigleyville, Clark Street choked with people in red shirts like the CPS protests times 50. Suddenly I realized that 6 Corners had thinned out, and I went outside and saw that the North-Damen-Milwaukee intersection was now overrun with revelers, just as it had been in 2010. Traffic was frozen in all directions. A 72 bus was stopped in front of SubT, and a Papa John's truck was stuck trying to go south on Damen.

Meanwhile, people were hoisting friends onto each other's shoulders, spraying champagne and beer, kissing inflatable Stanley Cups, and of course chanting "Let's Go Hawks!" and "Boston Sucks!" and, for some reason, "U-S-A!" There was even a man dressed as a Stanley Cup via tinfoil and masking tape, and he was marching around the intersection saying, "I am the Stanley Cup! The Blackhawks won me tonight. Take a picture with me!" Plenty of people did indeed pose for pictures with "the Stanley Cup."

Others posed for pictures in the crowd, with delayed motorists, with the people stranded on the 72, and with police. Camera phones were everywhere, filming the ruckus. I tried to take a picture, but my crappy old Droid would not allow it. Fortunately I ran into several friends, including one who took a picture of the two of us with his phone.

PART III: TALL TALES

I celebrate the 2013 Stanley Cup Finals in Wicker Park with Paul Matian.

I went back into 6 Corners and had another drink with my friend and some of his friends. Then, with the police cordially clearing the intersection, I walked home. I was barely buzzed and felt a greater intoxication of spirit than of body. I checked the time on my phone as I walked up Pierce, and as I turned onto Hoyne, I saw a man crossing the street toward me. I looked in his eyes. They were trouble.

"Hey," he said as he got onto Hoyne, about 15 feet behind me.

I kept walking, my phone in my hand at my side and my building now in sight. "Hey," he said again, rather casually, and I turned around.

"Yeah?"

"Put it down," he said as he cocked his pistol--click-click. I set my phone on the sidewalk. He neither approached me nor pointed the gun my way. We were staring at each other, still about 15 feet apart, his face in the darkness. "Wallet," he said, and I put my wallet on the ground next to my phone. "Take off," he said, and I turned and started walking. Then he asked, "Is there money in there?"

"There's a five," I said.

He sighed. "Keep going," he said. And then, changing his mind again, "No, go down the alley." So I turned left, walked down the alley that loops around my building, came out the other side back on Hoyne, looked around, and dashed home. Woke up my roommate to borrow his phone, called the police, and filed a report.

"What did he take?" the police asked me, and I described the unimpressive haul. I can only imagine this man's disappointment as he realized, yes, I did only have five dollars in cash, plus a debit card good for only a single fill-up at a gas station in Forest Park. All told, it was a rather unlucky night for my new acquaintance. One can only hope that he at least saw the goals.

Nov. 10, 2022, Windy City Gridiron
   Age 41

BOBBY DOUGLASS AND JUSTIN FIELDS: RUNNING MEN

"When I drop back, I'm thinking 100% to pass. But if there's a breakdown, I'll scramble." — Bobby Douglass, 25 years old, November 1972

"Oh, I loved running. But back then, quarterbacks weren't supposed to run. I would have loved to play for a coach who used my ability." — Bobby Douglass, 75 years old, November 2022

******

PART III: TALL TALES

It's Lions week! And I've got a Lions story for you.

But it's also Justin Fields week! And I've got a Bobby Douglass story for you.

Spoiler alert: They're the same story.

Growing up in the 1980s and really the 1990s, there were certain Bears quarterbacks I heard about from my father, uncle, grandfather and older relatives and friends. Obviously any Bears QB who comported himself halfway professionally summoned the name of Sid Luckman.

My dad's guy was Billy Wade, he of the '63 champs, and early on there were McMahon comps to Wade — both guided championship Bears teams in #9 — until finally it was all about Mac, and the pain of knowing "That Jim Harbaugh, I like him, he'll do, but he's no McMahon."

(The screams from my father's mother when news broke that we shipped Mac to the Chargers. We were out to dinner together and a news report came on at the restaurant. The SCREAMS, I tell you. The indignance. The OUTRAGE.)

So it was Luckman for the good and McMahon for the gutsy. When we had someone undersized out there (say, Rex), I heard about Doug Flutie. Someone uninspiring but steady (say, Orton), I heard about Bob Avellini.

But oh, if a Bears quarterback ran for with even a modicum of reckless success, we only heard one name.

Bobby Douglass.

"He's an amazing athlete," Raiders quarterback Daryl Lamonica said after Douglass shredded Lamonica's Raiders for 127 rushing yards in the 1972 season finale. "If I ran that much, I'd be in shape."

I don't know if that's a compliment, an insult, or something in between, but it does epitomize the feedback I always heard from my elders on Douglass. They talked about what he was and DEFINITELY delved into what he wasn't.

And that duality is a perfect introduction to a Bears history lookback that is fitting for this week's game against Detroit.

Let's go back 50 years, to Tiger Stadium, the day a Bears quarterback set an NFL record while taking a loss.

Bobby Douglass beats Greg Landry while Greg Landry beats Bobby Douglass

"It's a play that either works or doesn't," Bobby Douglass said on Oct. 15, 1972. He was describing his 57-yard touchdown run on a bootleg left, but he could just as well be describing the totality of the Bobby Douglass experience.

When Justin Fields rushed for 178 yards on Sunday, Douglass came up again and again. Fields broke two of Douglass's Bears records (more on that below), including rushing yards in a game by a quarterback. Douglass's mark was the aforementioned 127, which ended his record-shattering season at 968 rushing yards.

But because he nearly doubled the previous season record for rushing by a quarterback, his season record-setting game was not against the Raiders. It was six weeks prior, when the Bears traveled to face the Detroit Lions and quarterback Greg Landry.

One year earlier, Landry came into the final week of the season needing 19 yards rushing to break the QB season rushing record, then held by Green Bay's Tobin Rote, who ran for 523 in 1951. Landry gained 25 yards in his team's final game and set the new record at 530.

PART III: TALL TALES

Douglass destroyed that. After just seven games of the 1972 season, Douglass had rushed for 504 yards on 71 carries. His passing and rushing stats were shockingly close:

- 81 pass attempts, 610 yards, 6 touchdowns
- 71 rush attempts, 504 yards, 4 touchdowns

He'd already had a 100-yard game against Cleveland (the game with the 57-yard run). At 6'4, 225 pounds, he was an inch taller and a few pounds lighter than Justin Fields. He was also a lefty, which always adds an element of struggle for defenders.

As a passer, he was wild, explosive and inaccurate. In the Browns game, while rushing for 117 yards, he passed for only 62, completing just two of his nine attempts, but one of those attempts was a 41-yard touchdown.

Fans never quite knew what they would see next when Bobby Douglass had the ball. But they knew going into the Detroit game that Douglass would soon have a new NFL record.

"The question isn't whether he'll break the record, but whether he'll make 1,000 yards," Landry said before the Bears came to Detroit. "The record was 20 years old and everyone had forgotten about it until I started running last year. It took me 14 games. He'll break it in the eighth game."

So, Detroit.

This Lions game strikes me as just pitch-perfect Bearsdom. First, the good: Douglass did indeed break the record, carrying the ball seven times for 52 yards, giving him 556 yards on the season, breaking Landry's mark by 26 yards with half the season to go.

The irony — the Bearsdom — was that Landry outplayed him. He rushed eight times for 71 yards, including a touchdown, and the Lions blanked their NFC Central rivals 14-0.

"I don't care about the rushing record," Douglass said after the game. "I've got to gain some yards because it's part of our offense."

The loss ended a three-game winning streak and instead kicked off a five-game losing streak. Douglass started every game of that lackluster 1972 season. The team finished 4-9-1. And Bobby Douglass's team-leading 968 yards rushing stood as the NFL record until 2006, when Michael Vick became the first QB to rush for 1,000 yards.

And unless you were with an elder, that was the last many of us heard about Bobby Douglass.

Until this season.

Justin Fields passes the runner

You'll be hearing Bobby Douglass's name a lot more this season as Justin Fields continues to let 'er rip.

And he will, if anyone's listening to Douglass.

"There's so much room on the field," the 75-year-old Douglass told the *Sun-Times*'s Rick Telander the day after Fields diced up the Dolphins. "Give Fields the green light."

Fields has had it lately, and with a mix of designed runs and mind-blowing scrambles, he destroyed the Dolphins in historic fashion, setting the following records:

- Longest run by a Bears QB, 61 yards (passing Vince Evans's 58-yard run in 1980)
- Longest touchdown run by a Bears QB, 61 yards (passing Douglass's 57-yard run in 1972)
- Most rushing yards in a game by a Bears QB, 178 (passing Douglass's 127 against the Raiders in 1972)
- Most rushing yards in a regular season game by any NFL quarterback, 178 (passing Mike Vick's 173 against the Vikings in 2002)

PART III: TALL TALES

There is another record that Fields set that hasn't been talked about, one that helped create his rushing opportunities: his threat to pass. Whether the Matrix-esque bullet-time pump fake on his 61-yard touchdown run or his three TD passes, Fields created running space because of his passing, and created passing space because of his running.

The record in question? Of the now seven times in which a QB has rushed for 150 yards or more in a game, Justin Fields is the only one who posted a passer rating over 100.

"Dude's a baller," said Dolphins quarterback Tua Tagovailoa after the game, "and he was making some plays in the passing game as well."

Douglass was never on Fields's level as a passer. He threw for 1,246 yards in 1972, just under 300 more yards passing than rushing. That was his career high with the Bears (he threw for 42 more yards with the Saints in 1976). He did have a few games with a passer rating over 100, but his pass attempts were always low. He threw 30 passes four times in his career and his best rating in those games was 67.

He only had one season where the threw more touchdowns than interceptions: 1970, when he played three games, threw four TDs and was picked off three times.

"When I drop back, I'm thinking 100% to pass," Douglass said just before the Lions game. "But if there's a breakdown, I'll scramble."

"Oh, I loved running," Douglass says now, who Telander described as "still looking fit at 75 ...wearing a blue pullover and black shorts on a 50-degree day." What Douglass wishes he'd had is what Luke Getsy and the Bears are just now starting to give Justin: a playbook defined by his skills.

"Back then, quarterbacks weren't supposed to run," Douglass told Telander. "I would have loved to play for a coach who used my ability."

Justin has that. With 602 yards rushing, he's on pace for the franchise's first 1,000-yard rush season for a quarterback, which would break Douglass's record and bring him just shy of Lamar Jackson's NFL record of 1,206. But Fields has the passing down, too. In his last three games, he's completed 65% of his passes with a 104.7 passer rating and tossed six TDs against just one interception, all while averaging over 100 yards per game on the ground.

Fields is such a gifted runner that he'll always have that in his arsenal, but I imagine that as Ryan Poles continues to add weapons and protection around Fields, we'll see more of the passer we saw at Ohio State.

Which means that very soon, when Fields does something great, we won't be hearing about Bobby Douglass. Perhaps the name will be Johnny Lujack, who led the NFL in passing yards and touchdowns in 1949 and the next year became the first full-time quarterback to rush for 10 touchdowns, scoring 11, still the Bears franchise record for a QB.

But that's still rather niche, and Justin Fields is not niche. He is going to be our first true MVP candidate at quarterback since the man himself, Sid Luckman. He might well be the first Bears quarterback to win a championship — and give that team an edge — since Jim McMahon.

Yes, it's Lions week, and I've got Justin Fields on the mind. I want to see him out there again. As soon as possible. Making professionals look like high schoolers. Turning opponents into evangelists and hard-bitten fans into wide-eyed wonders.

When Justin Fields has the ball, I can see the future.

For now, at least, older Bears fans see the past.

July 9, 2010, ReadJack.com
   Age 28

BURN ON, BIG RIVER, BURN ON

A nine-year-old Cleveland boy woke up this morning a new man. His world crumbled last night when the words "South Beach" fell on his ears. He was sitting in his inflatable Cleveland Cavaliers chair when it happened, wearing the child-sized JAMES 23 jersey his parents bought him for his eighth birthday. It was the only item on his list that year.

His parents told him this might happen. They prepped him gently. And the boy thought he was ready. He'd matured since his Cavs had fallen to the Magic, and more after they lost to Boston. He listened to his parents as they told him: "He might not come back, son."

But he believed, in a way they couldn't. "His friends are in Miami, but I don't always go where my friends go. He's coming back. I know it."

His parents must have died a little, he thought. Somewhere on their journey, they lost their faith. *They can't see what I see. They're trying to help me, but they don't know: he's coming back. He's coming back.*

"This fall – man, this is very tough – this fall I'm gonna take my talents to South Beach – "

"Wait!" the boy shouted. He turned and looked at his parents, seated on the couch. He turned back to the TV, pulled the TIVO remote out of the cup holder in his inflatable Cleveland Cavaliers chair, pressed rewind. His parents watched sadly as their boy ran the feed back a few seconds:

"...this fall I'm gonna take my talents to South Beach, and join the Miami Heat."

He rewound it again. The words came again. The same words. "…take my talents to South Beach…"

The boy placed the remote in the cup holder. His forehead began to throb. He does not like to cry in front of his parents. He knew they were behind him on the couch, just as they were during Game 6 of the Boston series when the season slunk away. "We'll get 'em next year," the boy had said. "LeBron will come back and we'll get 'em."

He'd gone outside that night and shot hoops in the driveway. He'd held his Cleveland Cavaliers mini-ball and stroked turn-around jumpers and desperate layups while counting in his head "3, 2, 1… Cavs win! Cavs win!"

He did not feel like playing tonight. He switched the TV off and said, "I'm going upstairs." His parents let him go. He walked away, composed but not really. He got to his room and slammed his door harder than ever before. He paced. Short little steps, not wanting to face this. Not wanting to submit to that pain in his forehead where the tears were building.

He collapsed onto his bed, face in his pillow, and underneath his six-foot long WE ARE ALL WITNESSES poster, the boy began to cry.

Soft at first, and then more and more, his pillow case wet with pain until he pulled it up and dug his face into his mattress, pulling the pillow over his head. A knock at the door. Another. The door opens. His mother is sitting on the bed, rubbing his back as his shoulders rise and fall. His father is standing in the doorway, silent. Finally he turns over and faces them: "I never thought he'd do it. I just didn't think…"

He trails away, puts his head on his mother's lap, shakes his head as he looks at those outstretched arms in the poster above his bed, and now above his bedroom door where his Cleveland Cavaliers mini-rim sits, and now next to his closet where a life-size cutout of the man stands tall, and now at his desk where his Mac Book with the Cavs stickers covering the Apple casually rests as his Facebook page fills and fills and fills with notes...

******

He woke up this morning at his usual time. Looked at JAMES 23 slung over his desk chair, right where he'd tossed it after his parents finally left him. He picked it up and hung it in the closet. *They tried to warn me*, he thought as he brushed his teeth. *Dad said, "This is how the world works."* He finished brushing and looked deep into the mirror. He couldn't remember a time when he'd studied his own face like this. He looked into his eyes. They looked into his.

He got on the bus to go to camp. Not much was said. Not on the bus, and not during the day. The counselors tried to lift the spirits, but theirs were dampened too.

Autumn came. The first autumn Sunday. The boy's grandparents came to the house for dinner, as was the custom. Talk that evening was of the afternoon's football games, and the Cleveland Browns dud performance in Tampa, 14-3. The boy thought they would win that one, too.
"Wait till next year," his grandfather laughed.

His grandfather had said the same a year earlier when the Browns were whipped at home by Minnesota. As they talked about today's Tampa Bay game, the boy thought back to last year, and how he thought his grandfather was being unnecessarily negative. After all, the season had only just started!

"Wait till next year," the boy said, sadly miming his grandfather's countenance.

Last year, he did not understand. This year, he did. Since that horrible July night, he'd gone to the history books. Turns out his hero's departure was not the first time Cleveland's sports teams had been dealt a loser's hand. "So, I guess the Cavs aren't going to win a championship this year, huh Dad," he'd said a few weeks later, when it had all sunk in.

"Doesn't look like it."

"When was the last one?"

"The last one what?" his father asked him.

"You know. When did the Cavs win the championship?"

"They never have," his father told him.

"Never?"

His father shook his head.

"Well we still have the Indians." He looked at his father, who did not seem thrilled as to where this conversation was headed. "When did the Indians win a championship?"

"1948," his father said glumly.

1948, the boy thought, reviewing the year in his head. "But you were born in… when were you born?"

"1970," his father answered.

"Whoa…" The boy was silent for a long time after this. "And the Browns?"

"1964," his father said.

"1964," the boy said.

******

PART III: TALL TALES

The boy graduated from high school in June 2019. He was headed out of state, as far out of state as he could possibly travel. Off to Pepperdine with an academic scholarship and a trip to the j-school. He'd received a scholarship to in-state Bowling Green as well, but who wants to stay in-state? His mother, for one. Which was a perfect reason to get out.

Besides, he thought, it's enough already with this cold weather! Malibu... beaches... girls... the ocean... Yes, Pepperdine sounds lovely.

That summer, after four championships in nine South Beach seasons, LeBron James signed a two-year deal to return to Cleveland. There was no hour-long special this time; with Dwyane Wade enjoying retirement and three more Finals MVPs to his name, with Chris Bosh finishing his career in Dallas, the 34-year-old James announced his move home in a quiet press conference, his wife and children by his side and Cavs owner Dan Gilbert eagerly shaking his hand. "This is a proud day for the Cleveland Cavaliers," Gilbert told the cameras. "The prodigal son, home at last..."

The boy was not watching that press conference. On that night in mid-July, he was enjoying a beach bonfire with his closest friends, "the band of eight" his grandfather had dubbed them before he passed away.

The boy's iJolt twitched in his pocket. The news scrolled across the screen: "LeBron James signs two-year deal with Cleveland Cavaliers."

"Can you believe it?" the boy laughed. "*Now* he comes back! We just can't get that timing right, eh?"

He placed his iJolt back in his pocket and poked at the fire with a stick. Only two of "the band of eight" were staying in Ohio for school. But apart from the boy, all of them were staying within rock-skipping distance of the Ohio River. They'd known – as all high schoolers know – that their time together was ending. The feeling struck them the summer before, out on this very beach:

"Next year, guys. Next year, we'll be doing this, and it will be the last time. We'll come back for Thanksgiving, for the winter, for the summer, and we'll be together. But it will never be the same."

The boy thought back to those words. He smiled, a tinge of future nostalgia hitting him square. He would miss his friends, and yes, things might never be the same.

In his heart, though, he knew: it was time to move on.

PART IV:
THE OLD BALLGAME

June 4, 2005, "Bear Down and Get Some Runs"
   Age 23

FROM THE '93 SOX TO THE '98 CUBS: A SPORTS CONVERSION

Baseball was never that big in my house.

OK. That's not fair. Baseball was always big. But the Bears were BIG. We watched the Bears every week. We went to the games. We sang the songs. Papa made his picks for his pool, and later, so did I. And while Chicago has never been strictly a Bulls' city, I grew up at a time when the Bulls were on their way to becoming the biggest show around, on the strength of having a player who already was the biggest show around. On top of that, there was always such a choppiness with the Cubs. Two playoff trips five years apart, and yet two entirely different teams, with only Sandberg and Sutcliffe (and Scott Sanderson, if you want to be generous) stemming the tide from the '84 club to the '89 club. Meanwhile, the Bears were at their absolute best and biggest, and the Bulls were climbing: between '84 and '89 they acquired all six starters for the first Three-Peat, and promoted Phil Jackson to head coach.

So while baseball was always beloved, it was rarely the talk of the Silverstein household.

The Larmee household, on the other hand, was huge into baseball. But they were Sox fans, and as my friendship with Luke grew stronger I spent more and more time at his house hearing more and more Sox talk from Luke and his father Jay.

And what a time it was on the Southside. The year after the Cubs were rocked by San Fran in the postseason, a 22-year-old named Frank Thomas made his Southside debut, joining young Sox Robin Ventura (rookie in '89), Lance Johnson ('88) and Ozzie Guillen (Rookie of the Year in 1985). 1990 also featured breakout seasons for Black Jack McDowell (14-9, 3.82) and Bobby Thigpen (MLB-record 57 saves, 1.83 ERA, All-Star), along with the first season for Alex Fernandez. The 1990 White Sox won 94 games, nine games behind Oakland and out of the playoffs despite having the AL's second-best record. The Sox finished eight games behind Minnesota in '91 at 87-75, and then finished third in '92 behind both Oakland and the Twins, clocking in at 86 wins.

Still, the Sox were moving up with All-Star performances from Guillen (1990 and 1991), Thigpen (1990), Pudge (1991), McDowell (1991 and 1992), and Ventura (1992). No All-Star appearances for Frank between '90 and '92, but he was plenty busy himself, finishing third in the MVP voting in '91 while winning a Silver Slugger and finishing in the top ten in the AL in batting (.318, 9th place), home runs (32, 5th), RBI (109, 5th), walks (138, 1st), OBP (.453, 1st), Slug (.553, 4th), OPS (1.006, 1st), and runs scored (104, 8th). Yowza. By the spring of 1993, Luke and I were Best Friends, and the Sox were on the cusp of Something Big.

To this day, the '93 Sox remain one of my favorite teams. Along with Frank, Rockin' Robin, One Dog, Ozzie, Black Jack, and Fernandez, the Sox had added Rock Raines, Joey Cora, Roberto Hernandez, Wilson Alvarez, and Bo Jackson in '91. Ron Karkovice took Pudge Fisk's starting catcher job in '92, Gene Lamont took over the managerial reins from Jeff Torborg in '92, Jason Bere came along in '93, and the Sox traded a young, cocky outfielder named Sammy Sosa to the Cubs for the veteran George Bell. The pieces, as they say, were in place.

The '93 White Sox were exciting, much more exciting than anything happening on the Northside, and as the majority of Team Silverstein's attention was focused on the Bears and the championship Bulls, the Larmees' passion for Sox baseball combined with an incredible season pushed my baseball alliance to the other side. Frank made his first All-Star Game in '93, won his first MVP, Black Jack won the Cy, and the Sox took their division by eight games, capped off by Bo's incredible home run to beat Seattle and win the division. I was hooked.

But the White Sox season ended at the hands of the defending champion Toronto Blue Jays, and as Joe Carter's walk-off home run off of former Cub Mitch Williams cleared the fence and captured the '93 Series, the Sox waited at home. They came back strong in '94, getting another MVP performance from Frank and adding a huge bat in Julio Franco (.319, 20/98 in 112 games), but that all ended on August 12th when the players began the longest work stoppage in the history of professional sports.

Baseball returned in 1995 with a shortened season, with the Sox finishing under .500 for the first time since 1989 and the Cubs finishing above .500 for only the second time since 1989. Meanwhile, Northwestern began their Rose Bowl season in August, right around the same time that the Bulls acquired Dennis Rodman...and Michael Jordan began his first full season since 1992-93. In the summer of '96, the Sox got back to respectability, the Cubs faltered, and Michael, Scottie, and Dennis won their first title as a trio. In '97, Frank won a batting title, the Sox finished at .500, and the Cubs tanked out, losing 94 games to finish in last place.

But things changed soon after, as Sammy Sosa altered his brutal batting stance by dropping his hands and began popping Flintstones vitamins like nobody's business. By June 1st, 1998, the Cubs were a game-and-a-half behind Houston at 32-24, with Sosa and the rookie Kerry Wood supplying the buzz. By July 1st, the Cubs were seven games behind the streaking Astros, yet right in the Wild Card hunt. More importantly, Sammy had just finished ripping off the greatest single-month home run barrage in the history, cranking 20 balls out of the park to push his season total to 33 before the All-Star break. The Great Home Run Race of 1998 had begun...

...and it was during the first three months of that magical season that I began to notice some changes in my attitudes.

I was still very much a Sox fan, and yet my enthusiasm for this Cubs team was growing, doing so in a way much different than I could have imagined. Rather than simply being amazed by what Sosa and the Cubs were doing, I was Developing Emotions. Of course I said nothing. On the outside, I respected the Cubs for what they were doing, but I wouldn't dream of jumping on the bandwagon. I co-hosted a sports radio show at New Trier, and even as my co-hosts berated me on the air for being a Sox fan while the Cubs were In The Midst, I said nothing.

Of course, my parents never approved of my Sox fandom, particularly not my mother, who took it rather hard. But what is a parent to do? Rather than attacking and pummeling me with Cubdom, Mom allowed me to grow and find my own way, and as the Cubs' 1998 season revealed itself as Something Special, Mom kept an eye on me, waiting for me to crack.

And on Sunday, June 7th, it happened.

My parents took me and my bro to Wrigley for the third game of an interleague set formerly known as The Crosstown Classic. The Cubs had taken Game 1 6-5 in 12 innings, and then won the Saturday game 7-6. Sosa was streaking; he went deep in each of the first two games, his 17th and 18th of the season, his fourth and fifth of June, his average up to .342. The third game of the series saw Jeremi Gonzalez squaring off against Mike Sirotka, with Sosa hitting another home run and the Cubs prevailing 13-7.

There I was, my birth team against my adopted team, the sun shining bright at Wrigley as we sat on the first base side, half way up, watching the game. The feeling of Cubbie love had been growing inside me for three months, and I was finding it more and more difficult to keep it down, and then that game…

Cynics and skeptics will tell you that I was a fair-weather guy in '98, that my conversion took place when the Cubs were up and the Sox were down at a game at which the Cubs beat the Sox 13-7 to finish off a three-game sweep. They'll tell you I was faking, and frankly, if I took an objective viewpoint on my conversion, I'd come to the same conclusion. But I promise you that on that day, something clicked for me, and it had nothing to do with wins or home runs or beautiful days at the ballpark. It was The Love. The

Love clicked in, and when it did there was no use pretending any longer. The Seventh Inning Stretch came around, and my mom eyed me as we sang, and then all of a sudden it just burst out of me like Joliet Jake in the Triple Rock Baptist Church: "So it's root, root root for the CUBBIES!" and we finished the song, and I looked over at my mom and said, "Mom, I'm a Cubs fan," and she smiled, and said, "I know."

Naturally I took a great deal of crap from my friends, particularly my radio co-hosts, who called me out as fair-weather. Nothing you can do about that. It's the price one pays. But I stayed strong, and with the support of my family I was able to slowly show my friends and all others that I was a true Cubs fan. A born-again, if you will.

And I will, so there you go.

May 13, 2005, "Bear Down and Get Some Runs"
    Age 23

MY PARENTS, RON SANTO, AND MY ONE TRUE GLOVE

I didn't grow up with, "When I was your age, I had to walk to school 15 miles in the snow, uphill both ways."

I grew up with, "If you think that's bad, you should have seen the Cubs in '69."

There's no doubt that written history matters. You're talking to a guy whose favorite annual Chanukah gift growing up was the ESPN Sports Almanac. But your earliest passions come spoken. Parents, grandparents, aunts, uncles, cousins, parents' friends — each one shares with you a portion of your fan history, passed down through stories. The importance of the story is embedded in their voice.

Like the way my mother talked about the '69 Cubs. No one talked about that fallen team like Mickey Silverstein. She was 18 that summer, and this was her first iconic Chicago sports failure. She didn't have the Pistons terrorizing her before her 10th birthday. She didn't have the proud, bittersweet glow of the '95 Rose Bowl Wildcats. She had the Cubbies of Ernie and Billy and Ronnie and Fergie, gunning for their first World Series since five years before she was born and first championship since 15 years before her parents were born. They led the National League by nine games on August 14, up ten games on the Mets…

…and then those Mets, those Amazin' Miracle Mets, basically caught the Cubs on September 9, a game immortalized by the black cat at Shea Stadium sauntering past the Cubs' dugout. The Cubs lost that game 7-1, cutting their lead in the pennant race to half a game. The Mets overtook them the next day, ultimately winning the pennant by eight games, a gutting 18-game swing between the two clubs.

Anytime I was upset that the Cubs were losing, my parents told me about 1969 so that I knew how bad it could get. Anytime I was happy that the Cubs were winning, my parents told me about 1969 so that I knew it could all change in a heartbeat.

So I was quite curious today when I came downstairs and found my dad sitting in the TV room.

"Did you see what we rented?" he asked.

"No. What?"

"The Santo movie. *This Old Cub.*"

"Oh sweet!"

"Have you seen it?"

I shake my head.

"Want to watch it with us?"

"For a little bit while I eat. I called Luke because I felt like going out to play some catch, but he can't find his glove and he needs a new one anyways, so we're going to go out and get him a glove. But I was going to eat something first."

"Well as soon as your mother gets off the phone, I'm turning it on."

"Cool."

This Old Cub, a documentary about Ron Santo, was written and directed by his son Jeff Santo, and while it explores his life, playing career and battle with diabetes — and the positive spirit that, in a way, makes him the ultimate Cubs fan and the embodiment of Cubsdom — I'm most curious to see the sections on 1969, and watch my parents react.

The 1969 Cubs were on track to become one of the greatest teams in Chicago sports history. Instead, they became the single greatest sports tragedy in the history of Chicago, and possibly, just possibly, in the history of mankind. They turned into a symbol of this city's Murphy's Law mentality.

But they had another meaning in my house. In my house, the '69 Cubs were the best illustrator of my parents' differing attitude towards sports. My dad is a realist. When he talks about the '69 season, he sees the tragic aspect, but he doesn't live in that pain. He turned 19 in the middle of that summer, and the '69 Cubs marked the end of his childhood.

The early seeds of that team were planted when he was a boy, sitting in the bleachers to watch his heroes play ball. He tells stories of Ernie Banks standing outside of the ballpark and not leaving until every kid had left with an autograph and a smile. He grew up on the Northside in the Budlong Woods neighborhood, and among my favorite stories of his are from his days at Jamieson Grammar School, where he wrote for the Jamieson Journal.

DAD: "Because we were editors, my friend Sammy Wolf and I would have to go down to the printer to pick up the papers and bring them back for the school. There may have been someone else, but I just remember Sammy Wolf. The printer was down on Belmont, which is 3200, and we were at 5600, so we would take a bus south to Belmont but we'd get off at Addison instead and catch a few innings. We'd buy a couple of tickets and catch a few innings."

ME: *How much were tickets?*

DAD: "Well…I think good seats were about a buck and a quarter, maybe a little bit more. Bleachers were about eighty cents. We sat in the bleachers. I remember the programs cost fifteen cents each, so whatever it was it wasn't a lot. So we'd watch a few innings, and then we'd walk from the park to the printer, pick up the papers, maybe two hundred or so for the whole school, and we'd each carry two bundles of papers to the train, and take the El back to school. We usually missed most of the day. And they never really figured out why it took us so long to pick up the papers."

ME: *So, you did this once a week?*

DAD: "Oh no. No, no. Once a month. The paper came out once a month, and the season started in April, so April, May, June…we got out of school around the middle of June."

ME: *And then did you go again when school started up in August?*

DAD: "No, probably not. The school year didn't start until after Labor Day, so by that time there wasn't much left in the season. So it was really just at the beginning of the season and the end of the school year. Definitely eighth grade, probably seventh grade too. So, wow…" He thinks for a second. "It was probably only, you know, four, five, six times in my whole life that we did that."

For my dad, the '69 Cubs were a great team that, like most Chicago teams, just didn't make it. It was rough while it happened, but now when he looks back on that season, it's a snap of the fingers and a "that's the way it goes sometimes," but mostly it's the last great memory of a Cub team that he watched growing up, a team that was together for the better part of his childhood and teenage years. The Leo Durocher-led Cubs never had another season filled with as much promise as they did in 1969, and while there was pain in the outcome, my dad remembers that season as the most memorable year of his childhood team.

My mom does not. Mention the '69 Cubs to my mom, and you'll get a pained expression, followed by moans and groans and other nearly inaudible sounds. My mom is an optimist, and a very emotional person, and when she experiences something it stays with her. This was evident in many ways throughout my childhood, and it manifested itself in sports in three key places.

The first was her dislike for Tony Gwynn, who she held personally responsible for the 1984 Cubs' collapse in the NLCS. The second was her dislike of Isiah Thomas after 1991.

"I don't care how nice a guy he is, or how good a player he is, or if he was just really upset because they were swept," she would say. "You don't walk off the court like that. It's bad sportsmanship." I eventually got her to relent on Gwynn, and forgive Isiah.

But until her dying day, I don't imagine she'll ever grant the '69 Mets leniency. Indeed, anytime the Cubs are playing the Mets my mom is a little bit uneasy. While we joked about Tony Gwynn, I learned early on never to joke about the New York Mets. I was probably about eight or nine years old, and I had gotten into some kind of a stupid eight- or nine-year-old fight with my parents, and in an act of rebellion I declared that I would now be a fan of the New York Mets.

She turned towards me, slowly, and said without any trace of fun: "There are some things in life that you don't joke about." She turned her back, and walked away. I got the point pretty quickly.

And so it was when *This Old Cub* turned to the summer of '69 that my mom shivered and left the room. "I already lived this once. I don't need to watch a movie about it."

My dad and I stayed, watching clips of Mr. Cub and Sweet Billy and the greatest Cub third baseman of all-time, Ron Santo. There's no doubt my mom made the right decision to leave the room, and that my dad made the right decision to stay. He smiled at the good and saw himself in the documentary's stories told. Like Bill Murray working at the concession stand at Peter Jans Golf Course in Evanston, closing early so that he could listen to Cubs games. Or Dennis Franz shipping out to Vietnam that summer, upset to be missing a certain World Series after waiting so long for a team like that one. Or Dennis Farina sharing his days as a Chicago police officer in '69, noting how when bosses would ask officers about a given assignment, they would say that they "had it covered like Santo at third."

I watched a bit more of the movie with my dad, and then I left to pick up Luke, grabbing my glove from my room and tossing it in my car. The Cubs were playing the Washington Nationals, and I listened to the last few innings on 720. When I pulled up to Luke's house, he came out, hopped in the car and flipped it to AM 1000 to hear the White Sox.

"Knock it off."

"I want to hear the Sox game."

"Wait for a commercial."

But he can't, so while we drive to Dick's Sporting Goods store in Glenview, we flip back and forth between the two games, catching bits of both. We get into the store, and head straight to the baseball section to pick out a glove for Luke.

Now picking out a baseball glove is not like picking out a pair of shoes. There are similarities — shoes must fit right, and you want to get a pair that you like, since you'll be wearing them every day — but

PART IV: THE OLD BALLGAME

there is one aspect to picking out a glove that just isn't present in picking out a pair of shoes. While shoes have to fit right, they don't have to *feel* right.

With a glove, the feel is as important as the fit. The fit is about your hand; not too loose, not too tight. But once you've got a glove that fits, you have to leave it on to see if you have a glove that correctly *feels*. The feel is emotional. It's about the glove instantly bringing you back to your little league days. That's where the feel comes from.

Sometimes you'll be playing a pick-up game, and someone doesn't have a glove, so they'll borrow one from the other team. I've done that before. When you take a glove that's not yours, it may fit right, but it's just a tool. You trot out to the field wearing this foreign object on your hand, and you start pounding it and pushing it in an attempt to get the feel right.

Then, the next time you're playing ball with your own glove, you immediately feel the difference. It's like jumping into your own bed for the first time after a vacation. "Ahhhh," you say, sinking in. "*My bed.*"

When we find the baseball section, Luke starts trying on gloves. Outfielders gloves, infielders gloves, bigger pockets, smaller pockets, Rawlings, Wilson, Louisville Slugger—"I wouldn't buy a Louisville Slugger glove if I were you. They make bats. What do they know about gloves? It's the kind of glove that Edgar Martinez would probably buy if he ever had to wear a glove."—and as he's trying them on he tosses them to me to see what I think. Each glove he tosses to me, I try it on, give it a few punches to break it in, and then toss it back.

"There's no names on any of these," he says.

"I know," I say. "I think they stopped doing that."

"Seriously?" He frowns. "That sucks."

"Yeah. When I bought my glove, I was looking for one with a signature, but I couldn't find one, so I just signed it *Glenallen Hill*."

"Funny," he says, as he tries on another. "I don't remember who my old glove was signed by. You?"

"Dave Righetti. Old Yankee."

"Oh yeah. I remember that glove. Whatever happened to that?"

"I retired it. It's in the basement."

He tosses me another glove, and I try it on, give it a few punches, and then I pick up a ball from the basket and start throwing it into the pocket.

"What do you think about this one?" Luke asks, holding another one up.

"Eh, I don't know. I would never buy a black glove," I say, as I bend the top of the glove that I'm holding to improve its pocket. "I like gloves that are dirt colored. Nothing too dark, nothing too light."

"This one feels good," he says, as he pushes his fingers into one.

"What is it?"

"Rawlings." He pounds the pocket a bit. "Here. Gimme a toss."

He backs up, and I throw the ball to him. He throws it back, and continues to break in his glove, and then I reach into the glove I'm holding and throw the ball back, and I continue to pound on the pocket, pretending I'm at second base at James Park, waiting for the next pitch, hoping for a grounder, and I throw it back to him, and I push down on the tops of the fingers, getting the glove loose, like I would out in the outfield, wondering if a ball would ever come my way, and then I throw it back to him, and he throws it back to me, and as I'm pushing and pounding and getting my fingers comfortable…

"Dude, I might have a problem here."

"What?"

"This glove," I say. "I kind of like this glove."

"Oh yeah?"

"Yeah." And I continue working it in, throwing the ball into the pocket before throwing it back to Luke. "I really like this glove."

"Oh yeah?"

"Yeah, dude. I *really* like this glove."

"But you have a glove."

"I know. But what if it's the wrong glove. I mean, it feels right, but what if it only feels right because I haven't felt the right one yet. What if this is *my glove*?"

"Your one true glove."

"My one true glove."

He thinks for a second. "You might have a problem there."

"I know! Here," I say, motioning to him, "throw it back."

He tosses me the ball, and I catch it, and it feels really good. *Really good.*

"Oh man, dude. This glove feels really good."

"This one's feeling good too," he says, as I throw it back to him. "I think I'm gonna get it. It feels right."

"OK, but hold on." I'm still feeling the glove, imagining my days at James Park. "Just, just one second."

"Dude, you're not going to buy a second glove."

"Well, just hold on." I scan it. "There's no price."

"I'm gonna buy mine, and when I do you can have them do a price check."

We walk up to the counter, but I don't take my hand out of the glove. Luke buys his new glove, and a ball, and a three-quarter-length White Sox shirt. When she's done ringing up Luke's stuff, she looks at me.

"Is that all?" she asks, pointing to my glove.

"Well, kind of. Can you do a price check on it?"

"Sure." She swipes it. "$75.06."

"Oh." I think for a second. "Here's the thing. I didn't come here with the intention of buying a glove. I have a glove. I came to help *him* pick out a glove. But in doing so, I kind of fell in love with this glove. Do you see what I'm saying?"

"I guess so."

"However, I really can't afford to drop 75 bucks on a glove, particularly a second glove. It's just too much money."

"OK."

"But I really want this glove."

"What were you looking to spend?"

"Forty."

"I'm sorry, I can't do that."

"Come on dude," Luke says. "You're not going to spend that much on a second glove."

"I know."

"And don't you like your glove?"

"I really like it."

"So say goodbye to this glove, and let's go play catch. You'll feel better once you pick up your own glove."

And with that we left, but I couldn't help wondering if I had just left my one true glove behind.

When we get into the car, the Sox game is over. They were losing to the O's but came back to get the win, and we head back into Evanston while listening to postgame. Just east of Sheridan Road, down by the lake, there's a turf field where the Northwestern girls lacrosse team practices. It's left open and lit at night, and people go there to play football, soccer, ultimate or lacrosse.

There's a soccer game going on when we get down there, so we go to the grass field next to it and start playing catch. Luke is right: as soon as I put my fingers in my glove, I feel better, and though we start about twenty feet apart, we quickly move back so that we can both throw as far as we can.

We throw high pop-ups, and grounders, and bouncers, and line drives. We catch pop flies and then throw quickly to the other person, who catches the ball and swipes "home plate" to tag out the invisible runner. We throw balls that slip out of our hands, sending the other person chasing after it, and once we've chased after it we wind up and throw it back as far as we can, sometimes sending the other person running again.

The grass is damp, and there are a few thin areas where a bit of mud has collected, and as the ball gets slicker we wipe it off on our shirts to dry it, and then wipe our hands on our shorts to dry them. The ball flies back and forth, wet and dry, and we field grounders with the urgency that comes from playing the infield, and we camp out under high pop flies and catch them with the laziness that comes from playing the outfield, and bask in the moment when all the attention is on you before you throw the ball back to the infield and return to your lonely post in right field.

We do this for about a half hour, not talking, just playing catch, back and forth, from one person's hand to the other person's glove, and then back again, and just as we did in Little League, we stay close enough to maintain a game of catch but far enough away to be daring. And I don't care about 1969 anymore, or 1984, or 1989 or even 2003. I don't care about the Cubs and our lost season. I don't care about Sammy or Gracie or Ryno or Hawk, or Woody or Prior or Z.

Just wearing my glove is enough.

May 21, 2006, ReadJack.com
    Age 24

A PUNCH AND A LUNCH: BARRETT, PIERZYNSKI AND HERM'S

I didn't see the play.

My buddy Sven saw the play. He was at the Cell when it happened. Called me up to see if I was watching, and to find out what they were saying about it on TV.

"What happened?" I asked.

He told me.

PART IV: THE OLD BALLGAME

"Oh," I said. "No, I didn't see it."

So I didn't see the play. Most people, though, most people saw the play. And yet it seems that everybody saw something different. We're all in agreement that A.J. Pierzynski knocked over Michael Barrett on his way to the plate during Saturday's Cubs-Sox game. That much we're sure of. But everything else seems to be up in the air.

Sven, a Sox fan, says that after slapping the plate in celebration, Pierzynski tried to step around Barrett in an effort to grab his batting helmet from the dirt. That's when Barrett grabbed him, said something, and then laid him out with a stone-cold cold cock to the jaw. My buddy Davis, on the other hand, saw something else. Davis, a Cubs fan, says that after slapping the plate in celebration, Pierzynski gave Barrett an intentional shoulder bump on his way to the dugout.

That's when Barrett grabbed him, said something, and, well, laid him out with a stone cold cold cock to the jaw.

We all seem to agree on that.

One of my favorite aspects of sports is the way that one play can be interpreted in sharply contradictory ways, as well as how the competition on the field can mean different things to different people. The Pierzynski-Barrett brawl has shown the split between Cubs fans and Sox fans, but it has also shown the split between players and fans.

The fan split is obvious. Fans are loyal to a fault. Of course A.J. knocked into him. Of course he did. He's the game's great irritant. Makes perfect sense. On the other hand, it looks as if he really was trying to walk around Barrett. Yeah—yeah, look at him. He's walking around. *Look.*

I am a Cubs fan, as is my best buddy Ben. Ben didn't see the play, either. Like me, he saw it later, online. And though we are Cubs fans, we both agree that Barrett was in the wrong. Pierzynski made a great play; Barrett was in his squat, awaiting the throw, and seeing this,

Pierzynski bowled him over, an action that is perfectly reasonable, and perfectly legal. Barrett says that he told Pierzynski that he didn't have the ball, but how could Pierzynski know that? He's charging home. So he knocks him over, and he scores, and in the thrill of the moment, Pierzynski slaps the plate in celebration. Then comes the tricky part. Pierzynski's intentions as he passed Barrett.

Sven says one thing, Davis says another. Oh, to be an unbiased sports fan.

******

Regardless of Pierzynski's intentions, Barrett was clearly out of line. The situation simply did not call for a sudden punch to the jaw… there's no way to argue otherwise…and it was around this time in our conversation that Ben and I began to get hungry. We decided on Herm's Palace, Skokie's landmark of a hot dog joint. When we arrived, there were two people in line in front of us. The owner/manager Scott was behind the counter, taking orders in his usual way — fast. Anybody who meets him knows that he is friendly, inviting, and engaging, but the quality that new patrons hold to is his speed. He takes orders fast, and he totals up the prices fast. Nobody at Herm's uses a calculator or a cash register for determining prices. It's all done in their heads.

The people in front of us finish ordering, and Ben and I stroll up to the counter, thinking. But Scott's a step ahead of us. "Grilled Cajun chicken sandwich, large fry?" he says to Ben, as more of a statement awaiting confirmation than a question.

"Yes," Ben says.

"Two hot dogs, ketchup, large fry?" he says to me.

"Yes."

He smiles. "Then what the hell are you guys standing here for?"

Ben and I get our drinks and sit down in view of the television. Game 3 of the Cubs-Sox series is on, and the customers inside Herm's are geared up. When Michael Barrett steps to the plate in the top of the fourth, the fans at the Cell boo, and the Sox fans at Herm's dig their feet into the floor, trying to will a poor play from *this* ultimate instigator. Sure enough, the soon-to-be-suspended Barrett grounds out to third. When Pierzynski comes up in the top half of the fourth, everything is reversed, including the outcome. A.J. lets fly a two-out home run to deep center to pull the Sox even at two runs apiece, and the Cell erupts.

Take that, Michael Barrett! In a stoppage of play, you can sucker punch our guy all you wants. But out on the field, we are victorious.

And the fans at Herm's applaud, and high five, and shout for their guy Pierzynski. And Ben and I eat, watching.

******

The media saw the play.

They had the same reaction to the play that the fans had. *Hot damn!* This *is* a rivalry! Look at those two guys going at it, one in his White Sox pinstripes, the other in his Cubbie blue. And would you look at that? They play the same position. Two catchers, the backbones of their respective teams, slugging it out in the holy name of rivalry.

Or so we would hope.

But I think it's simply wishful thinking that a fan-based rivalry would mean nearly as much to the players as it does to the fans. Certainly the players take note of these rivalries, and feed off of the enthusiasm of the fans that surround them, both in the ballpark and in the universe at large…

…but how could we possibly expect A.J. Pierzynski and Michael Barrett, Chicago ballplayers for a combined three seasons before

2006, to fully appreciate the Cubs-Sox rivalry? To live it, to play it, to hold it dear? It's unreasonable and foolish, and though we support them and take up their causes, we the fans will never fully know what it is to be a professional athlete.

When Barrett punches Pierzynski or Jose Valentin mocks Sammy Sosa or Roger Clemens throws a bat at Mike Piazza, we rush to our sides in an effort to support our heroes, but there are things happening between the players that we will never be able to fully appreciate or understand or internalize; in a very practical sense, fans and players are separate entities who share a loose connection based on their involvement in sport.

And that's OK. Sports mean different things to different people. It is the great unifier.

Ben and I finish our meals, and head back to the counter to pay. Scott is there.

"Together or separate, guys?"

"Separate."

He compiles the totals, rapid fire. "Grilled chicken, large fry, water: $6.85 for you. Two hot dogs, large fry, was that a medium?"

"Yup."

"Medium Coke. $ 6.80 for you, sir."

We pay and leave. In the eighth inning, with the Cubs trailing four to three, The Great Michael Barrett steps to the plate with Todd Walker on first, and promptly smokes a triple to deep center field. On the next at bat, Jacque Jones dumps a ball into the Sox bullpen in left field to put the Cubs up 6-4. Cubs fans cheer wildly; Sox fans sulk. The Cubs' dugout leaps up in joy. Barrett passes Pierzynski at home, and then waits for his teammate Jones.

They high-five. Ben and I high five. Sven, presumably, slaps his hands together in disappointment, along with the rest of his fellow Sox fans at the Cell. Jones and the soon-to-be-suspended Barrett greet their teammates in the dugout. Meanwhile, Pierzynski, the Great Irritant, waits for the next pitch.

And I am happy.

Oct. 4, 2008, ReadJack.com
Age 26

THE AUDACITY OF HOPE

About a month ago, I realized that within two weeks of each other, the Cubs could win the World Series and America could elect a black president. That even one would happen seemed for so long a blink in the dark. But something flipped late this summer, something beyond statistics, beyond the NL's best record or the Dems' most delegates. That "oh what the hell?" feeling returned to me, the one that sweeps out the dusty corners of your cynicism and your nervous, desperate, don't-hurt-me-again guard. I just felt like it could happen, would happen, both, each one stacking upon the other, two impossibilities of varying weight yet equal myth, each remarkable in its own way.

Then the Los Angeles Dodgers came to town and siphoned the wind out of the Cubbies' sail.

Forget the walks and the infielding errors: two-love Los Angeles has been all about the bats. From Loney to Martin to the fly-swatting Manny, the Dodgers have reined in the hits, 20 in all over the first two games. With the Cubs trailing 4-2 in Game 1 and Edmonds at bat with Aramis aboard, I was certain the left-handed veteran would deposit the tying shot snug in the basket. He grounded to second instead.

And after DeRosa was discarded by Lowe's pesky pitching, it was that other Ramirez who fished out an 0-2 curve at his ankles and positioned it far above the Wrigley lights. Game 2 was much of the same, and though our Cubs traded shabby pitching for shabby fielding, it was still Los Angeles collecting hits, again and again until it made no difference. The series would return to the coast as scheduled, though with the underdog Dodgers packing the W's, the head-hanging Cubs packing it in.

I am happy to say that Obama is still on track, Thursday night's V.P. debate keeping the Hope'n'Change Express powering on. I watched Game 2 at my brother's because my roommate was having friends for the political game; when she asked me why I was leaving, I told her that "the Cubs need me more than Joe Biden does." This seemed particularly true following the embarrassing performance of our home fans Wednesday night. They seemed excited out of the gate, but Loney's granny and the homer from Manny set off a hush from which they never recovered. They should have. Instead they looked bored and annoyed. As my brother put it so well: "They look like they came to watch a movie instead of a ballgame."

Too true. Fazed by the cold and those hot Dodger bats, the home fans at Wrigley went into an inexcusable shell, and as we watched Game 2, we noticed that they'd broken out of that shell with a spray of boos for their beloved Cubbies, another reprehensible act. Boo poor effort till the cows come home, but don't boo a loss. Booing the home team makes as much sense as parents booing their children during a little league game. Booing the opposition just for being the opposition is pretty classless as well.

It's that bitter pettiness that has dimmed my sports fandom these past few years, the pettiness that made me shiver at an otherwise appealing Cubs-Sox series. Twould be a thrill to have the eyes of the baseball world stuck solely upon our fair city, but the boasting would surely leave it sullied. We can't amiably share a diamond during the regular season; no chance we'd do so with a ring on the line. A high-spirited, good-natured my team vs. yours…I'm all for that. But when fandom becomes all about bragging rights and dancing on the other guy's sadness, that's where I get bored.

Sadly, it looks as if neither team will be there, as both seem sunk in 0-2 holes. I've got faith in our Cubbies, though. Incredibly, as I sit and wait for Soriano to swing and miss at Ball One just hours from now, I feel better about this team's chance to rebound than I did a year ago against Arizona. Just got that feeling, I suppose. Of course, if we *do* lose, be it today, tomorrow, Tuesday, anytime before next season, that's when the real fear will set in. 101 years without a title terrifies me, because what are our seasons aimed at then? We've had that once-a-century thing resting safely in our back pockets for years now. The Bartman Game, the '04 collapse, the '06 debacle, the '07 sweep, all were tempered by The Coming of 2008. This whole season has been geared towards that anomaly of a celebration, a Cubs title becoming baseball's Haley's Comet, and wouldn't we be the lucky ones just to be around for it. *We'll get one in '08. We always do.*

Now we sit at the precipice. We lose this thing, and we're set adrift, floating away towards God-knows-where. 100 years had a rhythm that made losing palatable. Lose it this year, and there is no solace in 101, 102, 128, 145. We'll be lost in the unknown, the weight of 100 plus years without a championship falling on our shoulders in one fat lump.

But I have faith. Yes sir I do. Baseball will do that to a feller. It is by its nature a game of hope, a game that—defined by outs rather than minutes—allows those on the field and in the stands to reasonably expect victory even when nothing victorious has been seen. It's fitting, then, that the Cubs are a baseball club rather than something else. For them and for us, hope is a good thing, maybe the best of things, and no good thing ever dies. Hopefully.

June 2, 2009, ReadJack.com
Age 27

ALL HAIL THE CHICAGO BLUE SOX!

My friend Kristin and I were at the bar, playing a game called Question. It's simple: you ask a question, and then I ask a question. (Think Truth without the Dare.) Kristin is from Arkansas. She has lived in Chicago for five years. Her question:

"If you could change one thing about Chicago, what would it be?"

This was difficult. At first, every change I considered was simply something I would change about America and big-city living. School systems, housing, police, etc. Kristin reminded me that segregation is a much greater problem in our fair city than in many other American metropolises, and after a bit of consideration, I agreed.

But before that, my answer was:

"One thing I'd change? I wish we only had one professional baseball team."

"Really?"

I paused. And then: "Absolutely."

Though I'd never articulated that sentiment, it had been growing in me since 2005, when what should have been one of the greatest moments in Chicago sports was sullied by the split-screen that is Northside-Southside baseball.

Those 2005 White Sox were one of the great Chicago teams of my life. Lock down defense, timely offense, ten pitchers with ERA's in

PART IV: THE OLD BALLGAME

the 3's and an 11th (El Duque) responsible for a classic postseason Forgotten Man Performance (Game 3 of the Boston series). The lineup had nary a boring nor unsettled spot—not like Alex Gonzalez on the '03 team or the Cliff Floyd/Fontenot/DeRosa question in '07—and the playoffs produced a slew of fantastic games and impressive outputs, such as...

> ...the four straight complete games thrown by the Sox staff in the ALCS.
> ...Pierzynski's dropped third strike play in Game 2 against the Angels, followed by Crede's walk-off double.
> ...Crede hitting .368 with two home runs while making every key defensive play against those Angels.
> ...Ozzie's "big guy" hand sign for Jenks in Game 1 of the World Series.
> ...the Jermaine Dye phantom hit-by-pitch followed immediately by Konerko's game-swinging granny in Game 2.
> ...the Scotty Pods walk-off.
> ...the 14-inning Game 3, capped by Geoff Blum's pinch hit two-run shot and Buehrle getting the save in relief.
> ...the tense, 1-0 Game 4 Series finale.

From Contreras's first pitch to the final one from Jenks, the 2005 World Series was one of the greatest sporting events I ever viewed. Two of the four games were played less than 25 miles from my home. I followed it, loved it, felt good for my White Sox friends.

And I could not call it mine.

The Bulls defeat the Lakers for their first title and both sides of Madison Street rejoice. The Bears shuffle to a Super Bowl and delight everyone from Gary to Lake Forest. But the White Sox win the city's first World Series in 88 years, and it's accompanied by cross-town bickering, heckling, and taunting, with Cubs fans going out of their way to be bitter and Sox fans going out of theirs to deride. What's so great about that?

Better to unite the city's baseball fans around one team. We could donate the other to an MLB-less region. I nominate Omaha, home of the college World Series, a city in a state that loves its baseball yet is 200 miles away from the closest professional stadium.

Which club needs to go? Matters not to me. I say we flip for it. The other club heads off to Omaha and the American League (or the National League, if you like). We could even develop some kind of clause ensuring that the city's favorite players would remain with the team staying in town, just to be fair to everyone. And they could play half their home games at Wrigley and half at the Cell. I think that would be nice.

The name? I nominate the Blue Sox, a merging of sorts, as well as nods to the Cubs' roots as the Chicago White Stockings and the Sox blue helmets from 1970. The new ball club would officially be an expansion team—the Cubs' streak would end at 101 years, the White Sox would forever bask in 2005, and out of those franchises would grow the fabulous Chicago Blue Sox, a team for all of our children and grandchildren to share.

Imagine: it is October of 2010. Over the past nine months, our city has experienced a Cutler-led Bears team marching deep into the playoffs, Rose's Bulls taking LeBron and the Cavs to six games in the East Finals, and Toews and Kane leading the Hawks to their first Stanley Cup appearance in 18 years. Cutler and co. are now in their sixth week of the 2010 season, the U.C. will soon be rocking once more, but today, the city's entire fan population is locked into the fierce World Series battle between our beloved Blue Sox and those hated New York Mets (or those hated New York Yankees, if you prefer). Win or lose, we're in it together. And that is something I would never change.

Dec. 3, 2010, *The Sports Blog Network*
Age 29

A CUB TO THE LAST: A SALUTE TO RON SANTO

I never understood the bru-ha-ha over Ron Santo's heel click.

It is, when you think about it, the most benign of celebrations. When I think of heel clicks, I think of Bugs Bunny cartoons and old men bowling. If Derrek Lee or Paul Konerko let loose the occasional heel click, we'd chuckle and call them "old-timey." If Dorothy had jumped while trying to return to Kansas, and if, instead of being a young girl on her way home, she was a third baseman for the 75-44 Chicago Cubs in the summer of '69, the baseball press would have chalked her up as a gloater and suggested she stay in Oz until she learns some manners.

Santo was the embodiment of that '69 club. As my dad tells it, the 1969 Chicago Cubs were a rollicking good show, deft and powerful, afraid of no one. The same, he tells me, could be said of Santo.

Fitting then that it was Santo's heel click that baseball pundits pegged as the karmic catalyst for their fateful collapse, and that of all the players who could have been waiting on-deck when fans at Shea Stadium released a black cat upon the field, that it was Santo who watched this curs-ed kitten prance on by…

The heel click and the black cat. The saddest single season of a possibly cursed, definitely bummed-out franchise, and when the memories of '69 flood back, we think of Ronnie.

And yeah, we think of Ernie and Billy, of Fergie and Kenny, of Hundley and Beckert and Kessinger and Durocher.

Somehow, though, Santo became the symbol of that season. The power. The confidence. And the confusion as it all slipped away.

He was a metaphor for a franchise, and later, the voice of a fan base. That was *us* in that radio booth. When Santo delivered his most famous call in late September 1998 – "OH NOOOOOO!" – I was watching the television feed. Which was perfect, actually, because I wouldn't have heard Santo's anguished cry anyhow. No one in Wilmette would have. It would not have been audible over my own.

When that game began, we were huddled in the back of Mr. Senior's physics class listening to the feed on Jonny Corwin's handheld radio. The Cubs were going to beat the Brewers and keep their hold on the NL Wild Card, and we were going to live it.

When we left school that day, the Cubbies were leading seven-nil after six innings. All was well. September 23, 1998 was one of those lucky, last days of summer that sneak in every fall, and when we got home from school, my brother and I decided to celebrate the warmth and the Cubs with some long toss.

The Brewers scored four in the 7th. *Come on guys. Stop screwing around. Get this settled so we can celebrate.* Another run in the 8th. *Ha ha ha fellas. Yeah yeah. Very funny.* A groundout to start the 9th, with Cubs closer Rod Beck on the mound. A single for Mark Loretta, a double for Jeff Cirillo, 2nd and 3rd for the Brewers, an intentional walk to set up the force, a foul pop for out number two fielded by Cubs 3rd baseman Jose Hernandez… two outs now… two outs…

At this point, I am standing in the front yard with only my neck stretched some 25 feet back to the television, my eyes upon the screen, my brother awaiting my attention, *one sec Mike, one more out*, and now here comes Geoff Jenkins, and an easy fly ball to left to defensive replacement Brant Brown, *okay Mike, throw me the ball, Brown's got this under con* –

OH NOOOOOOO!

I didn't have 1969. And in the end, 1998 was a magical year of happiness and achievement. But right at that moment, right as that pigeon darted in front of Brown and the ball caromed off the base of his glove, right as Beck gasped in horror and Hughes screamed and Santo SCREAMED... well, I finally knew what my parents had been talking about all those years. "It's the *Cubs*," they told me, as if that was explanation enough.

That's what made Pat and Ron such a beloved pair. They were two generations of Cubs optimism. Pat the Son, the one who'd heard his father's stories and wished upon wish that the Cubbies would finally win one for the older folks.

Ronnie the Father, the one who'd Lived It, the one who knew it doesn't work out in the end, the one who felt a twinge of guilt for passing this inane, unrequited love to his innocent son, the one still shocked each and every time they did it again.

The Father is gone now, passing away yesterday at the age of 70, another Cub fan without a ring. But he never gave up. He knew, to the end, that if we just waited one more pitch, one more inning, *come on guys*, one more game, one more season, it was coming. The Cubs would win a World Series. The Cubs *will* win a World Series. It's gonna happen. Mark my words.

And when it does, you'll know what that waiting was all about.

April 2, 2013, ReadJack.com
  Age 31

PEOPLE WILL COME, JACK. PEOPLE WILL MOST DEFINITELY COME.

The email arrived April 1st at 12:35 PM, the very moment that David DeJesus was stepping to the plate in Pittsburgh to begin the 138th season of Chicago Cubs baseball, and already Doom was in the air. It was my buddy Ari, a ravenous Cubs fan. The subject head was:

Happy Opening Day

Shit, I thought suddenly, *they're back.*

Spring — and baseball — had snuck upon me yet again, and I was none too anxious to forge this river.

In my younger, naïve days, a new baseball season meant hope, forgiveness, acceptance, and yes, perhaps even VICTORY. I was James Earl Jones, eyeing the cornfield with curious anticipation, telling friends that the Cubs reminded us of all that once was good, "and it could be again."

But no more. Now the words "Opening Day" make me shudder. Now when I look at the cornfield, I see a new truth: there is nothing but corn.

I opened Ari's email. It was penned in classic Cubs fashion, with good cheer & realism (pessimism?) carrying equal weight:

> May our 105th year of championship-free baseball wash over you like a warm summer's day until greener fields are ours.
>
> Let's go for 72-90 this time! Go get 'em Shark!

Not long after, Anthony Rizzo hit a two-run homer for the Cubs' first runs of the year. By the time the sun went down, Cubs fans had weathered the full Cubs Fan Experience: We're winning — but we might lose. We won — but it might not matter. The pitching was brilliant — except when it was gruesome.

Meanwhile, Ari passed along a Google chat he had with our friend Dan, another classic Cubs fan, albeit one who resides on the opposite end of the IT'S GONNA HAPPEN! spectrum. Their conversation took place in the 9th inning, Dan assuring Ari that Carlos Marmol would give the game away, Ari pleading with Dan to avoid cynicism "at least until Game 1 of 162 is over."

"At a minimum, the tying run will come to the plate," Dan told him.

Somehow they were both right. Marmol struck out one batter, plunked another, allowed a stolen base and then a run-scoring single, and walked a man, allowing not just the tying run but the winning run to come to the plate. He was relieved after one-third of an inning, with manager Dale Sveum telling the press, "Yeah, he's still our closer."

And yet Ari was also right: he held out hope, he staved off cynicism, and the Cubs rewarded his faith with a win.

So the Cubs are 1-0, as are the White Sox, that other baseball team in Chicago, the one that wins without fanfare and loses without excuses. And I'm left in the middle, rewatching James Earl Jones, letting him suck me in just as he sucked in poor Ray Kinsella.

His words tug me, gently, innocently, calling me back to a time when I knew they were true. A time when they expressed everything I felt for the Cubs.

And then there is Mark, Ray's brother-in-law, the red-haired realist, the man telling poor Ray to just sell the damn farm already. *Be a grownup, Ray*, is what ol' Mark is telling him. *Make decisions based on what is HERE, not what is imagined. If you're not going to do it for yourself or your wife, then for God sakes man, think of Annie, your sweet little daughter. Do it for her, Ray!*

We know how this ends. Mark knocks Annie to the ground, she appears to lose consciousness, Archie Graham steps off the field, becomes Moonlight Graham, gives the kid a rudimentary tap on the back and dislodges a hot dog from her throat. Poor Annie was choking to death on that classic baseball food… the game was literally killing her…

Naturally, Mark The Curmudgeon suddenly sees the ball players and flips his whole act. "Do not sell this farm Ray," he says in a daze. "You gotta keep this farm." And those kooky Kinsellas are only too happy to oblige.

Of course it goes without saying that Ray & Karen are Cubs fans, if not in strict baseball allegiance then certainly in spirit & soul. I know Papa Kinsella's favorite ballplayer was Joe Jackson and that the 1919 White Sox sit at the center of the story, but the lasting legacy passed from father to son in *Field of Dreams* is not "Root for the White Sox." It is "Believe in ghosts until others believe in them too. Then sell tickets." It's right there in Terrence Mann's spine-tingling speech:

> People will come Ray. They'll come to Iowa, for reasons they can't even fathom. They'll turn up your driveway, not knowing for sure why they're doing it. They'll arrive at your door, as innocent as children, longing for the past. "Of course, we don't mind if you look around," you'll say. "It's only twenty dollars per person." They'll pass over the money without even thinking about it. For it is money they have, and peace they lack.

That's the brilliance of the speech: as the camera floats around Mann and the soundtrack whistles with mystery & nostalgia, this film lauded for capturing baseball's soul and returning its viewers to a simpler time actually lays out a rather insidious money-making scheme. James Earl Jones's smooth, soothing voice obscures the reality: he and Mark are allies, for goodness sake. *Don't sell your farm to the bank Ray — it's a Goddamn gold mine! You just need the right eyes. People will come, Ray, and they'll pay handsomely.*

Isn't that why we go to Wrigley? I know I do. The Cubs have beaten me within an inch of life, and yet beneath my grizzled exterior rests that boy full of hope, the boy who believes IT'S GONNA HAPPEN, the boy whose faith never left.

It's the man who resists Wrigley Field, who went several years without entering his gilded cage. Yet it's the boy who tugs the man's sleeve and whispers in his ear, the boy who tells the man to buy a ticket and cost be damned, because it's money you have and peace you lack.

And when the man creeps reluctantly through the Wrigley gate, it's the boy who takes every step after that. When I go to Wrigley, I move backward, from Moonlight Graham to young Archie. I am the line of cars at the end of *Field of Dreams*, wandering into Wrigleyville and not knowing for sure why I'm doing it. For nine innings, I am a boy again. It is the summer of '89, and I haven't heard of the Miracle Mets or the Billy Goat Curse, and the Cubs are in the pennant race and Steve Bartman is an unknown 12-year-old little leaguer and the Cubs will win the World Series because what kind of cruel world would this be if they didn't?

So now I'm here again, looking nervously at the baseball schedule. The 2013 season has started. The man and the boy are heading to Wrigley. The boy skips toward the cornfield. The man warns him it's only corn. The boy does not know why the man is hesitant. The man wants to open the boy's eyes without breaking his heart.

"Hold my hand kiddo," the man says. "I know how this goes."

But the boy smiles, deep & pure, and a voice tickles the man's mind. "Do not sell this farm, Jack," it says. "You gotta keep this farm."

**PART V:
THE BULLS ARE BACK**

PART V: THE BULLS ARE BACK

"They can't win until we quit."

— Michael Jordan, June 14, 1998, after winning his 6th championship in eight years

******

And then, just as suddenly, they couldn't win at all. In January 1999, just under 30 years after the '69 Cubs defined "collapse" in Chicago sports, Jerry Reinsdorf and Jerry Krause dismantled the championship Bulls in 10 days. My parents did not experience that the way I did, me, in my sports fan prime, them, deep in the duties of parenting. So while I do not have the '69 Cubs, they do not have the '99 breakup of the Bulls.

"The destruction of the dynasty was complete and devastating," I told Jake Malooley in late 2019 for his excellent 2005 Bulls oral history at *The Ringer*. "Suddenly it was this completely different team. The uniforms were the same, but the experience was totally different. I didn't think it was going to be as bad as it was. And I didn't think it was going to go on as long as it did."

The '99 lockout Bulls were like the '91 Bulls of losing. They flipped our identity and experience. The Bulls went from 62 wins to 13-37. In the '98 Finals, we held Utah to 54 points in Game 3, a record low for any game in the shot clock era. And then the very next season, we broke that record, but on the losing end, scoring just 49 points against Miami. As I continued with Jake:

> "You want to talk low points of being a Bulls fan in that era? We had four games in 2000 with John Starks in a Bulls uniform. Of all the indignities of that period, having to decide whether or not to root for John Starks for four games is up there.
>
> "Some time in '99, before I went off to college, I put my name on the Bulls' season-ticket waitlist. The Bulls were just

starting to get bad. My plan was that by the time my name would be up on the list, I'd be out of college, I'd have a job, I'd have money to afford the tickets, and the Bulls would be better. A year later, I get a call. It's the Bulls' season-ticket office: 'We're excited to tell you you've come to the top of the season-ticket waitlist.' I was like, 'No! That's not the plan!' People getting rid of their season tickets was a sign of how fast the bottom fell out.

"(Trying to strike it rich in free agency and landing Ron Mercer) – that was the big "uh-oh" moment—when it became clear that the Bulls could be losing for the long haul. After the first three seasons, I was reminded of the quote from *Macbeth*: "I am in blood Stepped in so far that, should I wade no more, Returning were as tedious as go o'er." In other words, I'd gone this far with the post-dynasty Bulls, I might as well keep watching them lose.

"Among those of us who were still watching the team during that historic run of losing between '99 and '04, there was a strange bond..."

April 24, 2005, "Bear Down and Get Some Runs"
   Age 23

THE BULLS ARE BACK! A TRIP TO THE UNITED CENTER

I woke up this morning ready to go.

Granted, I wasn't dressed or showered, nor had I eaten, and you can't very well go to a basketball game without getting out of bed, but all that aside, I was ready. The last time I'd seen the Bulls in the playoffs, I was a sophomore in high school with little idea as to where I'd be attending college. Bill Clinton was president, Dave Wannstedt was coaching the Bears, and Sammy Sosa was in the midst of a record-breaking month in which he hit twenty home runs and transformed himself from Sammy to *SAMMY*. Seven years and five Bulls coaches later, the Bulls are back in the postseason, and *I* am going to see them.

After showering and eating breakfast, I head upstairs to look for my game-day uniform. I've only owned one Bulls jersey in my day, a black Rodman jersey I got when he came to the team in eighth grade, and I can't find it anywhere. Great.

But I do have a lot of old Bulls t-shirts, and that seems like the way to go. My room was clean when I got here yesterday, (my parents for some reason decided that they would have to be able to walk through it while I was gone), but it is a condensed clean: you can walk around, but the closets are filled with old books and clothes, as is the storage compartment that's attached to my bed, and now there are boxes packed tight with stuff that my parents took off the floor while I was traveling.

It takes a while to get through everything, as I quickly look for any t-shirt from the glory days, and after searching the entire room I finally come to the last bag, a shopping bag that's sitting in the back of my closet underneath a blanket that I put on my bed during the winter. I open the bag, and I feel like I'm looking upon the briefcase in *Pulp Fiction*. About ten t-shirts that I've saved, and right there in the middle is the one that I know I'm going to wear. It's a black shirt from the third grade with pictures of Michael, Scottie, and Horace each dribbling the basketball accompanied by the phrase "Chicago Bulls' Triple Threat." Ball game.

"So tight!" as my brother would say, though the phrase takes on a literal meaning as well as the shirt is hugging the small gut I've acquired while on the road. But it's perfect, and once I find an old black Bulls hat from the garage and the black Bulls shorts that I got with the Rodman jersey, I know I've found my game-day uniform. I throw on a pair of red warm up pants over the shorts, lace up my shoes, and I'm ready.

Of course, at this point, it's only 1:15 or so, and Ben's not coming over till 2:30…

I go downstairs and grab the *Tribune* sports section and immediately begin pouring over every written word about the Bulls and this playoff series against Washington.

"Oh, that's awesome! They're gonna wear the black shoes!" I yell to no one.

"What's that?" Mom asks.

"It says here that the Bulls are gonna wear black shoes for the playoffs, which is what they always used to do back in the day. White shoes during the season, black shoes for the playoffs."

"Is that a surprise?"

"Well, I just wasn't sure if they'd do it, or if they'd remember to. It's just cool to see that kind of tradition, ya know? Just like the old days."

"I see."

The phone rings, and Mom gets it. I continue reading the paper, while Dad sits on the couch enjoying his Sunday, reading the paper and watching the Cubs. We're down 2-0 to Pittsburgh.

"I forgot all about the Cubs."

"Yeah. Pirates are up 2-0 in the third. Wood's pitching."

"You mind if I pop a tape in to get ready for the Bulls game?"

"What?"

"*Learning to Fly*. The Bulls '91 championship video."

"I'm watching the Cubs," Dad says in protest.

PART V: THE BULLS ARE BACK　　　　　　　　　　147

"Come on. Bulls baby. Bulls! Cubs'll still be on."

He relents. "Fine."

We put the tape in, and I'm brought back to the early days. All of the other championship videos focus solely on one season, but *Learning to Fly* looks at the rise of the Bulls, from Jordan's drafting to the signing of Pax and drafting of Scottie and Horace and the trade for Cartwright to the struggles against Detroit and finally to the '91 season. Just watching the video, I'm amazed at how emotional I still get at some of these scenes. During the sequence in which they recap the playoff losses to Detroit in '88, '89, and '90, I grimace and shake my head in disappointment.

After we go up two games to none in the '91 Eastern Conference Finals, and they show a clip of Laimbeer looking up at the camera, his eyes glaring creepily through the small slits in his clear face mask, I shiver in fear. As Scottie talks in the interview and says that Detroit is going to "have to accept the beating we was giving them," I get wide-eyed and smiley. And as we finish off the series, I pump my fist and grin.

Ben rings the doorbell as we begin the Finals against the Lakers. He's wearing jeans and a red t-shirt that says "1991 NBA Finals Bulls vs. Lakers." Perfect.

"WHAT TIME IS IT?" he exclaims.

I answer: "GAME TIME! HOO!" We high five. "Great shirt."

"Thanks man. You too." Ben eyes up Pip, MJ, and Horace. "Triple threat? That's a tight fit."

"No kidding. You ready?"

"I woke up ready."

"Same here!" We fist pound.

I say goodbye to my parents, and they wish us good luck and tell us to bring home a victory, and we jump in my car, turn on the radio, and head out.

There's lots of good stuff on, and it's tough to pick what to listen to. The Bulls games are broadcast on AM 1000, but there's no pregame right now because 1000 also does the Sox games, and they're playing Kansas City. So we flip to WGN on 720 to hear Pat and Ron do the Cubs game. While watching *Learning to Fly*, the Cubs came back to take the lead 4-2. It's now 5-2, with the Cubs trying to hang on and win. At the commercial, we flip to 670 the Score, and they're talking Day Two of Bears draft coverage.

"Oh man!" I say in surprise. "I totally forgot about the draft."

"Me too. I've been totally focused on the Bulls game."

"Yeah. Totally. Who'd we take today?"

"I don't know."

And then, as if they heard us...

"...and in case you're just joining us, we're talking about quarterback Kyle Orton of Purdue, the Bears' fourth-round draft choice."

"Hey there you go. Orton's a real good player."

"Yeah. That's a nice pick."

There's heavy traffic on the Kennedy — Bulls playoff traffic... awesome! — but it thins out a bit as a bunch of cars get off at Ogden. We decide to go all the way to Madison and head west from there to the stadium. On the ride there, the Cubs finish off Pittsburgh to hang on for a 5-2 win.

"OK, good win," I say.

"Let's get another one."

PART V: THE BULLS ARE BACK

The stadium looks great. It appears on the horizon, massive, peaking out over the left side of the landscape and then quickly dominating everything else in sight. Men in bright orange shirts wave flags and direct fans into their lots, less expensive than the lots next to the United Center, but we decide to park across from the stadium. The traffic inches slowly forward, allowing us to see the hoards of fans donned in red and black excitedly making their way to the gym. We pull into a lot, packed in tight next to the cars that pull in just before us and just after us, and then out of the car and out of the lot and across the street and now we're in the thick of Bulls fans, all ready for the playoffs.

The glory days are still well represented — everywhere you look there's a JORDAN 23 on somebody's back — but HINRICH 12, CHANDLER 3, CURRY 2, and GORDON 7 are also in abundance. We walk past the Jordan statue, which is surrounded by the usual group of fans, gawkers and photographers and enthusiasts and tourists, and we weave between families with little boys decked out in their Bulls gear, too young to remember Jordan's last shot and blissfully ignorant of the horrors of the Bad Boys, their faces aglow as they hold their parents' hands and listen to their stories of guys named Jordan and Pippen and Grant and Rodman and get ready to walk into a Bulls playoff game as if nothing out of the ordinary is happening.

The ticket windows are packed with hopefuls trying to get into the action, and scalpers walk among us with *you need two? I got two* slipping from their lips and then disappearing back into the crowd, but Ben and I have our tickets, and when we get to our gate we display them proudly, holding them up for the ticket rippers with big smiles on our faces. We are here.

"OH MAN!" I'm ecstatic. "Dude, we're at a Bulls playoff game! We're in the playoffs man!" Ben and I high five.

"What do you wanna do first? Get food or go to our seats?"

"I can't make any decisions right now. Let's get food. No, actually, let's go to the seats. I wanna see the court. I'm kind of hungry though."

"We'll go to the seats."

"Awesome."

We get up to the seats with about twenty minutes left on the pregame clock. The stadium is not empty, but it's certainly not yet crowded. All around the gym fans are settling into their seats, and blowing up those moronic "Thunderstix" that they pass out as you enter the stadium. I hate those things. So does Ben. There's a little kid in front of us smacking the hell out of his Idiotstix, and normally I'd be focused on him in the same way that you can't help but focus on a kid humming loud and off-key while sitting in a plane on the runway, but I'm so geeked up for the game that I hardly notice him. Fans continue to file in, and when the Bulls run out onto the court to start warming up the United Center comes to its feet, applauding our Bulls as they get into their layup lines. We get a kid behind us to take our picture, and then we head out for some food.

As we stand in line at the concession stand, I watch other Bulls fans walking around the concourse and I can't help but wonder how many of them have been there with Ben and me over the past six years. Do they remember Kornel David or Cory Carr? Were they dismayed by the Elton Brand for Tyson Chandler trade? Did they see the years of tough play and disappointing defeats? In the end though, it doesn't matter. This game means something to Ben and me, but that doesn't mean that it can't mean something else to other fans. Some people want to be involved for the whole ride, and other people can only get excited for the high points, and that's OK.

It's just like the High Holidays. Some people need and want to go to services every week, and other people, for whatever reason, only go for Rosh Hashana and Yom Kippur. It's just a question of what kind of a role Judaism plays in your life, just as this crowd is an example of what kind of role the Bulls play in their lives. And what this crowd really brings to light is what kind of role the Bulls play in the lives of Chicagoans.

No matter what the Bears do, Soldier Field will always be packed. We are a football city. When the Bears go to the playoffs, even if it's a surprise season coming off of a losing year like in 1994 or 2001, the fans at a Bears playoff game are all of the same people who have been experiencing the ups and downs with the team every Sunday. The schedule has something to do with it, as it's obviously much easier to attend eight football games than it is to attend 41 basketball games, but even still, the city's interest in the Bulls waxes and wanes with their performance. That's just the way it is.

Still, it's exhilarating to hear the roar of the crowd when the lights go out at the United Center. You can really feel it: these fans are truly excited for this game and this team. "Aaaaaaaaaaaand now…" A.D., Noce, Othella, Chris Duuuuuuuuuuhon, and Captain Kirk are introduced to applause and cheers and lots of "whoooooos!" and the lights come on, the refs jump it up, and we're underway.

During the game's opening moments the fans are pumped up and yelling on every possession, but soon after things settle into a nice rhythm and the crowd settles down, only getting jacked up for big plays. I haven't been to an NBA game since 2001, and I'd forgotten one incredibly obnoxious feature of today's NBA: they never let you rest. At every time out, time I usually spend relaxed on my couch watching commercials or flipping around, I'm assaulted with some kind of cacophonous entertainment ploy like a mascot race or a breakdancing contest or some other silly thing that asks for loud music and my attention.

I don't really care for this stuff, but it goes over well with everyone else, as fans cheer in celebration when Cuppy Coffee defeats the donut and the bagel in the Dunkin Donuts race. I guess the thinking is that we've paid so much for tickets, we may as well be pummeled with entertainment at every waking moment.

The Bulls trail by two at the end of the first quarter but quickly come right back in the second to take the lead. For a young team, the Bulls look like they've been playing playoff basketball for ten years. Paxson's decision to draft players with big-time college experience has been paying off all season, and at no time is that advantage more evident than today. What's Game 1 of a first-round playoff series to Ben Gordon, a guy who helped lead Connecticut to the national title last year? What's Game 1 of a first-round playoff series to Chris Duhon, a guy who became Duke's starting point guard during his freshman season and helped them win a title, and then brought them back to the Final Four last season? What's Game 1 of a first-round playoff series to Andres Nocioni, a guy who's been playing professionally in Argentina and just this past summer helped lead his national team to the Olympic gold medal?

Throw in Kirk Hinrich's four years at Kansas, including two Final Fours and a trip to the national title game in 2003, and you've got some big-time experience on the court. This isn't one-and-done Michigan man Jamal Crawford and a couple of high school guys; these are battle-tested players who have played big minutes in big-time competition. Hopefully, the success of these Bulls will lead other GMs around the league to mimic Paxson's blueprint, because talented high schoolers with big-time college experience are nearly always better suited for the NBA than talented high schoolers with little or no college experience.

PART V: THE BULLS ARE BACK

Behind Duhon, Gordon, and Othella, the Bulls begin to open up a big lead, and when Eric Piatkowski squares up and hits a three to push that lead to seven, the United Center explodes in cheer. But Washington comes back, and after they regain the lead at 52-51, Captain Kirk hits a jumper to end the half, and the Bulls go into the locker room with a one-point lead.

Ben and I decide to walk around the stadium during halftime, mingling with all of the other Bulls fans. Ben buys a beer while I go to use the bathroom. It's pretty relaxed, though every so often someone will yell "Go Bulls!" and get a few cheers. As I'm drying my hands, I see a young boy in a Bulls hat standing by the sinks, waiting for his father to finish up.

"You enjoying the game?"

"Yeah."

"Cool. What year were you born?"

He looks at me oddly. "1996. Why?"

I laugh. "No reason. Go Bulls."

I find Ben and we settle back into our seats for the second half. After a jumper from Wizard All-Star Gilbert Arenas — Washington's regular season scoring leader at 25.5 points per game was held scoreless in the first half by great defense from Duhon—Nocioni hits a three to put the Bulls up two.

"Noce is on fire," Ben says to me.

"No kidding. Has he even been out of the game yet?"

"He was out for like thirty seconds or something at the end of the first half."

"Wow."

Noce has been an animal on the boards, pulling down ten in the first half to lead the team. He also had eight points, and let out a scream you could hear from Argentina after every rebound he grabbed or basket he made. As the third quarter rages on, the emotion in the stands grows. Timeout entertainments are treated with less and less enthusiasm, the crowd anxious to get on with the game. A three-point play by Arenas puts the Wizards up seven with nineteen seconds to play, and a Duhon layup ends the quarter with the Bulls trailing 82-77. There's work to be done, and the players and fans are ready for the challenge. The Bulls walk off the court to the applause and encouragement of the crowd, which is now fully immersed in the game.

The Bulls open the fourth on a 13-4 run backed by ten points from Ben Gordon, who by now no longer surprises us with his fourth quarter magic. He cuts the Wizard lead to four on a jumper, and the crowd is with the team every step of the way. When Kwame Brown's weak floater is blocked by Tyson Chandler, the crowd pumps its collective fist in celebration. When Duhon steals a Juan Dixon pass and heads down the court, the crowd stands up and awaits the bucket that we all know is coming.

After Noce ties the game on a free throw, Ben hits a three to give the Bulls a lead they would never relinquish. Ben gets a steal and a dunk to put the Bulls up four, Noce hits a three to put the Bulls up five, A.D. hits a jumper to put the Bulls up seven, and after four straight missed free throws by Kirk and Tyson, Noce steps to the line and calmly hits a pair as the stands reverberate with chants of "No—ci—o—ni!" The final buzzer sounds, the Bulls win by nine, and the crowd stands and cheers and applauds the team. Game 1 is over. Final score: Bulls 103, Wizards 94.

"That's two playoff wins in a row," Ben reminds me as we high five.

"Hey, that's right! Winning streak. Awesome!"

We head into the bathroom, and it's packed and jumping. The lines go all the way to the back, and people are cheering and yelling and continuing the "No—ci—o—ni!" chant. "Go Bulls!" "Alright!" "Noce was awesome!" "So was Gordon!" We use the bathroom, give the Bulls one more cheer with the rest of the restroom constituents, and leave. Out the door and down the ramps and out onto the street, passing Bulls fans with smiles on their faces and a jump in their steps. We sit in my car, waiting for our turn to drive, and then it's out of the lot and down the block with the radio on, listening to Bulls post game and Bears draft coverage, and we drive back north on the Kennedy as the packs of Bulls fan thin out along the way. We pull up to Ben's house, and stop.

"Tell your friend thanks for the tickets," he says.

"Absolutely. Thanks for coming."

"Are you kidding? I wouldn't miss it."

"Get together for Game 2?"

"Sounds good. Later bro."

"Peace. Go Bulls."

"Go Bulls."

We high five, he leaves, and I drive home. What a great day.

May 4, 2005, "Bear Down and Get Some Runs"
     Age 23

THE OTHER SIDE: GILBERT ARENAS KILLS THE BULLS

"Would you have been happier had they lost by twenty?"

I'm sitting in my basement, having just watched one of the great gut-wrenching Bulls games of all-time, and all I can think is that I finally know what this feels like. Gilbert Arenas gave the Wizards the win and a 3-2 series lead with a buzzer-beating jumper not ten minutes ago, and as he was mobbed in celebration by his teammates while the United Center faithful stood in shock and disappointment, all I could do was think of Cleveland. And Utah. And New York. And Phoenix.

I racked my brain, trying desperately to locate a game in my vast ocean of Bulls memories in which my team had lost at the hands of a last-second shot, and for the life of me I could not come up with one. Certainly in all my years as a Bulls fan, I must have at some point watched a game in which the other team won with a game-winner, but obviously it was not a game that mattered.

All I could think of was MJ over Russell, and Pax in Phoenix, and MJ over Ehlo, and Kerr against the Jazz, and Ben Gordon's floater over the Knicks, and MJ over Gerald Wilkins, and always Jordan, again and again and again, until you get to the point where it's not even dramatic.

I remember Michael's last shot so vividly...Bulls down three, Jordan gets a layup, Bulls down one, Jordan gets a steal, and then down the court he comes and we're all just waiting for it, everybody's waiting for it, and then he pulls up and hits like we all knew he would. I didn't jump up and down in excitement. I didn't high five anyone. I clapped my hands and smiled. "Good ol' Mike. Always hittin' game-winners." After that shot, *Sports Illustrated* ran a cover photo of Jordan's game-winning pose from the front, face towards the camera, no one else in the frame. That's how it was for us.

But the better picture is the one from behind, because it's that picture that shows the full truth: Utah fans behind the basket, their hands on their heads and their mouths dropped to the floor and an empty look in their eyes that screams with pain. It's like the realistic side to an action movie. As a viewer, your concern is John McClane, and at the end of *Die Hard* Bruce Willis limps off the screen, wife in his arms, a hero to all. Cue happy music, the credits roll, and everyone leaves the theater having had a rip-roaring good time.

But what about the innocent people killed along the way? Sure, they don't matter to us, the viewer, because we understand that an action movie requires some innocent people to be killed, because bad guys kill innocent people, because if they don't then they're not bad guys and then John McClane need not worry about them and he can instead spend his Christmas kicking back by the fire drinking and having a good time with his family. But then we wouldn't have a movie, would we?

So for the good of the movie, innocent people must be sacrificed. We expect Michael to hit his shot and we expect the Bulls to be victorious, and that's all that matters to us, just as we expect John McClane to limp away laughing at the end of each movie. McClane wins. His wife survives. And all under two and a half hours. Perfect.

So now here I am sitting in my basement, and now I know what it feels like. My throat is still quite sore from yelling during the Bulls twenty-two point comeback, a comeback that accomplished nothing more than to give Gilbert Arenas a stage for a dramatic shot. The fourth quarter threes from Pargo, Kirk, and Ben — five in all — and the putbacks and rebounds from Tyson and all of the cheering from the Bulls bench and the fans at the United Center, all of it led to one thing: Washington fans were treated with a memorable victory.

And so my dad, with whom I watched the game, posed an interesting question to me, one I've yet been able to answer: "Would you have been happier had they lost by twenty?"

It's such a different feeling, getting blown out and losing at the end. I may be an intense sports fan, but in no way do I actually equate a basketball game to actual life and death matters.

That being said, the best way I can describe what these kinds of losses feel like is with life and death matters. Getting blown out is like having an old family member die of cancer. It's horrible, certainly, but it gives you time to prepare for the end, because it's only a matter of time until the clock runs out. You get time to come to terms with the end and what it means long before it happens. Losing a game not in a blowout but just because the other guys were clearly the better team is like losing a family member to old age. It's easier to accept because there's nothing you can do about it. It's "just the way things are."

Then there's losing a game the way we lost today. When you lose a game at the buzzer after battling back from a 22-point blowout, it's like having a family member get cancer, then having that person fight until the cancer is in remission, having them get out of the hospital, and then having them get hit by a bus the next day. Things are bleak, and then you're given just enough good to get your hopes all the way up, and then they're dashed cruelly and quickly, and a part of you is left wondering why fate had to mock you in such a nasty manner. "If only Washington had just pulled away, I wouldn't have to feel quite so terrible now."

My dad, on the other hand, did not go through what I went through, because he wrote this team off long before the final buzzer sounded. He wrote them off at halftime when we went into the locker room down 63-49, and again with a minute to play in the third when we were trailing 86-68, and again with eight and a half to go in the game down 94-82, and again with just under four to play down 102-90, and finally with 42 seconds to play down 108-98. My dad wasn't giving up necessarily; he was just being realistic and accessing the facts.

What my dad saw was a feisty yet clearly undermanned Bulls team that didn't have the fire power to hang with the Wizards. He saw a team that didn't look like it had much of a spark in the first half, just as they didn't have much of a spark in the two losses in Washington. While I was fired up and ready for a comeback built on desperate threes that were finding ways to drop through, my dad, ever the realist, knew that games can be won on one or two desperate threes, but not on six or seven or eight of them.

So my dad wasn't out of breath when Arenas took his game-winner, and he wasn't in shock when the ball dropped through, and he wasn't depressed by the final score. The facts pointed to a Washington victory, facts like their 56.1% shooting mark or their 49-36 rebounding edge

PART V: THE BULLS ARE BACK

or their two (and if Hughes had been healthy all year, three) All-Stars compared to our team of role players.

Having measured up the facts, and having seen the way both teams had played for the first three quarters — as well as since the start of Game 3 — my dad was sure that a Washington victory was in the stars. How we got there was not important, because he knew that every Bulls spurt and every Tyson dunk and every Pargo three was just delaying the inevitable. The movie will provide good drama and shocking twists and an outcome that's in the balance until the final scene, but John McClane will live and Hans Gruber will die because that's the way these things go, and having watched the Bulls for three quarters, it was clear to my dad that on this night, they were John McClane and we were Hans Gruber.

But then why rent the movie? What's the point of watching? I'm a smart guy, and a reasonable guy, and I know as well as my dad does that the Wizards have more basketball talent than do the Bulls and that you can't win games with nothing but lucky shots.

But maybe you can, and so I put my heart into the game and cheer throughout, even when things get bleak, even when we're playing poorly, even when I know that the Bulls will need to get awfully lucky to win this game. Sometimes that kind of hope and emotion pays off with a win, like it did when Illinois beat Arizona. And sometimes it doesn't. But you watch and you cheer and you enjoy every moment, because otherwise there's really no point.

The Bulls closed the third quarter on an 11-2 run to cut the Wizard lead to thirteen, and when the horn sounded my dad stood up to refill his water. "Well," he said, as he walked to the sink, "it's on to Game 6."

"Oh come on! What's a matter with you? We're coming back."

"We've been coming back the whole game. The Bulls just don't have it tonight. I wish they did, but they don't."

"It's down to thirteen. We've had some big fourth quarters this year."

"Well, we'll see who's right."

He was right. But I had more fun.

So now we head back to Washington, where we've lost ten in a row and two straight playoff games and where our season might come to an end in Game 6. Things aren't looking good for the Bulls right now. The losses of Curry and Deng are starting to show, and with Washington getting All-Star contributions from their All-Stars and solid games from their role players, the Bulls look like they might be in trouble. After dominating Games 1 and 2, talent may have caught up with the Bulls. It could be what Rick Telander called it yesterday on the Score: a delayed sweep.

But then again, maybe it's not. Game 6 is Friday, and a win in Washington brings the series home for Game 7. Can the Bulls rebound and even the series?

I don't know, but I'll be watching.

May 6, 2005, "Bear Down and Get Some Runs"
    Age 23

TO THE 2005 CHICAGO BULLS: A THANK YOU NOTE

The season is over.

The Bulls have just lost Game 6, 94-91, and I am strapped with an incredible feeling of loss. No second-round series with Miami. No Game 7 at home. After leading for most of the game and playing the kind of basketball that helped us earn the fourth seed in the East, the kind of basketball that had evaded us during Games 3, 4, and 5, the Bulls fell apart in the final two minutes and dropped a heartbreaker to the Wizards.

I watched the game at my house, solo, which was fine. I decided to tape the game, so that just in case we lost I'd have a tape of this Bulls team, but as the game got underway things were pointing to a Game 7. The Bulls came out hot and got off to a nice lead, and though Washington was able to tie it up it was clear that we were playing our brand of ball. Great defense, getting into passing lanes, challenging shots, beating them on the glass, hustling to loose balls. We led by three after one, by two at the half, and by six going into the fourth quarter.

But Washington wasn't going away, and they stayed close enough throughout so that I was never able to relax, even though it felt all the way like it was our game. We were ahead, we were ahead, and then as I realized that we weren't going to pull away and make it an easy win, it dawned on me that this might be the last chance I would get to watch this Bulls team play.

Suddenly, things were serious, and I focused in completely, not because the team needed my total concentration, but because I needed the team. I still felt like we were on our way to Game 7, but just in case...

Then the wheels came off. As Kirk went for what looked to be an easy layup, Arenas made an impossibly athletic clean block from behind, knocking the ball off the backboard and sending Hinrich to the floor. Washington gained possession, and Larry Hughes' layup cut the Bulls lead to two. Jamison stole the ball from Hinrich and hit a long deuce to tie the game at 91. The teams traded missed shots and the Wizards missed a couple of free throws, and then as Kirk prepared to inbound the ball to a streaking Chris Duhon, Du looked away and Kirk threw it in, bouncing the ball off of Duhon's back.

Jared Jeffries scooped up the loose ball and charged down the floor for an easy dunk. Down two, Pargo missed a quick three, and Juan Dixon grabbed the rebound and went to the line on a Hinrich foul. Dixon hit one of two, and suddenly the game had turned all the way around. Panic set in; this was the end.

Noce missed a three, and in a final sequence that typified the Bulls' late-game collapse, Tyson rebounded the miss with four seconds to go and shot up a two instead of kicking out for a potential game-tying three. The ball fell into the arms of Arenas, who tossed it into the crowd as time expired. Wizards 94, Bulls 91. Series over.

In a way, these details are all inconsequential. This isn't like Illinois losing to North Carolina, where they had a chance to win a championship. I didn't expect the Bulls to get out of the second round, and I'm not that upset that we lost to the Wizards. Washington is a very good team, and they played great basketball for four straight games. It would've been great to see this team advance to the second round, but losing in the first in no way detracts from what we did all year. This season is still a huge success, any way you cut it.

No, the loss that I feel right now, that I feel throughout my body, is from knowing that there are no more games to be played for the 2004-2005 Chicago Bulls. That's what sucks the most. I'd love it if we could go out and play Miami, but really I'd just love it if we could go out and play tomorrow. Any time. Any gym. Any opponent. They can scrimmage against the Charlotte Bobcats for all I care. I just want to see them play again.

I want to see Captain Kirk, all floppy-haired and sleepy-eyed, pulling up for three on a fast break and igniting the United Center crowd.

I want to see Tyson, long and slender and full of ferocity, extending his seven-foot frame as far as it can reach as he stretches for a rebound and roars after a blocked shot and celebrates with the front row fans after another exciting Bulls win.

PART V: THE BULLS ARE BACK

I want to see Ben Gordon, knifing through defenders and lofting up floaters that look like they'll kiss the Jumbotron before they dance sweetly through the net, changing the way we think about the fourth quarter.

I want to see Chris Duuuuuuuuhon in his defensive squat, arms out and eyes on his man, ready to swat away a dribble and lead a fast break.

I want to see Noce, barking and yelling at teammates and opponents, diving for loose balls and exploding into the lane for a game-changing dunk.

I want to see Eddy, lumbering down the court before catching a ball in the post, and in one motion turning and slamming it down so hard that the defenders know next time to just get out of his way.

I want to see Luol, a man with limbs from here to the Pacific, rushing in front of passing lanes and running the break and gracefully dropping in finger rolls that start from the foul line.

I want to see A.D., the old man of the group, battling for rebounds and defending his guys and smiling as he realizes what a special group this is.

I want to see Othella and Pike and Griffin and Pargo waving towels from the bench, not caring if they get in, but knowing that when they do they'll get the team going with a rebound or a box out or a pull up jumper or a spot up three.

And I want to see Coach Skiles working the sideline, keeping the guys focused but loose, because they know what he wants and he knows that they'll come through for him when he calls their number.

One of the big advantages of professional sports is that teams get to grow up together and play together and win together for more than four years. Win or lose against North Carolina, the 2005-06 Illini were sure to be a very different team than the 2004-05 Illini. That team will always be remembered, always be special, in part because fans knew that their time with that team was limited.

Pro sports are different. This Bulls team will improve, and they will be back, and come November we'll all be ready for the next step. We'll come out of the gate determined and prepared, maybe have an All-Star or two, grow stronger as a team and as individuals and have another exciting playoff run. We'll get to a point where the playoffs aren't the goal, but the expectation. We'll go to a conference championship where we have to prove all over again that we belong with the best, and maybe, just maybe, a trip to the NBA Finals, where we can all laugh and cheer and talk about what a ride it's been and how sweet it is to be here after all these years.

But we'll never have this year again, this 2004-2005 season. We'll never again have this exact group of guys, never again be the regular-season Cinderella story, never again go from 0-9 to the postseason, never again see the expectations change so dramatically that a loss in Game 6 of the first round would be deemed a disappointment in a season that began with fans hoping only for thirty wins.

So the season is over, and while the playoffs continue and the Bulls get ready for the summer, I say thank you. Thank you for never quitting, no matter what hole you were in, be it down 27 in the opener to New Jersey or languishing at 0-9 and 4-15 or losing your leading scorer down the stretch or trailing by 22 in Game 5. Thank you for back-to-back wins against the Knicks, for giving us that special feeling all over again, for showing us what a proud basketball team looks like. Thank you for winning with defense and hustle and heart and emotion, not to mention skill and speed and athleticism.

Thank you John Paxson, for having the vision and courage to put together a team that played the way you thought the game should be played, for choosing passion over potential and finding players that we could be proud of. Thank you Scott Skiles, for coming into a tough situation and showing that hard work and commitment can be just as rewarding as contracts and highlights.

PART V: THE BULLS ARE BACK

Thank you Chicago Bulls, our 2004-2005 Chicago Bulls, for giving us reason to cheer and a season to cherish. Thank you.

July 4, 2009, ReadJack.com
Age 27

GOODBYE TO THE MEMORY MAKER

Say what you will about Ben Gordon. It's been said before. Too short to defend two guards, too undisciplined to defend the point, too one-dimensional to run the floor, too streaky a shooter, too careless a ballhandler, too many pull-up threes that killed too many possessions, too much of a wild card to build a team around. It's not quite 22 two's, but then Ben Gordon was never quite what anyone wanted.

But here's what he *was*: a legit NBA scorer, a dude who could break you without breaking a sweat, a threat for 30 any time his sweet stroke was in rhythm, one of the most accurate three point shooters in the franchise's 43 years, and as of last season, the franchise leader in three pointers made.

So yeah, he made big shots. He made late shots. He made a whole bunch of threes. Most of all though, he made memories. Ultimately, that is where Ben Gordon's Bulls legacy will lie.

Removing the Bulls-Celtics series for a moment, (and Derrick Rose, whose rookie year reel is packed), what is your strongest memory of the BG-era players? My Captain Kirk moment is fairly obscure — 34 points in a double OT opening night loss to New Jersey in November of '04 — and remains only because I am diehard-diehard Bulls. My strongest memories of Deng, Noce, Duhon, Tyrus, Salmons, Eddy and Tyson are sparse for each and may be considered similarly obscure to the average fan.

But if you've been watching the Bulls and Ben Gordon since 2004-05, you probably remember: several game winners (my favorite was the

MLK Day floater at MSG in 2005)... tons of fourth-quarter magic... the Sixth Man trophy... the nine-for-nine against Washington... the 48 against Milwaukee... the 30 in Game 1 in 2005.

Then add the Boston series: Game 2's UConn shootout... the trey to send Game 4 into double OT (accompanied by his junk grab)... and his 33 to close out Game 7.

That 33-point effort was our final Gordon memory, and it was emblematic of his career. His detractors point to his game-high total in a losing effort, his live-by-the-Ben die-by-the-Ben attitude, his 30.4% shooting. Even his usual late-game heroics were reversed: after knocking down a pair from the stripe to pull the Bulls within three 89-86, the man once dubbed "Heir Gordon" converted only one of six shots, demanding the ball on every possession and failing to deliver.

On the other hand, Gordon got to the line a series-high fifteen times in Game 7, and knocked in all fifteen (including seven in the fourth). As great as Rose was in that series and in that game, he was unable to find the line even once in Game 7, a problem Gordon never had: the only dude on the team who could consistently create his own shot, get to the line, and get his points.

Of course, the days of Rose shooting only 25 freebies in a seven-game playoff series (and throwing up three goose eggs) will soon be over. At this moment, the 2009-10 Bulls starting lineup has only one spot absolutely positively locked down, which is fine, since Rose is the future and really, *really* good at basketball. Gordon is a fantastic NBA scorer and game-saver, but his role as both grew in part from the absence of anyone else to do the job. With Rose in the fold, the Bulls' need for Gordon the Gunner is gone.

Still, I will miss #7, even if his departure ends up being for the best. That is probably the reality, because exciting as he was, Gordon created many problems for the Bulls. It wasn't his fault. Simply the nature of things. The Bulls' brass could never admit they drafted an orgasmic bench scorer with the 3rd selection and nabbed Hinrich's starting mate 35 picks later. If Pax and Skiles had simply deemed

Duhon and Kirk the team's starting backcourt with Gordon the explosive bench man and leading scorer, the team would have been steady, contract negotiations with Gordon may have been a breeze, and five years later, had "Little Ben" still ended up on a bus for Motown, the number of Bulls fans, writers, and radio hosts satisfied to see it happen would have been far fewer.

…but then we may have made the playoffs in '08, and then Derrick Rose would be a Grizzly or a Timberwolf and not a Chicago Bull, and our futures as basketball spectators in Chicago would not be as bright.

For me, that's the end of it: we rode the Ben Gordon Experience, and it was fun. Being upset that the ride took us in a loop and not to a title would be like complaining that you can't drive to Florida in a roller coaster. Yes, I prefer a three month road trip to three minutes on Shockwave. But I also prefer three minutes on Shockwave to sitting in traffic.

For five seasons, Ben Gordon made it fun to watch the Bulls. He left his mark. I wish him the best as he moves to Detroit.

**PART VI:
THERE'S A TIMEOUT!
(WHERE?) ON THE FIELD**

Apr. 19, 2023, Windy City Gridiron
   Age 41

GOODBYE DEAR FRIEND: A LOVE LETTER TO SOLDIER FIELD

Dear Bears' Season Ticket Subscriber:

It's official! The Bears are moving to Soldier Field. This change should be considered as a temporary one as we are confident that a new stadium will be completed in Chicago within the next four years...

— Start of a letter from the CHICAGO BEARS FOOTBALL CLUB, INC. to season-ticket holders about how their Wrigley Field seats will be transferred to Soldier Field, dated May 17, 1971

******

Everything that Chicago fans like to think about ourselves starts in the elements. Our fandom doesn't work if confined to the United Center. Not even the chill in the air off the ice at a Hawks game can top an inclement day at Wrigley or the Cell. I've been to baseball games in April cold, August heat and standing in the aisles waiting out a rainout, and my Chicago fandom has been tickled.

And that's only baseball. What brings us all together, the Sox fans and Cubs fans, the hockey fans and hoops heads, are the Bears. While the mental and emotional side of my fandom started at home, the physical side started at Soldier Field. My grandfather was a season-ticket holder, one of the Wrigley-to-Soldier transfers. He got the letter. He made the move.

Slowly, my parents and my aunt and uncle went to more and more games, often without Papa. By the late 1980s, in his sixties, Mort Pierce was ready to give up the football Sunday grind completely, so he gave half the home games to our family and half to my aunt and uncle.

Nothing in my seven-year-old world could prepare me for attending a Bears game. You didn't just dress for the game, popping on a jersey or hat. You dressed for the weather. It was like a sports campout. I guess my parents deemed hitting the bathrooms with children tough enough. No point in adding the concession wait. So we brought snacks. We brought water. We brought binoculars. We brought spare gloves. The name of the game: stay warm, stay hydrated, stay loud.

"I have very early memories of Papa getting dressed with electric socks and a battery around his waist to go to Bears games," my mother told me recently. That was the standard. My parents spared us the coldest games when we were young (I never saw it but the stories of my Uncle Irv's full-body snowsuit with helmet are family lore), but even a crisp September day brought the possibility of a cold front and the need for your backup sweatshirt that upon arrival you wedged behind your back.

One time I attended a preseason game so hot that afterward, while we drove out of the parking lot at two miles per hour, my dad tried to buy pops from tailgaters to cool down me and my brother. I went to a game of such freezing wind-whipping cold ('07 Packers) that most fans, my friends and I included, spent halftime walking in the concourse because it was so packed that the bodies stopped the wind. I had sunny Bears games ('95 Vikes) and rainy Bears games ('05 Ravens). I don't remember hitting a snow games but I hit plenty of be-ready-for-snow games. You had to wear the right clothes.

Unless you wore nothing at all. Let your skin do its work. Nipples in the wind. I couldn't believe what I was seeing. Remember how Elmer Fudd would put his rifle in Bugs Bunny's face, and Bugs would turn the gun around at Elmer Fudd? And then Elmer turned it back to Bugs, who turned it back to Elmer, who turned it to Bugs, who then turned it… to himself. So Elmer Fudd turned the gun to himself, and Bugs turned it back to himself, and finally Elmer Fudd yelled something like "You asked for it!" and shot himself in the face?

That was these Bears fans in cold weather games. These fans, always in their twenties, always drinking beer faster than the beer man could double-pour, seemed to take the Bugs Bunny stance with the weather. *If I wear a coat, it's like I'm scared of the cold. But if I go shirtless, it's like the cold is scared of ME.*

I was in awe. Soldier Field wasn't a sporting event — it was a sporting expression. Fans sang more at Bears games. They cheered more at Bears games. They swore more at Bears games. I learned how to cheer by watching Rocky, a lifer a section below us in the yellow seats, the east side of the stadium. Rocky wore a custom #1 Bears jersey that said "ROCKY" on the back and led fans in chants with his megaphone. I've only recently learned his name was Bob Meehan. I always suspected he had a real name. But when you're standing behind him and he's leading you in "Bear Down," "Rocky" is all you need.

A "Rocky" wouldn't work the same way at Wrigley or the Cell. There are cheerleaders but it doesn't hit as hard. They're more like squatters lacking real authority. At a Bears game, "Bob Meehan" is the name in quotes. Everything is heightened. You walked into Soldier Field knowing this was it: THE home game for the next few weeks. Every Sunday took a mythic air. In 1995, my dad took me, my brother and my buddy Luke to a Bears-Oilers game. By chance, at halftime, the team was celebrating the 10th anniversary of the '85 Bears.

Ten years later, my dad and I attended a cold, rainy game against the Ravens. Game 2 of the World Series was at the Cell that night. The Sox led the series 1-0 and the Bears had a chance to get back to .500. The city was brimming with a united sports vibe. And sure enough, once again in a surprise to us, the '85 Bears were honored at halftime!

1985 was a special year for Chicago, and that made it a special year for Soldier Field. A stadium doesn't really feel like home until its home to a winner. The '85 Bears made Soldier Field our forever home. Those hallowed grounds returned the favor by giving us snowfall just as Wilber and the Fridge ran back the exclamation point.

And 21 years later, Soldier gave us snowfall again in another NFC championship game, the flakes falling as a deep ball fluttered to a lunging Bernard Berrian, the George Halas trophy presented to Virginia under the snowy lakefront sky.

As sports fans, we all want punctuation. When the scene around you is changing as you sit and cheer your team, that punctuation comes with texture of all five senses. I'll never forget sitting in the bleachers watching the Cubs punch a ticket to their first World Series since World War II, just as Papa never forgot sitting in the stands for a Bears-Cardinals game at Comiskey on Dec. 7, 1941, and getting word of an attack that would send the U.S. into World War II. When he described it to me in high school, he described the air. The cold. The wind. It's part of the story. As Chicagoans, weather is always part of the story.

At some point this decade, the Bears are likely giving up that weather. Their "temporary" home at Soldier Field in 1971 became a series of controversial, high-priced, often last-minute leases, the latest of which we signed in 2003 for 30 years upon completion of the spaceship. Today, the good money is on the club finally consummating its longstanding flirtation with the suburbs with a move to a new stadium in Arlington Heights. Kevin Warren is officially team president as of this week, and among his top credentials in a sterling resume is the work he did to bring a new stadium to the Vikings.

"[We're] continuing to focus on Arlington Park," Warren explained last month. "We purchased the land. And that's one of the things I'm looking forward to, to go to work on that. That was a big step. It showed our commitment to doing the right thing, especially solving a stadium solution."

The new stadium will have a dome. The Bears will own it. They'll host the Super Bowl. They'll play 21st century indoor football. They'll control the weather.

"I do envy the clubs enjoying new stadiums which give comfort to fans and pride to players," George Halas wrote in his autobiography in 1979 about the pros and cons of Soldier Field. "But if I had to choose between loving fans and a luxurious stadium I would stay with the fans."

It's a nice sentiment from Papa Bear, but ultimately we'll go wherever we can have a winner. I'll miss the old girl. All things must pass. And one day, I'll bring my children to a December Bears game in Arlington Heights, snow plastering the windshield on the drive to the park, and I'll sit with them in our stadium seats in our luxurious 70-degree controlled environment and tell them, with an odd, perhaps ridiculous pride, once upon a time, we were cold.

Ari Goldberg, Josh Frost and me at Soldier Field for the Bears' 35-7 win against the Packers on Dec. 23, 2007. The -18 wind chill at kickoff and 22 MPH winds puts this in the running for coldest Bears game ever. 4th Phase!

Jan. 20, 2005, "Bear Down and Get Some Runs"
 Age 23

THE FINAL GAME: A TRIP TO SOLDIER FIELD FOR THE 2001 PLAYOFFS

The joy of watching good playoff football usually comes with the pain of knowing that your team isn't good enough to be there. And when you watch the Chicago Bears, the pain of knowing that your team isn't good enough to get there is augmented by the pain of knowing that maybe your team would be good enough to get there if only ownership knew what they were doing.

Most of the Bears teams of the past 15 years have suffered from the same problems: an inability to win close games (coaching and quarterbacks) and an inability to run a team and evaluate talent. What impresses me most about this current edition of the New England Patriots is the way that they have instilled the team concept into every party of their organization, with Bob Kraft, Bill Belichick and Tom Brady embodying that concept with everything they do. If the Bears were only as eager to mimic the Patriots' broad approach as they were to mimic the 2000 Ravens' specific approach, when we went out and signed two massive d-tackles…

Unfortunately, this is not the case. The Bears had a promising 2004 in some respects, but we're a long way from being the kind of team that make the playoffs a yearly event. And so each year as the playoffs come around, Bears fans are left to reminisce on years gone by and our fleeting time in the sun.

The last one was just three years ago. It feels like 30.

On the strength of a suffocating defense, bulldozing o-line and some notable good luck, the Bears found themselves divsion champs at season's end, with a bye week to boot. After the Eagles trashed the Bucs, we were set to host Philly for a playoff game at Soldier Field. A few days before the game, my buddy Jake Bressler called me from U. of I. with the news. He had an extra ticket. The catch was that I was going to have to drive from Bloomington to Champaign, pick up Jake and a buddy of his and drive the three of us to Chicago. Within three minutes of hanging up the phone, I was packed.

When we got to Soldier two days later, I was overwhelmed. A playoff game is a different story. Dressed in my Marcus Robinson jersey over a Bears hoodie and a winter Bears cap, I was as excited for this game as any of my career. Meanwhile, on the same day, MJ was playing at the United Center for the first time since Game 5

PART VI: THERE'S A TIMEOUT! (WHERE?) ON THE FIELD

of the '98 Finals, though as a member of the Washington Wizards. Needless to say, it was a big day in Chicago. There was a feeling that even though some were at Soldier Field while others were at the UC and still others were at home or a bar or a friend's, we were all united, so if you were at either game you were watching it for anybody who couldn't be there.

That vibe was pervasive. Waiting in line outside the gate, I sang "Bear Down Chicago Bears" with fans I'd never met. When we stepped inside at last, I was ready. This was the final season at Soldier Field before the renovation. The Bears would spend the 2002 season at U. of I. With the Rams likely to win and host the NFC championship, this was looking like it would be the final game at this Soldier Field. We were going to send it out with a win, and my spirit was going to contribute.

But we didn't. The bad omen came before kickoff when the Soldier Field P.A. system blasted "Gonna Fly Now" from *Rocky*. Here we were playing the Eagles of *Philadelphia* and Soldier Field was getting fans pumped up with a damn Philly anthem! "What the hell is this?" I shouted as Bears fans sang and Eagles fans REALLY sang, grins on their pre-victorious faces. I should have known then and there that this was not our day. Indeed, while the Bears made a nice push with an end-around TD run by Ahmad Merritt and a TD pick return from Jerry Azumah, the game slipped away, and Philly walked out of Soldier Field with a 33-19 victory. Suddenly, the frozen air swirling around the park felt colder. I could feel it on my cheeks, like a slap, like it had been accumulating around me the entire game without my knowledge, and now that the game was over it belted me. I was surrounded by Eagles fans, all of them yelling and cheering, getting ready for a next game no longer promised to us, and all I could do was sit there, cold in my seat.

The last game at Soldier Field went by with little fanfare, the season over, our stadium as we knew it gone for good, nothing left but the cold in my cheeks. But then—and I'll never forget this— something came over me. A calm. For some reason, I felt okay, like losing was not the end. I felt this, through and through, and it shocked me, and it felt good. I could feel the smile growing on my face as my fellow Bears fans walked toward the exits engulfed in what felt like a sea of green, and in this moment of calm, I decided to say goodbye to Soldier Field by using the bathroom one final time.

As soon as I stepped in the door, I was in line. It was packed. I remember the feel of it, the overwhelming mood. Not only had we lost, but Soldier Field had seen its final game: construction crews began tearing out the seats as soon as the last fan left. No one said a word for the first two minutes I was in there. Finally someone in the back of the line yelled, "Let's piss on the floor. Not like they're gonna clean it." Another guy answered with "The sink looks good to me." Then, after about ten more seconds of silence, someone said, "It's been a great year."

It went from there. All of us peeing, and waiting to pee, reminiscing about a great season, cursing Hugh Douglas. This is what sports is about: the moments, both the moments of the season and the moments with the fans. Moments in bars and restaurants, time spent in the bleachers, moments after a huge game when you leave the park and feel the city vibrating, when you hear cars honking and you know why.

The bathroom moment after that Bears-Eagles game was one of those moments. It ended appropriately enough when a kid in front of me — no more than 10 — said loudly "Well, it'll all be okay if Brett Favre gets killed tomorrow." The bathroom erupted in celebration. Truth from a child.

Sep. 4, 2019, Twitter
   Age 37

THE BRYAN ROBINSON GAME: OUR SALUTE TO WALTER PAYTON

"When I get through with Chicago, they'll be loving me."

— Walter Payton, upon the Bears drafting him 4th overall in 1975

"Walter Payton picked me up in the air. I can't jump this high."

PART VI: THERE'S A TIMEOUT! (WHERE?) ON THE FIELD

— Bryan Robinson, after blocking a field goal against the Packers to seal a win in the first game after Walter Payton's death

✶✶✶✶✶✶

The (Player) Game. We love those. You know what I'm talking about. The Gale Sayers Game. The Devin Aromashodu Game. The James Allen Game. The Mike Brown Games. (Two!)

Of course this goes beyond the Bears. The Nate Robinson Game. The Sandberg Game. The Dewayne Wise Game. (Imagine having The Game on someone else's perfecto.)

You have to be special to get The (Player) Game. You have to be a legend's legend to get it after you die.

There is only one such legend.

On November 7, 1999, the Bears defeated the Packers 14-13 in a game that has been chiseled into Bears lore under two names: The Bryan Robinson Game, named for the Bears defensive tackle who blocked the game-winning field goal, and The Walter Payton Game, named for our beloved Sweetness whose spirit, B-Rob said, lifted him for the block.

"When I get through with Chicago, they'll be loving me," Walter said. We loved him long before he was through with Chicago. And long after.

Walter's skillset was as vast as it was deep. Yet that is not what defined him as a football player. What defined him were his intangibles: his heart, his will, his leadership, his toughness.

His spirit.

From the Flu Game — the *original* Flu Game — and his MVP in 1977, to the NFL's rushing record in 1984, to leading the greatest team ever to a Super Bowl victory, Walter Payton gave everyone who watched him and loved him a lifetime of memories. And we all know that "love" is not hyperbole.

Deepening the city's love of Walter — beyond his personal skills, achievement, personality and character — was his team. Generally speaking, Chicago sports fans root for one baseball team and one Chicago Stadium / U.C. team. But we all root for the Bears.

Even the term "Chicago sports fan" has fissures, with the sometimes strained relationships between the city and the suburbs, Chicagoland and downstate, Illinois and Northwest Indiana.

With Walter, none of those splits mattered. For 13 years, Sweetness was central. That's why, more than any other athlete, the news of Walter's illness shook us. He held a press conference February 2, 1999, to announce that he had a rare liver disease and was on a transplant list.

"It's out of my hands," he said in a tearful address. "It's in God's hands."

I can't speak for anyone else, but I know that during 1999, I was concerned for Walter, yet never ever thought he would pass away. For one thing, he was *Walter Payton*. For another, the survival rate after a transplant was reported as 90%.

Lastly, Walter was in the news that year for a lot of reasons that had nothing to do with his illness. He became the co-owner of Chicago's expansion Arena Football League team. He and Ernie Banks made news about opening a casino in Rosemont.

Also that summer, Barry Sanders retired less than 1,500 yards from Walter's rushing record. That kept the conversation around Payton the football player, and frankly, it made me feel as if he was even more untouchable. Barry was going to break Walter's record. There was no question about that. He needed just 1,458 yards to pass Walter, a total he'd cleared in each of his past five seasons, including a 2,000-yard season just two years before.

PART VI: THERE'S A TIMEOUT! (WHERE?) ON THE FIELD

When Barry retired instead of passing Walter, I remember thinking it was as if Sanders, one of sports' all-time good guys and arguably the running back GOAT, simply didn't want to interfere.

All the while, the Bears were in a transition period. A week before Payton announced his disease, the Bears hired Dick Jauron as their new head coach. When the '99 season arrived, the team had its most promising offense since the Payton days: recent 1st rounders at quarterback (Cade McNown) and running back (Curtis Enis), a deep receiving corps (led by Conway and Engram), an x-factor return man (Glyn Milburn) and a daring coordinator (Gary Crowton).

The Bears opened Sep. 12, beginning one of the oddest, most thrilling, most touching, most emotional seasons of Bears football I've ever seen. We beat KC 20-17 in Week 1; Mike and I were there and the vibe at Soldier was as renewed as Curtis Enis, slimmed down, wearing #44 instead of #39 and charging into the endzone toward us to give the Bears our first lead of the season. We'd started the past two years 0-7 and 0-4. A Week 1 win was electric!

We started 3-2, with last second losses to the Seahawks and Raiders and a ridiculous comeback against the Saints. There was a ton to talk about, from Enis finally looking like a 1st rounder to the team's questionable development plan for the rookie McNown (he would play the 3rd series of every game) to the madcap Saints comeback, in which Shane Matthews and Curtis Conway linked for two touchdowns in the final two minutes, turning a 10-0 Saints lead into a 14-10 Bears win.

All the while, Payton was out of the limelight. Then in the last week of October, word came that his condition had significantly worsened.

And just as sudden, the worst news possible. Nov. 1, 1999: Walter Payton had died.

Payton died of bile duct cancer, brought on by his liver disease. The city was wrecked. The state was wrecked. The Bears, the NFL, the sports world. I remember sitting in gym class the next day, a slack look on my face, holding back tears. Bears fans were traumatized. Walter's passing touched us all.

He died on a Monday. The Bears were 3-5, riding a three-game losing streak, with a trip to Lambeau Field coming that Sunday. The team announced that Saturday, Nov. 6, a memorial to Payton would be held at noon at Soldier Field.

The week was filled with stories of Payton's intangibles: his heart, his will, his toughness, his spirit, his leadership. Even facing death, he embodied his motto: Never die easy.

Attendance at Payton's memorial was estimated from 15,000 to 20,000. The team added a patch on the left shoulder: a football with "34" in it. The next day, a grieving Bears team with a roster in flux took the field in Green Bay to face the Packers.

This was the 158th game of the rivalry, and the height of Brett Favre's dominance over us. The Packers entered that game with 10 straight wins in the series, and a 12-2 record against the Bears with Brett Favre as their starter.

Yet 1999 had its own electric, bizarre feeling. Matthews and McNown had started games at quarterback. Conway was having a dominant year, got injured, and then Marcus Robinson plugged in and soared to stardom.

Meanwhile, the Bears had a kicking problem. By Week 6, we'd run through three: Northwestern's Brian Gowins, veteran Jeff Jaeger and finally former Cowboys and Eagles kicker Chris Boniol. The three kickers were 10-20 on field goals to that point. Gowins had missed a game-winner.

Just like that, it was Packers time.

They scored first, a 3-0 lead. Then McNown got injured and with Matthews already hurt, Jim Miller came in and changed the whole season. Miller steered two touchdown drives, and brought the Bears into the 4th quarter leading 14-10.

The Packers got a field goal in the 4th to make it 14-13, and Miller drove the team to the 16 with 11 minutes left. After two incomplete passes from Miller, Boniol came out to give the Bears a four-point lead, setting up for, of all distances, a 34-yard field goal!

AND HE MISSED IT.

So now we clung to a 14-13 lead, and after the teams traded punts, Favre took over to, once again, ruin us. Remember, Favre was very recently the NFL's three-time reigning MVP. In their 10-game winning streak against us, Green Bay had won by an average of 14 points.

With 3:19 remaining, #4 took over. He took 13 plays to drive from the Packers 17 to the Bears 16, coaxed us into two P.I. penalties, and left the field on 4th and 4 with 7 seconds remaining, leaving the game in the trusted foot of Ryan Longwell, for a 28-yard field goal.

I'm telling you — I could feel the collective breath-holding of my fellow Bears fans as Longwell lined up for this field goal. On the sideline, Big Cat Williams said to Jauron, "We've got to block it." Jauron responded as calm as can be. "Don't worry, we will."

AND WE DID!

It had happened! Bryan Robinson elevated and blocked Longwell's kick. Tony Parrish recovered. The clock was all zeroes. The team erupted — the game was over! We did it! WE DID IT FOR WALTER!

"Walter Payton picked me up in the air," Robinson said after the game. "I can't jump that high."

When Dan Pompei and Don Pierson were working on their Bears Centennial Scrapbook, and compiling their list of the top 100 Bears, they asked Virginia McCaskey for her pick.

That was easy.

Walter Payton.

What does this victory mean to you? a reporter asked Mrs. McCaskey after the game.

She signed deeply. "I just can't begin to —" and then she stopped, her eyes shut. "I'm sorry." She looked on the verge of both laughter and tears. She laughed, that Sweetness light seemingly running through her. "I just can't begin to tell you. The memories in this place. Memories of Walter through the week. And the way it happened today. It's incredible, isn't it?"

It was. Walter is one of those rare people on this Earth whose impact is felt by the generations who were not here when he was. Even now, 20 years after his death, Bears fans born after his passing speak of him as one of their own favorites.

He makes us happier sports fans.

We can't jump that high.

Jan. 5, 2023, Windy City Gridiron
    Age 41

SHE'S SEEN A CENTURY: REFLECTIONS ON BEARS FOOTBALL ON VIRGINIA MCCASKEY'S 100TH BIRTHDAY

I was stunned when our first child arrived on January 5, 1923.

A girl!

So wrote George Halas about his first born, Virginia McCaskey. She might not be the first person you think of when you think of the Chicago Bears. But whoever you do think of, she knows him. She traveled with Red Grange on his 1925-26 barnstorming tour, had a crush on Bill Osmanski in the 1940s, adored watching Gale Sayers, mourned Brian Piccolo, found her innocent love of the game rekindled by Walter Payton, and mourned him too.

And those are just the running backs.

Virginia McCaskey, the grand matriarch of the Chicago Bears, is 100 years old today. Anyone who lives to 100 is "our link with history" but rarely is that history so well known, so simple to map to that person's life. The franchise we revere was created more or less on September 17, 1920, as the Decatur Staleys, or the Staley Starchmakers as they were more frequently called, or even just "the Staley eleven."

The team was part of the new grid loop her father helped form, known briefly as the American Professional Football Association. In 1921, Halas moved the Staleys to Chicago, and in 1922 he renamed them the Bears and helped rename the APFA the National Football League.

And so Virginia, born to George and Min Halas the first week of January, 1923, technically only missed one season of Chicago Bears football.

The team was so young upon her birth, and professional football's future so uncertain, that when signing her birth certificate her father grew uncharacteristically bashful about his life's work. Under occupation, instead of writing "football club owner, manager, coach and player," he chose "civil engineer."

Mrs. McCaskey's birth certificate reveals her life story in another way, the family's fork in the road. As Halas described in his 1979 autobiography:

"I had assumed — and so had Min — that the new arrival would be George Stanley Halas, Jr. I already had visions of drawing my son into the thick of the Bears. We didn't even have a name for a girl. After some searching we decided on Mary Barbara, for her two grandmothers. But my brother Frank already had appropriated those names for his daughter.

"I filled in the baby's certificate of birth, leaving the name blank. Many years later, upon getting a copy of her birth certificate for a passport application, my daughter discovered that the name we gave her — Virginia Marion — had been inserted in pencil."

Her name was in pencil. That sums it up. Despite being first-born, when it came to the Bears, Virginia was going to be #2. Then in 1979, her brother George Jr., known since birth as "Mugs," died unexpectedly at age 54. Four years later on Halloween, their father followed. Papa Bear did not expect his daughter to inherit the Bears anymore than he expected his first child to be a girl. But there she was, and here she is, running the team for four decades.

"After dad died, at age 60 I started a whole new life," she told Dan Pompei in November of 2016. "It was pretty scary. A lot of people were saying we should sell. It never occurred to me to do that. I can't think of anything else I'd rather be doing."

Indeed, Mrs. McCaskey has become the matriarch not just of the Bears but of Chicago sports. She was born to this team, and even helped support it before she was a teenager, when her father told her and Mugs that to keep the team going, he needed to borrow the money they'd been saving from their grandmother's birthday and Christmas checks.

"He kept saying, 'I'll pay you back, I'll pay you back,'" she told author John Eisenberg in 2018. "I didn't mind. He could have had anything I had. I was just happy he could use it."

In her time as one of Chicago's major team owners, she is the only one who was never out front in public, steering the ship. Oh, we see her in her box during nationally televised games, the broadcast quick to announce, "And there she is, Virginia McCaskey..." We hear from her son when she is angry (most famously in 2014, when the team's free-fall led to George describing her as "pissed off"), and we see her when she is filled with pride.

The image that stands out for me is January 21, 2007, standing in her mink coat with the snow falling at Soldier Field, accepting the trophy that holds her father's name.

That was a beautiful day. A mournful, bittersweet one came seven years earlier, the other moment I think of when I think of Virginia McCaskey. November 7, 1999, the first Bears game after the death of Walter Payton, when Bryan Robinson stuck his big paw up and, perhaps with an afterlife boost from Sweetness himself, blocked a would-be game-winning Packers field goal at Lambeau Field.

"I just can't begin to tell you," she said when asked what that win meant to her. "So many memories in this place. So many memories of Walter through the week. And the way it happened today — it's incredible."

But from a football standpoint, it's hard for fans to say where exactly her influence begins and ends. She has never been Bill Veeck, or hell, even Dick Klein. She has never been Jerry Reinsdorf, Bill or Rocky Wirtz, the Ricketts family. Few fans lay our now generational struggles at her feet. She rarely grants feature-length interviews (Pompei called their 2016 discussion "her first extensive interview") and I can't remember seeing her in a press conference since the calendar struck 2000.

Since 1983 when she assumed ownership, the out-front faces of the Bears have been not her but her family members. Her husband Ed was chairman of the board from 1983 until 1999, while their oldest of 11 children, Michael, was team president during the 1980s heyday, and maintained that role during the 1990s "hey, what the hell??" days.

When she does step into team affairs, it's for moves at the top. Most famously in 1999, she made the unpleasant but necessary decision to relieve Michael of his duties as president and promote to the job the first non-member of the family, Ted Phillips. She introduced him at the press conference on Feb. 10, 1999, and on the topic of whether firing her oldest son (whom she then slid into her retiring husband's post as team chairman) was a "sad day," she offered a Papa Bear-esque rebuttal.

"You know when sad days are?" the 76-year-old McCaskey said. "When we lose games."

So she gave us Phillips and got out of the way, becoming, once again, Chicago sports's hidden hand. In the summer of 2001, when the *Tribune* ranked "the most powerful people in Chicago sports," Virginia came in 7th, behind even two Bears minority owners Andrew McKenna (ranked 1st) and Pat Ryan (6th). Steve Rosenbloom wrote the piece and couldn't quite put his finger on her influence.

"She isn't hands-on with player personnel…" he began. "The daughter of the late George Halas stays out of the spotlight, but she's not just collecting dividend checks. Probably could have more clout, but it's not her nature. At the same time, unused clout might be even greater than exercising it."

Ted Phillips was hers. Ed, Michael and George McCaskey were hers too. But what about their decisions? Are they hers? Is she the reason we won Super Bowl XX and reached Super Bowl XLI? Is she the reason the team has lost its seemingly insurmountable leads in the all-time Packers series or the NFL wins record? Is she the reason the franchise value rose from $319 million at the start of this century to close to $6 billion today? Is she the reason the team did not have a Black franchise quarterback from 1983 to 2021, or the reason we drafted Justin Fields? Is she the reason our stadium situation is always a mess? Is she the reason that, from the team perspective, it's only now getting fixed? Is she accountable for her franchise's use of taxpayer funds, or its role in the concussion settlement?

Fans never really feel confident in the answers to those questions. She reminds me of how Jerry Seinfeld once described wearing his father's swim trunks: "floating around me… somewhere." One of my earliest memories of attending a Bears game was seeing two fans walking between the seating sections at Soldier Field holding a life-size cutout of then-president Michael McCaskey, nasty words scribbled on his face, cursing him in effigy as seated fans hurled insults at cardboard. I don't know that Bears fans would have done the same to Virginia had she been running the team. But she hasn't, so we haven't either.

Instead she's maintained her position as a mostly lovable, unassailable figure of Chicago sports. Those who know her personally love her, honor her, cherish each moment. Everyone feels warmth around her. Jarrett Payton treasures her. In August, Jeff Hughes of Da Bears Blog penned a loving tribute to her. When the team tapped Pompei and Don Pierson to write its centennial book and rank the top 100 Bears, they sought her blessing, and she gave it to Sweetness.

She is not "Bears Football!" but she is Bears football, here since nearly the start. She has lived through all but the first of our nine championships. She has overlapped with the playing careers of all 29 Bears whose busts in the Pro Football Hall of Fame was earned primarily on this franchise. That includes her father, who played through the 1928 season, soon-to-be Hall of Famer Devin Hester, and everyone in between.

She has seen the championships and the title droughts, the team triumphs and tragic deaths. In her lifetime, her father had a hand in creating the modern pro football superstar, the first NFL playoff game, the NFL draft, the modern passing game, the shameful segregated NFL and the television era. She has seen her team help make famous the middle linebacker position, inventing the modern tight end position and delivering key innovations in special teams play, weight training, integrated player roommates, the 46 defense and league-wide diversity initiatives.

She was two years old when Red Grange came to the Bears, 11 when Beattie Feathers became the league's first 1,000-yard rusher, 20 when Sid Luckman became the first to throw seven touchdowns in a game, 42 when Gale Sayers tied the NFL single-game record with six touchdowns, 52 when Walter rushed for 275, 63 for Super Bowl XX, 83 when the Bears were who we thought they were and 96 for the Double Doink. She's had the curiosity of turning 100 before the Bears had a 4,000-yard passer but after they had a 1,000-yard rusher at QB. She's been through two home stadiums and possibly a move to a third.

On the home front, she's mourned the loss of her only sibling in 1979, her husband in 2003, and two of her children, including her oldest, Michael, in 2020. Those passings have increased the age gap between her and the next McCaskey in charge, until now, on the day of her 100th birthday, she sits alone at the top of the NFL's longest familial dynasty. The good and the great, the sad and the ugly, the touchdowns, sacks and all the surprises, Virginia McCaskey has seen a century of Bears football.

Her name was in pencil.

She wrote it in ink.

PART VII:
CURSE?

Oct. 14, 2003, Indiana Daily Student, the morning of Game 6 of the 2003 NLCS
Age 21

LET'S GET SOME RUNS!

Holy Cow! Despite a setback in Game 5, the Cubbies have a chance to grab the National League pennant tonight at Wrigley Field, the way it should be. With every twirl of Dusty Baker's toothpick I get more and more excited about this season, and the distinct possibility that in four days Kerry Wood could be pitching Game 1 of the World Series.

My giddiness has started to override my paranoid superstitions and has gotten to the point where I lay in bed for hours thinking about Sammy and Kerry and Harry and ivy, and the other night it got so bad (or good) that in order to quench my Cubbie thirst I had to pop in my tape of the 1998 one-game playoff against the Giants. Yes, despite the Southsiders' late-season collapse, baseball is alive and well in the Windy City, particularly at 1060 W. Addison, where the Cubbies have their 95-year-old fans thanking God for yet another chance to see a World Series champ at Wrigley.

"Ladies and gentlemen, welcome to the friendly confines of Wrigley Field, home of your World Champion Chicago Cubs!"

Does that sound right? Until Joe Borowski struck out Andruw Jones to send the Cubs to the NLCS, I never actually believed the Cubs could win the World Series. And I don't mean never this year. I mean never. Not in '89. Not in '98. Not after we clinched the NL Central. But after that final out in Game 5, I mapped out the probable pitching matchups for the NLCS, and that was the first time in my life that I'd ever seriously considered the idea of the Cubs playing in the World Series.

My worldview hasn't been the same since.

For years, I could always imagine the Cubs in the Series, but I never actually believed it. And now that it's more than a dream, it's frightening. I've crossed into a new level of being. I'd imagine that it's similar to dying. Logically, everyone knows that at some point they will die, but most people don't live their lives thinking it will happen. And then one day, you've got a disease or you're really old or you're about to crash into an oncoming Mack truck, and you realize that death can happen. You begin to deal with that sensation realistically, and your world is never the same. This is how I feel about the Cubs playing in the World Series. If it does happen, my entire perception of what it means to be a sports fan in Chicago will be altered.

To make things crazier, the equally cursed Red Sox are trying to win the American League, to set up a Cubs-Red Sox series. A lot of fans are hoping for this "dream series," but let me tell you something: Cubs-Red Sox is bad news. Both teams are trying to break curses, and if the Cubs beat the Yankees or the Red Sox beat the Marlins, then the curses will be defeated. But if the Cubs play the Red Sox, one of those teams has to win. Neither team has a chance to beat the curse, but instead one team will be mathematically forced into victory. That freaks me out.

But let's not get ahead of ourselves. This is still the Cubs, after all, and if the curse really does exist, then there's still time for something terrible to happen. At this point, I have to believe in the curse, because if I don't, it means the Cubs have been fielding a crappy, uncursed team for 95 years. I think we'll win tonight, but beyond that, I refuse to guess.

Writing this column was bad enough karma, so I'm going to stop before I jinx us any further.

**PART VIII:
HEARTBREAK**

Oct. 2005, "Bear Down and Get Some Runs"
Age 23

THE BARTMAN STORY, IN THREE HORRIBLE PARTS

On the morning of Sunday, October 12, 2003, I woke up on the couch. I was sleeping on the couch because my visiting parents were sleeping on my bed. I'd crashed out on that couch before, but that was the first time I purposefully slept on it. I think that's what threw me. That brief moment when I was coming out of a night's rest, and I opened my eyes just a bit to see, not the walls of my room, but the TV and front door. For that split second, I was not where I was supposed to be.

It was my senior year at IU, and my folks were in town for the IU-NU football game. The Cats had pulled out the big win, beating the Hoosiers 37-31 in overtime. Back to my apartment for cards, a movie, and although they were originally planning only to stay for the Bears-Saints game, I talked them into staying for another: Game 5 of the NLCS.

Game 1 was a dizzying back-and-forth affair at Wrigley that Florida eventually won in the 10th, followed by the Cubs taking three straight. Actually, 'taking' is putting it nicely. The Cubs obliterated Florida. Game 2 saw a 12-3 pounding with Prior allowing only two earned runs, and the Cubs' first three batsmen — Lofton, Grudz, and Sammy — combining for a 7-of-13 with 5 RBI and 4 runs scored. Game 3 was close, the Northsiders pulling out a 5-4 win in the 11th...

...and then came Game 4. The key game. Where a loss ties it up and a win puts you a game away from the World Series. You almost couldn't believe it was happening: we never had a big lead during the season — we were under .500 after the All-Star break and didn't clinch the division until Game 161 — and then all of a sudden we're in Game 4, and we didn't even realize where we were until we were there.

Which was exactly how the game began. Because Lofton, Sammy, and Moises all walked — *hey look at that, bases are loaded with one out* — and then Aramis came up and BOOM! clocked one with his big open swing, and like Pudge Fisk watching the ball drift high down the line — *damn, he killed that ball* — Aramis is just looking at it, and I'm looking at it, and everybody is just looking at it, and then it goes fair and Holy Hell! Did you see that? Aramis just hit a grand slam! We're up 4-nil! And it's still the first inning!

And that was the series. That was the season. Everybody just watching, not really processing the full meaning, and all of a sudden we realize, "Wait a second. Did the Cubs just go up 3-1 in the NLCS?"

Yes they did.

Suddenly we were one game away from a World Series appearance. Could it be? Was it possible? My folks came over for NU-IU, we hung out, and then I woke Sunday morning, and I opened my eyes, and instead of my bed I was on my couch. And that did it. My eyes adjusted, and the first thought of the day flashed through my head, a thought that frightened me, a thought that ended up haunting me until opening day of 2004: *Right now, at this very moment, the Cubs are FAVORED to be in the World Series.*

And it didn't feel right.

******

I shook it off. My parents and I were headed to Yogi's, my favorite Bloomington bar, for what was bound to be a wonderful day of sports, a double header with Bears-Saints at noon and Cubs-Marlins at three. SANTO 10 unbuttoned over ROBINSON 88, Bears hat on top. But the Bears were a bust, a lethargic 20-13 loss to New Orleans, leaving me anxious but focused on Game 5.

It wasn't to be. Josh Beckett threw a complete game, two-hit shutout and the Marlins won 4-0. Still, I was encouraged. When you get

PART VIII: HEARTBREAK

beat by a pitcher who is just too good, you don't feel quite so bad. Plus we were going home for Games 6 and 7 where we would have Prior and Wood and a chance to wrap the series in front of the home crowd.

The way it should be, I thought to myself.

******

It was back to Yogi's for Game 6. Luke, a bit distraught at this point, did not wish to venture out in order to watch the Cubs advance to the World Series, and so I went to the bar by myself, quickly sniffing out some legit Cubs fans and settling down to watch.

Man, I remember it so well.

The Cubs scored first — once again, it was Lofton, the guy who, to this day, I feel was the key to the '03 Cubs. He hit .327 for us during the regular season and just never stopped. After a leadoff single in the first, Lofton scored on a Sosa double. 1-zip Cubs on Lofton's eighth run of the series. Amazing. And the chit-chat begins.

So where are you guys from?... Oh cool... A senior... Yeah, I'm glad to be nearly done with it all...

Prior gets Miguel Cabrera to fly out to center to end the top of the third. The ace through three innings: two singles, one walk, one strike out, four runners left on base, no runs scored.

...oh, that's cool. How do you like that?...Understandably. Where did you say you were from again?

Sixth inning. Prior taking over. Powered by two strikeouts, he retires Florida 1-2-3. Marlins still haven't scored, and then it's back-to-back singles for Sammy and Mo to start the bottom of the sixth. Aramis grounds into a double play, and then it's rookie sensation and (sort-of) former Cub Dontrelle Willis relieving Carl Pavano. Willis gives up a wild pitch to Karros. Sammy scores from third. Two-zip Cubs.

I see. Interesting. One sec...Let's focus here...YES! YES! YES! (And then, almost under my breath, afraid to say it too loud...) *Holy crap! We're nine outs away...*

First up for Florida in the seventh: Mike Lowell. Game 1's hero flies out to Alou. *Eight outs away.* Next up: Jeff Conine. The lone remaining member of Florida's '97 World Series team flies out to Lofton. *Seven outs away!* And finally: the other Alex Gonzalez, and right on cue he flies out to Sosa in right. Three batters, three flyouts, left to center to right, Alou to Lofton to Sosa. Prior after seven: 26 batters faced, three hits (all singles), two walks, six strikeouts, no base runners allowed since Pierre's single in the fifth, no runs.

And oh, by the way...

SIX OUTS AWAY!

It was so exciting! Backup catcher Paul Bako singles to start the bottom of the seventh. At this point, I am standing up, my fingers gripping the back of my bar stool, and then off as I high-five my new Cubs friends, nearly holding their hands. Prior bunts Bako to second, Lofton K's, and then it's Grudzielanek singling in Bako, and now the Cubs lead 3-0. *Climbing, climbing, building...*

Sosa singles, but Alou flies out to end the inning, leaving Sammy on first. And now we go to the eighth inning, six outs away. *I can still feel it...*

Mark Prior takes the mound to begin the eighth. He has been spectacular — no: *brilliant* — and now he is getting set to take us to the World Series. The World Series! I'm nearly jumping with every pitch now; I've taken my Santo jersey off due to sweating, and now it's slung around my neck John Thompson-style, and I'm squeezing it and holding it to my face in anticipation and constantly rubbing the stitches around the "C" on the chest for good luck. Mike Mordecai to start things off, and he flies out to left, to Alou, and there's one out in the eighth. *FIVE OUTS! FIVE MORE OUTS!*

PART VIII: HEARTBREAK

Pierre doubles to left. *He's a slippery one.* Still, one out, Cubs up 3-0, top of the eighth, Game 6 of the NLCS, eventual-Cy Young winner (*assuming he doesn't win it this year...he is incredible!*) Mark Prior on the mound. I'm applauding. I'm jumping. The entirety of Yogi's is watching. But I'm not concerned with them. I'm focused on my karmic connection with Cubs fans around the country. And Chicago. Always Chicago...

Up walks Luis Castillo. Pierre at second. One out. At this point, I couldn't even follow the pitches. I had no idea what the count was on Castillo. All I knew was that each additional pitch meant that we were *that much closer* to an out, and each additional out meant that we were *that much closer* to the World Series.

Castillo swings, fighting off a Prior pitch, and the ball floats into the stands, surely out of play...

And now Alou approaches fast / and now he leaps so high / and now the air is shattered by the hands of some poor guy...

WHAT THE #%$@&!!!???

It was so confusing. And of course, Alou made it worse. When he slammed his glove to the ground in disgust, it was the signal to the rest of us that Things Were Bad. And so we began yelling and shrieking and looking around in a panic. If we were in the stands, we began pointing at the headphone-wearing fan, who sat silently, possibly just as confused and panicked as we were, though maybe for different reasons.

And if we were watching on television, we were pointing as well, waiting for the announcers to tell us that, perhaps, just perhaps, fan interference would be called. *But wasn't Alou's glove over the wall? Ya know, in fan territory? Hold on, they're showing it again. Yeah, it was. So that's not interference, right? And plus, he's a Cubs fan. They won't call anything, right? Right?*

Nobody knew.

Castillo walked on a wild pitch. Pierre took third. First and third, one out. *We're still up 3-0, right? I mean, they haven't even scored. We're fine... right?*

Pudge singled. Pierre scored. *It's just one. Still 3-1. Relax.*

And then Cabrera bounced to short. *YES! That'll do it. No! No! No! Gonzalez booted it! Please let this be over. If I close my eyes, maybe it will be over...*

If we had been watching with Clear Heads, perhaps we would have turned and blamed Gonzalez for the whole thing. After all, it was still just three to one. Months later, we would hold him almost entirely responsible, but not yet.

Still confused by the Unidentified Fan (and to think, he was actually unidentified for that first 24 hours) we shook ourselves, trying to understand what was happening, and we looked at the fan, who was now being pelted with beer and napkins... and now he's being led out of the park by security... what's happening to us?... and then, with the bases loaded from the Gonzalez error, Derrek Lee rips a back-breaking double to left field, the ball dropping in front of the still-flustered Alou. Two runs score, tie game. Just a tie game. Cubs still have two more chances...

And now Dusty is going out to get Prior, who looks spooked, and now it's Farnsworth, and one after another, the runs come pouring in. Lowell intentionally walked, Conine sacrifices to score Cabrera. 4-3 Marlins. Todd Hollandsworth pinch-hitting with the runners again at second and third, and again it's an intentional walk. And now it's Mordecai. They've batted around. And Mordecai doubles to clear the bases. 7-3 Marlins. And Mordecai is standing alone on second base, elated. And now there is no doubt, and Remlinger comes in for the Farns, and Pierre singles to score Mordecai, and Remlinger gets Castillo to pop out to second, and the Cubs go six up-six down the rest of the way, and now it's on to Game 7...

PART VIII: HEARTBREAK

One of the Cubs fans I've been watching with turns to me, with purpose.

"We're driving up tomorrow. We're going. We've got tickets. You can come if you want."

"No, I'll stay here."

I remember that even in my complete state of shock, I still thought that the Cubs would win Game 7. I remember really appreciating the offer, but feeling that driving in for Game 7 was a desperate move. And who needs desperation? We aren't desperate! We've got Woody tomorrow! This was just a setback. The team was fine. We would win tomorrow...

******

It was back to Yogi's the next night, this time running into a few guys who graduated with me from New Trier. SANTO 10 once again on my back, and this time, a different section of the restaurant.

Pierre triples to start the game, Castillo flies out, Pudge walks, and then Cabrera unleashes a monster shot to give the Marlins a three-nil lead. And our hearts sink, and it feels as if we are about to trudge through a leach-infested swamp, barefoot and pantless, just to get to a guillotine.

But in the second, things turn around. Karros singles with one out, Gonzalez doubles Karros to third, and then Damien Miller grounds into the fielder's choice to score Karros. 3-1 Marlins, with Kerry Wood coming to the plate, and he works the count full, and after two consecutive balls, BAM! He launches one to left-center... *shades of Game 1 against Atlanta...* and as the ball sails high I swing my feet up to the top of the waist-high stool, and now I'm squatting on it, and the ball doesn't bang off the wall but flies over it instead, and now I am standing on top of the bar stool screaming like a child and actually jumping up and down *on top of a high bar stool*, and my loose jeans fall to my knees and I don't care. Nobody else does either. Three to three, and Wood puts the Marlins down 1-2-3 in the third.

Up come the Cubs, and after Mark Redman plunks Sosa on what would have been ball four, Alou comes to the plate. First pitch: ball. Second pitch: a swing and a drive and OH MY GOD THAT BALL'S GONE! CUBS LEAD 5-3!

At that point, I was convinced the Cubs would win. It made sense. *Finally, things are different.* I felt certain that the Bartman play was going to go down as the turning point, the play that in past seasons would have killed the Cubs. *But not this year. Not in 2003.* That's how I felt.

Brad Penny replaces Redman for the fourth, retiring the Cubs in order. Brian Banks pinch-hits for Penny to lead off the fifth, and in his first AB of the series Banks draws a walk. *Come on Kerry. Not now.* Pierre flies out, and Castillo works the count full before drawing a walk. And then Pudge… always Pudge… Pudge comes up and doubles to score Banks, and then Cabrera grounds out to score Castillo.

And now the game is tied, and then Derrek Lee singles, and now it isn't.

6-5 Marlins.

And that was that.

Marlins 2003 hero Josh Beckett replaces Penny for the fifth and pitches four innings, striking out three and giving up one run on one hit, a solo home run from Cubs' reserve Troy O'Leary with two outs in the seventh. Florida had already added three runs at this point, so O'Leary's shot only makes it 9-6.

Remlinger and Borowski fight off Florida in the eighth while Beckett brushes aside Grudz, Sammy, and Moises, and after Borowski gets

PART VIII: HEARTBREAK

the last out of the top of the ninth, Beckett hands the ball over to Marlins' closer Ugueth Urbina.

Aramis hit by a pitch.

Simon hitting for Karros.

Simon strikes out swinging on 1-2.

Gonzalez strikes out swinging on three pitches.

Bako flies out to left. Cubs slink away.

Stunned faces.

Florida celebrating on our field.

Me walking out of the bar.

A guy in a Cubs shirt crying while his girlfriend consoles him.

Me in shock.

Me calling my parents.

My mother's warm shoulder.

My father's cold water.

My apartment.

My bed.

And it's over.

******

Now then…

Did I believe in the curse? No, not really. I come from a fairly supernatural family, but as far as sports are concerned, curses are kind of silly. To be fair, I probably used the curse more as a fall guy, perhaps as a defense mechanism to deflect the feeling that, quite often, this team has been very bad as well as very unlucky. No, there was never a curse, and there isn't one now.

What there *is*, however, is a horribly negative energy mixed with some bizarre and twisted luck. *If it wasn't for bad luck, I wouldn't have no luck at all...*

The negative energy at Cubs games is a brutal force. What makes it particularly powerful is the fact that Cubs fans at Wrigley are typically positive and hopeful. We're not a bunch of Philly fans out there, snarling and growling and always expecting the worst. We usually expect the best. So when something bad *does* happen, everything flips. The sheer speed of the turnaround is most frightening. *Oh no. What now? We're up ten with two outs in the ninth. Why does that double bother me? How are they gonna blow this one? How will it happen? How?*

That's the big one. How. Hitting the Nervous Point is bad enough. When it comes in a way you didn't see possible even when you've already seen everything that is possible, well, it's unsettling. And over the past twenty years, Cubs fans have been unsettled many times, most notably:

1. The Cubs blowing a 2-0 lead in the '84 NLCS to the Padres, including...
2. ...a pre-Buckner Buckner error from Cubs first baseman Leon Durham in the seventh inning of the decisive Game 5 that led to four runs.
3. A 26-year-old Greg Maddux winning a Cy Young in '92 and then being allowed to leave for Atlanta, where we watched in horror as he won three more Cy's and a World Series.
4. Brant Brown. Nuff said.

PART VIII: HEARTBREAK

When your recent history contains all *that* — not to mention plenty of losing seasons and horrible yet unmemorable games — watching one of your own fans knock away what appears to be a sure out when you are only five outs away from your first World Series appearance in 58 years… well, you can see why we would be nervous. And then Alou's outburst confirmed our fears, and we all went just a little bit crazy.

And when over 40,000 fans in a contained space all go just a little bit crazy, that's when trouble happens. After all, if a team can thrive on the positive energy of its fans — and they can (and do) — then certainly they can be affected by a sudden shift in fan-mood. What effect did Bartman have on the players that night? Who can say. But it's probable that, at the very least, they noticed our collective nervous breakdown.

Bartman didn't *do* anything, but he definitely felt like a Sign of Things To Come. Perhaps our energy distracted Prior just enough to get him to throw the ball four wild pitch to Castillo. Or perhaps it made Alex Gonzalez antsy, causing him to over-think on the Cabrera ground ball. Again, it's hard to say.

A sports-curse is all about design and effect. What will the embodiment of the curse look like, and what will be its ultimate effect? The negative energy thing explains the effects of the Bartman play.

As for the design, I always found it interesting that the ball landed where it did. If you watch the tape, there are a bunch of fans reaching for the ball. It could have hit any of them. But it hit Bartman, a 26-year-old white male with a sad-sack face, a distinct outfit, and a memorable name that was easy to pronounce. Would fans have been so quick to attack him on the spot if he'd been a woman, or a kid, or a senior, or a minority? Would he have been as memorable if he didn't have the Cubs hat, glasses, and grey turtleneck?

And of course those headphones. And not just any headphones, but very specific headphones, the old ones with the thin silver connector piece that arches across the top and the circular black felt.

And what about the name? His name could have just as easily been Swearingen or Syrjamaki or Larrecq or McCarthy-Frankenheimer. But no. It was Bartman. Sounds like a cartoon character — perhaps a super villain. And then a "Steve" right in front of it. Easy to remember, easy to say.

It may not have been the result of a curse, but everything about the play stood out. It was almost *too* obvious, like a bad movie director sacrificing subtlety in an effort to create Something Memorable.

In the end, it was simply a one-of-a-kind situation that preceded a lot of bad baseball. It was Prior and Gonzalez and Dusty and Farnsworth. It was Cubs fans at Wrigley, and, somehow, everywhere else. And though we don't like to admit it, I have to say: it was fun. It may have been twisted and sadistic, and it may have been a horrible mess at the time, but in the end, it was fun.

Why not? Think back on Bartman. Go ahead. Think back. It's almost so far-fetched and absurd that, in retrospect, it's kind of funny. It's awful, yes, but admit: It's funny. In the end, it's a memory, and that's all we really want.

Feb. 4, 2007, ReadJack.com
   Age 25

TO MY FELLOW BEARS FANS

It is 9:36 PM.

My team just lost the Super Bowl.

This sucks.

PART VIII: HEARTBREAK

Is it all bad? No. It's not *all* bad. Some would say that it's not all bad because I root for the second best team in the NFL. Some take solace in that. I do not. *That* is not the reason why it's not *all* bad.

The reason why it's not all bad is that I root for the Chicago Bears. That makes me feel good. The Chicago Bears are my team, and I love them. And it's not just the franchise. I love *this team*. These 2006 Chicago Bears. The Bears of Lovie Smith. Urlacher and TJ and Briggs and Peanut and Kreutz and Mike Brown and Berrian and Vasher and Alex Brown and Hunter Hillenmeyer and Wale and Ian Scott. I love all those guys. Chris Harris and Tommie Harris and Dev Hester and Jason McKie and Mark Anderson and Israel Idonije and Cameron Worrell and Robbie Freakin' Gould. I love them too.

And yes, I love Rex. Still.

I said all week that if the Bears lost, it would be because they did a lot of things horribly wrong. And they did. Not just the obvious, the fumbled snaps and the picks. We missed a bunch of tackles. We couldn't stop their run. We couldn't keep Peyton off the field. We couldn't run the ball until the second half (apart from the TJ 52-yard dash) and even when we were running well, we weren't running often. We carried the ball only 19 times against their 42. We were 3 of 10 on third down conversions. We were unable to pressure the quarterback.

So that was bad.

But it's not *all* bad, because the Chicago Bears are still my team, and even if that means that I am beyond sad *right now*, life is good. Yes, it sucks to lose the Super Bowl. I know that now. And even though there is an instinct to say that all is well because this Bears' team is At The Beginning, I think that's missing the point. I do not know what will happen in the future.

Will we get back? We should. But will we?

One never knows.

What one does know is that the Chicago Bears are my team, and that's enough. For 25 years I've been a Bears fan, and barring something extraordinarily freakish and sad, I will be a Bears fan for the rest of my life. The majority of those seasons have been "bad." The majority of the rest will probably be bad as well.

But I enjoyed those teams. Everyone will remember Payton and Butkus and Singletary and Urlacher. Only the Bears fans remember Donnell Woolford and Marty Booker and Raymont and Dante Jones. And the same can be said for any other fan of any other team.

That's what this is about. It's about dedication. It's about giving yourself to a team, about taking the highs and the lows. Cliché? Sure. But it's the truth.

So, yes, I feel like crap right now. I can only imagine how the team is feeling. What bothers me the most is that we played like straight ass tonight; we failed to show the football fans of America just what made this team great. This was arguably the worst game we played all season. Worse than Miami, worse than Green Bay, worse than any of the "Bad Rex" wins. This was all kinds of bad. Certainly not the way that you want to end your season.

But it's one game. It's just one game. It does not mean that we are a bad team, and it does not mean that we had a bad season. All it means is that we didn't win the Super Bowl. That's it. Ah well. So it goes.

I made a t-shirt today, one that I was very excited to throw on. It was a navy blue shirt with orange lettering. The front reads "SUPER BOWL CHAMPS". The back reads "AND DON'T IT FEEL GOOD?". I was so excited to wear that shirt tonight. Now I wonder if I'll ever take it out of my drawer.

So we lost one game. A big one, but just one, and what we are left with is a wonderful football team that gave us a wonderful season. And maybe this team will be Back With a Vengeance. And maybe they will be back in the Super Bowl. And maybe they'll win two in a row as did the '71-'73 Dolphins, and maybe they'll drop four in a row as did the '90-'93 Bills.

Or maybe everything will fall apart with injuries and free agency, and by the time the Bears are back in the Super Bowl it will be a new team with a new coach in a new decade. Who knows. But we'll put up with the Rex-bashing, and we'll deal with the pain of losing, and we'll head into the 2007 season happy and healthy and ready for more.

And you know why? Because we're fans, and that's what we do.

I am a fan of the Chicago Bears.

And don't it feel good.

Oct. 7, 2008, ReadJack.com
   Age 26

THE POINTLESSNESS OF HOPE

They got swept.

Can you believe it? In its way, this was as bad as the Super Bowl. Worse, maybe, exacerbated as it was by the whole 100-year thing. Game 3 had been a dull ache throughout, yet one masked by enthusiasm, faith, hope. When those failed, when Soriano checked his final swing and the Cubs' death knell echoed no more, all that was left was that ache.

I couldn't talk. Couldn't think. Couldn't do anything other than shake my head and fumble the same words again and again. *I can't believe it. I just can't believe it. I mean, I can't believe it can't believe it just can't.* What happens now? What happens when you spend 162 days building a house and watch it burn a week later? What happens tomorrow?

What if they never win?

That's what gets me most. Because I believed in 100. Maybe if we'd followed up our 96-loss 2006 with similar natural disasters in 2007 and 2008, I would have been prepared. Perhaps if we'd followed last year with disappointment, the way we did in '85, 1990, '99, or 2004, I would not have thrown myself aboard this ride. I claimed all season: I will not let my guard down until we clinch.

Yet even that guardedness was brushed aside in the thrill of this incredible run, a season that saw the Cubs atop the NL Central from May 11th through the end save one day late July tied with Milwaukee. Six players with 20 or more home runs, a rookie catcher as All-Star starter, joined by two veteran pitchers in new roles, a stacked lineup up and down the order, a no-hitter tossed for good measure. Useless, all of it.

And now 100 slaps me. 100 and beyond.

What if they never win? I mean, what if they never win? They might never win. They just might never win might never do it. And that's the thing. 100 felt like a predestination. 101 feels like banishment. The Cubs return home, where they will have six months before another regular season game, an additional six before even a whiff of another chance at last week. Right now, the 2008 postseason continues without them.

After becoming Chicago's first baseball team to post consecutive postseasons since those other '06-'08 Cubs, this year's bunch set these other notable marks in division series play:

- They tied the 2003 Braves for the biggest positive win differential of a team that lost an LDS. (The Cubs won 13 more games than Los Angeles.)
- They became the third team to be swept in the LDS after posting a league-best record (2000 White Sox, 2001 Braves)
- They became the third team to be swept in consecutive LDS (Dodgers '95-'96, Rangers '98-'99), and the only one of the three to have home field in either series.

PART VIII: HEARTBREAK

Yes, it's fair to say had we not been the 97-win hitting, pitching, and fielding machine we'd been all season, I would not have felt quite so despondent Saturday night. But we were, so I did, and considering this L.A. collapse followed Leon Durham, Will Clark, Brant Brown, Bartman/Gonzalez, LaTroy/Victor Diaz, those damned Diamondbacks, seven 90-loss seasons, the jettisonings of Palmeiro, Maddux, Luis Gonzalez, Gracie, Steve Stone, and the failures (on some level) of Walton, Patterson, Sosa, Prior, Wood, (Pie?), Hawkins, and Dusty, and since all of these took place during my nearly 27 years on Earth, I would say it's remarkable how rapidly, strongly, and consistently my vulnerability can be restored.

Of course, for the players themselves, this is all periphery. They carry this 100-year experience like a hiker with a backpack, relieved of its weight once the trip is completed. Their sporting experience is related to ours, but we are cousins, not siblings.

If late in the 8th inning, for instance, you and I and Alfonso Soriano had been sitting on our couches or bar stools or dugout benches with our cheeks on our hands, we were probably not all thinking the same thing. My guess is that when Soriano and the fellas distress, they aren't pondering tragic thoughts of black cats and heel clicks and billy goats and one eight-run inning from a game five years ago.

They are probably thinking only about their own personal failure as individuals and as a team, about the way they were inept at their chosen profession, the gaze of half a gajillion spectators trailing them as they bungled their way through three disastrous baseball games, the embarrassment of knowing they'd been the National League's best team for 162 games and its worst for the next three.

That is plenty reason to be distraught.

Still, like the home fans in Game 1, I kept wishing our team would kick themselves out of their funk. Isn't baseball supposed to be a game of short memory? I kept shouting at the screen: "Buck up guys! It's a two-run game! Lou, kick 'em in the cleats man!"

It was no use. After getting trounced in Game 1, this team deflated. After fumbling away Game 2, they decayed. And after leaving two on in the top half of the 1st only to watch Los Angeles score two in the bottom half, they were defeated, each inning more defeating than the last.

It was sad, the whole thing, us and them together, the only series I can recall where the fans failed the players and the players failed the fans.

So off we go, each on our way, them spending the winter wondering if their group of Cubs will get another chance to win it all, us wondering if any group of Cubs ever will. I asked my father about it ten minutes after the final pitch. He has lived with 31 more years of this than have I. As such, he is 31 years closer to watching Cubs games from that big lounge chair in the sky. I figured this must have brought him a panic.

"They might never win it. Ya know?" I said to him.

"They might not." He opened his Alexander Hamilton biography, set down his bookmark, and began to read.

That urgency may have been beaten out of him, but not me. And it still hasn't. Even here, three days later, I am already beginning to feel my confidence restored. It's still a terrific group, and just about everybody should be back. And, you know what? 101 years is kind of a perfect total to wait for, ya know? It's got that good symmetrical look to it. People are always listing 101 ways to do something, as if it's just a bit cooler than 100. 101, it stands out. It pops.

This was good. This was meant to be. Capturing that title after 101 years of misery was meant to be. We'll do it after 101 years. 101 years. 101 years. After 101.

PART VIII: HEARTBREAK

Jan. 31, 2011, The Sports Blog Network
   Age 29

THE TURF IS ALWAYS GREENER

I still can't believe I was back on the floor.

For the Super Bowl, we were at my parents' place. Kelvin Hayden crossed the goalline and I was on the floor with my head bowed and ten fingers in the air. Ten points. The biggest comeback in Super Bowl history. We were down 12.

The game wasn't over. But it was over.

This one had that feel earlier, yet also later. When we realized Jay Cutler was out, and would not return, the air in my apartment evaporated. We'd seen Todd Collins. Two games, one start. One win, not from him. Across two games: 10 completions on 27 attempts, 68 yards, no touchdown passes, five interceptions.

Now he was all that stood between us and the Super Bowl. In for Cutler in the 3rd. Down 14-0. Soldier Field crowd beat back. Incomplete pass. And another. And another. We trade punts. Ball to the offense. Two runs and a fourth incomplete pass. We trade punts again and that was it for Collins. Over to the third stringer.

Caleb Hanie.

Suddenly, shockingly, the game was back! Hanie led a touchdown drive. 14-7 with 12 minutes to play. The storyline rejuvenated me. Could the third-string QB lead us to the Super Bowl? Could it be?

We force the Pack to punt. And then we punt. And then they punt and we're on our own 10. Two short gains. Third and five and… damn man. He blew it. Just didn't take that extra half a beat. Pass to his left and boom, the big d-tackle B.J. Raji plucks it like an apple from a tree. Eighteen yards. Touchdown. 21-7. Ballgame…

…but no! Three straight completions for Hanie, and then a weird sideline pass to Earl Bennett, who slips between and past two defenders and darts down the sideline for 35 yards and a touchdown. Bears were still in this! I was rallying the party. The third stringer was going to do it!

The third stringer did not do it. But man, he *almost* did it. Drove us 11 plays down 21-14, and we weren't out of it until an interception on 4th and 5. XLI left me crushed but weirdly hopeful. 2010 broke me in a personal way. There's nothing worse than losing the Super Bowl. But losing at home to the Packers to *go* to the Super Bowl was closer than I wanted to get. Even now, a week later, I can't get this taste out of my brain. And all I can think about is that Tony is marching on.

******

A few days ago, three days after the Bears lost The Most Important Bears-Packers Football Game of the Past 70 Years, I stopped into Poitin Stil in Rogers Park to congratulate Tony the Packers Fan on a well-earned victory. He was there, and greeted me with the same underhand grin he had in my basement on January 26, 1997, the only person in my entire house happy that the Packers won Super Bowl XXXI.

"The Bears," I began hopelessly, "played a helluva game. We've had a rough line all year. No surprise when the quarterback goes down." I paused, breathing. "Helluva game."

"Yeah," Tony agreed, "and if you have a helluva game and also win they give you these sweet hats." He pointed to the hat on his head reading GREEN BAY PACKERS 2010 NFC CHAMPIONS.

I sighed. "That's a great hat."

That's about as bad as it ever gets with Tony. He respects us, we respect him, but he has amassed a powerful fan confidence during these 15 seasons, holding edges over my Bears in regular season wins (150 to 113), playoff games (19 to 7), playoff wins (11 to 3), Pro Bowl quarterbacks (2 to zero), Super Bowl appearances (3 to 1), and Super Bowl championships (1 to 0).

That last one could jump if Cool Aaron Rodgers can best the fearless Steelers de-fense. It is a mighty task, but Rodgers enters the Super Bowl playing as well as any team could hope of its quarterback, including the Packers, remarkable considering Brett Favre was in the midst of an MVP three-peat when he led the green and gold to its last Super Bowl.

Favre played a long time after that, including ten more seasons in Green Bay. All told, #4 started every game for the Packers from Week 3 of 1992 until the 2007 NFC Championship Game, a stretch during which media members enjoyed highlighting the quarterback disparity in the Bears-Packers rivalry by showing graphics like…

Bears starting quarterbacks since Brett Favre took over in Green Bay

…which was then followed by this list: Jim Harbaugh, Peter Tom Willis, Will Furrer, Erik Kramer, Steve Walsh, Dave Krieg, Rick Mirer, Steve Stenstrom, Moses Moreno, Shane Matthews, Cade McNown, Jim Miller, Chris Chandler, Henry Burris, Kordell Stewart, Rex Grossman, Jonathan Quinn, Craig Krenzel, Chad Hutchinson, Kyle Orton, Brian Griese.

That's 22 quarterbacks and not one Pro Bowler, unless you count Harbaugh with the Colts, Krieg with the Seahawks, Chandler with the Falcons, or Griese with the Broncos, which I don't.

Meanwhile, backing up Brett Favre were a bevy of future Pro Bowlers and NFL stars, including Mark Brunell, Kurt Warner, Matt Hasselbeck, Aaron Brooks, and the now-great Rodgers.

That last one came about through unfortunate circumstances: the 49ers nearly selected Rodgers first overall in the 2005 draft, but chose fellow quarterback Alex Smith instead, allowing Rodgers to drop past the Bears at number four, all the way to the Packers at 24, who, despite already employing Favre, thought it might be a good idea to nab the QB who was nearly the first overall pick.

Tony called me ten minutes later, taunting: "We just found our Favre replacement. Enjoy the next ten years, Jack."

Indeed. After three years riding the pine, Rodgers took the handoff from a reluctant Favre, and now, in three seasons as the starter, is 27 and 20, with two playoff appearances, one Super Bowl appearance, and one Pro Bowl selection, while becoming, at least for now, the NFL's all-time leader in passer rating.

And here's where it gets really startling: in only three full seasons, Aaron Rodgers' stats put him in the running for greatest quarterback in *Bears* history. He would be second all-time to Harbaugh in completions, fourth in attempts, second to Luckman in touchdowns, and tops in completion percentage, passer rating, and yards.

But wait: giving Jay Cutler a 2011 commensurate to his 2009 and 2010, Cutler would rank first in Bears history in passer rating, second in touchdowns, fourth in completions and completion percentage, and fifth in yards and attempts. If he continues at this pace, it will take him only five seasons to re-write the franchise's passing record book.

And yet when the final gun sounded on the Bears' 2010 season, the word in Chicago was that Jay Cutler was not fit to lead this team to a Super Bowl. Evidence used to support this claim was Cutler missing the game's second half with a knee injury that turned out to be a sprained MCL, and that he was seen "sulking" on the sideline.

PART VIII: HEARTBREAK

Cutler, by the way, was sacked 87 times in his two Bears seasons and still only missed one game, but whatever.

The real problem with Cutler is that he is a Chicago Bears quarterback, and Bears fans are only satisfied when their quarterbacks win championships, a list with only three names. One is Sid Luckman, the Bears great of the 1940s whose 14,686 yards are the third lowest total among franchise leaders.

The second is Billy Wade, who joined the Bears in 1961 as a 31-year-old, was the team's full starter for four seasons, and Dilfer'd us to a championship in 1963.

The last, of course, is Jim McMahon, who was immortalized on a team with nine defensive Pro Bowlers, three Pro Bowl offensive linemen, and Walter Freakin' Payton. Swap Cutler for McMahon, and Big Jay is the beloved punky QB while McMahon spends the 2010 NFC title game on crutches, having long ago been battered to the IR on one-too-many collapsed protections.

In my life, only McMahon was good enough for Bears fans. Harbaugh (the only Bears QB to start 16 games in consecutive seasons) was "soft." Kramer (the only Bears QB until Cutler with multiple 3000-yard seasons) was "boring." Steve Walsh (8-3 in his one full season as starter), played only one more game in Chicago after the '94 playoffs despite being only 28. Jim Miller went 13-5 from '99 to '01, passed for 422 yards in a game, led the Bears to a division title, and lost his job to a 37-year-old Chris Chandler.

When Kyle Orton was 11-4 in his rookie year, we wanted Rex. When Rex was 13-3 after returning from three season-ending injuries, we wanted Griese. When Orton won the job, started 15 games, and barely missed the playoffs, we yearned for Cutler.

Thank goodness we passed on Rodgers. We would have hated him.

Aug. 25, 2011, ChicagoNow — Eye on Chi
    Age 29

AN ODE TO THE 2011 CHICAGONOW SOFTBALL TEAM

Losing sucks.

Especially when you're undefeated and a victory away from a championship game and down to your final three outs in a 9-5 ballgame and nothing is going right, *ESPECIALLY* if the team with nine is a publicly funded radio station you cremated 15-1 in the season's first game way back in June before those bastards employed ringers.

As they surely must have done.

But what's great about the diamond sports is that they are as much about memories and sensory experience as they are about wins and losses. Thus when I look back at the 2011 ChicagoNow softball team, I will think of smells and sounds and joyful moments.

There was Jimmy, our fearless manager. Jimmy's email in June got the ball rolling, his talent in filling out a roster eclipsed only by his Santo-esque plays at 3rd, his mighty RBI-driving bat, and his ferocious competitive spirit. And his extended jaw-line when angry, his lip curling like Thayer's Casey, while his boy Eli played Angry Birds, none-the-wiser.

There were Kissko and X, our unshakable 1st basemen, they of the big mitts who scooped every throw and bopped pitches over the lip and shook opponents with their sarcasm and growling, respectively.

There was smart-ass Nikki, a mom who drinks and swears and plays catcher like Pudge, and Denise, who maintained high energy even through injury.

PART VIII: HEARTBREAK

There was Margaret's long-legged hustle, David's imposing grin, Brandi's smiles and high-fives, and there was spirited play and teamwork from Andrea, Joe, Courtney, Michael M. and Andy F. There was on-field filmmaking from Jen Ka-no-del and stellar substitute play from Kissko's friend Chelsea.

There was Paul Banks, Captain K, humming pitch upon pitch past the knee-trembling batters, his own knees battered but his arm smooth as butter.

There were the talented Alexanders, Michael and Bianca, committed to sustainable living and world peace and stomping on WBEZ loudmouths. If it came to that.

And there was the outfield of dreams — wise-cracking Jeremy, hard-drinking Alan, swift-running Scott, sweet-swinging Curtis, and me, ol' High Socks. We were glad to get Curtis out there with us after his early stint on the mound, and nobody read the field quite like Scotty, who once dashed in front of me to make an out as I eyed the ball and nothing else. Didn't even see the dude until the ball was nearly in my hands, and then *whoooooosh!* he shot past me and the ball was in *his* hands for the end of the inning like Kelly Leak.

I'll remember post-games at McGee's with Alan and Paul leading the shot-slurping fun, and Big League Chew and seeds for all, and come-from-behind victories week after week until we thought, "Yes yes, here we come again…"

I'll remember scoring the winning run from first on Alan's big bat in our final regular season game, and watching Jimmy stroke triples and homers on opening day, and Michael A.'s Bermuda Triangle de-fense at short.

I'll remember pre-game email trash talk amongst ourselves, visions of a limousine arrival and trophy-hoisting departure dancing in our minds.

I'll remember thinking we were on our way to that limousine when Curtis started our semi-final game with a legged-out triple, sliding into 3rd as I yelled "Down! Down!" from my spot at 3rd base coach, a Trebes Park mushroom cloud hiding the outcome until it floated away, revealing the streaks of dirt on Curtis's pants and his foot safe upon the bag.

I'll remember the BEZ bru-ha-ha in which our team stood as one.

I'll remember the game slipping away, the errors piling up, our bats catching air while theirs caught flight.

I'll remember that final come-from-behind victory that never came, that shitty feeling upon the final out, that hopeless frustration, that moody, reluctant sportsmanship.

And the last McGee's, and the last goodbyes, and wings and chicken fingers and buckets of Bud till we all felt healed and our season felt whole. And photos and video and trash talk and high-fives, and hugs and we'll-get-'em-next-year's and we-all-had-fun's.

And little Eli playing Angry Birds, none-the-wiser.

April 29, 2012
  Age 30

THE DERRICK ROSE INJURY

Well that sucked.

For so many reasons, and for so many people, starting of course with Derrick Rose, who in one foul misstep was stripped of his livelihood. Think of it: 23-years-old in the throes of your passion and atop your profession, and then snap — all gone.

Not for good, of course, but for a while, and definitely for the remainder of this postseason. When word came back that Rose's scary knee injury at the conclusion of Game 1 was a torn ACL, I felt sad for this man so hungry for greatness. More than anywhere else, my thoughts are with the displaced Rose.

As for the remainder of my emotions, this is an odd position for a sports fan. What does it mean to be a fan of a team? Despite the positive energy put forth by Rose's teammates and the #WinItForRose Bulls fans, how would fans really feel about this team winning a ring without this player?

I don't mean to suggest that you shouldn't continue supporting the Bulls or that you're wrong for wanting them to win a title even without Rose. I'm simply asking because it's something I have not yet sorted out in my own saddened, Bulls-loving heart.

This isn't about doubting the collective talent of players 2 through 13. If any team is equipped to roll without its superstar, it's the Bulls.

This is about a man who should be there when the deed is done.

Even if this team has carved its niche as The Team That Can Win Without Its Star, its true identity includes Rose as its leader. The heartwarming scene of the Bulls handing their injured captain the Larry O'Brien Trophy notwithstanding, a Bulls championship without Derrick Rose would feel incomplete.

But this is our team, and we move forward. As Kyle Korver wrote to the fans online, "We are going to keep going strong. One quarter, one game, one round at a time. Until it's over. That's how we gonna do it."

Spoken like a Rose protégé. I just wish the mentor was there too.

Jan. 10, 2019, Windy City Gridiron
  Age 37

THE PREMATURE PAIN OF THE DOUBLE DOINK

I'm not ready to talk about Vic Fangio.

I'm not ready to talk about Ed Donatell or Steve Wilks or Gregg Williams or Dick LeBeau.

I'm not ready to talk about Cody Parkey or Robbie Gould.

I'm not ready to talk about the draft or free agency.

Four days ago our beloved Bears went home way too soon. The conversation has moved on to next year. But not for me. I'm not ready. Because it's this year still and this year stings.

It didn't occur to me until now, but the loss to Philly was a first for me. As it turns out, it was a first in Bears history.

PART VIII: HEARTBREAK

The loss to Philly was the first time that we won the division, were favored in the Wild Card round, and lost.

Perhaps that seems a frivolous distinction. I assure you it's not. What it signifies — assuming your expectations were close to mine — is the largest gap we've ever faced between the amount of time we expected to spend watching the Bears in the playoffs and the amount of time we'll instead spend watching a Bears-less playoffs.

Look at this. Here is our history in the Wild Card round, along with our record and division finish:

- 1979: +6.5 at Eagles, lost 27-17 — 10-6, 2nd in Central
- 1990: -6.5 vs. Saints, won 16-6 — 11-5, Central champs
- 1991: -3 vs. Cowboys, lost 17-13 — 11-5, 2nd in Central
- 1994: +6 at Vikings, won 35-18 — 9-7, 4th in Central
- 2018: -6.5 vs. Eagles, lost 16-15 — 12-4, North champs

Setting aside the fact that I wasn't alive in 1979, and the probability that an eternally positive Bears fan such as myself would have likely been surefire convinced that we were going to beat the Eagles in Philadelphia, the '79 Bears never led the division.

In 1990, we won the division and won in the Wild Card round.

In 1991, we lost the Wild Card game at home to the Cowboys. That was a game I expected to win — again, I am the preeminent positive Bears fans — but we'd closed the season with a 52-14 loss to the Niners on Monday Night Football, and I remember thinking that no team was a powerhouse that could lose by nearly 40 points.

And in 1994, we finished fourth in the Central and upset the division-champion Vikings in Minnesota.

In the years we lost, I wasn't expecting us to play beyond the divisional round. In the years we won, I either thought the ride would end before the Super Bowl (1990) or I was thrilled just to get the Wild Card victory (1994).

We've also had four home losses in my life in the divisional round, each one painful in its own way. In '86 and '87, I expected a championship. In 2001, I thought we would have a tough time with the Rams. In 2005, I harbored all year this weird notion of winning a title "too soon" and didn't quite know what I wanted.

The point here is that when you lose in the divisional round, you only have the conference championship and the Super Bowl remaining.

When you lose in the conference championship — as we did in '84, '88 and 2010 — you watch the Super Bowl with the weight of absolute gloom, but at least the whole thing is over after the Super Bowl.

And of course losing the Super Bowl is the worst feeling I've ever had as a fan, but at least when that game was over, the entire NFL season was too.

That's the gap I'm talking about. That's what I'm staring down right now for the first time in my life. We have three rounds of football left. As a baseline, I expected the Bears to be around for one if not two of them. I thought a Super Bowl appearance was legitimate, and in fact my confidence was so strong that my outward attitude even at the start of the playoffs was a championship.

After all, the 2018 Chicago Bears gave me one of my favorite regular season fan experiences of my life. This was the first surprise Bears team of my life that was not only superlative on defense but capable of ass-kicking on offense. The Prophecy may have seemed silly to some but it embodied a truth that I felt to my core.

This team felt both historic and playful. Powerful and loose. Mitch's six TDs and Fast Eddie's runbacks. That goofy Giants near-comeback and the soul-snatching Rams game. The arrival of the Mack. The domination of the North. The promise fulfilled of Kyle Fuller. The Dream. The Grind. The Missile. Prince Six.

The way the Bulldozer remained relevant. The way the receivers danced for days.

PART VIII: HEARTBREAK

"I don't care what anyone says anymore," I wrote. "They're winning this whole damn thing."

I started to get nervous in the 3rd quarter, yet I still never thought we would lose. Even when Parkey hit the iced field goal and lined up for the second, I never thought we would lose. Even after the second doink, before I could see which way the ball was bouncing, I never thought we would lose.

No joke, as the ball hit the crossbar, my brain said, "Wow what a cool story: Parkey hits the upright and the crossbar and it bounces in for the win. That's awesome! On to L.A."

Now I sit here four days later amidst defensive coordinator trackers and an impending placekicker hot stove and our reserve/future signings and debates on players we'll add for next year and I'm over here like WAIT A SECOND I'M NOT IN NEXT YEAR YET.

Bears fans are turning the page to the 2019 season, and I get it — fans always look ahead. The days march on. That is true. But that's a lie. We're not turning the page to the 2019 season because we're burning with interest in OTAs. We're turning the page to the 2019 season as a defense mechanism. We're turning the page to the 2019 season to avoid the unbearable truth.

And the truth is this:

It's still the 2018 season. We're just not part of it anymore.

PART IX:
LOST IN THE WILDERNESS

Oct. 15, 2012, ReadJack.com
Age 30

THEY SHOOT BASEBALL TEAMS, DON'T THEY?

1.

When Marlon Byrd struck out way back on April 5th to wrap the Cubs' third straight opening day loss, I was at a doctor's office four blocks from Wrigley Field dealing with an inflated bill for an STD test now 18 months old. I had suggested to my new lover that we get tested, but due to an insurance snafu committed by my doctor known as a "miscoding," I was not covered for the test and was saddled with a bill that was probably 10 times my expected co-pay.

But why? I couldn't figure out the beating I was taking. I'd been *responsible*, for God's sake. I held no concern that I would fail the test — it was a formality in the name of safely enjoying sex and love. I aced the test as I knew I would and as I always have whenever I get tested. The only difference this time was that I was being financially ransacked by bureaucratic hustlers through a bookkeeping error of their own creation.

So that's what I was doing when the Cubs were busy losing their first of 101 games of 2012. The doctor was the third in a series of afternoon errands, and I was following the game on my phone with, I suspect, the same hopeful reluctance my parents used to employ when watching me stride to the plate in little league. *Maybe he won't get hit by a pitch this time. Maybe he'll draw a walk. Maybe he'll ground into a run-scoring fielder's choice. He's still my son. Athletic excellence isn't everything.*

That was me with the Cubs. *Maybe they'll salvage their dignity. Maybe they'll play entertaining baseball for eight innings. Maybe they'll... gulp... win.*

Instead of winning, they called upon Kerry Wood and Carlos Marmol, who promptly gave the game away.

This was a sickening twist — the Cubs were ahead 1-0 when I got off the train and went to a Vienna stand for a hot dog. When I stepped into the doctor's office and began speaking with the woman at the desk, I heard Len & Bob on the waiting room television, but it wasn't until I turned around to call billing that I saw the scoreboard 2-1 in favor of the Nationals.

Fucking Cubs, I mumbled as I dialed. It's been four years since I last followed the team on a daily basis, and watching this opening day go-from-ahead loss felt a lot like running into your ex-girlfriend — you know, the one who'd recklessly bulldozed your heart despite your friends' warning that she was "not the safest bet."

And she wasn't. But now you're free! Sure, it took being cheated on and ignored and publicly embarrassed, but at long last you'd escaped! You removed yourself from the cancerous relationship. You rehabbed your emotions and healed your soul. "I am better without her," you tell yourself. "I am *stronger* without her. Good riddance."

Then you run into her, right there in the doctor's office, and she's beautiful and alluring as ever. You remain cautious. But she creeps in. *She smiled, so I guess I can smile back*, you think. *And I suppose a hug won't hurt.*

A few weeks later you're crying over your beer and your buddies are rubbing your back, and even though they're supportive you know they're pulling away. They're staring right through you, restraining themselves from looking you in the eye and saying without mercy, *Yes, I am your friend, but you brought this on yourself.*

2.

So you can imagine my chagrin when, a few weeks after Opening Day, I learned my ex was now dating my dear friend Alex Heldman.

"What??" I asked in disbelief. It was no dream. My thoughtful, careful friend Alex, from *Cincinnati*, with no familial influences to blame was, at the age of 27, *willingly* becoming a Cubs fan.

Strike that: it was done. He *had* become a Cubs fan. I was too late. It was accomplished.

"What can I say?" he told me. "I'm in love." I heard his smile on the phone. It put a chill down my spine. Good God — he was babbling like a 12-year-old on Valentine's Day! "And guess what!" he told me. "I'm going to Wrigley tomorrow!"

Great. Just what we need. We'll never get him back! "But why?" was all I could muster.

"It's Wrigley Field!" he shouted. "Everyone should see a game at Wrigley Field before they die."

"Sure," I said. "The problem is that it's a *Cubs* game. I'd love to go to Wrigley and see the Dodgers and the Giants."

"Jack, hush. I know the Cubs have broken you, but so what? I *love* this team. I'm wearing my Cubs hat as we speak." That I did not need to hear. It's those visuals that knock you out. "Don't worry Jack. Tomorrow is going to be beautiful."

And it was. The Cubs pummeled the visiting Brewers, shutting them out 8-0 for their second win of the season. Sure enough, I got a text from Alex shortly after the game reading "Go Cubs Go."

"Oy vey," I responded. "Get out now! Get out while you can!!"

"Explain to me why and perhaps," he said.

With pleasure, I thought…

…but as soon as I started thinking, I was stalled. What arguments can I make to someone who has never been in love? What can a bitter, broken-hearted, been-around-the-block man tell a young pup of 15 who has finally gotten a date with his first crush? "I've been there kid. It ain't good. It seems fun at the start, but it wears you down."

"Ah, you're just an old man who messed with the wrong gal. That's not going to be me. This girl *loves* me! I *know* she does!"

I tried to talk him down, attempting to barrage him with a list of reasons to avoid Cubdom. *You're too old to start!* I told him. *You wouldn't start smoking cigarettes at this age, right?*

"It's not the same," he said arrogantly.

But this was no time for judgment. I had to save my friend.

3.

Here's what I should have told Alex about the Cubs, but didn't, because I couldn't articulate it until I'd settled my emotions: They might never win. We take it as an article of faith that they will, but they might not.

Or they will, but we'll be long dead, and a lot of good it will do when our grandchildren place Cubs hats upon our headstones.

A week before Opening Day, I saw a pair of 70-year-old Cubs fans walking south on Sheridan Road toward Irving Park. One wore a classic Cubs hat, the other a blue Cubs windbreaker, and they were strolling, smiling, talking merrily about whatever it is that 70-year-old Cubs fans talk about.

And I thought to myself, *When they were my age, the Cubs already hadn't won a World Series in 27 years.*

That's what makes the whole 103-years-and-counting thing so unnerving. Looked at from our 2012 perspective, "103 years without a World Series" is an abstraction. A frightening abstraction, but an abstraction none-the-less. It's like saying you're younger than Shakespeare.

After all, die-hard sports fans enter historical and contextual sports consciousness around the age of ten, so unless you're a 113-year-old Cubs fan, you've only waited 90, 75, 50, 30, 15, or even 10 years for a World Series.

And as it happens, there are only four Americans alive who would have been at least ten on Opening Day 1909, and they were born in Tennessee, Italy, South Carolina, and Florida, respectively.

But when you look at this century of futility from the perspective of someone in the *past*... well, that's when Cubs fandom stirs the imagination to madness.

I know the analogy here is to love and marriage, but at least when a woman breaks your heart you get to find a new one. Because it's not love you want to give up on. It's *her*. The filthy demon-goddess who stole your innocence, ground it into a fine powder, and scattered the ashes into the outfield grass. What did Steve Goodman call it? That's right: the ivy-colored burial ground. That's Wrigley Field. A graveyard of broken souls.

Indeed, while there are many new women out there within the unchanging arena of "love," there are no new Cubs teams. Oh, there is roster turnover, and if you return after a five-year abstention you might not recognize the stars, the role players, the management, or even the ownership.

But the shirts are the same. The park is the same. The demon-goddess's sweet siren song, her alluring wink that could puncture your eye — it's all the same.

Yes Steve, they still play the blues in Chicago. Some poor folks just think it's rock and roll.

4.

And yet, Wrigley Field.

There was a time when, as a rule and a pleasurable habit, I frequented Wrigley at least five times per summer. I bought tickets in advance, was invited to games, or just showed up with friends and suckled the will-call teet. No matter the reason, no matter the season — it was always worth it.

But times change, and on July 17th, 2012, I entered the park for my first Cubs game in three years.

It started when I got an email from my friend Jimmy Greenfield, a man who, as a 16-year-old in 1984, kicked a hole in his parents' wall after the Cubs lost a game... in April.

Six months later, after the Cubs dropped three straight to blow the NLCS, a distraught Jimmy left the house in tears to wander the neighborhood.

It's no surprise that today, Jimmy is the author of *100 Things Cubs Fans Should Know & Do Before They Die*, a collection of heroes and goats, comebacks and meltdowns, games, myths, legends, and facts.

Nor is it a surprise that he made fast friends with Ira Frost, the father of a great friend of mine and a supreme Cubs fan himself, a man who sends regular Cubs-oriented emails to friends and family. Jimmy & Ira met at a family dinner — turns out they share in-laws — and soon the three of us made a date for a trip to Wrigley, a night game against Miami in mid-July.

I called Alex on my way to the ballpark. I'd heard from him throughout the season as he toughed it out (I would wake up to messages about "Keep hope alive" and "Stay positive, Jack!") and even as his hometown Reds ambled into first place, Alex was adamant: "Jack,

I *am* a Cubs fan," as if this were a state of being and not a horrific choice. "Deep down in my heart, I've *always* been a Cubs fan. I just hadn't come out yet."

"So it doesn't bother you that this brilliant, beautiful, heartwarming team you've *always* loved is 14 games out of first?"

There was a pause, and some sort of shuffling. "Not at all," he said, though his voice cracked at this next part as he crawled through the words "You win some, you lose some."

I met up with Jimmy & Ira at John Barleycorn's for a pregame bite, and after we left the bar and security inspected my bag, we entered the park and walked through the concourse to the steps leading to our section. The national anthem was in progress, and we waited at the base of the steps behind a throng of fans. Over their heads I could see the blue of the sky, and then the anthem ended and the applause and cheers began, a rolling coil of sound that circles the grandstand and signals both patriotic release and sporting anticipation.

And finally up those steps, and then that field, and as we hunkered down in our seats in the shade, I smiled.

Yes, the slow crawl of advertising is creeping around the park like that mirror-goop in *The Matrix* sliming its way up Neo's arm. Even the "good" advertising is gone: the famous red Budweiser rooftop beyond left field is now an imposing blue UNITED sign, and the homey TORCO Oil logo over right field has been replaced by a rotating Miller Lite billboard.

I shook my head in smug self-defense. *She sure sold out*, I thought. *How did I once LOVE her?*

Still, enjoying Wrigley has always meant disregarding certain unavoidable annoyances, and I've never had trouble zoning in on the peace and majesty of the park.

We were seated behind home plate on the 3rd base side, and as I reshaped my back into her form-fitting chairs and began filling out my scorecard, the faintest of smiles filled my cheeks. I heard her familiar siren songs — "Beer here! Buuuuuudweiser here!" — and I saw her loving wink as the doomed players in blue took their outfield posts.

It's good to see you, she said as I shifted uneasily in my seat. *You're looking well.*

I struggled to make small talk. *I see you're still packin' 'em in.*

Oh, she said with a giggle, *I do okay.*

It was no use fighting it — she had me. It *was* good to see her? Who am I kidding, it was *great* to see her. All of a sudden there I was again, snuggling into the woman I loved, just like I did long ago, back before I knew any better.

5.

I don't have to tell you how this ends.

The Marlins broke a scoreless tie with three runs in the 4th inning, followed by a 5th inning grand slam from the old Sout'sider Carlos Lee, capped off by a run-scoring single. 8-0 Marlins.

Throughout the madness, I watched as Jimmy dug his way further and further into his chair, possessing the unhappy slouch of a boy sitting through an adult dinner party mixed with the grim countenance of a man who's been here before.

Meanwhile, the older and unceasingly jubilant Ira was seated upright, checking his scorecard and watching the proceedings like a grandfather patiently observing his two grandsons in the backseat of his Lincoln as they slurp ice cream cones on a summer day, knowing as he watches them, *There will be ice cream on the seats. But I'm going to have a great time with my grandchildren.*

PART IX: LOST IN THE WILDERNESS

And that's pretty much how it went, as the Cubs put up just enough of a fight to get our hopes up without doing anything quite so drastic to unilaterally crush them.

So now here we are, the postseason underway as the 2012 Cubs mercifully sit at home. After winning the final two games of that Marlins series, the Cubs lost 48 of their final 73, dropping over 30 games behind the first-place Reds. In that time, they had losing streaks of 8, 7, 6, 4, and 4. They lost games 12-0, 5-0, 10-1, and 15-4. They eclipsed the 100-loss barrier by losing to the equally shameful Houston Astros.

A lot of Cubs fans made a big stink out of 100 losses, but my take is simple: when you've lost for 100+ years, what's another 100 games?

Alex didn't take it quite so well. I got a call from him on a Sunday in the middle of August, a few hours after his hometown Reds had polished off three wins at Wrigley. The Cincinnati faithful had produced an impressive show of numbers that weekend — everywhere you turned there were flocks of Reds fans, VOTTO 19 and PHILLIPS 4 and even DAVIS 44 on the backs of these invading strangers.

"Hey buddy!" I said when I answered the phone. "How are you feeling?"

There was a deep pause on the other end. I could hear him breathing, building to the words he couldn't speak. "You tried to tell me," he said softly. His voice was low and weak, without its usual bubbling confidence. "You warned me," he said.

I stood quietly. This wasn't an I-told-you-so moment. It was more of an everything's-going-to-be-okay-little-buddy moment.

"Are you going back to the Reds?" I asked honestly.

"Absolutely not," he said. "This is where I belong. But man..." he said, babbling on, "I just, I had no idea." He paused again. "I mean, goodness. How do people do this for so long?"

That's the question, ain't it? My friends who still die with the Cubs tell me that this 2012 season was all about "building," whatever that means.

"Basically it's like this," said my friend Ari, one third of my holy trinity of Cubs fan friends, a man who once did a naked marathon wearing nothing but Mark Grace's jersey in body paint. "Usually the Cubs are bad because they don't know what they're doing. But now they're bad because they know what they're doing."

Sounds like the same old song to me. *Tell me lies, tell me sweet little lies*, right? IT'S GONNA HAPPEN, right?

Here's the thing: I'm no longer sure you have to believe in the Cubs. But I'm also not sure that belief in the Cubs is what's expected of us. Maybe what's important is not that we believe, but that we forgive. Forgive the Cubs for their perpetual failure. Forgive our ancestors for their slamming-our-heads-into-an-ivy-covered-wall ways, and for passing down that unfounded dedication to us. Forgive ourselves for not giving up and never giving in, for believing in something so blatantly ridiculous and obviously impossible.

I don't know if my last trip to Wrigley was a return to my old love, but it definitely was a day of forgiveness. It taught me two things: the Cubs will never win a World Series, and I can live with that.

PART X:
TWO SAVIORS

March 15, 2009, ReadJack.com
Age 27

APPRECIATING CLARK KENT: A SALUTE TO ROOKIE DERRICK ROSE

In the third game of the 1989 Bears season, a rookie running back for the Detroit Lions named Barry Sanders ran for 126 yards on 18 carries, scoring once in a 47-27 Bears win.

This was the fall of '89, and even with the Cubs wrangling a division title, our emotion was locked square on our beloved Bulls. Only three months earlier, the young guns in red and black had dropped their second straight series to the hated Bad Boys. For Chicago fans in the late 80's, nothing mattered like the Pistons.

And for the 2nd grade fellas of Orrington Elementary School, the pain of that struggle was exacerbated by our friendship with Aaron Wightman, Detroit-native. Regardless of the happenings at recess or in gym, we all knew deep in our souls that Aaron's ties with the Pistons elevated him beyond the rest of us. No insult could touch him, not so long as Isiah, Laimbeer, Rodman, Dumars, and the Microwave were on the warpath.

So you can imagine my dismay when number 20 got his first crack at the Bears. Beyond unfair, I thought at the time, that Aaron should now be armed with this squirrelly, dominant tailback when he already had Daly's crew. And then it hit me: "...and we have to watch him do this twice a season for the next ten years." Ugh.

I had the same trembling realization in 2007 when a rookie named Adrian Peterson sliced us up for 224 and three scores in a Vikings win. *Twice a year. Here we go...*

Peterson has amassed 554 yards and eight touchdowns in four career games against the Bears, and I'm not expecting Years Three through

Eight to soften the blow. But while Sanders added to our Pistons grief, it has been Derrick Rose who has made everything okay in the city of wind. *82 times a year! Here we go!*

It is our good luck that a point guard's lifespan far exceeds that of your average running back. Sanders hung 'em up after only ten seasons — Rose could easily be ours for fifteen. Of course, that all depends on contract negotiations and the team's success, but Rose leaving Chicago before his 30th birthday would be a disaster, infinitely dumber (should we trade him) than shipping Brand, infinitely more upsetting (should he want out) than losing Maddux. I'm not one for long-term predictions, but the only obstacles to Derrick Rose playing ten seasons with the Bulls would be career-ending injury, death, or the fulfillment of the 2012 Mayan calendar prophecy.

Speaking of those 2012 Olympics, Team USA's probable starting point guard, Chris Paul, was at the UC Saturday night. And though Paul greatly outplayed him, Rose's stature is already such that a showdown with his position's top man is truly a showdown.

Saturday was an off night for the man "From Chicago." But more than the numbers or the wins, I'm watching for those wonderful moments that only the best athletic competitors provide. Like midway through the opening quarter, when Rose kicked himself into a second and then third gear on a routine drive to the hoop. At the top of the key he was covered. One blink later: uncontested layup.

For me, that's enough. That one moment where greatness seems inspired, not assumed. Where the man who has done it all does it again in such a way that even his most weathered fans drop a "He just did *what*??!!!" at their highest pitch.

And that's the thing about Derrick Rose: he's full of 'em. Full of those moments that make posters and youtube clips and give columns to the columnists. Wins and losses? They still matter, but not like they once did. I was seven turning eight in 1989. At that age, players aren't players. They're superheros and villains, mythical beings that exist in trading cards and video games and in each one of us every time we picked up a ball.

In that way, I missed out on the true brilliance of the 90's Bulls. I wasn't able to marvel at Michael's dominance or Scottie's versatility because I was not experiencing those games as acts of athletic competition. They were full-on battles between good and evil on which my very emotional wellbeing and quite possibly my status as a human hung firm. I was no more capable of appreciating the unique physicality of MJ's famous "switch-hands layup" against the Lakers as you might be of Superman leaping a tall building in a single bound. That is simply what Superman does.

Now it's just sports, just some dudes playing ball. Yet I watch Rose play now and I get to experience determination, joy, courage, leadership, frustration, beauty, and a whole slew of Well-Hot-Damn-I-Don't-Believe-I've-Ever-Seen-A-Human-Do-That-Before's. At seven, Rose would be a superhero, nothing more. At twenty-seven, he's some kind of concoction: Iverson's quickness with Kidd's strength with Jason Williams's sudden and crazed clutchness at Duke, or perhaps he is the 21st century evolution of an Isiah and Dumars backcourt fused into one body.

82 times a year?? For the next ten years??!!!

Hot damn.

April 3, 2009, ReadJack.com
    Age 27

HERE COMES CUTLER! (AND PACE!) (AND CONVERSATION!)

The text message came in at 4:43 Thursday afternoon from Ben. It said:

    No. 6!

So, I thought, *we got Jay Cutler.*

Sure enough, ESPN.com confirmed:

> BREAKING NEWS
> Cutler Headed to Chicago

Like most Bears fans who follow the news, I'd spent the past few weeks mulling over the cons and pros of collecting the Denver signal-caller. Now, having heard it certain (barring a physical), I began examining his statistics with a newly-critical eye. He did not seem necessarily better than a healthy Kyle Orton, but there it is: in Cutler's two seasons as the Broncos starting quarterback, he has started and then finished all 16 games. No Bears QB has gone back-to-back on fully healthy seasons since Bob Avellini went 14 for 14 in 1976 and 1977. Only four Bears have done it in a 16-game season. None did it again.

So that seemed positive. Then I saw that they were giving up two first rounders to get him, and just as I was getting set to call Ben and discuss the deal, my phone rang. Brian Glickman — big Bears fan.

I laughed as I answered. "Afternoon sir."

"Well… what do you think?"

"Seems alright. I liked Orton. Cutler seems… healthier."

"And better." He paused. "What about the first rounders? I guess the idea is that Angelo's record on first rounders is so brutal anyhow."

"Plus they're costly. And that's even more vital now. And Angelo or no Angelo, the success rate of first rounders still isn't that impressive. And with this defense, we kind of have to win now anyways. Now's the time. I don't care all that much about first rounders, even the next two."

"We still need receivers."

"We don't need receivers so much as we need to learn how to use receivers. Do you realize that all five receivers from the '05 team were terrific for *other* teams last year? Berrian and Wade were 1-2 in Minnesota, Gage led Tennessee, Moose was second in Carolina..."

"Cutler throws a nice deep ball. Hester will like that. And he could turn Olsen into a Pro Bowler."

"Exactly. Our receivers are not nearly the disaster they are made out to be. Especially when you include Olsen and Clark. And come on: Devin Go Deep! The best play in the Bears' book! Remember in that Saints game when they finally figured out that Hester was a guaranteed monster pickup every time he ran a fly because he would either catch it or get mugged for the interference call?"

"Devin Go Deep. I like it."

My phone beeped. I was getting a call from my cooperating teacher Jeff.

"Glick, getting another call."

"Go Bears."

"Go Bears."

I click over. We exchange quick hellos. And then:

"Just wanted to call to see what you think."

"We'll see. We'll see," I said. "Cutler's exciting. But we still need the same, like, four things to go well, just like every year. Strong o-line, a tailback on his game, baller pass rush, and dudes have to stay healthy. That's it. That's the season."

"There's talk we might sign Orlando Pace."

"I've heard that. Now that would get me amped. You know, when the team gets good, and you spend all sorts of time being excited over the position players...ooh, Marty Booker! Whoa, check out Nathan Vasher! Dude, Bernard Berrian is fast!...and what you miss is how good the line is. That '01 team, all five guys started all 16 games. And we were rock solid '05-'06. Then Miller and Tait and Ruben Brown got old and impossible, and we all started wondering why Rex and co. were looking sorry."

And it's true. More than any other position on the team, the Bears' offensive line affects the way I feel about myself during football season. I know that sounds entirely insane. So be it. I don't feel like a bum when the Bears are losing, but I do feel like a king when they are winning, and when that winning stems from a powerful, dominant offensive line… there's just something about a group of five massive men who are experienced as a single unit and are responsible for protecting your leader and creating space for your spark plug that makes me feel strong.

Jeff and I break down the defense and discuss the new offense and then hang up.

I go back to ESPN.com where CUTLER TO THE BEARS is still breaking news, and then I see it, off on the side, in tiny print: Bears sign ex-Ram Pace.

"Yes! Yes! There we go!"

My phone rings. It's Luke. He's getting married on Saturday, so the man has plenty to think about. And yet:

"How about those Bears?"

"We got Pace!"

"Isn't he old?"

"Reallllll old. But if he's got one season left, then that's one season of a Hall-of-Fame, former-Pro Bowl left tackle. And if he's totally done, then with the new guy Omiyale and the young guys a year older our line will still be better, and now we've got a Hall-of-Fame left tackle showing these dudes how to train."

"I'm pretty pumped about Cutler. He's a Pro Bowl quarterback! When was the last time we had that? McMahon, probably."

We chatted a bit more about Cutler and Pace and Forte and Hester, wished each other well, and hung up with nary a mention of his impending nuptials. I still had yet to call Ben, or my dad, or Tony the Packers Fan, or a slew of other people who I knew I'd be on the horn with sooner or sooner. Say what you will about Cutler for Orton. At least they've got us talking.

Sep. 21, 2009, ReadJack.com
Age 27

PASSING IS FUN!

Following Pittsburgh's first touchdown in yesterday's Bears-Steelers game, Jay Cutler orchestrated a three-and-out. It was unspectacular in every way that a three-and-out can be. A pass complete to Greg Olsen for a gain of six, a Matt Forte run for a gain of one, a pass incomplete to Olsen. As the punt team took the field, my father laughed:

"Wasn't Cutler supposed to, you know…change our lives, or something?"

Since Angelo made the move for Cutler on April 2nd, Bears fans everywhere have been waiting for the offensive messiah to lift them to previously unknown heights, the kind we've cursed from afar whenever Favre or Manning or Marino or Montana were on the screen.

And in the preseason, Cutler delivered. He played stellar football, revealing a command of the quarterback position Chicago fans have not seen since the radio days. He tossed balls all over the field with such ease and efficiency that we gave ourselves permission to believe in The Power of The Arm.

Four picks and a loss later, Bears fans were drooping. Early in the first quarter of Sunday's game, our spirit was no better.

But Cutler ended up righting the ship with several flicks of that magnificent right arm, leading the Bears on three extended scoring drives that produced two touchdowns and the game-winning Robbie Gould kick in a 17-14 win at Soldier Field.

As he did a week ago, Cutler made throws that brought the "Holy #%@!" out of even the tight-lippiest of Bears fans. Like the Week 1 sideline throws to Hester and The Hustlin' Johnny Knox, Cutler laid out the most beautiful of balls for Olsen in the second quarter. The pass resulted in the near decapitation of our young tight end, who, fortunately, went on to play and play well.

But Olsen was on the bench for this drive: 13 plays, 97 yards, Cutler going six of nine for 62 yards and a score.

And what a score! Third and goal from the six, 23 seconds to play in the half, Bears trailing seven-zip. Cutler looks left to the blanketed Knox, and then pivots his head to the right, taking two quick steps and machine-gunning a ball to Kellen Davis that sticks on his massive right shoulder as he absorbs a "take that!" hit from James Farrior.

Cutler's second score was no less impressive. Now trailing 14-7, Cutler and the Bears took over at their own 28. Big Jay made three incredible throws on this drive, the first coming on a third-and-three from the Chicago 35 in which Cutler evaded the blitzing Farrior to his left, stepped forward and away from a diving defender, and then fired a ball twenty yards to Hester in double coverage. On the very next play, Cutler went play action and spun to his right, casually flipping a pass down the seam over the heads of three Pittsburgh defenders to a wide-open Olsen at the 25.

Five plays later, third and goal from the seven, Cutler in shotgun with an empty backfield and Knox lined up wide to the right. Of all the

PART X: TWO SAVIORS

passes I've seen Cutler fling in the navy blue, this was the one that absolutely killed me.

The Steelers brought pressure on the right side of the Bears' line, and something went wrong, because a blink after the snap the Steelers had not one but two dudes untouched and preparing to remove Cutler's legs from his waist. At this point, Knox was at the four, not even into the first step of his break. And Cutler was screwed. A pump fake? A hopeless scramble? Probably a sack, one of those painful-to-watch body slams in which the ball carrier's doomed escape attempt succeeds only in setting himself up for a more dramatic twisting and tossing of his useless frame...

Instead, Cutler uncorked an impossible throw off his back foot with one defender leaping to bat the ball away, and this God-blessed football traveled at top speeds from the fifteen all the way to the leaping Knox, who cradled it a step inside the goal line for the touchdown.

From snap to two-feet-down, the entire sequence covered three seconds.

How the hell did he do that? How did this human being throw a ball that far that fast to that exact spot that quickly without setting his feet while staring down two monstrous men each a step away from ending his life?

If this is what Pro Bowl quarterbacks look like, sign me up.

And sign me up for the Bears' pass-catchers, especially those much derided wideouts Hester, Bennett, and Knox. Hester has turned into a versatile receiver—we all know about his speed, but he goes over the middle, has great hands, and runs better routes than most will credit. And Johnny Knox...Holy #%@! Those two plus Bennett, Olsen, and Kellen Davis all made outstanding catches of the leaping, stretching, darting, ducking, QB-saving and defender-evading variety, all in a win over the Super Bowl champs.

I don't know about you, but two games in and I'm having a ball.

Jan. 26, 2010, ReadJack.com
  Age 28

THE SOUND OF GREATNESS: THE DRAGIC DUNK

Hear that? That's the buzz.

The buzz is pulsating, especially in Chicago. You see it in the bullhorn of national press and the personal pokes of status updates. You see it in the Saturday-night bar crowds that, a year ago, had their eyes on their beers and their minds on each other regardless of what He was doing on the screens beside them. You see it on youtube and ESPN, see it on the Score, see it bursting into the general discussion, see it from people who tell you they haven't watched the Bulls since Jordan, but man, they're watching now.

Did you see Rose last night? Oh man! That dunk on the break, sick two-handed flush right in dude's face. Dropped 37 and the game-winner against the Wiz. Went for 32 on Nash. Straight killing it right now! Bulls baby! Bulls!

The buzz is Derrick Rose. The buzz is "this kid from Chicago." The buzz is performance and entertainment and athletic amazement.

Last Wednesday, Bill Simmons wrote a wonderful essay about LeBron James and the yet-to-be-witnessed "greatest highlight ever" that only someone with James's unique physicality can unleash.

But one night after he dropped The Dunk on Phoenix, our man Rose pulled off a move that I'm not sure I've ever seen…ever…from anyone.

Late in the second quarter, Rose rebounded a Luis Scola miss and turned up court. Upon finishing his first dribble, he found Rockets point guard Aaron Brooks a half step behind on his right hip with Scola directly in front of him. Instead of committing a charge or pulling up his dribble to let Brooks fly by and his teammates advance, Rose decided that continuing forward was the only choice. He could split them, maybe, but the ball was in his left hand and the space between Scola and Brooks was to his right...

...so without slowing his gallop or changing direction, Rose went behind his back with his left hand squirting the ball between the two Rockets and regaining control of his dribble at midcourt. Now a full step ahead of Brooks (and well-past the confused and turned-around Scola), Rose was two-on-one with Taj Gibson against Houston's Kyle Lowry, and no sooner did Lowry step up to face Rose did Number 1 flip the ball to the streaking Gibson, drawing the block on Lowry as Gibson put down the dunk.

From rebound to dish, this sequence took three seconds.

The second half of that play was the perfect example of why Rose makes basketball so easy for his teammates. When the ball is in his hands, everyone is open. It's not just his Favre-like ability to thread passes through narrow spaces, though that helps. It is his foot speed. Rose is so fast and can change directions so quickly and fluidly that he alters the angles on the court. A guy covered under the basket is open as soon as Rose approaches because of that split second when the defender freezes, not sure how to handle this blur of a guard darting towards him. His instincts betray him as he pivots *just that much* towards Rose, and in that instant the ball is gone, dropped in the hole by that now-open teammate.

I am sure that this is why the Suns love playing with Steve Nash, why the Hornets love Chris Paul, why Utah loves our old friend Deron Williams, why the teammates of Magic, Stockton, Isiah, Cousy, or any other great point guard found life on the court such a joy.

And while Rose is not yet in the league of Nash, Paul, and Williams as a passer, his physical attributes make him a more dangerous scorer. More explosive than the first, bigger than the second, faster than the third. Other than his speed and hops, his best offensive advantage is his ability to adjust his body mid-air, especially when avoiding the charge. He basically curls his torso around the side of a defender as if independent of his legs, his arm continuing that movement so that he swoops the ball to the backboard while his legs re-adjust beneath him and join their up-top limbs on the other side of the confused defender.

All this and still learning. Posted his first regular season 30 on December 19th, and has three more since. Added a one-handed floater to his arsenal this season that he can make going right or left, (a maneuver that beat the Wizards in double OT earlier this month). Improved his jumper with the extra shot reps gained in Ben Gordon's absence. Is shooting a career-best .510 from the floor in January, scoring 23.3 points per game despite not yet figuring out how to get to the line whenever he pleases as do Wade, Nash, and Paul.

And in two days, when the All-Star reserves are announced, Derrick Rose's name may well be called. It should be. The buzz continues.

Jan. 23, 2011, The Sports Blog Network
    Age 29

FINAL THOUGHTS ON A TEAM WITH A SHOT

We would not be here without Jay Cutler.

This statement is as true as it is forgotten. The NFC Championship Game kicks off in less than two hours, and the Chicago Bears might not be participants – let alone hosts – if not for the prowess of #6.

The Bears' de-fence comes close to matching the playoff units of 2005 and 2006, but the offense – with its hodgepodge o-line – was out-passed by the 2006 team and outrun by both. Cutler is the difference; not Rex nor Orton or Griese could have withstood the

PART X: TWO SAVIORS

pounding delivered upon Big Jay's noble frame, and a lasting injury at quarterback in 2010 meant Todd Collins or Caleb Hanie under center and 'home' for the Bears, watching from instead of playing at.

Cutler makes throws untried by his predecessors, and escapes would-be sackers with legs unseen by a Bears QB since McMahon (or, fine, Kordell Stewart). Just imagine the beatings Grossman or Orton would have taken with this line!

The line has gelled, though, over the past six weeks, and while the team's use of eight starting linemen is a franchise-high for a post-merger Bears playoff team, all five men – Kreutz, Omiyale, Garza, Chris Williams, and the rookie Webb – started at least 12 games. The lineup has gone unchanged since the bye week, a stretch the Bears have mastered with an 8-2 record, including last week's playoff win.

Meanwhile, the defensive line of Peppers, Idonije, Adams, Toeaina, Melton, and the recently rejuvenated Tommie Harris give the Bears an all-around strength up-front they have not seen since 2005. The team's last tandem at end to notch at least eight sacks apiece was Richard Dent (12) and Trace Armstrong (10) in 1990, while the 1441 rushing yards allowed is, since 1990, second only to the 2001 team.

The pass catchers Knox, Hester, Bennett, Olsen, and Forte are a dynamic bunch; The Hustlin' Johnny Knox is the team's best deep-threat since Marcus Robinson, while the running back Forte is the team's best receiver out of the backfield since Payton.

And the defensive leaders at linebacker and DB – Urlacher, Briggs, Tillman, and Chris Harris – are a formidable foursome whose veteran resolve match their athletic feats.

Still, it is the arm, legs, and torso of Jay Cutler that has filled the gaps in the offense and given an aging defense room to breathe. The excitement of April 2, 2009 was tempered by redzone picks and a bounty of sacks, yet for the patient viewers truly paying attention, the trade that brought Cutler to Chicago has given the team and its fans something unusual: a quarterback to believe in. On the cusp of the Super Bowl, that's something to celebrate.

May 8, 2012
  Age 30

THE BULLS' LIVING NIGHTMARE

"You can just see it," announcer Hubie Brown said during Sunday's Game 4 loss to the 76ers. "It's like a nightmare unfolding."

That comment came after a missed shot by John Lucas III and another Sixers rebound, the Bulls trailing 66-63 early in the 4th. Made on a rainy, dreary day in Chicago, Brown's comment was, I thought, a fitting eulogy for these 2012 Chicago Bulls. Hubie probably didn't mean it that way, but no matter. His words were truth:

This postseason has not been a death sentence.

It's been a nightmare.

As if Bulls fans had, after Game 5 of the 2011 East Finals, dreamt of the 2012 playoffs and ended up with *this*.

You know the feeling, when your team gets knocked out in the playoffs. You say to yourself, "I wish we didn't have to wait a whole *year* to get back to this point. I wish next year's postseason could start tomorrow."

Well, tomorrow came. And our point guard blew out his knee.

Then the Sixers rocked Game 2, Joakim Noah sprained his ankle, and Games 3 and 4 slipped away like rainwater down a slanted street.

PART X: TWO SAVIORS

These are the plot points of nightmare. Hell, even Noah's injury was fraught with irony, as our heart-and-soul center turned his ankle while running a 3-on-1 fastbreak, a job usually reserved for Rose.

The series has been so bleak that late in Game 4, I pled with the basketball gods to allow the Bulls to pull out the victory and save their season. Ten days ago, no one thought this team would face a do-or-die Game 4. But they did, and they did, and now tonight's game is their final hope.

I expect the Bulls to give the home fans one last thrill, yet even if they win Game 5, their season appears over. The rain may stop now and again, but it's never gone. It covers the streets and sticks in the air. It leaks from tree branches and rests on cars. It has disrupted outdoor life for most of this week. It is raining in Chicago and we have no umbrella.

Feb. 25, 2015, ReadJack.com, after Derrick Rose's 3rd major injury
Age 33

FOR 1.

All I want to hear is love.

Don't talk to me about prospects — ours for the playoffs or the talent that might replace him.

Don't talk to me about fault — his or his coach's or anyone else's.

Don't talk to me about the future — his with us or ours without him.

Don't talk to me about legacy — about Penny or Prior, about Fields or Woody.

Don't talk to me about pain — unless it's his.

Don't talk to me about anything other than what he means to you. As a Bulls fan. As a Chicagoan.

That's it.

That's all I want to hear.

For once, let's strip his latest injury of any context other than empathy and sympathy. Let's wish for goodness and joy to be heaped upon this man. For him to do what he loves safely and successfully.

Let's close our eyes and picture him. The beauty of his body.

Dribble. Cut. Slice. Jump. Release. Splash. Smile.

36 and 11 assists in his first playoff game.

"Stop it! Stop it! What are you doing Dragic?"

"Why can't I be the MVP?"

44 against Atlanta.

Three wins from the Finals.

Yes, we should remember all that.

And then think about his Adidas press conference.

Think about the man who has bankrolled a stranger's funeral and regularly attends others.

The man who wanted to be announced as "From Chicago."

The man whose quiet t-shirt protest spread through the league and professional sports so that everyone watching knew that just because you've made it doesn't mean the breathing's easier.

Think about this man, not a rose that grew from concrete but a Rose that bloomed in Englewood, a man who wants to inspire not just the adults who pay to see him but the children who dream to be him.

Think about him and only him. Not the man in the jersey. The man.

Send him the smiles that he's given us.

Send him care and support.

His name is Derrick.

May 9, 2015, BlogABull
  Age 33

D-ROSE PUMPS SWAG TO 11 WITH FIRST BULLS PLAYOFF GAME-WINNER SINCE MJ

When the shot banked in, when the swag meter hit 11, when the United Center erupted and the city of Cleveland swooned, my buddy Phil Kijak dropped a tweet that summed it up:

> @readjack That was worth the last 3 years.

Derrick Rose. Playoffs. Game winner.

From Game 2, 2012 to Game 1, 2015, we waited. Waited for his return, not to mention his Return. Waited for 1 to be whole. Waited for 1 to be 1.

Lost to Philly, upended Brooklyn, caved to Miami, crumbled vs. Washington.

Finally, this year, we caught glimpses. Moments when the 2011 MVP looked like himself again. 30 and a win vs. Golden State. 34 and a bigger win — a PLAYOFF win — vs. the Bucks.

That series also saw him lose an opponent on a game-winner. They said he lost a step.

But Derrick Rose is built for this shit.

I will admit: I wasn't sure this play vs. Cleveland was going to him. I was thinking Dunleavy would get a pass back after inbounding the ball. The inbounder, they say, is the most dangerous man on the court.

My buddy Pat thought the play would run to Jimmy Butler. According to Taj Gibson, that was the plan.

But Jimmy's stutter-step on LeBron — toward the arc, toward the hoop — proved fruitless.

And while Butler tried to break free, dragging LeBron down low, Derrick — who had streaked past Butler & Gibson — crossed in front of Dunleavy as Shumpert tried to follow.

Dunleavy gave one look to Butler and, finding that option sealed, looked back at Rose, who had halted his run and cut back behind Kyrie Irving, who was defending Dunleavy on the inbounds.

Dunleavy looked as if he was going to pass to Rose over the top of Irving, and then thought better of it as Rose streaked back. Rose caught Dunleavy's bounce pass and wheeled to his left, with Gibson screening Shumpert.

Rose took two dribbles as he curled around Gibson. He was now guarded by the 6'9 Tristan Thompson, who switched off Taj after the screen.

With 1.5 seconds, Derrick Rose raised up.

PART X: TWO SAVIORS

He released the ball.

His hands shot to his sides.

His shot flashed through the air.

The orange hit the glass.

The ball ripped through the net.

Bulls 99. Cavs 96.

"AHHHHHHH!!!!"

My arms flew into the air at the bar as Pat practically tackled me, the two of us plunging into an ottoman as a guy caught us and cheered in our faces.

The shot was a killer on its own.

But it meant something else too.

After Rose's winner, I combed my Bulls-fan-brain-bank for the most recent Bulls playoff game-winner. I thought of Jannero Pargo's three in '05, and Ben Gordon's three in '09 and Nate Robinson's running deuce in 2013.

But those weren't winners.

Pargo's set the stage for Gilbert Arenas' dagger. Gordon's sent Game 4 of the Celtics series to double overtime, where the Bulls won. Nate's was nearly a game-winner, but Joe Johnson tied the game two seconds later and the Bulls eventually won in triple overtime.

And of course we suffered Arenas' game-winner, and Ray Allen's triple in Game 2 of 2009, and Andre Iguodala's season-ending foul shots in 2012, and Jerryd Bayless' season-saving layup in Game 4 this year.

And then it came to me:

It's been 17 years since the Bulls hit a playoff game-winner.

6,171 days.

81 playoff games.

You might remember it. Jordan. Russell. Championship #6.

It was significant that LeBron guarded Buckets, not Rose, for the game's final play. Significant, too, that Derrick broke the MJ streak.

This is the man who, since June 26, 2008 (10 years and 12 days after Jordan's farewell stroke) has been The Man Who Will Get Us Back. We lived and died with him. Cheered for him. Gasped for him.

It's fitting he got this bucket, a shot that is, so far, the biggest of his career.

There's something else though. Take a look at his celebration. Or lack thereof.

This is Rose's version of the MJ still-life fist pump from the '97 Finals.

It's the I'm-the-only-one-here-who-knew-I'd-make-that-shot face that he nearly pulled off in 2012 against the Bucks.

In that game, his soul blinked first. His stone face cracked as he famously pounded his chest with his right hand, then his left, a sneer curling his lip like Thayer's Casey.

This time he jumped into the arms of Joakim Noah and stared, dispassionate, masterful, a calm in the United Center storm he created.

This time, D-Rose was back.

PART X: TWO SAVIORS

This time, the Return was here.

It bloomed from concrete.

It brought us home.

Phil, you're right — it was worth the wait.

Oct. 1, 2015, *Windy City Gridiron*
Age 33

SEE? THAT IS WHY WE WANT JAY CUTLER BACK

Jay Cutler is no Aaron Rodgers.

We know that.

Shoot, after watching Tony Romo cheer teammates on the sideline with an injured clavicle, it's clear Jay's not even Tony Romo. Obviously he's not Tom Brady. He's not Drew Brees. He's not Andrew Luck. He would have been sent to the nearest orphanage if somehow he'd been born a Manning.

He does not belong on that list. But he doesn't belong on that Moreno-Burris-Quinn-Collins-Horrible-Bears-QB-X list either.

When you've lived that list, you learn to appreciate what you have.

We have Jay. He's far from perfect but he's ours. Jimmy Clausen's ours too. You'll see the difference Sunday.

— My column, Sep. 24, 2015

✶✶✶✶✶✶

I'm a stat man, and the stat I can't quite wrap my head around is the Bears offense going 10-for-10 on possessions ending in a punt. Before we move on to the Raiders or discuss the so-called fire sale, let's sit in that for a moment.

Ordinarily a team down 20 with zero points to their name will take a shot on a 4th-and-long and secure at least one possession that ends in a turnover-on-downs. Not these Bears. Losing 20-0, 23-0 and 26-0 late against Seattle, these Bears punted on 4th-and-1, 4th-and-2 and 4th-and-5.

They didn't even turn the ball over, becoming the first Bears team since at least 1940 to get shut out without committing a turnover.

That's a special sort of incompetence and incapability. Jimmy Clausen, welcome to the record books.

A few hours after Clausen & Co. placed that hideous bow on that horrible affair, Jake Arrieta won his 21st game for the Chicago Cubs. Arrieta's performance has been just about as big a surprise as the playoff-bound Cubs for which he plays, but even if the team weren't headed to the postseason Jake's 1.82 ERA, without the wins, would be something to celebrate.

I mention that because how Cubs fans view Arrieta's majesty is how I've viewed Cutler's since 2009. "Holy crap, can you believe we got a guy who can do THAT?"

When I wrote last week that I would miss an injured Cutler because "he's the best QB in Bears history," I wasn't being hyperbolic but I think I failed to underline the significance of that assessment. I don't care one lick if you agree with me about Jay being the best,

PART X: TWO SAVIORS

or if you think it's Sid Luckman or even Jim McMahon. That's not important.

What is important is that Luckman retired in 1950, McMahon last played for the Bears in 1988, and here's this guy Cutler capable of some of the finest quarterbacking physically possible in the NFL, and he's ours, all ours. That's what matters -- that even if you think McMahon was a better QB, you're talking a 20-year period between his departure and Jay's arrival when the pickings were slim as Jake Arrieta.

(And fine, there were some people who responded on Facebook or these very message boards that Erik Kramer, by virtue of 1995 alone, is a finer QB historically than Jay. If you feel that way, I just don't know how to talk to you.)

Chicago sports fans don't know how to talk about their athletes, either. Our responses to our stars often make as much sense as 10 punts on 10 possessions.

Derrick Rose is reviled for getting injured and for talking about the very same career objectives that every other Chicagoan discusses -- financial security.

Jay Cutler gets pounded into the turf for six years, and because he doesn't smile and is married to a reality star and throws more interceptions than we like, we collectively treat him like a tooth ache that just won't stop pulsing, mucking up our otherwise gorgeous smile.

I don't buy it. In a season shaping up to be historically atrocious, Cutler's talents should feel to us like an uninjured arm in a vicious car wreck. "I can't walk, my jaw is wired shut and I lost vision in one eye from that wayward dashboard, but hot damn, I can still write!"

Naturally, as the Bears tumbled toward oblivion against Seattle, Bears fans clamoured for Cutty. Of course plenty of others remained stubborn, claiming that "We'd still be losing even with #6 back there." Again, not the point. We all know this season will be rough. As I told my colleague Brian on Monday, "Pace yourself -- we have 13 more."

Do whatever you need to be able to appreciate Cutler. Pretend he is Matt Forte if you have to. Strip him of any positional importance and just enjoy the show that he, and no other Bears quarterback in at least two decades, can give us.

If you're looking for upside, Jay practiced this week. Raiders coach Jack Del Rio said he is preparing his team for both Cutler and Clausen.

Trust me: You want Cutler back this week. If I've taught you nothing else, let me teach you that.

If you're looking for additional, weirder upside, the last time we started 0-3 we bagged our first win against the Oakland Raiders. And the night we did, the Cubs wrapped their first postseason series victory since 1908. So perhaps we are in the midst of a footnote-laiden historical sports loop, and when I sit down to write this column a week from now our beloved Bears will be 1-3. I'd like that. I'm sure you would too.

Those 2003 Bears, by the way, rallied to finish 7-9. Coaxing seven wins out of this Bears team would be as much a miracle as the 2015 Cubs. I hope we get there. In the meantime, I just want something fun. Jay Cutler is part of Something Fun. Ignore that at your own peril.

June 22, 2016, Facebook Live
    Age 34

UNTITLED (BULLS TRADE DERRICK ROSE)

It is June 22, 2016, downtown Chicago at 4 o'clock, and I feel pretty much exactly how my face looks right now after this sad day in Chicago sports: the end of the Derrick Rose era. Drafted in 2008. We probably should not have even gotten him with a 1.7% chance at the #1 pick. But we got him. And (pause) man.

What I'm seeing from everybody today is what I've seen for the last four years, which is something between pleasure and resignment. People saying that he's trash. "You gotta get rid of him." People talking about 'injury optics.' What it looks like versus what he actually went through. And this has been something that has been on my mind for a while and it was really crystallized with Derrick's last four years.

We talk about being sports fans. Sports fans of what? What are we fans of? Are we fans of players or are we fans of ourselves?

And I think too often the answer is that we are rooting for our own happiness. Which is certainly part of the equation. And I know that it's important. Look at what's happening in Cleveland today. You've got a city of under 400,000 people — that's Cleveland's population — and conservative estimates put their parade at a million. I've seen a million and a half. I don't know where all of these people are coming from. I guess Akron and Columbus and Cincinnati and Canton. I don't know. But they're not all from Cleveland.

Obviously we know the importance that sports hold for folks, and that's good, but the whole Derrick Rose thing the last four years, everybody dogging this guy because — what? He made too much money? He was injured? I don't understand it. I don't understand saying you are a fan of a team which comprises its players. That's it.

What else is a team? It's us. It's the old "cheering for laundry" thing. But it's got to also be about the people who play on that team.

It's just infuriating when you have a day like this. This guy should have retired as a Bull. And I'm happy for him if this is a better situation, and I'm happy for the Bulls if ultimately it's a better situation for us. But all of the people who are Chicago Bulls fans who spent the last four years saying, "Oh man, we gotta ditch this guy. We gotta get rid of him. This guy's a bum" and all of that…

Look, I know there are more important things than sports. Look at what's happening in D.C. today with the sit-in. Look at what's happening in Chicago today with people protesting for school funding and police accountability. Obviously in D.C., House reps are staging a sit-in for gun violence.

But look at Derrick Rose. This is a guy who stood up for anti-gun violence. He stood up for Chicago schools. He stood up for Chicago youth. He wore the "I Can't Breathe" shirt and started the "I Can't Breathe" t-shirt movement that spread throughout the NBA and to the NFL.

So yeah, there are things that are more important than sports, and this dude was about them all. It's just agonizing to see sports fans talking about, really, themselves. That's it.

I wish Derrick the best. I hope it works out in New York. And I'm disappointed in Bulls fans that he reached the point where he needed a fanbase to embrace him, and it wasn't in his hometown. This could have been like LeBron. And hopefully he comes back in four years and gives us what LeBron just gave to Cleveland. It could have been that. It should have been that. And it wasn't that. Because the last four years, Bulls fans really turned on this dude.

Yes, he could have used some media training, obviously, but this guy had two knee surgeries. He dragged the Bulls to the playoffs in 2009 as a rookie. In 2010, when we were 10 games under .500 in March, got us back to .500 and got us into the postseason. Became MVP. It's just not the way that this should have ended. Any Bulls fan today who gets this news and says, "He's garbage, I'm glad we're moving on" — I hope we're moving on from you.

Dec. 3, 2016, Windy City Gridiron
　Age 35

6 QUESTIONS ABOUT #6

Jay Cutler, we hardly knew ye.

(Wait that's not right. Hold on.)

Jay Cutler, we knew ye all too well.

(Much better.)

Now that Jay Cutler's 2016 season is over, Bears fans are wondering if his Bears career is over too. The WCG staff teamed up to examine that question, and five others, about #6.

Should Jay be back next year?

JACK: Drafting our quarterback of the future and retaining Jay in 2017 are not mutually exclusive options. If Ryan Pace thinks cutting him loose is the best plan, fine. But let's have a plan, whatever we do. "SCREW CUTLER! HE SUCKS!" is not a plan.

What is the single biggest factor that has prevented the Bears from winning the Super Bowl in the Cutler era?

JACK: I want to say offensive line performance in 2010 and 2011. I really do. Jay was sacked 51 times in 37 games in Denver. He was sacked 106 times in his first 37 regular season games in Chicago.

And yet...

Aaron Rodgers was sacked 50 times in 2009; he won the Super Bowl the next year. Tom Brady was sacked 41 times in 2001; he won his first Super Bowl that year. He was sacked 40 times in 2013; he won his fourth Super Bowl the following year. Joe Flacco was sacked 40 times in 2010 and won a Super Bowl two years later. Ben Roethlisberger was sacked 50 times in 2009 and has topped 40 sacks six times.

It's Jay. He's the biggest factor. Not him personally per se, but the decision the team made to build around him and make all decisions based on him. I'm a huge Cutler supporter and always will be, but he's the one constant from 2009 to now.

Of Jay's eight seasons in Chicago, which is the biggest missed opportunity for a Super Bowl championship?

JACK: You can make a great case for 2010 or 2011, but I'll take 2012. We were 7-1 and finished 3-5. The 2012 season came down to the Flacco-led Ravens and the Kaepernick-led 49ers; neither team was an all-timer. We needed to make it happen in the back half of 2012 and we didn't.

When it's all said and done, what will you remember FIRST about Cutler's time in Chicago?

JACK: I hate to say it, but the 2010 NFC championship game. I don't blame Jay for leaving that game; he did, after all, have a torn MCL. But our defense gave Aaron Rodgers the business -- his 55.4 rating is his lowest ever in the playoffs -- and we nearly sent the game to overtime with Caleb Hanie.

Okay, okay, we've heard all the negatives. What is your favorite memory of Jay Cutler, Chicago Bears Quarterback?

JACK: His passing abilities! That sounds basic, but nothing about the Bears quarterbacking in my life prior to Cutler even reached "basic." When we traded for him, I was in awe of things like "his arm" and "his height." He made passes the likes of which we've never seen in Chicago.

My favorite was probably the 56-yarder to Brandon Marshall that led to a game-tying field goal against Seattle in 2012. No other Bears QB could have made that play.

Knowing what you know now, if you could go back to April 2, 2009, would you still trade for Cutler?

JACK: I could be a real bastard and say no, only because I can say in retrospect exactly what would have been better: roll with Kyle Orton in 2009, draft Clay Matthews with our abandoned 2009 first round pick, draft Mike Wallace in the third round, and then land our QB of the future in 2011 with Andy Dalton.

But that's not fair to Bears management; you can say something similar every year in every sport. I'm glad we took the shot on Jay. No matter what else, it's been a fun ride.

PART XI:
ONE SAVIOR

March 2005, "Bear Down and Get Some Runs"
  Age 23

MOVING ON: THE TALE OF SCOTTIE PIPPEN AND THE 1994 BULLS

My mom told us while we were getting dressed for school.

It must have been something for her, hearing the news and knowing she had the responsibility to tell my brother and me. I can imagine her downstairs, getting ready for her day in the classroom, making our sandwiches and listening to the radio as she would on any other morning, and then comes the report, and her own personal reaction, and the sudden decision that had to be made of how to tell us.

This wasn't a death; a family member, or even a pet, passing away. This wasn't a building bombed or a country going to war; it wasn't a house burning down or a near-fatal car accident. This was just a man deciding he no longer wished to play basketball. That's all it was. Yet she knew it was more than that, we all knew, the city knew, and so she walked up the stairs and stepped into our room and gave us one final moment of innocence before telling us what we never thought possible.

"Boys, I've got some bad news." We stood and looked at her. "Michael Jordan retired."

At first I thought she was kidding, because any news as drastic as that must surely be a joke. But the look in her eye told me she was serious, and I didn't know what to say. Even though word had spread the night before during the White Sox playoff game, I still did not believe it. Athletes had retired before, guys we wished would play forever, but not guys like this. Not guys who were not only at the top of their game, but also at the top of everyone else's. Not guys who had won seven straight scoring titles. Not guys who had gone to nine straight

All-Star games. Not guys who had won three straight championships. Not guys in the prime of a Hall of Fame career and only 30, a month away from what would surely be another glorious season. Not guys who were the biggest star in the game, in the city, in the world. Not Michael Jordan.

When I arrived at school that day, most of my classmates were experiencing it all as well. Kids walked the hallways, stunned. Teachers did their best to keep us on the ball, but even they knew this was no ordinary day. Two of my friends made a sign that read "Say it ain't so, Michael!" and carried it from class to class. Everywhere you turned you saw JORDAN 23 on somebody's back, as kids had undoubtedly heard the news that morning and changed clothes in order to... what? Support him? Mourn him? Celebrate him? We weren't sure.

There are some events that have an immediate impact, even while we attempt to sort the meaning and make sense of our emotions. This wasn't like Jordan's second retirement in January of 1999; that was expected. He was 35 by then, the NBA was in the midst of its lockout, and everyone had a pretty good feeling that 1998 would be his final year. No, this retirement was a shock. It was a blindside tackle. It was your girlfriend dumping you on Valentine's Day, or going in for a promotion and getting fired instead. A month before the season, the Bulls looking stronger than ever, fans wondering if we would become the first "Four-Peat" since Russell's Celtics, and the greatest player the city has ever seen walks away.

When something like this happens, it makes you question *everything*. Your universe is fundamentally changed. It'd be like waking up one morning and finding gravity obsolete. Michael Jordan's first retirement felt like an alteration of our basic, Earthly laws. Life would continue, the world would go on, and basketball would still be played, but in Chicago we wondered what the three would be without Michael Jordan. What did it mean? Is nothing guaranteed? With this in the books, what other mind-blowing events would take place? Perhaps we'd go to the ballgame one day and find the Cubs now playing at '69 Mets Field, or Comiskey Park II. In a world where Michael Jordan

PART XI: ONE SAVIOR 277

plays for the Chicago Bulls, that could never happen. In a world where Michael Jordan retires one month before the season starts despite the fact that he's only 30 and is still quite clearly the best player in the L, the impossible is possible and reality is faulty and everything we know as sports fans, and dare I say, human beings, is suspect.

******

But if the retirement threatened to end us, the timing was our savior. Instead of having a whole summer for everyone to sit around and think about it, the team and the fans had but one month. The 1993-94 season already promised to be an interesting one. Would MJ be the same after a difficult 1993 postseason in which the press came down hard on him for gambling, and after the horrible murder of his father? Would the team be burned out in another bid for a title? How would the "Croatian Sensation" Toni Kukoc fit in with Jordan, Pippen, Grant, and the rest of the team?

All of those questions and more were replaced on October 6, 1993, with the biggest question of all: how would the Bulls fare without The Greatest Of All-Time?

For me, the answer was simple: the championship Bulls were more than just one man, and the 1993-94 team would prove that. I was in the minority. Many were writing these Bulls off, including the Chicago media. The *Tribune*'s Bulls writers were seemingly all picking the Bulls to free fall. I remember one of the previews very specifically, something to the effect of: "Record: 41-41. Reason: The Los Angeles Clippers were 41-41 last year, and the Bulls without Jordan are the Los Angeles Clippers."

Over the years I forgot the writer, but I never forgot the words. I looked it up recently and was not surprised to find that succinct cynicism coming from the pen of Bernie Lincicome. Did he honestly believe that? Did he think that you could simply add MJ to the '92-'93 Clippers and make a champion? The brilliance of the Bulls was not just that they had the league's best player, but also its best coach, second man, bench, GM, coaching staff. Michael was among the best in the biz, certainly, but so were Scottie, Phil, Krause, and Tex. The Bulls would not be a championship runaway, but they would still be contenders. *Just you wait. Just you wait...*

...and indeed, I was proven right, though not at first. A year earlier, the Bulls were 8-2 after ten games; in 1994, they started 4-6. The critics hounded, but by the forty-game mark the Pippen-led Bulls of '94 were a game better than the Jordan-led Bulls of '93.

The surprises kept coming.

For the tenth straight year, a Bulls guard was voted a starter on the Eastern Conference All-Star team, but this time it was B.J. Armstrong. The Kid joined Scottie in the East's starting lineup, and Horace Grant joined B.J. as first-time Chicago All-Stars. Scottie scored a game-high 29 to capture the game's MVP while leading the East to a 127-118 victory.

This was the story of the season: Scottie emerging from the shadows of Number 23 as a legit MVP while Michael's famous "supporting cast" demonstrated just how vital they'd always been. This was like *The Godfather Part II* making due without Brando. Scottie put together his best all around season: career highs in points (22.0), assists (8.7), and steals (2.9). He was named All-NBA 1st team for the first time in his career, and was named to the All-Defensive 1st team for the third straight season.

But the most important statistic for Scottie Pippen in 1994, the hands-down, balls-out, far and away most important stat, was the Bulls' record. Led by Michael Jordan, the 1992-93 Bulls won 57 games. Led by Scottie Pippen, the 1993-94 Bulls won 55. That was good for the East's third seed, only two games behind both New York and the surprising Atlanta Hawks.

Two wins. The Bulls lost the best player in the league, and were able to reproduce all but two wins. Meanwhile, the Los Angeles Clippers went 27-55, last in their division.

41-41 indeed.

PART XI: ONE SAVIOR

******

In the playoffs' first round, the Bulls met a familiar foe. The Cleveland Cavaliers — the bizarro Team of the '90s — were on their last legs. The classic patsies Lenny Wilkens and Craig Ehlo had both scattered to the Hawks, and now the Cavs, still with old foes Price, Daugherty, Hod Rod and Larry Nance, were heading to Chicago for yet another showdown with the (now-Jordanless) Bulls.

Surely this would finally be the year that Cleveland overcame Chicago, the team that had toyed with them and made their basketball lives miserable lo those many seasons. Finally, Cleveland would have their revenge...

Sorry fellas.

Bulls sweep easily, winning Games 1 and 2 by a combined eighteen points before finishing the Cavs off in Cleveland 95-92. Meanwhile, the Knickerbockers were squaring off with their tri-state rivals, those pesky New Jersey Nets, a team that they would dispose of in a tightly contested four-game series.

Now was the time. Bulls vs. Knicks. Fourth consecutive postseason meeting, fifth since 1989. True, there was little pressure on YOUR *World Champion* Chicago Bulls. They were the lower seed, facing off against arguably the league's best, and doing so without Michael Jordan. They had already accomplished more than nearly anyone thought they would. And yet, there they were, ready for more.

To say that this was a hard-fought series is to say that Hunter S. Thompson probably did some drugs. The Knicks took Games 1 and 2 at the Garden, winning by scores of 90-86 and 96-91. The Bulls played well, yet it was clear that this was a different team than the ones that had won the past three NBA titles. Beyond the loss of Jordan, the '94 Bulls also saw former starters Pax and Mr. Bill getting old. Meanwhile, the team was incorporating many new talents into their lineup, most notably Toni, Luc, Steve Kerr, Bill Wennington, and Pete Myers. These were men who had yet to truly experience the postseason, and Games 1 and 2 were their basketball fire baptisms.

The Knicks were beyond physical in these two games, The Enemy John Starks even resorting to tripping Scottie after he beat him on a fast break. It was The Clothesline all over again, and just as they had the year before, the Bulls went back to the Stadium down 0-2.

This was where the series took form. This was where the series took life.

The final five games would be defined by three plays, all of which would involve Scottie Pippen.

Play number one: Game 3, Knicks up 2-0, score tied at 102, Bulls' ball, 1.8 seconds remaining.

As far as his fiercest critics are concerned, Game 3 of the 1994 Eastern Conference Semifinals is the defining game of Scottie Pippen's Hall of Fame career. The Bulls were fighting for their playoff lives, literally and figuratively, as Game 3 featured a classic hoops brawl when New York's Derek Harper and the Bulls' reserve guard Jo Jo English began a tangle that ended up with both teams entwined and spilling into the stands — right in front of the Commish David Stern, who was in attendance. Whoops!

The game went back and forth, and finally, with 1.8 seconds remaining and the game tied at 102, the Bulls went to the huddle to see the play that Phil had drawn up. Much to Pippen's surprise and dismay, Phil wanted his MVP candidate to inbound the ball to the rookie Kukoc. Scottie pouted, sat himself on the bench, and watched as Toni knocked down the jumper to win Game 3.

The Bulls were victorious, back in the series, and the Pippen Detractors had their proof. After the game, a distraught and nearly tearful Cartwright chastised Pippen for his selfish play.

Play number two: Game 5, series tied at 3, Bulls leading 86-85, Knicks' ball, end of the fourth.

Ah, Hue Hollins, you unholy son of a bitch.

PART XI: ONE SAVIOR

With the Bulls up one in the crucial Game 5, the Knicks' Hubert Davis launched a desperate trey from the top of the key. Scottie defended beautifully, with a long arm and a hand in his face. The shot missed badly. The Bulls would close out in Chicago...

But no.

Hollins blew his whistle, signaling a foul on Pippen, sending Davis to the line, and effectively turning himself into one of the great outside villains of Chicago sports. Bill Laimbeer, John Starks, Charles Martin: say hello to Hue Hollins.

Davis knocked down both shots, the Bulls failed to score — though they did have a possession, and enough time...everyone forgets this — and the Knicks escaped with the win and a 3-2 series lead.

Play number three: Game 6, Knicks up 3-2, Bulls up by fifteen, 6:01 to go in the third.

Two downers... nothing bittersweet about 'em.

The first, a selfish, frustrated moment.

The second, a theft. Pure and simple.

By Game 6, the Bulls had experienced two beatdowns in New York, one agonizing win, one easy win, and one horribly agonizing loss. The Bulls knew what a crippling Game 5 loss could mean in a 2-2 series. The year before, the Charles Smith Game sucked the life out of MSG.

This time around, it was the Bulls who were coming off of the Game 5 loss. In its own way, the Hue Hollins-Scottie Pippen-Hubert Davis Phantom Foul Call was as improbable and inexplicable and mind-bendingly awful as Charles Smith having four consecutive shots blocked cleanly under the basket... two of which, incidentally, were blocked by Pippen. Perhaps Hue Hollins' foul call was simply retribution from the basketball gods. Perhaps.

Still, odd twists of (possible) fate aside, players still have to play. Bartman didn't kill the Cubs; the rest of the 8th did. Buckner didn't kill the Mets; Game 7 did.

Hue Hollins was not going to kill the Bulls.

And once again, it was Pippen making the defiant statement. A year earlier, it was his #1 off the trey. This time, it was one of the great in-game dunks ever.

With the Bulls already up big midway through the third, B.J. pushed the ball on the break. The play developed quickly into a 3-on-3 situation, with B.J., Scottie, and Pete Myers on the attack against Ewing, Starks, and Derek Harper. With Myers streaking on the right, Armstrong grooved him a perfect bounce pass. Harper fell as the pass crossed him up, but Starks was able to get nice position in front of Myers.

Myers, however, was a step ahead, and rather than trying to continue his offensive pursuit of the basket, he stopped short and swung around to his right to dart a chest pass to Pippen. This pass gave Ewing, who had been plodding slowly up the court, just enough time to get right under the basket in the middle of the floor, and as he filled the lane Pippen caught the pass.

Suddenly, Pip was in the air. Ewing's jump was reactionary, and a moment late, and Scottie extended his picturesque basketball body, viciously engulfing the Knicks' big man. Ewing raised his arms, and Pippen threw down the archetypal Tomahawk Jam, slicing his long arm between Ewing's. Pippen's legs came on either side of Ewing's body, and as he slammed the ball down, an off-balance and totally overwhelmed Ewing fell backwards, but Pippen was still coming, and the Bulls' MVP stepped right over Ewing, pushing him backwards further as he came down. Ewing swatted feebly at Pippen, like a frustrated younger brother does after his older brother has just given him three dead arms in a row.

That entire play, more than any other, symbolized the 1993-94 Chicago Bulls. A complete team effort with everyone contributing, and then Pippen, the forceful, final, punishing punctuation. That dunk made the possibility of losing Game 7 bearable…

******

…and yet, we went into Game 7 with confidence. There was a feeling among Bulls fans that all was well. The Ewing Dunk was one of the great statement plays in my memory, right there with Elway's Helecopter Leap, Torii Hunter's smashing of Jamie Burke, Michael's dunk on Ewing in the '91 playoffs, and, yes, Starks' baseline jam over MJ and Horace. At the very least, we knew that there was no longer any doubt in the basketball world: the Bulls were good enough to win a championship. And now that we were confident that everyone else now agreed with us, we felt good.

That was the feeling after Scottie's dunk. We had three wins in the series, we had one loss heavily influenced (but not decided) by a horrible foul call, and we had taken care of business at home and sent the series back to New York. If the Knicks were going to win, it was going to be due in large part to their home court.

On the day of the game, James Park was in full gear. It was a Sunday, late May, and we were nearing the end of our regular season. I was playing for Maday Auto Body that season, as I had the year before, and though nearly every team played on Sundays, most of us were more focused on Game 7 than on our own games. I remember sitting on a set of bleachers, huddled with a large group, kids and parents alike. Somebody had brought a portable television. We sat, quietly, and watched our Bulls lose Game 7. The last time we had seen them eliminated in the postseason, it was another Game 7, Detroit in 1990. The famed Scottie Pippen Migraine Game, the start of the Pippen-bashing.

Now here we were, four years later, where Pippen had become The Man. He had been the Bulls' rock all year, Game 3 aside. He had seen a call go horribly wrong against him, and rather than crumbling, he rose above, making sure that a referee's whistle would not define his season. He had brought us all with him — his teammates, his coaches, Bulls fans everywhere — and as the final ticks ticked off the Bulls' 1993-94 season, Bulls fans applauded. We sat there, watching the end of the game, and were at peace with the outcome.

The game ended, the Bulls lost… and we smiled, and returned to our fields. The situation was so different than the past three years, yet in many ways it felt the same. It had been a great season, and a great team. Still to this day, one of the best I've ever seen.

**PART XII:
SO I CREEP**

April 25, 2010, ReadJack.com
Age 28

SPORTS AND THE GOOD LIFE IN SUNNY CALIFORNIA

GEORGE: "Alright. Tell me the rules."

JERRY: "Okay. No calls the next day."

GEORGE: (processing) "So you have the sex... next day you don't have to call... that's pretty good." (impressed. more processing) "Go ahead."

JERRY: "You ready for the second one?"

GEORGE: "I gotta tell you: I'm very impressed with the first one."

— Seinfeld, "The Deal"

******

It's Day Six in Los Angeles, where everything is cooooool. Bedrooms have large windows that look upon mountains, sun, and sky. Houses are built on hills with little consideration for either. Waking up is effortless. Walking more relaxing. Bananas tastier. Illegal drugs legaler. And pedestrians always have the right of way.

Stunning! Another curious California contradiction distilled to hilarious perfection: a town where drivers treat the freeway like a cruel death course while also granting travelers on foot unwavering respect and safe passage.

I have been waking up between 6:30 and 9, partially because of the beautiful world announcing itself through the window, partially because of my Chicago clock that translates those times as 8:30

and 11. But it's 6:30 a.m. in Los Angeles, and the day is long and waiting.

My trip is long and waiting. We arrived by way of Phoenix, I-10 for many miles. My brother lives in a house with three of our friends, all four working together through either direct collaboration or simple motivation. This sounded like a terrific set-up for *them*, but I never wished to join, for two reasons.

One, I did not think L.A. was for me. Two, even if it was, I was not up for living in the Super House with Everybody. I still think I'm right…

…and yet as soon as I arrived, saw their three-story house on the hill, saw the mountains and sun, saw the sweet colors of trees and sky, saw the space to work, I had to say: "Damn. This is terrific."

So I changed my train ticket home from yesterday evening to this coming Thursday, and decided to treat this trip more as a trial than as a vacation. To think, I spent an April afternoon yesterday on the deck in what must have been 75-degree April weather, enjoying burgers and conversation and music and a book, shirt off, sunscreen on, the sun upon my eyelids. Train's twin sister Shannon is in town, and she was good enough to buy groceries and cook up a full-scale barbeque that in Chicago would only be possible a month from now. After lunch, Train, Schwartz, and I played basketball for 90 minutes, *outside*, at a park where two soccer games and two baseball games were in progress. Then I watched the sun drop out while reading a bit more…

Hot damn! It's guilty out here! I feel like I'll get home and the first thing out of Chicago's mouth will be, "So, how was it?" I'll stammer a bit, turning away. "I thought of you every day. I missed you terribly." She'll sense my evasion. "Did she… did you…"

"Baby, don't think those thoughts! I love *you*! You're my town! My home! My life!"

In a way, I have felt more tapped in to Chicago than ever, especially with the playoffs in Full Swing. The Bulls have a win in their pocket

PART XII: SO I CREEP

and a certified Death Match less than two hours away, while those masterful Blackhawks are locked into a grueling first round showdown with the Nashville Predators. What would my grandfather, who raised my dad and uncle on Original Six hockey, think of his beloved Hawks mixing it up with an 11-year-old franchise from Tennessee? Hard to say.

During deck time, Schwartz came out with News. He'd received a call from Tony the Packers Fan asking if he was watching the game, which he wasn't, so he flipped it on. And then: "Hawks were down 4-3 and short-handed on the penalty, but scored the game-tying goal with about 13 seconds left."

"Excellent! Who got it?"

"Kane."

"Overtime?"

"Bout to start."

I was not handed hockey as a boy. Chicago is a Bears town with a deep passion for baseball; MJ made the Bulls toast of the Stadium and the Hawks faded away...

They're back now, younger and faster and scarier than ever. All things even, the city will always embrace hockey over hoops, and the resurgence of the once mighty Black Hawks has brought our city's hockey fans to the fore. I took notice during last year's postseason run and five-game OT tangle with the Red Wings. Even if I hadn't, I'd have to be some kind of sports fascist to not rush inside to watch sudden death overtime in Game 5 of the Playoffs! My oh my! What kind of monster do you take me for?

What's great about a Game 5 is that even if you are unfamiliar with the series, the season, or even the sport, any serious Game 5 transports you to all previous Game 5's you've ever watched. The Charles Smith game, the Hubert Davis game, the Jannero Pargo game, Reggie

Miller's 25-point fourth quarter, Soriano's walk-off single in the 2001 World Series, the Pujols death blow home run in Houston, and even the epic do-or-die Nuggets-Sonics series capper in '94.

These Hawks remind me of those Supersonics. Young, world-class athletes talented beyond belief, talented possibly beyond their own imagination, lacking the experience and wisdom to match that talent with the intangibles needed to turn All-Stars into champions.

I was thinking about this as overtime began. We were watching on Ben's computer thanks to a bootleg television website, and the reception was splotchy. The puck was nearly impossible to follow, what with players "jumping" from one spot on the ice to the next like a video game with bad graphics. Every time there was a shot on goal, we needed confirmation from the announcers, players, and crowd as to the result.

"Man this team is good," Ben said in knowing amazement as Antti Niemi stopped a Nashville shot. "These guys are SO fast and skate SO well and are SO good at keeping the puck in the zone."

There was about two minutes left on the Predator power play. "Wait – where was the penalty?" I asked.

"That's from the end of the third."

"Holy hell! Manslaughter?"

"We just have to ride out these two minutes," Ben said, eyes in the screen. "Get back to full strength."

It was Marian Hossa in the box, a five-minute penalty for something called "boarding." I would see the replay after the game: it was a vicious hit, and Hossa was definitely Guilty. Minute and a half left in the power play, minute, 30 seconds – "Ride it out. Come on guys." – 15 seconds, 10, 5, and Hossa was back! "All right…" Ben clapped. "All right…" The Hawks were now at full strength and controlling the puck in the Nashville zone, and the screen was clicking along as they

PART XII: SO I CREEP

worked it around. Bolland behind the goal line, passing quickly to Sopel at mid-ice, Sopel slapping one toward the goal that bounces off a Nashville stick to Hossa by the crease GOOOOOOAAALLL! Goal Hossa! Hawks win! The United Center goes berserk!

Yes sir, all is well in hockey once more. It's bad enough for a team that nearly captured the conference's top seed to fizzle out in the first round, even worse when it's the old school Black Hawks dropping a series to an 11-year-old club from the South. I suppose we can blame Wayne Gretzky for the league's southern migration. He too was seduced away from a more honest life to spoil himself in the Los Angeles sun...

And why not? Life is good out here. We can now rest easy with the Hawks up three games to two and a Game 7 at home in Chicago should they need it. There are floorboards covering that ice right now, where Derrick and the gang will try to wrestle Game 4 away from the Cavs and send the series back to Cleveland deadlocked at two. LeBron will be Angry and in Rare Form – I was not joking two days ago when I predicted a minimum of 45 points and a possible quintuple-double. The Bulls have their work cut out, as do the home fans at the U.C., who must drown the great James and send him dejectedly away from our beautiful city...

Yes, yes, sweet home Chicago. I will be back in your loving arms on the first of the month. Los Angeles has not seduced me, but we're talking and laughing and drinking on the deck. Her fingers are in my hair and I am not objecting.

**PART XIII:
THE BLACKHAWKS ARE BACK**

May 16, 2010, ReadJack.com
Age 28

THOUGHTS AND MEMORIES ON A SPORT WITH NO TEETH

I never understood hockey. It was the one sport of America's Big Four that remained uncelebrated in the Silverstein household. My brother and I played Little League baseball. We played flag football at Orrington Elementary School and hoops as well. I recall my brother trying hockey once. He was flipped in the air by a fellow skater's errant stick, smacked hard against the ice, and promptly returned his skates.

My father and his brother were Black Hawks fans. Indeed, the first Hawks game I remember watching came one evening when Uncle Eddie was babysitting.

My father was 10 when the Hawks wrapped the title against Detroit. Eight years later he graduated high school. Ten years later he was a working man in Boston. Two years later he was married. Five years later he had two sons. Three years later he had a mortgage. 15 years later his sons were high school graduates. Eight years later they were working men in Chicago and Los Angeles. The 10-year-old boy is nearly 60 now, still waiting for that second Cup.

The Hawks remained competitive, of course. From 1959 to 1997, they missed the playoffs only once. Grade school became high school, college became career, girlfriends became marriage, condoms became children, summer remained the Cubs, Sundays remained the Bears, the Bulls became Da Bulls!, the Hawks slid away...

And that is, more or less, how a 10-year-old hockey fan goes on to birth a 10-year-old hockey novice.

My father's childhood love for the Hawks did rub off on me, if only indirectly. My Neil Funk imitation is a direct descendent of his imitation of Hawks radio man Lloyd Pettit, a flurry of words and hockey phrases that would pour from him, always sounding to my 8-year-old ears like: "To Hay to Hull to Nesterenko back to Hay abamanaramadonerater GOOOOOOAAALLLLLL!!!"

I had problems making it work with my hockey fandom. Whenever I *did* watch a game, I was always, somehow, looking away when any goal was scored. Friends would cheer, and my head would flip back to the television to see celebratory sticks in the air, the siren/light blaring/spinning. In fact, I did not see an NHL goal with mine eyes until March 4, 2000, a random ESPN game between the Penguins and Flames that I watched in Wilmette with Josh and Sven.

One of my favorite columns ever written was about hockey. Penned in 1998 or 1999, Rick Telander wrote "a letter to Bill Adee" (the *Sun-Times* sports editor at the time), asking Bill to run a photo of a recent fight between, I believe, Tie Domi and Bob Probert, promising to "come up with some words to go with it." It was a satiric column about fighting in hockey, and I was very excited to share it with my New Trier hockey friends.

"Isn't this a sharp comment on the state of the sport?" I asked them.

"No," they answered.

That was sophomore or junior year — I had started eating lunch with these hockey players, and was eager to learn the game. They were eager to teach, and I found it all quite thrilling during the playoffs, but I could never accept the idea that punching was part of the game.

I still can't. And yet the evolution of my fandom mixed with the renewal of the Blackhawks has brought me into a place of greater appreciation for the sport.

For starters, I understand now what I was missing every time my head was pointed in an unfortunate direction. Hot damn, hockey goals are exciting! I realized this during Game 3 of the Bruins-Flyers series, a game I watched at a Boston friend of mine's while we hashed out details of an upcoming comedy shoot.

Neil was dressed in a stitched Bruins jersey, focused intently on our work. He wrote the series, it's his baby, I am involved at his request, we are working out the blocking and discussing BRUINS ON A BREAKAWAY HERE WE GO SHOT ON GOAL! NOOO! MISSED IT! HE FREAKIN' MISSED IT! how we will rearrange the set to maximize our shooting space. A really successful meeting: our shoot the previous Sunday had been something of a disaster, and our shoot last Sunday was OH! OH! THERE HE GOES! AND... GOOOOOOAAALLLLLL!!! GOAL BRUINS! MAHK RECCHI! ATTABOY B'S! THERE WE GO! a certified success.

But there's no success quite like a hockey goal. It packs the importance of a touchdown with the thrill of a homer. Touchdowns are EXCITING, but we always know approximately when they will strike. When teams are consistently punting between their 30's, where the hell's the thrill?

And that is why hockey goals get the people crazy: the fan advances from The Calm to The Orgasm just like *that*. (snaps fingers.) Each goal is more important than any one homer, and certainly any one dunk. Imagine if basketball players scored once every twenty trips near the rim... that's pretty much what's happening here.

Which also explains why soccer fans go ballistic with such regularity. Those goals occur less frequently than even hockey goals; combine that tension/release with the all-in nature of European sports (they don't have a Big Four to dilute their interest), and is it any wonder why soccer fans are prone to the occasional riot?

But that is a question for another day. The World Cup will be upon us in one month, and we will have plenty of time then to dissect the world of futbol. I have to go now. Puck drops in an hour and a half.

May 24, 2010, ReadJack.com
Age 28

LIFE'S A BEACH WHEN YOUR TEAM IS UP

SUMMER!!!

Summer.

Summer in Chicago.

It was quarter to two in the afternoon, a Sunday afternoon, a Chicago summer Sunday afternoon, the first of 2010. I was on my way to the Damen Blue Line for a roundabout trip to Firkin and Pheasant, a bar on Diversey prone to mad Blackhawks celebrations. Not that one needed a train ride to find Hawks fans. They're everywhere now. Jerseys, hats, flags. Everywhere.

The Hawks have been on their way back for three years, but now they're Back, in full, no question. The big tip-off? When 24-year-old Wrigleyville girls replace their blue LEE 25 tees with red KANE 88 tees… when every block features at least three guys in neatly pressed, just-off-the-racks, stitched and certified Hawks jerseys… when Wicker Park bars are sponsoring playoff hockey pub crawls… That's when you know for sure.

And all it took was strong player development, solid free agent signings, a few good trades, a new head coach, the additions of back-to-back top 3 picks, and new management by way of death.

The celebratory mood on Sunday afternoon was one of anticipation. Anticipation for the summer, that glorious season that makes the shoveling, space saving, and high heating bills of December to March (October to April?) totally worth it.

PART XIII: THE BLACKHAWKS ARE BACK

And of course there was the anticipation for Game 4, the hope of a Hawks sweep, the possibility of the city's first Cup appearance since 1992, its first Cup hoisting since 1961.

Summer in Chicago. The first Sunday beach day. The Chicago Black Hawks hosting a close-out game. Nothing better.

I stepped on the train. The car was packed, everyone traveling to a TV for Game 4 or the beach for the sun. I stood next to the door as I always do; next to me were two guys around my age and a man in his late 50s who looked late 60s.

"How's everyone's day going?" I asked.

"Great!" responded one of the twenty somethings. This one was wearing red-framed Ray Bans and holding his bike. "Summer in Chicago, huh?"

"Love it."

"Glad it's here," said the older man, "as long as there's a breeze."

"Don't like the heat?" Red Ray Bans asked.

"I work in a bakery," said the older man. "100 degrees in there, all day. A breeze would be good."

The older man was wearing a navy blue t-shirt, blue jeans, and Timberlands. His head was free of any hair, large ridges in his forehead, deep eyes.

"Excited for the Hawks?" I asked.

"Oh yes. Yes yes."

"They might actually do it," I said.

"Oh, they're *going* to do it. Absolutely. These guys are…" He smiled. "Too bad we can't do it against the Habs. That'd be nice to get that revenge. Doesn't look like it will happen though.

"They broke our hearts in '71. Just terrible. Up 2-0 in the series, up 3-2! Lost back-to-back games to lose the series. And at home!

"I couldn't believe it. And we were up in Game 7. Up two to nothing in Game 7. At the Stadium. And Montreal won 3-2 to take it. Henri Richard scored two goals. He was old… geez, 35? 36? I couldn't believe it.

"Everyone was still there. Hull, Nesterenko, Mikita. They were old, but they were there. Tony Esposito…

"We had these two young defenders, just got 'em. One was this guy named Jerry Korab. King Kong Korab. His job was to stand in front of our net and keep the other guys away. He was good at that. (Laughs.)

"That team should have won three, four Cups. Just sad.

"These young guys, though… The kid Toews is the best center I've seen since Yzerman. Not sure if he's better. But he's there.

"This group will be together for a long time. All these young guys. Fast, tough. They're gonna win this year, and many years on. Four or five Cups. We'll see."

May 29, 2013
Age 31

COREY CRAWFORD WATCHES BRENT SEABROOK END THE RED WINGS

It was over.

It was all over.

With 1:47 remaining in regulation of Game 7, the Blackhawks's Niklas Hjalmarsson unleashed a fierce shot past Detroit goaltender Jimmy Howard, giving the Hawks a 2-1 lead and a glimpse of advancement. The crowd roared in ecstatic approval as the players celebrated.

But near mid-ice, a whistle had blown. A dual-roughing call on Brandon Saad and Detroit's Kyle Quincey.

No goal.

From the opposite end of the ice, Crawford watched in disbelief.

"Hammer made a great shot," Crawford said with a laugh about his teammate Hjalmarsson. "It was a great goal by him. And I guess everyone didn't hear the whistle. The crowd was so loud. It was obviously a little frustrating. We were mad at first. But we just settle down and forget about it and keep playing hard."

Crawford reflected on the crowd. On a night where the cheering faithful included Charles Tillman, Israel Idonije, and Scottie Pippen in a crisp, red Patrick Kane jersey, the real stars were the everyday fans. Their screams echoed off the cavernous walls of the United Center from the National Anthem to the last refrain of "Chelsea Dagger."

"It was probably the loudest game this year," Crawford said. "It was a lot of fun to play in. I can't think of a better feeling or a better game to be in than that one."

But if he was loose and cheerful now, it wasn't too much earlier that Crawford and his teammates sat in the locker room awaiting an overtime period. They were no longer angry, just focused. And when a Brent Seabrook wrister ended the overtime, the game, and the series, Crawford's sightline was as good as they come.

"I actually had a really good lane," he said about his view for the game-winner. "I believe it went off the stick there and went upstairs over [Howard's] glove." He laughed again as his teammates entered the locker room to change and give interviews. "It's a crazy feeling," he said. "I don't think it gets better than that at that point of the game."

"Excited for L.A.?" a reporter asked him as the team closed the locker room.

"Yeah," he said. He nodded goodbye to the reporter and leaned back with a smile. At long last, his day was done.

May 17, 2013
   Age 31

WHY WE NEED THE BLACKHAWKS DOGS

If you've ever owned a dog, you know the importance of finding the perfect name. It's the name you'll use for commands and praise, and the name your dog will make his or her own. Maybe you picked a family name, the name of a childhood dog, or even the name of a city you love.

For dog specialists Bridgid Nolan, 36, and Sue Naiden, 41, there was a different source of inspiration: the Chicago Blackhawks.

Nolan owns and operates Project Rescue Chicago at 1535 N. Dayton, an agency that rescues homeless and abused dogs and finds them homes for adoption, while also running Unleashed, a doggy daycare at the same location.

She partners with Naiden, whose organization Trio Animal Foundation (516 N. Ogden) raises money to pay for the dogs' medical bills. They are friends as well as business partners, and while they have each run their respective organizations since 2009, their shared love of dogs and the Blackhawks converged in late 2011 when they learned about a dog in New York in need of their help.

"There was a pit bull that was really beat up," said Naiden of Roscoe Village. "My dog Trio had just passed in the end of November. This dog looked just like her. He was going to be euthanized — he was hit by a car: broken leg, broken hip. It was the cathartic, 'Gotta go do it,' you know what I mean?"

"It was a once-in-a-lifetime thing," said Nolan, of Lincoln Square, about going to New York to adopt. Most of their dogs come from the Animal Welfare League at 6224 S. Wabash.

"We were trying to think of a strong name that represented something that we loved," said Naiden. "We thought of Hossa. It went from there. The next one was 'Shaw.' It was Shaw's first game, and he got in a fight and had a cut on his face, and we had a dog that was slit from ear to ear from its collar, so from that we got Shaw."

From there, the two friends began naming dogs after members of the Blackhawks based on the dogs' looks, injuries, and personalities. There was Toews ("super chill… a good leader of the group"), Kaner ("runs in circles and has all these little deak moves"), Stalberg ("super speedy and very handsome"), and most recently, Carcillo ("a scrappy, little meatball").

Most dogs were given one name — Toews, Kaner, Sharpie, Crawford — though Brandon Saad got a full name (since naming a dog "Saad" bums out potential adopters who mistake the dog's name for "Sad") as did Duncan Keith (since naming a dog either "Duncan" or "Keith" misses the point).

With the exception of Michel Handzus, who the Hawks acquired in April, the entire roster is complete. And while the Blackhawks dogs make up a small percentage of the dogs PRC has assisted with TAF, they are among the most popular.

But that's only in Chicago. As Naiden points out, some of their non-Chicago clients are none too happy about adopting a Blackhawks dog.

"I was like, 'People are going to love it and rally around it,'" said Naiden. "Well people from… Pittsburgh, they don't appreciate a dog named Hossa. People from Michigan and the Detroit area especially don't appreciate a dog named Hossa. So you have to be cautious."

Though they admit, they would be the same way. "'Sid Crosby?'" said Nolan with a laugh. "I don't want that."

Naiden and Nolan can regularly be seen wearing Blackhawks gear, and try to attend as many games as possible. But while many fans treat sports as escapism, these two women are escaping from the gruesome images of abused dogs. Dogs have arrived with ripped mouths or slit throats, while others have been delivered in garbage bags. Naiden calls attending Hawks games her "saving grace."

"It literally keeps me sane," she said. "There have been times we've gone where we literally haven't talked. You're straight-faced. The only time there's any excitement is if they get a goal. Even when they have the video at the beginning and the national anthem, I literally get goose bumps because everything bad goes away. It's the best escape possible.

"You think about it non-stop. I can barely sleep at night thinking about the things I've seen in the shelter. The abuse cases that come in are so horrific. So to be able to go to [Blackhawks games] and escape – I have a very humble living. I don't have much, but that's one thing I will spend my money on."

PART XIV:
FOR A WINNER

March 26, 2008, ReadJack.com
Age 26

GIVE MY BEST TO STEVE GOODMAN

My grandmother died today. She was 85.

There is a lot to think about when a close relative dies. Sometimes the death is horribly sad; other times it is a sad relief. Priorities get shuffled. You have to contact work and school, and figure a way to keep both moving forward while you schedule the funeral, update The Outer Circle, file paperwork.

There are the other thoughts that spring to mind, the ones that seem inappropriate, and maybe they are. But they are hard to help.

Nana was a Chicago sports fan. She knew the lyrics to every Big Ten fight song, excluding Penn State and including the University of Chicago. And of course she knew *Bear Down*, and sang it with us after touchdowns. Because she called my cell after touchdowns. And after bad first halves, big home runs, pre-game shows, post-game shows, and any time the Bulls were leading or trailing by 20.

And oh how she loved her Cubs! When the Cubs were winning, in '69 or 2003 or even a year ago, Nana was thrilled. But she did not hate the White Sox, not one bit, and when it was their turn, she was dedicated. Geoff Blum's homer in Game 3? I was sleeping, having made the mistake of leaving my TV room after the 13th to watch the game in bed. Not Nana. I spoke with her the next morning:

"You were up for the whole thing?"

"Of course," she said, dragging out the 'or' in 'course' the way she does at her house when you ask if you can have a cookie. "I wouldn't have missed it."

That was Nana: always loyal. My guess is that as she got older, the CHICAGO meant more to her than did the WHITE SOX. She was 85 years old, an old Cubs fan just like her late husband, and that's when it hit me: here is yet another Northsider who lived a lifetime and never saw a championship.

Trivial? Perhaps. When you are preparing to bury your grandmother, everything else is dimmed. But there it was, and less than a week before the Cubs began their 100-year anniversary season. 99 years without a title. That theme will surely be exhausted by June, but there is no denying that there is something very real here.

I am reminded of a quotation from Antoine de Saint Exupery's *The Little Prince*. The Fox is talking to the Little Prince about the latter's rose, which the Little Prince misses very much. And the Fox tells him: "It is the time you have wasted on your rose that makes your rose so important." That word, *wasted*, has always stood out to me. Is the time we spend on the ephemeral a waste? The time we spend on a sports team?

As any Cubs fan will tell you, what makes this club so important is the time we have all wasted on them. The trips to Wrigley, the afternoons watching WGN, the Old Styles and hot dogs, the El runs and cab rides. The Cubs are Ernie and Billy, Santo and Sandberg, Brickhouse and Harry and Santo again. But for me they are also Tapani and Walton and Glenallen Hill. I am sure that you have your own. These are the everyday Cubs, the ones only you and I will remember, the Monday through Fridays.

But then comes the weekend: a chance to celebrate! And then comes a wedding, a child birth, a birthday (we get those once a year, no exceptions). And though the majority of our time is spent on 355 normal days, it is the other ten that hold so many of our favorite memories, the other ten that give us cause to embrace our loved ones, to hug and kiss and clap and dance and sing, to tell stories, to make stories. We loved our Cubs in 1945, 1969, 2003, and we loved our Cubs in 1915, 1951, 1980. But oh! How we must have loved them in 1908!

PART XIV: FOR A WINNER

It is time for another celebration. It is long since time. And though I am a man who celebrates each day simply for coming, I am also a man who knows the value of those ten days, and now I think back on last October 28th when I got a call from a Boston friend of mine. It was Game 4 of the World Series, and my friend was at Nic and Dino's Trapoli Tap, a Boston bar in our city, and he asked me to join him and his Red Sox buddies for a celebration.

And when the final pitch struck the catcher's glove, my friend and his stood and cheered. They hugged and kissed and clapped and sang — *Oh I love that dirty water!* — and they told stories, and they made stories. This, a group that until three years prior was our spitting image in sadness.

And now two titles in four years, and as the champagne flowed and the high-fives flew, I sat there, watching, and thought: "Yes, yes, I think I could enjoy this."

PART XV:
WITH NEW EYES

Feb. 3, 2008, ReadJack.com
Age 26

ONE YEAR LATER: A LOOK BACK AT SUPER BOWL XLI

One year later, here's what I remember.

I remember...

...waking up and showering. Both were swift.

...putting on my Soldier Field game day best: Marcus Robinson jersey, blue warm up pants, blue Pumas with orange laces (bought specifically), and Bears hat, the baseball cap rather than the winter wool one. In addition to this dress, I remember being very excited as I put my homemade GROSSMAN handband on. I felt this was important for two reasons: support of our quarterback, a nationally-battered player, and as a rather fitting homage.

...going to the Wilmette Bike Shop on that very morning to pick up the t-shirt I'd ordered the day before, blue with bright orange text. On the front:

> SUPER BOWL
> CHAMPS

And on the back:

> AND DON'T
> IT FEEL
> GOOD?

...taking that t-shirt home and placing it at the bottom of my t-shirt drawer, telling no one. And when the great Urlacher gave his postgame interview in his SUPER BOWL XLI CHAMPIONS t-shirt, I would join him in my own. Awesome.

...not being able to stop barking "SU-PER BOWL! SU-PER BOWL!" as I marched around my parents's place, as well as not being able to stop actually barking, Otis Wilson-style.

...being certain that we would absolutely deconstruct the Colts. I saw it so plainly. Hester hasn't hit in the playoffs yet, and you know *he's* going to break one. And Thomas Jones? That first score he had against Seattle, when crossing the goal line literally transformed him from a tailback to a woofing, ball-shaking maniac—remember that? He's going to be that times *fifty*. Rex'll be steady, and the play-pass is gonna be outstanding with Jones and Benson, and defensively we'll be able to get at Manning with enough pressure to keep him off. We have the secondary to hang with their receivers, and wait'll you see Alex Brown. He's going to be a madman. I'm picking him for three and a half sacks, two forced fumbles, two batted balls, and the MVP. You'll see.

...talking to my friends in Miami, including my buddy Ric, who was wearing the shirt I'd made following the overtime win against Seattle: ROBBIE FREAKIN' GOULD!!! Another friend of mine was wearing a shirt that read I CAME IN FROM AMSTERDAM TO GO TO THIS GAME, and without knowing of their mutual acquaintance, my two clever shirt-wearing friends greeted each other with an excited Bears-fan shake.

...feeling a thrill from the thought that, right now, at this very moment, 90 million people are thinking about MY football team, my Chicago Bears.

...being unshockingly calm during Hester's touchdown runback. While the rest of the living room flock was on hopping foot, behaving wildly, cheering their lips off, I stayed seated, placing only my pumping fist in the air.

PART XV: WITH NEW EYES

...shaking my head as Nate Vasher dropped a sure interception. "Peyton's not gonna get many breaks like that."

...being, again, unshockingly calm as Chris Harris picked off Manning, giving the Bears the ball, a 7-0 lead already in their hands.

...the first big "aww nuts!" of the night, when Manning, nearly sacked, slipped away from Tank Johnson and heaved a ball deep to Reggie Wayne, who entered our TV screen with no blue shirts to be found. The Bears' young safeties had botched the coverage. Wayne strolled in untouched. A TD return, an interception, some near picks and near sacks...everything wiped out by one blown coverage. But then, a missed point after. Maybe? Maybe?

...the beginning of an ugly turnover night: the Bears fumbling the kickoff to the Colts, followed by Manning fumbling the ball right back.

...my first true "get up and holler" of the night, TJ heading over left tackle at our own 43, cutting back to the right, and breaking through for a 52-yard scamper setting up a first and goal. Brick on first down, brick on second, sweating on third as Rex dropped back to throw, sweating more as his pass zoomed behind Moose, but then: bam! Moose with the pluck! 14-6 Bears, as the rain began to fall.

...hoping for a field goal and a 17-6 lead, knowing that the biggest deficit a winning team had ever turned was ten points.

...Bob Sanders laying serious stick on Cedric Benson, the second-year tailback coughing up the football like a kid with a cold coughing up phlegm. And then one drive later, Benson twisting his knee on a carry, limping away, out for the game, a meager end to his second pro season.

...Indy's ten straight points in the second quarter, a field goal from Vinatieri and a TD from Dom Rhodes. 16-14 Colts in the slushiest Super Bowl ever.

…Peanut Tillman playing like a man possessed, pulling a triple play on the Colts' Bryan Fletcher: holding him upright on the wrap-up, punching the ball free, recovering the fumble. Alright! Here we go! You wanna win a Super Bowl? You need statement plays from guys who are willing victory. Jones' 52-yard run was one; Peanut's strip and scoop was another. That is the way to do it.

…shaking my head as Rex gave the ball right back on the very next play. Aww nuts.

…watching Vinatieri miss a field goal at the end of the half, my team running to the locker room, their jerseys damp with rain, trailing by two. After a racing start, what?

…not eating during halftime, while the rest of our party stocked up on dinner.

…the Colts grinding us out in the third quarter, bagging another field goal. 19-14 Colts. *No one is running away with this one,* I thought, which meant that a loss would be due to a chip job, not a beat down.

…gripping my GROSSMAN headband at a Rex sack and another Rex fumble, the rain slamming down. Were we really going to lose the first Super Bowl played in Bears weather, and to a puff-ball indoor club like the Colts? Were those carpet-treading weenies really going to beat us by grinding out the clock and making big hit upon big hit? I want to vomit.

…watching another Colts field goal. 22-14 now, down by eight. Chip, chip, chip, closer and closer to that death-count of 10.

…watching the Bears begin their next drive inside Colts' territory (courtesy of a roughness call on Indy), and mustering only a Robbie Gould field goal. Still in it at 22-17, but our points were all on three somewhat fluky plays: Hester's TD return, Jones' 52-yard run, and the roughing penalty. Into the fourth quarter, clutching tightly to life…

PART XV: WITH NEW EYES

...the final choke-out from the Colts, or perhaps from Rex, or perhaps from that unholy bastard Ron Turner. Down five, a blanket of rain, no one able to handle the ball, a leader at tailback, and a first and 10 after a 22-yard pass. And what do we do? Go right back to the air, Rex to Moose, and an easy pick by Kelvin Hayden. And he's running, and I'm watching, squatted down in front of the couch, and he's still running, *come on, someone get him,* and down the sideline and into the endzone, and that is that. 29-17 Colts, up by 12, my head in my knees as I remain on the floor, and I hold ten fingers above my head as the booth announces to the viewing public that "no team has ever erased a deficit of more than ten points and won." Over 11 minutes remaining, and my team seems cooked.

...keeping the faith. What else would I do? "Come on guys! Be the first! Make history!" And now I believe, and for a moment I think it will happen, and then Rex throws another pick. Back to the floor.

...trading possessions, watching the clock die. 29-17, 29-17. That's how we're going out.

...the clock running dead. The realization that our story was complete, and it was of a team that no one outside of Chicago much feared or respected. In the end, as far as they were concerned, they were proven right. The Bears, anyhow, had done nothing to disprove them.

...looking at the ill-fated t-shirt, deep in my drawer, never to be unveiled.

...the feeling of loss. True loss.

...dealing with the L by gathering my thoughts, composing myself, and writing a column. Feeling better about everything. Feeling at peace. And feeling stone-certain that the Bears would be back in a year. We would be champions; the shirt would one day be worn, even a year late...

And now, one year later, I'm watching pregame coverage for Super Bowl XLII, New England set to face the NFC champion Giants, while my team sits at home, a sad 7-9, with nearly as much to do with this game as me.

Aww nuts.

Sep. 24, 2006, ReadJack.com
Age 24

NOSTALGIA COMES EARLY: A SALUTE TO THE 2005 WHITE SOX

We were sitting in Tommy Nevin's Pub in Evanston the other day, and after about an hour of barely hearing the conversation over the juke box and barely listening to the juke box, a song came on that grabbed us. Grabbed Luke in particular. Luke is a raging White Sox fan. The song was *Don't Stop Believing* by Journey. His face sagged.

"You know what this is?" I asked him. He did not respond, and so I proceeded. "Nostalgia."

It should be noted that while I am a Cubs fan, I have never been a Sox-basher. Three of my best friends growing up — Luke included — were mondo, legit Sox fans, and so I support the Sox in that I support the happiness of my friends. Furthermore, as a sports fan, I've learned to appreciate, and at times mildly support, any team in football, basketball, or baseball that I deem plays the game The Right Way. The team can be one that grabs me on a strategic level or an attitude level. For me, the 2005 White Sox satisfied both categories.

PART XV: WITH NEW EYES

A fundamentally sound team, the '05 Sox excelled in classic Chicago sports fashion: scrappy, get-it-done offense mixed with top-notch defense. In this case, defense includes pitching, where the Sox were the best in the Bigs without any perennial All-Stars on the rotation. White Sox pitchers finished first in the AL in ERA (3.61), wins (obviously), saves (54), complete games (9), and innings pitched (1475.7), while finishing in the top six in four more categories.

It is true, yes, that the Sox did not have a single .300 hitter on their roster (not including Joe Borchard and his .417 average off of 12 ABs). Despite that, they were a very effective, productive bunch. They excelled at small ball, (second in the AL in hit batsmen and third in stolen bases), but they also had a good deal of power (fourth in the AL in home runs, seventh in Slug).

But oh, how unsatisfying numbers can be when set against the experience, which is exactly what the 2005 White Sox were: an experience. Boy, were they ever. Dominant through and through, yet rarely overwhelming. That was them. From the first pitch thrown by Mark Buehrle to the final one from Bobby Jenks, the White Sox frustrated opponents by never really seeming *all that good*, even though, of course, they were. From April to September, the Sox were the kings of baseball, revered by writers and adored by fans, just as it should be.

Then came the near-collapse, as Cleveland erased a double-digit lead in games to pull to within a game and a half in the division. And then came the Sox, righting the ship, saving the dream and their fans' sanity. And then came the first show of extended dominance in an obvious manner, as they muscled the Red Sox in Game 1 en-route to a sweep before smothering the Angels in five on the strength of four consecutive complete games from their rotation.

Then came the World Series, where the Moments piled up. From Ozzie's classic pantomime request for the hefty Jenks to shut the door in Game 1, to Paulie's granny and Pods' walk-off in Game 2, to Geoff Blum's Game 3 pinch-hit homer in the wee hours of the morn, and then back to the park and Houston's weary fans for Game 4, inning upon inning, scoreless, waiting…

It was, throughout, a wonderful season, one that Sox fans will carry with them every day for the rest of their lives. The 2005 Chicago White Sox were an experience, one that will never be replicated, and now as the curtain to this 2006 season falls unwittingly upon Ozzie's team, Sox fans are left wondering why it had to end *this way*. To your credit, you Sox fans have been more grateful than bitter, more understanding than angry. You wanted to see your team back in the postseason, to see them defend their championship. Any fan would.

In a way though, that's what has happened. Let's just call the past month the qualifying round, with the Sox being knocked out by Minnesota, Detroit, and Oakland, three of the teams that will "advance" to the final tournament. No shame in that. Sox fans, like all fans, simply wanted a chance to see what their team was "made of." Well, this past month was it.

And now we say goodbye, and focus in on the Bears and Bulls and maybe even the Blackhawks, and in twenty years we will go to the local Jewel to see Geoff Blum and Willie Harris and Pablo Ozuna and Neal Cotts signing autographs, and we will stand and cheer and beat our hands together in welcoming Ozzie and Paulie and Jermaine and A.J. and Crede and Rowand and Buehrle and Contreras and the rest to World Wide Cellular Field, and we will look down at our children and tell them about *this team*. And maybe the Sox did indeed win another title or two in '08 or '09 or 2010, and maybe they didn't. Maybe they simply ended up being the team that won the World Series once and us forever.

If only all fans could be so lucky.

April 26, 2010, ReadJack.com
  Age 28

SHOT THROUGH THE HEART

ED. NOTE: *Game 4 of the Cavaliers-Bulls series left Mr. Silverstein confused and agitated. He contacted us last night through an "emotional interpreter" who told us that the writer was unable to produce or file any copy. After much coaxing and some early-morning deal-making, Mr. Silverstein released the following column.*

I am out of new ways to describe LeBron James. Yesterday's half-court jumper was a basketball act I'd never considered realistic. I have never been more demoralized or impressed by a third quarter jump shot. Just an absolute nightmare of an amazing J.

I repeated these statements endlessly from the fourth quarter onward. Spoke with dozens of fellow basketball enthusiasts. Almost everyone was in agreement: this man is playing a different game than the rest of the league.

Combined with his buzzer-beating deuce to end the half, *this* shot seemed to power James like a video game. It was the Star to his Mario, the "He's on Fire!" to his NBA Jam Scottie Pippen… once that shot fell, the only thing missing from James's easy-does-it fourth quarter was a pulsing glow and a Power Meter on the side of the screen with the red bar all the way up and the words DO NOT ATTEMPT TO STOP flashing and blinking in bright neon.

Seriously: that was one helluvan encore performance. It was like a baseball curtain call, only instead of waving his hat to the crowd from the dugout's top step, Mutant Captain James was given a few more AB's with batting practice pitches just so he could smoke a few more home runs onto Waveland. Yes. And it counts.

To recap: he entered with 9:25 remaining in the game after the Bulls had made a cute go of it, cutting the lead from 23 to 19. Rebound LeBron. Assist LeBron. Three more treys (one straight-on banker), a couple more rebounds. Back to the bench for good at 4:58. 113-88 Cavs. Thanks for playing.

At the start of the series, I was excited to watch my Bulls battle James and the Cavs. Now I am ready for peace. My time watching LeBron since his rookie year has been relatively low – relative, that is, to the frequency of his amazing feats. Every All-Star game, a featured Sunday tip here or there, and I try to catch as many showdowns with Kobe, Wade, or Melo, etc.

Before this week, the most extended stretch of LeBron I ever watched was back in August of 2008 during the eight Olympic games. James was remarkable: other than being uncharacteristically abysmal from the line (11 of 24), he was second on Team USA in scoring and assists, third in boards, and tops in blocks and steals.

The rest is history, yes? Those Olympics kicked off these mind-numbing soon-to-be back-to-back MVP seasons, and now here we are four games into a hypothetically seven game series and I am spent.

I now understand what opposing fans went through with Jordan. I get it now. I get why Steve Smith referred to a week of guarding Jordan as "hell," why fans of the Knicks, Pacers, Heat, and Jazz did not enjoy The Jordan Years.

I understand why friends from other cities did not enjoy speaking with me from April to June, and why Ewing, Barkley, and Malone always looked just a touch deflated when Jordan was announced and the game was soon to start.

I understand why opposing fans just wanted Jordan to go away. For good. Forever. It's easy to be a Bulls fan and argue: "But I am also enjoying this OBJECTIVELY as a Basketball Fan, and you should too."

Which is kind of like telling a friend who has not been laid in years to objectively enjoy the beauty, friendship, and sexual mastery of your own girlfriend.

PART XV: WITH NEW EYES

I understand it all, and James has not even won a ring, let alone six. Please forgive me for any arrogance I may have displayed between 1992 and 1998. I was young and it was wrong.

The Cavs are now the Bulls, and the Bulls are now the Cavs, and that's the way it is. Derrick Rose is great fun, and Great, and I will have plenty to write about him in the coming years. Joakim Noah can rebound with the best of 'em, and has wrangled together some nifty low-post moves. He does not use Rodman's ethereal outlet pass to start the break. Heck no! He brings it up himself, with Rose and Kirk and Deng on his wings, crazy eyes straight ahead as he dribbles.

And help is coming... help is coming...

So what now? Had Game 4 been close, LeBron's triple-dub may have been 50-20-15 instead of the pedestrian 37-12-11 he posted. He is better than Jordan, no question, but not yet Greater. As his teammate and Aristotle-admirer Shaquille O'Neal can remind him, "We are what we repeatedly do." Upcoming series against Boston, Orlando, and the Lakers will pose more challenges than this warm-up act with our beloved Bulls. James will need to embrace his total greatness to capture Ring #1...

And yet no roster on Earth possesses the player who can defend him, especially not when Jamison is at full All-Star status and those shooters are shooting with fearless grace and efficiency.

Game 5 will be here tomorrow, whether we like it or not. These were the games when Jordan sniffed death. The Bulls impaled opponents, and His Airness made it known who held the sword...

I have written more this morning than I could have imagined, and will now stop. The sun is shining in Los Angeles, and thank goodness, because LeBron is playing basketball tomorrow and I need to rest. God save us.

Oct. 15, 2013, Cubs Den
    Age 31

FINAL THOUGHTS ON FAN INTERFERENCE AND THE 2003 CUBS

1.

I'm writing this on the 10-year-anniversary of Game 7, lest we forget there was a Game 7.

Most of the focus, (naturally, I suppose), ends up on Game 6.

You know the one. The one with the nickname. It's not called the Looney Game. But damn, it could have been.

Just think: the wind blows a bit more toward the plate, and the baseball hits a Cubs fan named Pat Looney instead of you know who. The Cubs still lose Game 6. They still lose Game 7. Looney goes into hiding. And we spend ten years re-hashing "The Looney Game."

I mean, isn't that just perfect? Doesn't that sum it up? What better name for Game 6 than "Looney"?

But it was not to be. Just as fate was against the Cubs that vicious October night, it was also against that poor sap Steve Bartman. Steve got no help that day from the wind, the fans, the Marlins, the Cubs, and certainly not from Moises Alou, whose animated reaction gave an unlucky play the stink of impending doom.

And like that, "Bartman" was born. The Bartman Game. The Bartman Ball. The Bartman Seat. Billy Goat... Miracle Mets... Leon Durham... Brant Brown...

Steve Bartman.

2.

That's the treatment this man received, an eternal judgment cast upon him for a crime that he didn't so much "commit" as had foisted upon him. Because really, what does it all have to do with him?

I'll ask you again: what does it all have to do with HIM?

Many fans reached for that ball. Many fans hoped to touch history. But history touched *him*. History floated down to *him*. History grazed *his* hands.

Grazing was enough. The ball bounced off his hands as surely as anonymity slipped through his fingers. It was a sequence befitting a Cubs fan: hoping for a souvenir and a trip to the World Series, Steve got neither. The ball that changed his life forever was never even in his possession.

Ain't that just how it goes when you're a Cubs fan? Hey hey, holy mackerel, no doubt about it.

3.

Here's why Steve is alone in this mess: there's no one else to lump with him. That's because no one else allowed themselves to be lumped.

Think about what happens when a beggar boards a train and starts requesting charity from the other passengers. No one wants to talk to him because no one wants to be responsible for him. No one makes eye contact. No one listens. No one sits near him.

That was Steve. As the footage so clearly depicts, not even his friends want to talk to him. He seems isolated. No one protects him. No one shelters him. His "I am Spartacus" moment never comes.

No one wants to be Steve Bartman.

4.

Here's another reason Steve is alone: there is no singular Cubs culprit to blame for the breakdown.

The various suspects – Mark Prior, Alex Gonzalez, Kyle Farnsworth, Dusty Baker, Moises Alou, and even Kerry Wood – have each received some degree of forgiveness, if for no other reason than that there is little consensus among Cubs fans as to who among them was most responsible.

Most say it was the Gonzalez error, though some people think even a clean play would have only yielded one out. Dusty takes a lot of heat, while Farnsworth takes too little.

Prior must be responsible somehow – he was pitching when "The Incident," as he calls it, occurred – while Wood of course suffered an equally catastrophic inning the next night, when he allowed three runs in the 5th that gave Florida a lead they never lost.

And of course some people place the bulk of the inning's culpability on Alou for his unforgettable freakout.

But for those who think that the most important factor in Game 6 happened off the field of play, Steve is the only fan to look at. He is the only one to blame. He was the only one to reach the ball. He stands alone.

Or sits alone, if you prefer.

5.

The bitch of it is, fan interference DID cost the Cubs their lead. I can prove it. Watch.

Cubs fans who don't hold the fan interference responsible tend to point to the Gonzalez error, a ball that looked like an easy inning-ending double play.

"If Gonzo fields that ball cleanly," the thinking goes, "the Cubs get one out for sure, and perhaps two."

But Gonzalez made the error. It wasn't an anomaly. It can't be changed. It was a fact. It happened.

And from watching the replay, it seems just as probable that Alou would have made the catch. Even Prior & Paul Bako – the game's starting battery – thought he had it. This is important, because the fan interference play only matters if you assume that Alou would have caught the Castillo ball.

So instead of wistfully revising history with the Gonzo play, or anything else that happened on the field, let's isolate the fan interference. Let's pretend that the fans in aisle 4, row 8 shouted to each other to let Alou make the play. Let's pretend he did.

Now, obviously, if you can hypothetically change one event you can hypothetically change them all. I got into a Twitter debate on Sunday with several Cubs fans that dealt with that very issue. So for the sake of simplicity, let's pretend that the rest of the inning was destined to play out the same way. Here's a look then at our alternate version of events, AKA The Marty McFly Version of the 8th Inning of Game 6 of the 2003 NLCS.

LUIS CASTILLO
ACTUAL: Walks on a wild pitch, Pierre takes 3rd
MCFLY: Flies out to left field, second out of the inning, Pierre stays at 2nd

IVAN RODRIGUEZ
ACTUAL: Singles to score Pierre, 3-1 Cubs, 1 out, runners at 1st & 3rd
McFLY: Singles to score Pierre, 3-1 Cubs, 2 outs, runner at 1st

MIGUEL CABRERA
ACTUAL: Safe on Gonzalez error, 3-1 Cubs, 1 out, bases loaded
McFLY: Safe on Gonzalez error, 3-1 Cubs, 2 outs, runners at 1st & 2nd

DERREK LEE
>ACTUAL: Doubles to score two, game tied 3-3, 1 out, runners at 2nd & 3rd
>McFLY: Doubles to score Rodriguez, 3-2 Cubs, 2 outs, runners at 2nd & 3rd

This is where Dusty Baker brought in Kyle Farnsworth. However, I emailed Paul Bako to ask him about it, and he said that with the Cubs still leading 3-2 in the Marty McFly world, Dusty would have probably left Prior in.

Regardless, either pitcher would have intentionally walked Mike Lowell to set up the force. So forget the pitching change and just look at the next two batters:

MIKE LOWELL
>ACTUAL: Walks intentionally, game tied 3-3, 1 out, bases loaded
>McFLY: Walks intentionally, 3-2 Cubs, 2 outs, bases loaded

JEFF CONINE
>ACTUAL: Sacrifice fly to right, Castillo scores, 4-3 Marlins, 2 outs, 2nd & 3rd
>McFLY: Fly ball out to right, END OF INNING, MIDDLE OF 8TH, 3-2 Cubs

6.

In chess, it doesn't matter how good your attack is if your opponent is able to implement his attack first. You'll always be a move behind, stuck reacting instead of dictating.

Baseball is similar because of the mathematical certainty of outs vs. runs. That's why the Cubs were "5 outs away" from the World Series.

But unlike in football, basketball, hockey, or soccer, there is no "running out the clock" in baseball. Protecting a lead means action. You have to record outs. *You* have to do it.

PART XV: WITH NEW EYES

That's why the most we can say conclusively about the fan interference is its effect on the 8th inning. Nothing else is certain. Game 6 was Florida's fourth come-from-behind win in the 2003 playoffs; Game 7 was their fifth. Would a motivated Marlins team trailing 3-2 in the top of the 9th have scored to tie the game? Would they have won in extras?

Meanwhile, let's say the Cubs did manage to eliminate the Marlins – would they beat the Yankees? That's the real question. Because as much as we talk about just wanting to win the pennant, the real goal is to win a championship. That's the source of the misery of Cubs fans.

That's why a fan interference became the most famous play in franchise history.

7.

5 outs away. 5 outs. 5.

Can we soak in that for a moment?

Not how close they were, but how far.

Because what matters is winning a ring. And by that measure, the Cubs weren't 5 outs away. They were 113 outs away. 5 to win Game 6, and 108 to win the World Series.

When you look at it that way, it seems beyond just silly or shortsighted to blame a fan for the Cubs' demise. It seems stupid.

It IS stupid.

Blaming a fan is stupid.

Think about how much can happen in 113 outs. Or hell, even one out. Look at the Texas Rangers in the World Series two years ago. In Game 6, they were one STRIKE away from winning. This happened twice: in the 9th and the 10th. Both times the Cardinals tied the game.

The Cardinals won it in the 11th. Then they won Game 7. The Rangers got nothing. Their drought – 53 seasons and counting – goes on.

Ask Rangers fans if just making the World Series was good enough.

Ask Rangers fans if "one out away" was close enough.

8.

So no, fan interference did not cost the Cubs a championship.

And no, the fan who happened to touch the ball is no more or less responsible than the fans who would have touched it if they could have.

But "The Incident" was weird. That's for sure.

This was baseball S&M – Strange & Memorable. It wasn't "the curse," but it felt like one. It didn't cause eight runs, but it preceded them.

It's easier to blame a fan than to accept the reality that you root for an un-cursed franchise that has played crappy baseball for over a century. Or the reality that the Marlins were the better team.

Wait – the Marlins? Yes, the Marlins. The team with more wins. The team with a starting pitcher who led his teams to championships in 2003 and 2007. The team with the Hall of Fame catcher, the future MVP rightfielder, and a 1st baseman who won a batting title two years later.

Yeah, those guys. They were the better team. We just didn't know it yet.

9.

There's one other entity that deserves its share of responsibility for 2003. And that's the Cubs, of course.

Or, to be more precise, the 1909-2002 Cubs.

That's a lot of failed dreams right there. A lot of trophy-less seasons. A lot of pressure building on an otherwise innocuous foul ball.

It was the fans who gave those 94 seasons of trophy-less baseball their destructive power. We did it. The downtrodden, sad-sack, never-say-die Cubs fans.

Why? Because we're sports fan survivors strengthened by that unfathomable futility. It's what makes Cubs fans special. It's why we like to think of ourselves as a different breed.

I'm not talking about those dopey Wrigley revelers, mind you – the people out for a drink and a picnic. I mean the *true* Cubs fans. The kind of fans who never lose hope. The kind of fans who just want to cheer their team despite the chaos around them. The kind of fans who wear Cubs hats. The kind of fans so locked in that they bring headphones.

The kind of fans who come to the ballpark hoping that if nothing else, maybe, just maybe, they can catch a foul ball.

June 27, 2021, Windy City Gridiron
    Age 39

WCG 30-DAY CHALLENGE: MY MOST PAINFUL BEARS MEMORY – SUPER BOWL XLI

Kelvin Hayden scampered down the sideline and my nightmares came true.

All around me, my friends and family were groaning and pleading and crying for his capture at the hands of desperate Bears defenders. But I was silent. On my knees, silent. Eyes affixed, silent. We knew these runbacks. Since the team hired Lovie Smith two season prior, we'd returned 10 interceptions and three fumbles for touchdowns. You always look for the linemen. Once your man is passing the linemen and the receivers and running backs are blocked, you've got six.

At the 20, I could tell that Muhsin Muhammad — the intended receiver on the play — was not going to catch Hayden. The rest of the Bears in view of Hayden were linemen. He dove and rolled into the endzone. I put 10 fingers in the air.

A few hours earlier, it was a fist. Devin Hester had returned the opening kickoff of Super Bowl XLI for a touchdown, and while my friends and family around me stood and screamed and cheered and Arsenio'd, I stayed quiet. Raised my fist in the air. Nodded. Said, "Okay, let's get started." I'd predicted Devin would get one. I felt no surprise nor now great thrill when he did. My expectation was a dogfight, ruled by our greatness, yielding victory. Had Alex Brown as my game MVP. Hester was the appetizer. This was to be the greatest night of my sports fan life.

For a while, it was. We led 7-0 on the Hester touchdown and 14-6 at the end of the 1st quarter. We didn't fall behind until late in the 2nd quarter and went to the locker room down 16-14. I spent halftime pacing up and down the building's stairwell, wearing a white headband on which I'd written "GROSSMAN" in Sharpie. Missed Prince's performance. We trailed by five at the end of the 3rd. Not great, but still right there.

The Hayden return was where my heart stopped. As a Super Bowl historian, I was all too aware of the foreboding stat of the day: the greatest deficit overcome in a Super Bowl was ten points. As Hayden ran back the pick, I just kept hoping we would tackle him. Up five, we could hold the Colts to a field goal and tie the game with a touchdown and two-point conversion.

PART XV: WITH NEW EYES

A touchdown, though, meant a 12-point lead midway through the fourth. *If he scores,* my brain kept running, *we're in a two-possession game and a battle with the gods.*

Sure enough, the first words out of Jim Nantz's mouth after the extra point: "No team in Super Bowl history has ever come back from a margin larger than 10 points down." The game wasn't over — we had more than 11 minutes remaining — but I felt crushed in a way I never had before as a fan. Eleven minutes and change of game time later, that feeling was all I had left.

The question for today's 30-day challenge is as simple as it is devastating: Write about your most painful Bears memory. Considering I was four years old in January of 1986, Super Bowl XLI was *MY* Super Bowl. That was the game that was going to define me as a Bears fan.

Unfortunately, it did. There is no other choice for most painful Bears memory. Every now and again during the season, a fan will drop a poll asking for the most painful recent moment in Bears history, and the NFC championship scores pretty high. I even see ones where the Double Doink finishes first. To each their own, I guess, but there is nothing like the Super Bowl. If you're a generation ahead of me, you're probably a tad too young to have felt the impact of the 1956 NFL championship game, AKA Sneakers Game: Frugality's Revenge.

In fact, on the all-time Bears heartbreak list, Super Bowl XLI ranks high no matter how you cut it, and will take its place with 1956, 1942, 1934 (AKA Sneakers Game: A New Hope) — and, if you are literally George Halas.

So no, not only is this not a question for me from a Bears fan perspective, but it's not a question for me from a Chicago sports fan perspective. Super Bowl XLI is my most painful sports memory, period. Thinking about it now feels like if the Bulls never got past the Pistons. That's the best comparison.

My other most painful moments are the 2003 and 2008 Cubs. I needed 2016 to wipe those off the books. But at least those are series, and at least neither was in the World Series. What if the Cubs had lost the 2016 World Series the way Cleveland did — would that be worse than Super Bowl XLI? I ask myself that all the time. I think the answer is no. First of all, I still felt like the 2016 Cubs were a year ahead of schedule, which made a possible loss bearable — and boy, down 3-1, I thought that was coming. The 2006 Bears were ripe.

Second, the unique spotlight of the Super Bowl dominates anything else. Game 7 of the 2016 World Series is one of the greatest sporting events I've ever seen, while Super Bowl XLI is a relatively run-of-the-mill Super Bowl. Here are their ratings and total viewerships:

- Game 7: 21.8 rating, 75 million total viewers
- XLI: 42.6 rating, 140 million total viewers

The Super Bowl is singular: There is no other experience in American sports akin to knowing that 140 million other people watched your favorite team endure their greatest professional heartbreak.

Third, in Chicago, the Super Bowl was all hands on deck, because the Bears belong to all of us. If we lost Game 7 of the 2016 World Series, "we" would just be half of us. The other half won their title 11 years prior. My Sox fan friends were great to me after we won, a result perhaps of my having been great to them in 2005. Yet there is still that divide.

When the '85 Bears won, we all won.

When the '06 Bears lost, we did that together too. The pain hit harder.

And we weren't even on the team.

PART XV: WITH NEW EYES

In the years since Super Bowl XLI, I've had the chance to get to know a number of players from that fabulous team. To a man, they all talk about the anguish of losing that Super Bowl. Some are more upbeat than others, some more downtrodden, but for each of them, the game stands as a point of no return.

Thomas Jones watched every Super Bowl of his life until XLI and hasn't watched one since, calling it a pain "that will never leave." Olin Kreutz acknowledges that while football has given him and his family everything, the Super Bowl was "the worst game in the world to lose." Charles Tillman said that while he didn't have any regrets because he gave it everything he had, losing the Super Bowl left him "sick to my stomach."

"I cried after the game," Tillman told me in 2016. "I sat in the locker room and I cried. I was disappointed in the outcome. It wasn't what I envisioned."

These guys and the rest of that team are champions in my book, and I know that they know the greatness that they accomplished together. But they don't have that final piece. Instead, they have a hollow space that will last forever.

"It does something to you emotionally — it's like a girlfriend you never really got over," TJ shared with me in 2016. The NFC championship game was "a kid's dream," he said. "And then two weeks later, the worst feeling of your football career. A two-week swing. The best feeling ever in your football career to the worst."

After that game, I had to write a column just to temporarily and marginally shake free of the weight of that loss. Now, a decade and a half later, I keep those guys in mind when I think about XLI. No matter how bad it was for us, we will never understand how bad it was for them. That's what I remind myself.

And then I am shattered by the flip side. If we can't understand what they feel, then what they feel must be unbearable. Because boy oh boy, it was for us.

June 23, 2023, Bulls Confidential
    Age 41

BULLS FANS NEED NEW NOSTALGIA

You deserve more than this old fan's nostalgia.

Unfortunately for you, nostalgia season is never over. The high season? Sure, the high season ends. It starts April 24, picks up at Memorial Day weekend and runs to June 20. The peak of high season is June 14, the day of the '92 comeback and The Last Shot. You weren't around for those. Not even that second one.

Think of it: You've been a Bulls fan for two decades and you weren't even around for that second one.

So the high season is over. But as we've learned, 90s Bulls nostalgia is always in season. An MJ anniversary? In season. A fake, new day on Feb. 3, 2023, that folks called "2-3, 23" and hence "Michael Jordan Day"? What the hell: in season too. 90s Bulls nostalgia is like the Three Dobermans: relentless.

But you don't want to hear about that anymore. I wouldn't either if I were you. In 2023, the 90s Bulls are a VR headset. The actual Bulls are what happens when you take off the goggles. The 90s Bulls were the party of a lifetime. The actual Bulls are a quarter-century hangover. For five magical years, from June 12, 1991 to June 14, 1998, Bulls fans were treated with six nights where we saw the breadth of our domain and wept, for there were no more teams to conquer.

Until next season, that is.

But one day, next season didn't come. In a mere 10 days during the first month of 1999, the Bulls punctured their ball and watched the air go rushing out — Jerry Krause, the man walking the plank while thinking it a bridge, Jerry Reinsdorf, the owner of the boat who could always jump to his other boat. For the next six years, though we walked the desert as the stars of our greatest glory sparkled in other skies, our bellies were full with the championships of days only recently gone by.

The franchise returned to the playoffs in 2005, made it again in 2006, reached the second round in 2007, had a deeply frustrating 2008 season that brought us a surprising lottery win and the gift of gifts: Chicago's own Derrick Rose.

By this time, if you were a Bulls fan who was born the year of our first rebuild, you were turning eight. When I was eight, the 1990 Eastern Conference Finals became my first sports heartbreak. If you're old enough for sports heartbreak, you're old enough to know why sports matter.

So I imagine that you, an eight-year-old Bulls fan in the summer of 2008, knew that it was a pretty big deal to have the #1 overall pick. Derrick was better than advertised. Dragged us to the playoffs as a rookie. Won Rookie of the Year. Helped take the defending champs to seven games. Dragged us to the playoffs again in year 2, making his first All-Star team. Lost to the team with the best player in the world.

And then came the summer of 2010, and here is where you might have noticed that all those championships you read about might not be coming back.

"I think the biggest question (about the Bulls) that you think about has to be loyalty," Dwyane Wade said that May, as he and his future teammates LeBron James and Chris Bosh were in the process of choosing their next team. "I see Michael Jordan is not there, Scottie Pippen is not there. ... You know, these guys are not a part (of the franchise). That is probably one of the biggest things for me, because I am a very loyal person."

That sentiment represented, if not the final nail in the dynasty, then certainly the biggest nail. Here was an Illinois-native and childhood

Bulls fan with a chance to continue his basketball journey for his hometown team, and he passed. Yes, there were great reasons to stay in Miami, but Wade didn't simply choose the Heat. He rejected the Bulls.

And while Derrick took a lot of heat for not going harder in recruiting Wade and LeBron, years later we learned via Ric Bucher that during the Bulls free agency meeting with LeBron in 2010, though Reinsdorf seemed hopeful that his Bulls could sign James, he also gave James a piece of advice that Bulls fans were none-too-pleased to hear.

"I told him he should stay in Cleveland," Reinsdorf said.

On Twitter, I asked Bucher to clarify whether Reinsdorf spoke in jest. "Jerry told me he believes the league is better served when players stay with their teams," Bucher wrote back. "It wasn't said in jest."

Here was a franchise flashpoint if ever there was one, a time when our beloved Bulls could have cashed in on all they built in the 90s, and instead the hometown guy said the team isn't loyal to its biggest stars while the team owner tells the opposing star to be loyal to his team.

The irony is that Jerry Reinsdorf is, in many ways, incredibly loyal. To close the book on the dynasty, he hooked up Pippen, Longley and Kerr with lucrative sign-and-trades that vastly increased their salaries despite getting barely anything for them. In the post-dynasty world, he spent heavily on extensions or long-term deals on Rose, Luol Deng, Joakim Noah and Kirk Hinrich.

He was spectacularly loyal to many retired players to whom he's given myriad jobs (front office, coaches, broadcasters, scouts, ambassadors), and went above-and-beyond with generous offers to both Jay Williams and then Eddy Curry, whose catastrophic health issues threatened to end their careers, or at least their time with the Bulls.

Lastly, there is the loyalty Reinsdorf showed Krause. I asked Sam Smith about it in 2020, seeking clarification as to why Reinsdorf would choose loyalty to Krause over loyalty to Jordan. Sam found my question comical.

"If you're the CEO of the most successful company in the world, why should you be fired?" he said. "In effect, Jerry Krause was the CEO of the most successful basketball team in the world. Whether he was liked by his employees or not is irrelevant. He is producing the highest level of production for his equity owners, the board of directors, whatever. They keep that person. You don't lose your job if your company is successful."

I get all of that. I do. But the fact remains that the Bulls of the 90s were a source of seemingly unlimited goodwill and one of the strongest brands in American culture, all of which could have been parlayed into the next Bulls championship era, perhaps even with Michael Jordan recruiting the next generation of Bulls legends the way Magic Johnson did for the Lakers or Dwyane Wade does for the Heat.

Instead, we lost out on LeBron, Wade and Bosh, Miami knocked us out of the playoffs twice in four years while they won two titles, our superstar was felled by the cruelest injury and eventually traded long before his 30th birthday.

All that remains are the memories.

Strike that: All that remains are *my* memories. And little good those are to you.

This is all pretty simple. I'm not going to stop talking about the 90s Bulls. No one should. When I tell you that it was incredible... THAT SHIT WAS INCREDIBLE!

That's what I want for you. Your own nostalgia.

Jerry Reinsdorf had a vision. He wanted to build a franchise in the model of his beloved New York Knicks of the early 1970s, and he did it, hiring a fellow Red Holzman devotee in Krause, who rescued one of Holzman's key acolytes, Phil Jackson, and made him their coach. He gave this city six championships, and as someone who came of age as a fan during that era, I will always have a soft spot for The Chairman. I think you can understand that.

But I hope Bulls fans of my age can understand why you will not. The Bulls were your birthright, and your birthright was squandered. Jerry didn't sell it to anyone in particular, and he didn't get much for it. He just made one calculation after another that left it ruptured and flooding and let the rest leak to a slow drip. What was is no more.

And that's heartbreaking. Because you would love a championship Bulls team. You deserve one. You've earned one. And here on what someone will surely claim is "Michael Jordan Day" (6.23.23), I don't know when the next one's coming.

May 27, 2021, readjack.substack.com
  Age 39

THE WALKOFF: A LOVE STORY

The broadcast doesn't show when the planning started but it was brewing throughout the fourth quarter in the form of Bill Laimbeer, the baddest of the Bad Boys. He had been on the bench since about six minutes remaining in the third quarter, nothing to do but stew on 24 hours of disrespect. On five years of disrespect. On his chickens coming home to roost. On bodyslams delivered and punches absorbed. On Michael Jordan and Phil Jackson. On newspaper reporters and national commentators. On David Stern, the grand puppeteer.

It was all there for Laimbeer, as the fourth quarter wound down in Game 4 of the 1991 Eastern Conference Finals, the back-to-back defending champion Detroit Pistons watching their reign run out. Somewhere in that stasis, the idea took root. When you watch, you can see him pitching it to teammates, an acerbic curtain call befitting this most defiant of champions.

"Let's give them the torch like they gave us the torch," John Salley remembers Laimbeer telling him on the bench in the fourth. "Them" was the Chicago Bulls. "They" was the Boston Celtics. Salley knew what Laimbeer was suggesting. He approached head coach Chuck Daly.

"Let me get back in the game," Salley told his coach.

"Come on Salley, you can't get any more stats than you have."

"No," Salley pleaded, "there's some shit going down I don't want to be a part of."

******

Chapter 1: The Supervillains

I don't cultivate sports beefs like I once did. It's impossible. You get older. Priorities change. Sports fandom's raw intensity dissipates and you learn to see athletes as people first, rather than heightened characters in an ongoing battle of good and evil. Today, for example, I can hear Isiah Thomas on NBA Open Court express the frustration that he and his teammates felt about what they perceived as a double standard of treatment from the NBA and its adoring public. I can hear that and I can empathize.

"Everyone and every team could play and act like the Pistons and adopt our philosophy — except the Pistons," he said in their defense.

And that's true — to a point. Yes, the NBA of the 1980s was physical. The hard foul still existed. The "no layups" rule was real. But even with all that, this much is true: There was no team like the Pistons.

That's because there was no player like Bill Laimbeer.

"I wore the black hat," Laimbeer said upon his retirement in 1993. "Somebody has to play that role. I accepted it. Even in high school, the other teams disliked me."

I will never like the Bad Boys, but I've come to appreciate and respect them. Yet even now, 30 years later, I detest Bill Laimbeer. It starts with his face. That pious glowering. His teeth when he smiled. The way his eyes would tighten when he said things like, "I don't give an inch at all on the court. I don't give anybody any respect."

I bet that if I ever meet him and rap with him, I'll find something I like on a personal level. He's probably a good storyteller, and I bet people in his presence are inclined to become willingly complicit in support of his on-court batteries. But there is a part of me that even to this day squirms and braces and rages when I look at him. Perhaps it's only childhood residuals, but talk about residuals!

In the *Detroit Free Press*' 1988 NBA preview, writer Johnette Howard named Laimbeer one of three players on her All-Thug Team, and asked Laimbeer whether he would take a swing at himself if he were an opposing player.

To which he answered, "Yeah, I guess I would."

"He was a dirty player," Larry Bird said a few years ago. "Ricky Mahorn, he'd hit you … but he didn't try to maim you. Bill tried to hurt you."

"I am not a dirty player and have never tried to hurt anybody," Laimbeer said during the '89 Eastern Conference Finals against the Bulls, a series the Pistons would win en route to their first championship. "That image was started by the press in Boston and promoted by the league."

During the '87 Eastern Conference Finals against the Celtics, the late Pistons GM Jack McCloskey defended Laimbeer's rep too on the technicality that "He has never thrown a punch."

"I've only thrown one punch, against Brad Daugherty," Laimbeer said during the '89 Finals. "I'll push somebody, but I won't swing at anybody."

He didn't have to. McCloskey, Laimbeer and anyone else can say whatever they want, whether in 1987 or 2021. Laimbeer was different. He was just different, man. He relished the fight and instigated them, a reputation that has obscured the rest of his game. He was a deeply skilled player who made four All-Star teams. He won the rebounding title in 1986 and was one of the first big men to consistently shoot the three. He was an iron man, going 10 straight seasons of 81 or 82 regular season games, plus deep playoff runs for much of that time. He was a leader — the acknowledged co-ruler of a two-time champ alongside Isiah Thomas, the 1 to Laimbeer's 1a.

And he elbowed and tripped and clubbed opponents until they snapped and threw punches at him.

He enjoyed the Bad Boys moniker, bragged after retirement about his team's influence on the roughness of the game and starred in the only Super Nintendo game that, to this day, I refuse to play: "Bill Laimbeer's Combat Basketball," set in a futuristic 2031 in which Bill Laimbeer is commissioner of the NBA and allows not just on-court fighting but explosive devices.

"Laimbeer is very dirty in terms of — you've seen Laimbeer: He doesn't jump well. He can't block a shot. This is true, it's not to knock him," Jordan told Arsenio Hall in 1990. "So to see him coming at me full steam ahead, it's only to knock me over or knock me off balance."

McCloskey chalked up much of Laimbeer's physicality to his being "clumsy." He was certainly awkward. But when I think "clumsy," I think Bill Cartwright, whose violent elbows caused the league's chief disciplinarian Rod Thorn to ask Cartwright if he would wear elbow pads during games.

Yet that was the extent of Cartwright's physicality. Laimbeer had an arsenal. Opponents hated Cartwright's *elbows*. No one reduced Laimbeer to a body part. They hated *him*.

"A physical game by Piston standards is when everybody is bleeding from the mouth," Rick Mahorn said as the '88 Finals got rough. Just think: Mahorn, one half of Washington's "McFilthy and McNasty" — well, Mahorn was Detroit's *other* rough player. And Dennis Rodman was third. Third! Laimbeer-Mahorn-Rodman was the Bird-McHale-Parish or Magic-Kareem-Worthy of bullyball. McHale could have been a #1 option in this league. Worthy too. Put those guys next to Bird, or Magic and Kareem? Watch out.

"We've got the reputation of being Bad Boys — throwing elbows, throwing people down," Rodman said during the '89 Eastern Conference Finals. "You've got to live with it. But we shouldn't change the way we play."

They didn't. And only Jordan scored on them with regularity. Over Detroit's three-year Finals run, MJ scored 20 or more points against the Pistons in the playoffs 17 times. Second best were McHale and Worthy, each with 6.

"Chuck Daly said, 'These are the Jordan Rules: Every time he goes to the fucking basket, put him on the ground,'" Rodman said in *The Last Dance*. "We tried to physically hurt Michael."

So when we finally flipped the script in 1991, when Scottie and Horace came of age, when everyone knew why Bill Cartwright mattered to this team, when Pax was locked in as the other guard, when the bench got tough and organized, when our coaching staff knew every angle, it made sense to us that the Pistons would walk off the court. *A punk move for a punk team*, we all thought. The Pistons fled the scene. Showed their bellies. Revealed themselves the snakes we knew they were. The walkoff fit the story. *Our* story. We needed that ending.

In fact, I'll be real: We liked that ending. The win was so much more satisfying with the walkoff. For Bulls fans, it was vindication. Validation. Confirmation that we were on the side of good and had vanquished a pox upon sport. Beating the Pistons would have been sweet in seven games. It would have been sweet even if they'd offered up postgame handshakes.

But nothing was as sweet as seeing the Bad Boys slink off the floor with the clock running down. It was, as I said, petty and perfect. So long fellas. Don't let the door hit ya.

To this day, a part of me can't help but smile.

******

As Salley finishes the game, his star teammates are on the bench talking. Reflecting. Feeling it out. Laimbeer's pitch. You can see it during the close-ups, the cuts from the action. Isiah and Laimbeer next to each other, talking, laughing. Aguirre between them, listening. Isiah then gets up and walks to Dumars, telling him something. Later, he is talking to Rodman, again in conspiratorial fun. He and Laimbeer are gleeful. The Pistons fans are cheering. They know this team is not going to three-peat. They love this team.

They also hate the Bulls. The Pistons know it. The Bulls know it. Everyone knows it, in fact, because the home fans begin chanting, "Go L.A.! Go L.A.!" cheering the assumed eventual Western Conference champion Lakers, the team their beloved Pistons battled in consecutive Finals just two years prior.

They're down to 1:45 remaining on their season, and at this point, your attention switches from Laimbeer to Isiah. The camera catches him standing near Chuck Daly, the two men talking, Zeke still smiling, Daly flustered. The coach turns his back on his superstar and folds his arms. Cut to the court, and then back to the sideline, the two men still talking. Stoppage of play with 35.2 seconds remaining, and now Daly walks away from Isiah and shakes his hand in a negative fashion, as if to say, "Don't do it." He looks perturbed. You can't say for sure, but watching it, Daly seems to make a "No, stay there" wrist move.

Isiah is listening, still standing, swinging his hands. Accomplice energy. The Pistons score — 24.8 remaining. Isiah leans down to tell Laimbeer and Aguirre something as Daly walks away. The camera pans left with the Bulls bringing the ball up, 22.9 and ticking. Our last view of the Pistons bench shows it bubbling. Percolating. And there is Isiah, swinging his arms...

******

Chapter 2: Revenge of the chosen heel

What stands out to me today are those fans. Those screaming, cheering, adoring Pistons fans. More than anyone else, they seemed to understand immediately what their Pistons were doing. It took me a few seconds to process what I was seeing, and not just because I was nine years old. You can hear it in Marv Albert's voice as he calls the action. There's a moment where reality kicks in for Marv, an NBA lifer.

"The Pistons just LEFT," he declares, dumbfounded. But Pistons fans — they got it. They knew where their guys were coming from, why they would do *this*.

"It was intentional on my part," Laimbeer said a year later.

"No, why would I regret it now, today?" Laimbeer said 28 years after that.

Okay okay, fine, he's low-hanging fruit. Of course Bill Laimbeer was an unapologetic Bad Boy.

But try this one on for size:

"I don't know if it's been good for the league, but it was damn sure good for me. I've gotten two rings. I don't give a damn if it's good for basketball."

That was Joe Dumars, "The good Bad Boy," Memorial Day 1991, reflecting on the team's "Bad Boys" image. To understand the walkoff from their perspective, you have to go back to the start of that famed

PART XV: WITH NEW EYES 347

moniker itself. January 1988. The brainchild of former sociology minor and NBA superstar Isiah Thomas.

"I learned in my sociology classes about the labeling theory. When you apply labels to individuals, they tend to stick, and people begin to form opinions about these individuals based on those labels," Thomas writes in his 1989 book "Bad Boys!" which he co-authored with his dear friend Matt Dobek, the Pistons longtime spokesperson. "Soon, these opinions become closer to fact than mere opinion."

Thomas was reacting at the time to Michael Jordan's comments about the Pistons after the famous Mahorn-vs.-Everyone fight, which started when Mahorn fouled Jordan particularly hard on a drive.

"There is no doubt in my mind that Mahorn and (Adrian) Dantley were attempting to injure me, not just prevent me from scoring, and that's what infuriated me," Jordan said after the game.

Thomas read Jordan's comments and decided to lean into that reputation. By fostering the "Bad Boys" image, the Pistons could give themselves the type of mystique that the Lakers had through Showtime, that the Celtics had through their leprechauns and clovers, and that both teams had through their banners.

Thomas knew that reporters would inadvertently get players off their game by asking them about the leprechauns instead of about Bird and McHale. Now, reporters would get Pistons opponents off *their* games by asking them if they were ready to fight the Bad Boys.

But Thomas heeded for himself a warning: "We better let this work for us, because if we don't it's going to work against us."

That's exactly what happened. Dennis Rodman lamented during the '88 Finals that their reputation was hurting them with the refs. Isiah, Laimbeer and Mahorn talked about how much more the Pistons were fined compared to other teams, even for the same actions; during the '89 Finals, the *Los Angeles Times* reported that the Pistons had been fined more than $29,000 that season, more than triple the amount of the next most heavily fined team, the Trail Blazers.

Even when the Pistons said that they were retiring the name after the club let Mahorn leave in the '89 expansion draft, they continued hyping it amongst themselves until '91, and into the present day. In 2014, the entire team participated in ESPN's 30-for-30 documentary about them, titled "Bad Boys."

Yet what I think really bothered the Pistons then and now — and what was a major contributor to the walkoff — was their realization that David Stern and the NBA were benefiting financially from the Bad Boys image, even as they were publicly condemning it.

"The 'Bad Boys' came from the league, actually," Laimbeer said years later. In February of 1988, during halftime of its nationally televised Sunday afternoon Celtics-Lakers game, CBS aired a feature on the Pistons called "The Bad Boys of Basketball." The clip referred to the Pistons as "The Raiders of the NBA." Watching the game, Raiders owner Al Davis was inspired to send the team a care package of Raiders gear — the start of the Pistons' black-backed skull-and-crossbone branding.

A few months later after the season ended, the Pistons reached the Finals, losing a famed seven-game dogfight with the Lakers. When the league released the Pistons' team video after the 1988 season, the title was no surprise.

"It was titled 'Bad Boys,'" Laimbeer said. "David Stern always says that he regrets the day that he approved that title — I disagree. I think he knows what a great moniker it was. It will live forever and will always be associated with our ball club."

What Laimbeer saw – or, perhaps, what he saw *through* — was that the NBA seemed fine promoting the Bad Boys image so long as the team was coming up short each season. But champions are the face of the league. If the Pistons never won, I think the league would have been more comfortable with the Bad Boys image. Instead, they won not one but two championships, and the league was stuck with a champ it did not want to promote.

So it didn't.

In 1989, 1990 and 1991, the league seemed to treat the Pistons just a bit differently than it did other great champions. The first NBA-licensed video game was released in 1989, after the first Pistons championship and second Finals. The video game was called "Lakers versus Celtics and the NBA Playoffs."

As an introduction to this cutting-edge video game series, I guess it made sense to wrap up the 1980s celebrating the two teams that combined for eight championships, five runners-up, and six league MVPs. But in 1990, after the Pistons won again, the game was not released. The next version in the series came out after the Bulls won in '91, with a game called "Bulls versus Lakers and the NBA Playoffs."

The national television schedules didn't favor the Pistons either. Not in 1989 (coming off their NBA Finals performance), 1990 (as defending champs) nor 1991 (as two-time champions) were the Pistons the top team on national TV. The best you could say is that in '91, they led all teams with eight appearances on NBC, but when adding the cable games on TNT, they dropped to fourth overall behind the Lakers, Celtics and Bulls — against whom the Pistons swept in the playoffs across 1989 and 1990 in four total series.

League award voters weren't any more generous. Rodman and Dumars were honored defensively, but voters ignored the Pistons within MVP and All-NBA. In both '89 and '90, Isiah and Dumars tied in the MVP voting with one vote apiece, coming in last both years (13th and 17th, respectively) among those receiving votes. And All-NBA? In 1989, the year the league expanded All-NBA to three teams, the Pistons became the first 60-win team in NBA or ABA history to get shut out of all-league honors.

To this day, 70 teams have won 60+ games, the NBA championship or both. The '89 Pistons are the only one of those 70 with zero All-

NBA players. They finally got another in 1990, when Dumars was named third team.

The NBA's ambivalent promotion of the Pistons as champion was transparent compared to how it celebrated the Lakers, Celtics and — much to the Pistons' consternation — a pre-champion Michael Jordan.

"All I can say is, he hasn't been in the league for one month yet, and the refs are treating him like a god," said Kings fifth-year guard Larry Drew in October of 1984, MJ's first NBA preseason.

That treatment only grew. In 2017, in an interview with longtime Bulls beat writer Melissa Isaacson, John Paxson recalled head NBA official Darrell Garretson laying the league's chips out on the table, as it were.

"He told us, 'Look, we all know the fans are here to see the great players like Michael Jordan, so if there's a play where Jordan and Paxson are together and there's a foul and Jordan smacked the guy on the arm, I'm giving the foul to Paxson because the fans don't want to see Jordan foul out of the game.'"

For Isiah Thomas, a man whose lone significant deficiency compared to Jordan, Magic and Bird was his height, and for the Pistons, a team that was scratching and clawing for leaguewide respect and hardware, there was natural frustration over the league showing promotional favoritism to every team *except* for theirs, especially the Bulls, a club they were defeating annually in the playoffs.

And then finally, in September of 1990, David Stern and the owners of the other 26 NBA teams settled into the business of making life a little bit harder for the two-time defending champs. At the annual league meeting in Boca Raton, Florida, several major rule changes under consideration for the 1990-91 season would have an adverse effect on the Pistons, none bigger than one the league adopted for the next season, 1990-91: the addition of the "flagrant-2."

This new foul category would give a team two free throws and possession of the ball. The problem with the flagrant foul rule in its previous incarnation, Rod Thorn explained then, is that it came with an ejection for the player. And in a star-driven league, refs didn't want to eject players, so they were disinclined to call flagrants.

"Hard fouls in the half court have gotten ridiculous," Thorn said at the time. "You can't go for a guy's head when he's up in the air, or when he's not involved in the play at all."

While Thorn specifically cited a 1990 foul by Charles Barkley, it was clear that the flagrant foul rule would heavily impact the Pistons as a whole. In the 1991 Eastern Conference Finals, officials called three flagrants on the Pistons in Game 2, causing an eight-point swing for the Bulls in what ended up an eight-point win. There were also the usual spate of technical fouls as well as just standard personal fouls. In the first two games of that series, at home in Chicago, the Bulls enjoyed a 79-40 free throw advantage.

Which is not to say that the Bulls won because of the refs. Far from it. By 1991, we were flat out better. We were better than Boston, better than Cleveland, and yes, better than Detroit, with a major boost from Pippen compared to the prior three years.

But from the Pistons' perspective, the officiating was just the latest example of the league chipping away at their power. And then, with the Bulls up three games to none, Jordan took the mic.

"The people I know are going to be happy that they're not the reigning champs anymore," Jordan said before Game 4. "When Boston was the champion, they played true basketball. Detroit won. You can't take that away from them. But it wasn't clean basketball. It wasn't the kind of basketball you want to endorse."

Of course, MJ was right. Not only that, but to me, that's an example of what Salley — who shook hands with the Bulls on the court while his teammates walked off — calls "(killing) you from start to the double-zero" before "going back to become human." Jordan speaking candidly and saying what everyone was thinking constituted killing the Pistons from start to the double-zero.

"I don't feel we're overconfident," Jordan said, "but we want to kill this team."

Everybody did. Everybody, that is, except Pistons fans. The Pistons did everything on their own terms, so why not this too? Looking back on it now, 30 years later, I think the walkoff was an opportunity to stick it to David Stern, to stick it to Rod Thorn, to stick it to the Bulls, to stick it to MJ, to stick it to everybody except their fans, to whom they gave this gift of defiance. Again, listen to their fans as they depart. Just listen to them. Those cheers are pure love. If the Pistons could get it nowhere else, they could get it there.

******

The Pistons score with 24.8 seconds remaining, and the last thing you can see of the Pistons bench is Isiah leaning down to tell Laimbeer and Aguirre something as Daly walks away. The camera pans left with the Bulls bringing the ball up, 22.9 and ticking, Isiah still swinging his hands, but there's movement now, and Pistons fans are applauding as the Bulls dribble out the clock, the camera moving left and leaving the Bad Boys behind.

Except then you realize this is not a standard ovation. The Pistons fans are reacting to something. The cheering increases as the Pistons players are walking down the sideline. Aguirre is in front, followed by Laimbeer and Isiah. It's hard to tell at first their purpose. Your mind calculates. Are they on their way to greet the Bulls? That can't be right. But the alternative is that they're leaving the floor while the game is ongoing. That can't be right either. NBC cuts to a wide shot with 9.2 seconds remaining, the clock running, and they're really doing it, they're walking off.

The scene is bizarre. Logic retreats. "I think the crowd is cheering here for the Bulls right now, and the Pistons as they leave the court," says color man Cotton Fitzsimmons. NBC cuts back tight to a profile view of Isiah, walking right to left on screen, trailing Aguirre and Laimbeer, and the clock stops at 7.9 seconds. Whistles blow. Neither team has called time. There is no injury. There was not a basket. The clock has stopped because one team is leaving.

"I don't think they're cheering for the Bulls," Marv Albert responds, flatly astounded, still processing. NBC cuts to a close-up of Jordan and Scott Williams. They are stunned and serene. The feed cuts back to the profile shot of Isiah, as Marv corrects Fitzsimmons. "I think the greeting is for the Pistons, as they are headed off as time runs down." And just as he's saying this, Isiah ducks his head down as he begins to pass the Bulls bench.

******

Chapter 3: The Isiah Effect

The walkoff wasn't anything new for Bill Laimbeer. He was born to play the villain. It wasn't anything new for Mark Aguirre or Dennis Rodman. It didn't matter to James Edwards or Vinnie Johnson. It didn't change anything for John Salley or Dumars, who also shook hands with the Bulls after the game.

But it mattered to one man — the one man with more to lose than anyone else.

Isiah Lord Thomas III.

He's the one guy in all this I really feel for.

"I've paid a heavy price for that decision," Thomas said last year about the walkoff, during the airing of *The Last Dance*. "And in paying that price — I understand that this is the sports world ... but at the same time, looking back over it in terms of how we felt at that particular time, our emotional state, and how we exited the floor, we actually gave the world the opportunity to look at us in a way that we never really tried to ... project ourselves."

Okay... there's a lot there. On the one hand, Isiah is playing both sides of the truth. As he wrote in his book, and as was clearly the case with that team, they absolutely did project themselves as the Bad Boys.

"I know it's all bullshit," MJ said during the doc about Isiah's walkoff remorse. "Whatever he says now, you know it wasn't his true actions then. He's had time enough to think about it. Or the reaction of the public has kind of changed his perspective. ... There's no way you're going to convince me that he wasn't the asshole."

Jordan's right. And one thing I would have loved in *The Last Dance* would have been the filmmakers using their iPad watch-and-react style to ask interviewees to react to their own words. Had they done that, they might have waited for Isiah to finish his, "That's just what was done at the time" explanation, and then played him his own statement from November of 1991:

"At that time we were mad, we were upset. And for me to sit here now and say, 'We didn't really mean it,' that would be a lie. Because at that time, we meant it. Was it unsportsmanlike? Yes. Was it the wrong thing to do? Yes. But at that time, was that the way we felt? Yeah, it was a very emotional response..."

On the other hand, what Isiah said last year is true in two key ways. First, he's talking again about labels and myth-making, and the walkoff solidified in the public's collective mind that the Bad Boys were everything they'd made themselves out to be — and not, additionally, or moreso, a team that embodied the best of basketball and team sport: the cohesion, teamwork, fighting spirit, discipline and pure, raw talent.

So that was the team fallout. The other point Isiah makes is a personal one. The price *he* paid. The price no other member of that team was in a position to pay: a historical downgrade that started with his snub from the Dream Team. The team had other pro snubs, with Dominique Wilkins at the top of the list. But the only man whose exclusion felt like a birthright betrayed was Isiah.

PART XV: WITH NEW EYES 355

"You see him? You see Isiah?" I remember my father saying to me in the late 1980s as we watched yet another Pistons beatdown of the Bulls. "He's from Chicago. Yet he plays for the Pistons. And B.J. Armstrong? He's from Detroit yet he plays for the Bulls."

That was the beginning of my Isiah respect. He was short, like me. He had a chip on his shoulder, like me. He played the way I liked to play, with equal parts intelligence and passion. Everything about Isiah resonated with me — expect, of course, his jersey.

Walking off the court was poor sportsmanship. I knew that then and I know that now. But even then, I didn't think that warranted exclusion from the Dream Team. I don't judge Scottie by his 1.8 seconds, I don't judge Jay Cutler by the 2010 NFC championship game, I don't judge Dennis by what he did to the Bulls in Detroit, and I don't judge Isiah based on the walkoff.

And yes, it was the walkoff that kept him off the '92 Olympic team. Dream Team historian Jack McCallum thinks that Thomas's disrespect of Bird from 1987 played a major role in his Dream Team snub, but by the time the players were selected, that was four years in the past. Magic wrote in his 2009 autobiography with Larry Bird that Thomas's reaction to Magic revealing his HIV-positive test was to speculate on Magic's sexuality, and that that was the reason Isiah was not selected — but Magic learned of that test in late October of 1991, and the first 10 members of the Dream Team were chosen the month before.

In fact, less than a week before the selection, Isiah was one of five groomsmen at Magic's wedding. Mark Aguirre was another, while the other three were Magic's three brothers.

Yes, Isiah's reaction to Magic having HIV could have prevented him from being awarded the final spot for a pro — that went to Clyde Drexler in May of 1992. But by that point, the Dream Team opportunity was gone for Isiah. The camaraderie factor, along with the overall level of animosity, is I'm sure why Jordan told McCallum in 2011 for his Dream Team book: "I told Rod [Thorn] I don't want to play if Isiah Thomas is on the team."

Still, while I agree with Jordan and others (Magic, Malone, Pippen…) that Isiah would not have fit in, his dye was cast when the NBC cameras showed to the world Isiah ducking his head as he passed the Bulls bench, and then walked directly behind him for that long run from the Bulls bench to the Pistons tunnel. That's another major difference between the Pistons walkoff and the Celtics walkoff: perspective. The power of the picture. Everyone who cared about the NBA felt viscerally linked to that walkoff due to that broadcast. Headline writers had a field day:

- "Bulls sweep vile Pistons from playoffs"
- "In the end, Bad Boys nothing but crybabies"
- "Pistons bow out in the lowest way possible"
- "Bulls make NBA safe for 'solid' basketball"

"All over the world, when basketball fans think of the NBA, they think of six names: Dr. J., Kareem, Bird, Magic, Michael, Isiah," *Detroit Free Press* columnist Michelle Kaufman wrote in early September 1991, before the selection. "Those six players are the pillars that bolstered the once-floundering league and raised it to heights other American sports leagues should envy. … (The U.S.) should send Michael, Magic, Bird and Thomas."

They should have, but they didn't. Despite his political deftness within league matters, Isiah did not realize (or did not believe) that his place on the Olympic team depended on him mending fences, with both Jordan and the league powers who made up the selection committee and were reportedly disgusted by the walkoff.

"The Olympic team was a political battle," Laimbeer told McCallum, "and if there was one team and one player that wasn't going to win a political battle, it was the Detroit Pistons and Isiah Thomas."

That is my best guess as to why Isiah has gone round and round on the walkoff — why over the past 30 years he sometimes seems remorseful, other times vindictive, and still other times dismayed. He felt he should have been respected and promoted at the level of Jordan, Bird and Magic, and should never have needed to stoop to the walkoff in the first place. In a way, his original assessment might have been his truest one of all.

"It was a happy time," he said after the game. "For the first time in five years, we can lean back and say, 'Whew!' It's been a cruel kind of torture that we've had to endure physically and mentally. I don't think anyone looking from the outside can understand that."

If you can't understand *that*, I don't know what to tell you.

******

"Pistons wasting no time in getting out of here," Marv says as Isiah passes MJ. The camera pivots to join a single-file line, behind Isiah — and now the whole of the basketball-loving world is looking at those bright blue names stitched into white fabric: LAIMBEER ahead on the left of the screen, and THOMAS, bold, clear, filling the frame. "Now a timeout was called."

The crowd is roaring, and suddenly, Marv seems to understand what's happening. The meaning of it all. He knows what he's looking at. You can hear it in his voice. The clock on screen is frozen at 7.9 seconds remaining, and the instant legacy of the action clicks in for Marv.

"They LEFT the BENCH, although there are seven and nine-tenths seconds remaining," he says. Laimbeer high-fives and then hugs Jack McCloskey just outside the Pistons tunnel. "The Pistons just LEFT..."

******

Chapter 4: The Bad Boys and The Dynasty

Every superhero needs an origin story. The Pistons were ours.

And that origin would not have been the same without the walkoff.

"Detroit's been very successful with their style and other teams tried to copy it because they were successful," a prescient Jordan said after Game 4. "And that's not good for the game."

Oh, and speaking of prescience…

"They still haven't proved anything. They've got to win about five or six championships before they're a great team."

That was a frustrated Dennis Rodman after Game 4, one of several Pistons who dismissed our victory and dumped on us after a chippy, emotional game. The most famous play was probably Laimbeer and Rodman converging on Pippen on an open drive to the basket; Laimbeer wacked him across the body and face with his left arm, and when he landed, Rodman threw him past the basket into the front row of seats.

Incredibly, that was not one of the four technical fouls that the Pistons received, nor the one flagrant. Rodman did receive a tech for arguing with the refs, as did Daly and assistant Brandon Suhr.

Laimbeer earned a technical and a flagrant, separately, and spent his postgame interview coldly repeating, "They won." On the Bulls side, Jordan kept both barrels blazing.

"You see two different styles of play with us and them — the dirty play and the flagrant fouls and unsportsmanlike conduct," he said. "Hopefully, that will be eliminated from the game."

Jordan even stated something that Pistons players gripe about to this day: the notion that the Bulls complaining to the league caused an increase in disciplinary attention.

"We may have complained about it and told the teacher, or whatever, but we never tried to lower ourselves to that level," he said.

So there they were: the proverbial Two Teams That Just Don't Like Each Other. The Pistons did what they had to do to win championships. Theirs was not the template of a standard NBA champion, starting at the top with Isiah, who had every bit of the greatness of Jordan, Magic and Bird, and was one of the most talented players to step into this league, but was only 6'1.

"If Isiah were five inches taller," Chuck Daly said in the mid-1990s, "he'd be the best basketball player in NBA history."

Detroit pushed the era's standard physical play to its limit, and had the mental toughness to take what came of that. This was the mystique factor that Isiah talked about building, and it worked! They beat Jordan up because that was the only way to handle him.

"He by far is the best I've ever seen," Isiah told Arsenio while the Pistons were champs. "And Earvin's my boy, but, you know, Air…" Isiah said, fading out in awe.

As the decade wore on, the Bulls fended off bruising challengers in Riley's Knicks, Riley's Heat and Reggie's Pacers (coached by Larry Bird). With each new team, I said to myself, "We handled the Pistons, we can handle anyone."

In a bizarre twist, Dennis Rodman wound his way to the Bulls in 1995. James Edwards and John Salley did too. The 1996 Bulls are possibly the greatest team in NBA history, and 25% of them were displaced Bad Boys. We embraced those guys — I was the world's biggest Rodman fan — but the one guy we would not have accepted was Laimbeer. He remains in the exact same headspace today about the rivalry as he was then, with no alternate perspectives or insights.

He and Jordan share that: If "…and I took that personally" applies to anyone other than Jordan, it's Laimbeer.

As Jordan said in that 1990 Arsenio interview, ask all NBA players to identify the dirtiest player in the NBA, the answer would be easy.

"I say 95% would say Laimbeer, or Larry Bird," Jordan answered. This caught Arsenio off guard, but Jordan went on to define Bird's style of dirty play as "smart ... not really cheap."

That assessment defines the perception of the Pistons. They were like the Richard Nixon of basketball teams: "If the president does it, that means it's not illegal," and if the Pistons do it, that means it is. It's a tricky balance, even with 30 years of hindsight. "Dirty" is a value judgment, so let's stay away from labels and just describe what we all saw. They hit you. They tripped you. They tried to hurt you.

"As soon as he steps in the paint," Salley said about Jordan during *The Last Dance*: "hit him."

But so it goes. We won six and became the second greatest dynasty in league history after Russell's Celtics. They won two and carved out a legacy unlike any other, giving something beautiful to their fans. That to me was their most damning sin. What made them intolerable to the NBA powers-that-be was not the physicality. It was their success. They won. And not just a few key games. Championships. They were the league's ultimate villain. The Bad Boys. And world champs twice over.

"I can't sit here and whine about the reaction to what's happening right now," Dumars said last year about *The Last Dance* on B.J. Armstrong's podcast. "I played for the Bad Boy Pistons." He paused, letting those words sink in. "And you know what you signed up for when you play for the Bad Boys Pistons. So you can't sit here and be sensitive about criticism. It's the walk we walked. We got rings. We got trophies. We got banners. Right? I'm not going to sit here and walk the walk with my teammates and then cry about the reaction."

Amen, Joe. Thanks for the battles.

******

PART XV: WITH NEW EYES

As the fans at the Palace cheer and wave, a tearful Jack McCloskey embraces Isiah. "That's a three-pointer!" Marv exclaims, indicating that, yes, the game is continuing.

But no one is watching it or even thinking about it. The TV viewers aren't. The fans at the Palace aren't. The Pistons stars certainly aren't. The camera is close behind Isiah with a shot straight at a crying McCloskey as they hug. We can hear the buzzer sound signifying the game's end. The reign's end. Isiah is smiling, cheering up McCloskey.

The fans are going bonkers as Isiah and McCloskey walk arm-in-arm to the locker room. McCloskey stops and turns back toward the court, but Isiah still has his right hand on Jack's shoulder and he pulls him back. Speaks softly to him. Smiles with him. Isiah is in control, guiding his beloved general manager to the locker room.

And all is well in the Pistons world.

**PART XVI:
THE FAN FAVORITE**

Jan. 10, 2017, Windy City Gridiron
Age 35

THOMAS JONES: PAIN, POWER, PRIDE

Thomas Jones is one of the greatest Chicago athletes of my life.

He is also one of the greatest what-if Chicago sports stories of my life.

In 2004, in the first minute of free agency, the Bears reached out to Jones, the fourth-year running back who had just rejuvenated his career in one year in Tampa. The Bears wanted him bad, viewing him as filling the Priest Holmes role in new offensive coordinator Terry Shea's offense. He had a career year in 2004, rushing for 948 yards in 14 games and setting a Bears franchise record for receptions by a running back in a season with 56.

He had a career year in 2005, joining his childhood hero Walter Payton as the only Bears to rush for 1,300 yards in a season, while also leading the Bears to a division championship.

He had a career year in 2006 as one of the unquestioned leaders in the locker room of the NFC's best team, becoming the first Bear to rush for 100 yards in multiple playoff games and leading the Bears to the franchise's first Super Bowl in 31 years, where he rushed for a team-high 112 yards on just 15 carries.

Then he got traded.

"I think I'm the first running back to ever get traded after running for 100 yards in the Super Bowl," he told me with a mix of pain and bemusement. "It makes no sense. But it happened."

That trade sent Jones into what amounts to an alternate timeline of sports history. Jones wanted to finish his career with the Bears. But for this trade that he decidedly did not want, he likely would have, and would have been just as big a part of the franchise as Peanut and Lance, for instance, who arrived in Chicago only one year before TJ. He played five more seasons with the Jets and KC, ending his career with a rushing total that would have placed him second in Bears history behind 34.

In fact, if you really want to get into the what-if game, the number one question about Super Bowl XLI that all Bears fans, and *players*, have is why Ron Turner did not keep feeding TJ in a game in which he was clearly hot. Imagine this: Instead of abandoning the run, Turner and the Bears ride Jones all game. If we win, Jones is Super Bowl MVP.

If Jones is Super Bowl MVP, we don't trade him.

If we don't trade him, he stabilizes the team through the QB carousel of 2007. It's possible we get back to the playoffs in '07 or '08, or both, and maybe don't make the Cutler trade. With the starting QB job securely with Kyle Orton (who much of the team, Jones included, loved), we keep our 2009 and 2010 1st round picks and have another shot at a Super Bowl in 2009, a season in which Jones set career highs in rushing yards (1,402) and rushing touchdowns (14) with the Jets.

And if all of that happens, Thomas Jones is roundly regarded as one of the greatest ever to suit up for the Chicago Bears. In 2019, the Bears named the top 100 players in team history and held their 100th year celebration; Jones was not on the list, and was not even invited to the celebration where, instead, fans chanted his name and his teammates gushed about him on stage.

"No I wasn't invited but never any hard feelings," he tweeted when a fan asked if he was invited. "I'll always have love for the #Bears organization and the priceless memories from my time there at Halas Hall and Soldier Field. So cool to still feel the love from my short time there."

PART XVI: THE FAN FAVORITE   367

The love is eternal. He holds a rare place in Bears history, a man whose impact and power on one of the greatest sports franchises in U.S. history far exceeds his truncated three years of play.

In recent years, TJ has reconnected with his teammates, the franchise and Bears Nation. He is roundly beloved. He and I connected in 2016 for an interview and have since stayed in close contact. At Jones's request, I worked with him on a video celebrating his Bears career. My WCG colleague Robert Schmitz edited it. Fans loved it. His teammates loved it. We all loved it, because we all love Thomas Jones.

Our 2016 interview, published in January 2017, is excerpted here. Our conversation drives at the ultimate question around Jones's Bears career, the one that eats at fans and his teammates alike: Why in the world did we trade Thomas Jones?

******

SILVERSTEIN: You had four touchdowns in the 2006 NFC playoffs — two against Seattle, two against the Saints. Then it's off to the Super Bowl in Miami. What was the offensive game plan?

JONES: We ran the ball really well against New Orleans, and Indianapolis was smaller up front. Small and quick. It rained a lot, so of course we figured we'd run the ball the majority of the game. And, uh — (pause) I don't know. I really don't know. It's one of the weirdest situations I've ever been in. I look back at that game and I don't have the answers.

The number one thing we did: we turned the ball over. You turn the ball over in any game, you're going to lose. You turn the ball over in a Super Bowl, you're definitely going to lose. And we turned the ball over way too many times. Unnecessary turnovers. Things that you look at and you're like, "Man, this is the Super Bowl." Yes, mistakes happen, but this is the biggest game ever. Every game you've played in — as a kid, as a collegiate athlete, as a pro — has been to get to this one game. And some people just aren't meant for that big stage. It's just too big for certain people.

That's understandable. It's a huge opportunity to shine. Or it's a huge opportunity to drop the ball, literally. And that's kind of what we did. Indianapolis played a great game. They did what they had to do to win. But we didn't help ourselves at all. The gameplan? I think it just took a mind of its own.

I ask because when I was watching, as a Bears fan, I just kept saying, "I don't understand why we're not running the ball more." Was that something you and Coach Turner and Lovie were discussing? Was it something you were wondering about? You only had 15 carries but you went for 112 yards.

I think a lot of it had to do with the two-back system that they had established with me and Cedric. I think they wanted to make sure they got Cedric in as well to get him some carries and maybe possibly try to wear them down. But I think you have to be strategic. This is the Super Bowl. I felt as though it was one of those games where I was in a zone. Every couple of series, we'd rotate. I'd go two series and Ced would go in two series, which was great. We wore defenses down and it helped us get all the way to the Super Bowl.

But in that game, I remember I came to the sidelines and I knew that the next series would be my series out, and I said, "Don't take me out." I just remember saying, "Don't take me out, don't take me out."

I was in this zone. I had figured out what they were doing on defense. I had broken this long run. I'd watched so much film during the week that I understood exactly what they were going to do. They were going to come up the field — and I was going to tell the coaches, "Run this play, run this play." There were two or three plays that I wanted to run. And the coaches have to make their decisions. They're the coaches. I play, they coach. I really felt that was going to be a game where I would go for 200 or 250 or something crazy.

Sometimes as a running back you have this special feeling in a game that, "No one can stop me." And if you get taken out of that space and the game gets out of hand, and then the play-calling has to fit the way the game's going, you get out of that space. And I think that's what happened to me.

We gave them a chance to figure out what was going on by not letting me continue to attack them. Even the linemen — I went up to Olin and Ruben Brown and Tait and Garza and Fred Miller and said, "We're gonna kill these guys." And they were looking at me like, "We know." I was like, "Run draw and inside zone. Draw and inside zone. Draw and inside zone. We'll kill them."

(Pause) But it's in the past. Hindsight's 20-20. That might not have worked. Who knows? That's just what I felt. So I would never throw anyone under the bus. We all did the best that we could to help our cause and it just didn't happen for us for whatever reason. And it sucks, because that's one thing that I'll never get over. Every year around playoff time you kind of get a little depressed subconsciously. I haven't watched the Super Bowl since we lost. It's too hard to watch.

Are you serious?

Yeah. I haven't watched one Super Bowl since we lost. I don't watch it.

Did you watch it growing up?

Oh yeah. Every year.

Did you watch it in your playing career prior to 2006? From 2000 to 2005?

Yeah.

So you watched every Super Bowl until the one that you played in, and since that time you haven't watched any?

No, it does something to you emotionally. It's like a girlfriend you never really got over. It's that serious. You go from beating the Saints, and literally looking at guys — I remember looking at Desmond Clark after we beat the Saints and he was in tears. He was like, "We did it. We did it." And I was just looking at him like, "Is this really happening? Are we really going to the Super Bowl?"

We were in Chicago. It's snowing. This is a kid's dream. The Chicago Bears are going to the Super Bowl. And I just remember looking at Dez Clark and he was in tears. And then two weeks later, the worst feeling of your football career. A two-week swing. The best feeling ever in your football career to the worst.

It's raining. It's wet. They're pulling the ropes out. They're ushering you off the field so they can pull the platform out for the Colts. I'm in the locker room, and I didn't know how many yards I had but I knew in my mind that I could have had more. I'm thinking, "What else could I have done? Maybe on this run, if I would have cut left — "

You're just constantly beating yourself up about it. Every year, somebody will call me. Brian Urlacher will call, or I'll call Lak, or on Twitter we'll reach out to each other. "How did we lose that game? How did we lose?" That was 10 years ago. That will never leave. It was tough for a while. It was pretty depressing.

I read about your reactions to Jovan Belcher and Junior Seau. I assume that you've seen the news about Rashaan Salaam. What health issues do you deal with on a day-to-day basis? How are you doing, man?

I broke my ribs in Arizona when I played for the Cardinals, my rookie year. I was misdiagnosed. I had three ribs that came out of my sternum, (*Ed. note: this led to breathing problems*) and the trainers, they misdiagnosed me. They told me I had everything from asthma to valley fever to a hundred other things that were completely wrong. They sent me to see a psychiatrist. (Laughs.) I was like, "Listen, I can't breathe. I'm not crazy."

But because they didn't send me to a chiropractor first, they didn't understand. I went to the Cleveland Clinic to have an endoscopy on my stomach to see if acid reflex was causing the shortness of breath and chest pains. I literally went through twenty or thirty thousand dollars of hospital fees to try to figure out what was going on. And then a local chiropractor in Virginia figured out what was going on and he adjusted my ribs. But because my ribs had been out for so long I've had shortness of breath. So I played with shortness of breath for the rest of my career.

That's probably the main thing that bothers me now. I still have spurts of that sometimes because I developed a shallow breathing pattern. And then obviously my knees. I didn't have any major surgeries but I was one of those guys who just played hurt. I could be hurt and you would never know. I would stay in the cold tub. I would go to the facility at 2, 3 in the morning and sit in the cold tub just to get the inflammation down. I'd wear a brace, or get super taped up, take a Toradol shot, and I would play.

A lot of those things now, they affect me. A lot of numbness in my hands. Numbness in my arms. One morning — it's not funny, but my whole left leg had gone numb from my hip down. I wasn't laying on my hip. I was laying on the opposite side, actually. I tried to get up and run and I fell because my leg was numb. It scared me. My dogs were barking at me like, "What are you doing?"

When was that?

This was probably about five months ago. I mean, your body — we are not meant to play football. We created these games and we make it normal but it's not normal to crash into people daily. It's not normal for your brain. It's not normal for your bones, your muscles, your joints. So of course there are going to be problems.

I have a lot of physical issues I deal with. And I still try to go to the gym. But you just accept it. I'm 38. I get up to go to the bathroom and it's like, you slide. (Laughs.) You scoot. You scoot to the bathroom. It takes you about 10 minutes, because you have to get warmed up. So I slide. It's like I'm roller skating, because my ankles and everything are so stiff and tight. It's like everything is locked up.

I had turf toe in my right toe. I had a hairline fracture in my left ankle. So when you get up, you can't just take off. I scoot for maybe the first 10 minutes around. People look at me and are like, "Wow, you look like you're in great shape." Yeah, I take care of myself, but my body is still beat up. It's bad.

If you had to do it all over again, would you still play football?

That's a million dollar question, man. (Pause.) No. No, I wouldn't. Especially not with what I know about football, some of the injuries and things that come with it. Some of the consequences. And it's not even just the physical. The emotional issues that come with it. Football is a very emotional job. You make it to the NFL and there's a lot on the line. Your namesake is on the line.

I was in Arizona and I was called a "bust." I didn't live up to the expectations they had. And that was my fault. It wasn't "My situation." It wasn't the fact that the team I went to was never good. It wasn't any of those things. It was me. I am man enough to accept that, and I did.

But it's tough when people come up to your family, or they overhear people saying, "Your son's terrible. He's trash." Or "Thomas Jones is terrible. Thomas Jones is a bust." It's tough, man. It's hard on your family. It's hard on people who love you. And then from a financial perspective, you literally come into a situation that you're not used to, especially if you're not used to being a millionaire. You become an instant millionaire and there are a lot of things you don't know. There are a lot of things the people around you don't know and don't understand. Some relationships get tainted and tarnished. People change. The people you think love you run away from you and the people who don't know you run toward you.

It's super weird, man. There is a lot that goes on as a professional athlete, and especially as an NFL player. And then because of the physical demands, there's a psychological element that comes along with that. You don't just play as an NFL player and not have violent tendencies. It doesn't make any sense. And unfortunately no one tries to see that side of it because people only know what happens. No one wants to figure out why it happened. They just know it happened. So I think sometimes we're put in a tough predicament. And then the decisions that we make, the environment that we're in on a day-to-day basis isn't taken into consideration.

That's a trip. So last thing: final legacy for you of that 2006 season. When you think of it, what comes to mind first?

The Super Bowl. Those people on that team, Cedric Benson included, are my family for life. I'll always love those people. Any and everyone who was associated with that team. Lovie, Jerry Angelo, Cedric Benson — everybody. There's no way you can have a year like that and not be connected to everyone in some capacity. The ups and downs. That will go down as one of the best years of my life.

I would have dreams of the parade. Because when we stayed at the hotel in Chicago downtown during playoff time, they would show the '85 Bears parade on the TV and monitors, and in our room they had a channel with the parade. And it was like, "Man, that could be us twenty years later. That could be us."

(Sighs.) That's the only thing I regret — that we didn't win a Super Bowl for that city and go down in history as the next team to win the Super Bowl. But that was one of my most proud years of my life. I'll never forget that. How could you? We had so much fun, man. It was such a fun year. It was like I was in high school on my high school team. We literally kicked people's asses. We were physical. We were tough. We were mean. We didn't care. We did things our way. We bullied people. We literally bullied people. We bullied grown men that year. It's just an adrenaline rush, man. Something I'll never forget.

And back to Benson — I just want to say one thing about Benson: Cedric Benson went on to have a great career. His career was a little bit like mine: we started out on a team where it didn't work out, and he went somewhere else, a couple teams, and he did his thing. I'm proud of him. I'm proud of Cedric Benson. I'm proud of his accomplishments and what he did. He's a super talented kid. Super talented.

I know what it feels like to fight your way out of a tough situation like that. You go to a major market like Chicago or New York or one of these cities and you don't do well, early? It's tough. It's a tough crowd, man. They want to win now. When you go to a team like that, it's very tough if it doesn't start off well.

The NFL's a grown man's job. It's no place for the faint of heart. No place. It's just in the air. It's a really unique environment to be in. And sometimes I miss it. Sometimes I do miss it. But I haven't been to a game since I retired. Not one. I haven't even been to a football field since I retired. The last football field I was on was Mile High Stadium at Denver. I have not been to a football game or on a football field.

You would get such an ovation going to Soldier Field. I can tell you that.

Listen man, I'm in L.A., and every day or so I see a Bears fan. It's incredible. The Bears fanbase is like a cult. They're everywhere. Somebody sent me a picture on Twitter and somebody was in South Africa with my jersey on, on a bike. I went to Rio in 2011 and there were four Bears fans there at the same hotel I was at. To play for the Chicago Bears is really an honor. If you're going to play football in the NFL, the Chicago Bears, man (pause) — I went to the Super Bowl with the Chicago Bears. Nobody can ever take that away from me. Period. When it comes to football, it doesn't get any better than that.

But I'm very grateful that I had the opportunity to play. I'm thankful that I had the opportunity to experience those things. When I say I wouldn't play again I'm not saying that because I didn't appreciate the experience.

It's just some of the things that I deal with now and the things I see other guys deal with — my close friends — it's heartbreaking to see some of the things guys go through. It's tough to watch, because these are people who I love and care about. There are a lot of people who are out here struggling and no one knows what's going on in their heads. It's tough. It really is. You get close to these people and they become your family, and when something like that happens it hits home. Like, that could be me. That could have been me.

******

At the end of the interview, I thanked Thomas again for speaking with me and giving me his time. I then reiterated that if he ever did decide to come back to Soldier Field, he would be warmly and joyously embraced.

"Thank you so much," he told me. "And, please make sure you put in the article that I love Bears fans. I love everyone who has ever supported me in my career and as a Chicago Bear. I'm forever grateful to them and the love they have. And I did not want to leave Chicago. I think if we could have kept the team together, maybe another year, we could have done it."

Three years later, in October 2019, the Bears held a reunion, inviting the Lovie Smith-era players to Soldier Field for an afternoon Bears game. The alumni donned their orange jerseys and shot out of the tunnel to incredible cheers. Among those in attendance were three members of the Bears Top 100 — Urlacher, Briggs, Tillman — and many others who have been central to the extended media life of that marvelous team the past decade.

The man they chose to lead them out of the tunnel: #20, Thomas Jones.

Thomas Q. Jones 🌿
@thomasqjones

Much love to the #Bears organization for inviting me to be a part of this alumni weekend in Chicago at Soldier Field. Haven't been to a NFL game since my last game which was Jan 1st 2012. Can't wait to reunite with my teammates from 04 to 06. My brothers for life.
#BearDown

PART XVII:
CLIMBING THE MOUNTAIN

Dec. 4, 2005, "Bear Down and Get Some Runs"
    Age 24

TAKE THAT BRETT! BREAKING THE FAVRE CURSE

"Isn't it weird how we just keep winning?"

I've just gotten home from Buffalo Wild Wings, where I watched the Bears beat Green Bay 19-7 at Soldier Field. It was their first win at home against the Packers since 1993, and it broke a streak of 26 straight Bears-Packers games in which Brett Favre threw a touchdown pass.

Though the score is impressive, this was not the full-on dominant performance that we saw against Carolina, or even last week against Tampa Bay. The Bears allowed a season-high 198 yards in the first half. They got great field position, but did nothing with it. All the offense could scrape together was four Robbie Gould field goals, and only two of those came from long offensive drives. The other two were products of turnovers, including one at the end of the first half, when Brett threw a lazy jump ball towards the endzone. The ball got caught in the wind, floated left, and was easily intercepted by Peanut, who hopped out of the endzone and returned it 95 yards to set up the field goal that gave the Bears a 9-7 lead heading into the locker room.

In the second half, the Bears produced a 67-yard drive, led by Bernard Berrian and both TJ and Adrian Peterson. But after a nine-yard pick up on first and ten for Peterson with the Bears inside the Packer 30, AP was stuffed on second and third down, forcing the Bears to kick yet another field goal. The Bears forced and recovered fumbles on consecutive Green Bay possessions in the fourth quarter, but ended up punting on both of the following drives.

Then, on the third straight Packers possession, the Bears put pressure on Favre on third down. Favre did his little body going backwards/arm going forwards pass, a pass that zipped towards his receiver... who was not looking. Nate Vasher jumped the route, made the pick, and took the ball 45 yards for a touchdown. Green Bay drove down the field on their final drive, but couldn't score. Time ran out. Bears 19, Packers 7. A good score, but not one indicative of the game we'd watched.

To see what kind of game the Bears played compared to the past two weeks, just look at the final play of each. The Bears finished off both the Panthers and the Buccaneers with game-ending sacks on fourth down, both from Ogunleye. This game ended with the Packers picking up a fourth-and-long, but having the game clock run out. We didn't snuff them out on their final drive; the game ended of, shall we say, natural causes.

So while the result is the same, the feeling was different, and while it is always super sweet to beat the Packers, and while the Vasher TD was an entertaining capper to an otherwise lackluster performance, I am a realistic Bears fan who is always looking at the big picture. This eight-game win streak has been amazing, but more important than the wins is the week-to-week improvement. Any team can luck out a win here or there; nobody can luck out a Super Bowl victory, and since that is the ultimate goal in competition, a true fan is always looking for signs that indicate their team's chances to win a championship.

The past two weeks were clear markers of a team on the rise; this game was a bit murkier. There were a lot of negatives this week — we had zero offensive production, and the passing game, which has been competent for most of the season, was absolute garbage — and while I am enthused that we were able to find a way to win even when we weren't playing our best football, and while my excitement levels went through the roof in the "living in the moment" area, this game did not leave me entirely satisfied in the "big picture" area.

As soon as I answered the phone and heard my dad's question, I could tell that he was feeling the exact same way that I was. The win

PART XVII: CLIMBING THE MOUNTAIN

is great, but what did it tell us about our team? I'm not sure, and so for that reason I was not over the top in the "big picture" department.

But something else was bothering me as well, something that I've never felt as a sports fan, a feeling that, as soon as I properly identified it, frightened and shamed me.

I didn't want the Bears to win.

******

When the Bulls won their first championship in 1991, it was a culmination of the journey they had embarked on over the previous three years. They finally got over the Pistons hump in '91, Michael finally proved that he could make his teammates better, Scottie came of age, and the team made The Leap from very good to CHAMPION.

When the Bears won the Super Bowl in 1985, they were capping off a three-year ascent that began with the 1983 draft. That draft planted the seeds. In 1984 they climbed the ranks of the NFC, going all the way to the NFC title game where they lost to the eventual Super Bowl champion 49ers. And in 1985, they put it all together and won the Super Bowl.

In my twenty-four years as a Chicago sports fan, I have experienced the thrill of eight championships on some level or another — as a wee pup in '85 with the Bears, six for the Bulls in my teenage years, and this year with the White Sox as a borderline participant. I've seen Northwestern go to (and lose) the Rose Bowl, the Blackhawks go to (and lose) the Stanley Cup, Illinois go to (and lose) the national title game in hoops, and the Cubs and the Sox each go to (and lose) the LCS. The majority of my joy in watching Chicago sports during my life has stemmed from the players and the teams, not the championships.

On the other hand, the Florida Marlins have won two World Series in their thirteen years of existence. Both of those teams were surprises, as they were not successful in the years leading up to their championships. And both of those teams were one-and-dones, as the Florida management decided that they could no longer afford the players who had brought them a championship, or that they just didn't want to, or something.

So Florida Marlins fans — whichever ones there are — have been given two World Series titles without having one single player that they can hang their hats on as a classic Florida Marlin. Maybe Jeff Conine. Maybe. In that same time span of 1997-2003, the title-less Chicago baseball fans were able to watch Ryne Sandberg, Frank Thomas, Mark Grace, Sammy Sosa, Magglio Ordonez, and Paul Konerko.

Championships are nice, but what moves me as a sports fan are the lifetime players, the memorable teams, the guys who I will one day tell my kids about. Maybe that's just a Chicago sports defense mechanism, but I doubt it.

Which brings us back to the 2005 Chicago Bears, a team with more swagger and legit talent than the 2001 team, and as the wins keep coming, and our defense continues to play well, I began to wonder more and more if the Bears can win a Super Bowl this year. And as I wonder that, a part of me is feeling nervous, as if winning a Super Bowl this year out of nowhere will somehow lessen my overall enjoyment. Can I enjoy a championship without the buildup? Without the playoff losses and growing pains?

Well, the White Sox just won a World Series in that way, and nobody seemed to care. They hadn't been to the playoffs since 2000, the year that they won the most games in the American League and were promptly swept out of the postseason by the Mariners. The team that won this year was devoid of Mags, Carlos Lee, and Frank (more or less), three of the biggest stars on that 2000 team, and three guys who were all significant contributors up until this season. A.J., Iguchi, Uribe, Pods, Jermaine, Contreras, Garcia, Jenks, and Dustin Hermansen were all acquired either this season or in 2004, and long-time prospects Aaron Rowand, Joe Crede, and Jon Garland hit their potential this season. So this really was a surprise team, and everybody enjoyed them. I never got the feeling that the championship was in any way cheapened by their sudden rise.

But then again, 162 games is plenty of time to grow fond of new guys, and the length of a baseball season has always negated any possibility of a fluke-championship. This is not the case in football, where a team can come out of nowhere to win a Super Bowl as the '99 Rams, 2000 Ravens, and '01 Patriots all did. There is a part of me that is truly afraid of the Bears winning a Super Bowl this season...

But wait! Isn't that fear unfounded? Even if they were to win a Super Bowl this year, the Bears would not dish out their players. We're not going to have a Marlins fire sale. We're not over our heads in salary, and we're not vying for a new stadium deal. On top of that, isn't our situation similar to the 2005 White Sox? The Sox missed the playoffs in 2001, 2002, 2003, and 2004, but since that 2000 season they have had a team on paper that could compete for a championship.

I always felt that the Bears' 1999 and 2000 drafts would be the foundations to championships, and when they went to the postseason in 2001, I felt vindicated. We were brutal in '02, '03, and '04, but wasn't that due to silly front office meddling? Isn't this 2005 team rooted in the same base as the 2001 team? The defensive leaders of this year — Urlacher, Mike Brown, Azumah, and even Michael Green — were all members of the 2001 team, as was Olin Kreutz, our best offensive player since 2001. Maybe this team really is more of a culmination of those earlier drafts and the earlier success than we all like to think.

Or maybe the foundation of this team is the 2003 draft — the one that brought Briggs, Tillman, Ian Scott, Wade, Gage, Todd Johnson, Rex, and Michael Haynes — and this year will be our 1984, with a Super Bowl champion coming next year.

No matter what happens, I am sure of one thing: when you build your sports fan identity on the lessons of losing, winning blows your mind and gets you thinking thoughts you could have never imagined. More than winning, and certainly more than losing, sports fans want to be given life. We want the full spectrum, the full story, the ups that feel better because they were born of downs. The '85 Bears and the '91 Bulls, they gave us championships, but more than that, they gave us life and everything that life entails. They were full experiences, and with this Bears team there is a small part of me that fears missing out.

******

Or maybe not.

After much analysis, I still don't know entirely what all of this means, but maybe my answer can be found simply in my emotions during the Packers game.

The Colts were playing the Titans on CBS yesterday at 1, which meant that FOX did not carry a game in Indianapolis. So I headed over to Buffalo Wild Wings to watch the game, which frightened me since all three of the Bears' losses this season had come when I was watching the games at sports bars. The place was packed, and I ended up sharing a table with two other Bears fans.

When meeting Chicago fans outside of Chicago, the first question I always ask is, "Where are you from?" The person usually says "Chicago" or one of the suburbs, but sometimes they are from someplace else in the country, and when this is the case the immediately add in, "…but my family is from Chicago."

So it was with great surprise that when I asked the first of these two fans — a guy a little bit older than us named Mel — where he was from, he responded "Puerto Rico," and nothing else.

"Really?" I said, wondering what the rest of the story was. "Is your family from Chicago?"

"Nope. We're Puerto Rican. But we got WGN, and so I became a Cubs fan…"

"That's amazing!"

"...and then from there I just became a Chicago fan all around."

Mel's friend Rob came in from parking the car.

"This is Jack."

"Good to meet you," Rob said, sitting down as we shook hands. "Rob."

"Jack. Where are you from?"

"Orland Park. You?"

"Evanston and Wilmette."

The game had a slow pace to it to start, which was fine since I was suffering from unspeakable levels of nervousness and twisted excitement. We backed the Packers up inside their fifteen on their first drive, forcing them to punt. It was an ugmo, and the Bears took the ball inside Green Bay's thirty. But on the very first play, Orton's pass bounced off of Desmond Clark's hands, flew up into the air and was intercepted. We stuffed Green Bay again, and again they dropped a short punt to us, and again we punted back to them.

"Watching the Bears is like a manic depressive's worst nightmare," Rob said, laughing. "But I like our strategy. The Packers punt to our thirty, we punt to their twenty, they punt to our forty, we punt to their ten...if we keep going like this we'll be in field goal range in no time."

"We're not getting pressure on Favre like we did against Carolina and Tampa Bay," I said. "They're playing loose." (A clear sign that Rob is much more relaxed than I am: he's making jokes, and I'm already dipping into the Serious Analysis jar.)

The game was still scoreless at the end of the first, and in the middle of the second, around the time that my burger was arriving, the Bears put up a field goal. They stuffed the Packers and got the ball back, but Green Bay sacked Orton on consecutive plays, forcing and recovering a fumble on the second. Favre drove them 60 yards for a score, a short run by Samkon Gado. 7-3, Green Bay.

Now it was 7-6 Packers, late in the first half, and Favre was leading them back down the field and back towards the endzone. *Here we go again* was the general mood at the table. We'd all seen this look from Favre plenty of times. He's like Clint in the Mexican standoff scene from *The Good, the Bad, and the Ugly*: confident to the point that you suspect he knows something you don't.

"Shit, Favre's going in," said Rob.

"You gotta stay confident," said Mel.

I didn't say anything. I was watching for trends, looking for the Big Picture. We weren't attacking Favre the way we'd attacked Delhomme and Simms. This worried me. We had to get at Favre, to knock him on his ass. We couldn't be afraid of him anymore.

The Packers kept moving the ball.

They ran a reverse to the left, and Favre was out in front as the lead blocker. He threw his body in front of Vasher, sending them both to the ground. Then, getting up, he slapped Vasher on the ass.

It was the kind of gesture that makes Brett Favre impossible to dislike.

It's the way that he engages the opposition, the way that he sparks the players on the other team to play their best. It's the way that he fosters an atmosphere of respect, respect for the opposition, and respect for competition, for competing as hard and as true as you can, because that's the only way to play.

But still, this is Brett Favre, quarterback for the *Green Bay Packers*, and as much as I respect the guy, he's still the quarterback of the other team. Brett was leading the Pack right down the field, and we were letting him do it. If this guy was playing his final season, then that meant that he was playing his final game at Soldier Field, and I didn't want the Bears going down without proving that after thirteen years, the tables were finally turned.

Come on fellas. Stop him here. Put the clamps on. Knock him on his ass.

And then...

"Here it comes," said Mel, smiling oddly. "Our defense is getting a turnover right here, and we're gonna take it back for a touchdown."

The Bears crowded the line, put a nice rush on Favre, and as he was falling back he lofted a pass towards the endzone. It faded to the left, like a wounded duck or Judge Smails' slice into the woods, and Peanut jumped up and snatched it.

"Yes! Peanut!"

Tillman brought the ball out of the endzone, and as our table and the table of Bears fans behind us began clapping and yelling and cheering, all of us on our feet, Tillman galloped 95 yards before being taken down at the eight with six seconds left. Robbie Gould came out, nailed a field goal, and the Bears went into the locker room with a 9-7 lead.

The teams started slowly in the second half, but the Bears were growing more confident on defense. *Attack-attack-attack. You have to attack.* The third quarter was scoreless, but it took a toll on Favre, who we knocked down repeatedly. *Alright now. Get at this guy. Don't be afraid.* The Bears got another field goal in the fourth quarter... 12-7... but we were still only hanging on. We were getting to Favre, which made me happy; late in the third, Mike Brown crushed Favre for a sack on a blitz, and Favre was left wincing, holding his right hand. Green Bay's backup quarterback Aaron Rodgers began warming up, but I knew better.

"No way Favre comes out," I said. "I don't care if every bone in that man's hand is broken. If the skin is still intact — I don't care if his hand is like broken egg shells inside of a glove — if the skin is attached from the elbow to the tips of the fingers, Brett Favre will figure out a way to throw the football."

And I was right.

Favre stayed in the game, and not only did we continue hitting him, but now we were forcing turnovers. Tommie Harris struck first, sacking Favre and forcing a fumble that Lance Briggs recovered. Tillman came unblocked on a corner blitz on Green Bay's next possession and knocked the piss out of Favre from the blind side, forcing a fumble that Ogunleye fell on. Still the Bears were unable to produce on offense, and so back the ball went to Green Bay on yet another Brad Maynard punt.

I was getting antsy.

Yes, we were beating the Packers. Yes, it looked as if our defense was growing stronger as the game went on; they had certainly regained the dominant form that led us to victories during the past two weeks. And yes, I was enjoying the game. A win is a win is a win, and a win over Green Bay is the best win of all. And yet throughout, I felt like something was missing. I was nervous that we were going to win without *earning* a win, I was nervous that we were going to win without making a statement, and there was still the possibility that we wouldn't win at all, that Brett would rally the troops and somehow lead the Packers to a 15-12 win. Again, I didn't want to lose to the Packers, but even more than that, *I didn't want to beat them accidentally.*

After the second fumble, the Bears again failed to move the ball, and so it went back to the Packers for yet another shot at the endzone. On first down, we played them loose on the line. On second down, we did the same. *Come on guys! Get at him! Do it like you've been doing it! Don't be intimidated.* On third down, the Bears stacked the line and showed blitz, and I exploded.

"Alright! We're gonna get one right here! We're getting another turnover RIGHT HERE! Come on guys!"

PART XVII: CLIMBING THE MOUNTAIN

Favre went back to throw... pressure on him... bad throw... Vasher jumped the route... HE GOT IT! Vasher's gonna score! Go! Go! Go! Go! Holy hell! Touchdown Bears! Touchdown Bears! Touchdown Bears!

We were all screaming like that, high-fiving each other, and I just continued screaming as my phone rang, and without looking I picked it up, yelling.

"Yes! Yes! Yes! Touchdown! Aaaaahhhhhhhhhhhhhhhh!" I was yelling and barking, exorcising the spirits Otis Wilson and Dave Duerson and Richard Dent. And then... "Who is this?"

"It's your mother!"

"Oh! Hi Mom!"

"What a play, huh?"

"You're goddamn right!"

"Well, just wanted to say hello."

"Hello!"

And we hung up.

I was still out of breath, and my throat, which hadn't yet fully recovered from the Tillman interception, was now completely shot and scratchy. The Bears now led 19-7, but there were two minutes left, which meant that while the odds of a Green Bay comeback were remote, it was still entirely possible. I'd seen it done — TD, onside kick, TD — many a time. *Let's get a stop! Let's not just 'not lose.' Let's win this game. Come on guys, put it away.*

Brett was leading the Packers down the field, but the clock was running. It looked like the Bears would win, but I didn't just want a win; I wanted to snuff them out, like we had against Baltimore, Carolina, and Tampa Bay.

Well, it didn't happen.

Instead of a Last Stand, a Beat Down, a Snuff 'em Out and Send 'em Home, the Packers drove the field and managed to move the ball inside our ten. Their final play of the game was an 11-yard pass to Tony Fisher that picked up a first down. Then the clock hit 'zero,' and that was it. The game was ours.

And you know what?

It felt good.

I mean, really good.

We didn't look great, and we didn't end the game with an emphatic stuff. And yet, within the confines of the game, I felt great. I left Buffalo Wild Wings smiling and in good spirits. We beat Green Bay. For sixty minutes, we were the better team. It wasn't our greatest performance, but it wasn't luck, either. It was just a win, a win in which the team that made the most big plays won, and to my surprise, I loved every minute of it.

Separate from the Big Picture, separate from Orton's poor play, separate from Green Bay's final drive, separate from anything that the hard-bitten, tough-loving, analytical Jack M. Silverstein may have been *thinking*, I enjoyed the game. Loved every minute of it. Loved the feeling of watching my team play. Loved the feeling of watching my team win. For sixty minutes, the Bears made me feel good.

And if we win the Super Bowl this year, fall apart in 2006, and never compete again with this team, you know what?

I'll always have this season, just one, single season, and that's all you can ever really hope for.

Oct. 16, 2005, "Bear Down and Get Some Runs"
Age 23

THE WHITE SOX TO THE WORLD SERIES!

So here we are again, back in what should be the most exhilarating and wondrous place for a sports fan, and yet I find myself terrified and anxious. Illinois-UNC? Forget it. I was cool. Bulls-Wizards Game 6? No way. I was still pumped, and that's considering that we'd just lost three straight, including the heartbreaker in Game 5. Cubs-Marlins 5 and 6? Nope. I was pumped up for those too. Even Game 7 had an excitement to it. Now, staring down Game 5 of the ALCS with the Sox up three games to one, I know this team isn't too far from putting the city through 2003 all over again.

As usual, I am most nervous in situations where I should be most calm. Any time a Chicago baseball team is favored to win a series or key game, I get nervous, because we've made the mistake of putting ourselves in a sticky position in which we *have to win*, lest we choke. And we all know how good we are at *that*.

Of course, there's a part of me that is so amped right now it's unbelievable. That's the part of me looking at The Facts, facts like three straight complete games from Buehrle, Garland, and Garcia, Sox bats on fire, and of course Vlad Guerrero, walking nightmare.

But more exciting than The Facts are The Possibilities. Imagine: a Chicago team in the World Series! Nothing I've ever known as a sports fan approaches that, and even though my emotions are not fully engrossed in this team, my objective side is still damn-excited.

I care deeply about football, baseball, and basketball, and the World Series is the most historic and holy of any of those championships. The NBA Finals? Exciting and important because it's a championship, but not over-the-top in the areas of myth and lore. The Super Bowl?

Amazing, a true pinnacle, and obviously I'd rather see the Bears win the Super Bowl than seeing the Cubs (and certainly the Sox) win the World Series. But there's so much spectacle, and it's just one game, and since I was only four in January '86, I can't honestly say that I was more excited/anxious for that than I am this. When the Bears go back to the Super Bowl, I will be infinitely more excited. But for now, this tops January of '86 simply because of my age.

I've experienced just about everything as a sports fan. Teams I've rooted for have won a Super Bowl and six NBA titles along with appearances in the Stanley Cup Finals and the Rose Bowl. The World Series? Never. Not once. So close and yet so, so, painfully, far.

So now that Chicago has a chance to go to the World Series, even if it is the other guys, I'm expected to remain calm and in control? How is that possible?

It will have to be possible, because until I see a final count that says the White Sox have won four games out of seven in the ALCS, and until I've confirmed that count with at least three friends or family members as well as three separate, unbiased media sources, and until I've slept, and then woken the next day and found the count still standing, I will not get excited. I refuse to revisit 2003... and even though it won't be my team on the field today, the possibility of experiencing some sort of horrible flashback has left me rather cautious. You'd better believe I won't be counting outs during *this* game.

I call Luke, who can hardly hold the phone to his face. "Here we go...!"

And here we go.

Paul Byrd begins the game by striking out Podsednik. Byrd won Game 1, putting together Anaheim's most complete starting pitching performance of the series, the only guy other than Washburn who seems to have equaled the White Sox starters.

His opponent is Jose Contreras, who came up two-thirds of an inning shy of a complete game in their Game 1 matchup. Contreras has been wonderful in the postseason, and makes short work of the Angels in the first.

Soon after, the Sox get on the board. Rowand clocks a ground-rule double to right, Pierzynski lays down a bunt to move Rowand to third, and Crede sacrifices to center to score Rowand. 1-0 Sox on the Ozzie-Ball maneuvering.

Rain is falling. Not hard enough to get the game canceled, but beating down. The Angels tie in the bottom of the third off an Adam Kennedy single, but the Sox answer in the fifth: a Uribe double, a walk to Pods, and after Iguchi flies out Jermaine ropes a double to left-center to score Uribe. 2-1 Sox, and out comes Paul Byrd with a nice hand from the crowd at Angels Stadium. Too bad. I was really starting to like Byrd; he seemed like a guy who could have battled Contreras all night.

Their starting pitcher gone, the Angels turn to their pen and their bats, and with Kennedy on first, the much-maligned Chone Figgins rips a ball to right on an off-balance swing that energizes the Angel crowd. The hit-and-run is on, and Kennedy is rounding second before the ball hits the ground, and as it skips off the grass and makes its way for the wall, a fan cloaked in red flips his hand over the rail and snatches the baseball.

A good souvenir... oh, and by the way, you just cost your team a run as Kennedy was rounding third on the reach. Kennedy stops at third, Figgins at second, and the crowd's mood drops from euphoria to betrayal...

...though it takes a little while for the L.A. fans to dig what's happening, as they never seem fully engaged in the ballgame. Mike Scioscia scoots out of the dugout to argue fan-interference... and, in what seems to us an unprecedented turn of events, fan-interference is granted. *Wait a second! They actually do that?* Kennedy takes home, the game is tied, and every Cubs fan watching wonders why we are never quite that lucky.

Figgins stays at second, and when Orlando Cabrera hits a high chopper to Iguchi, Figgins takes third on the out to first. Then it's Garret Anderson, who sends a deep fly to right field. Figgins tags and scores easily. 3-2 Angels, and that's where it would stay until the seventh…

******

Late in the game… late in the game… this has been the White Sox' time: they outscored Boston 3-0 in the seventh inning or later, and so far in the ALCS they have outscored the Angels 4-0 after the seventh. Ozzie's White Sox have been an intelligent, defensive-minded squad all season. That's how they were built; their dominance during the final three innings of their postseason games has been confirmation of their strengths.

Sure enough, the New Mr. October slams the second Kelvim Escobar pitch he sees well over the fence to tie the game. HOT DAMN! What a hit by Crede! Sox fans in the house are seen choking rally monkeys, and on FOX's let's-hear-what's-happening-in-the-dugout shot, Pierzynski lets out an exuberant "Fuck yeah!" which is promptly ignored by Buck, McCarver, and guest Lou Piniella. Crede is the first batter Escobar has faced since Crede himself, when the Sox' third baseman ended Game 2.

On a whole, however, Anaheim's pen has been pretty sharp. FOX flashes a stat comparing the teams' relievers…

- WHITE SOX: 2/3 innings, 7 pitches
- ANGELS: 17 1/3 innings, 245 pitches

…and even though they've worked a slew of innings, the Crede home run is only the third earned run allowed by the Angels' pen. Scot Shields has been the best of the lot; he just completed his fourth appearance in five games, and has given up only four hits in six innings, walking one, K-ing five, allowing no runs. Kudos to the Angels' pen... but it's not good enough when your starters are averaging under five innings per start.

Into the eighth. Don't say it Jack...

Escobar strikes out Konerko and Everett to begin the eighth. And then: more madness. Rowand walks on a 3-2 breaking ball that misses away, and Pierzynski comes up. A.J. is greeted with boos from the Angels' crowd, and he settles in to face Escobar, and now we've got the matchup that spawned the controversial game-changing play of Game 2. A pick-off move to first to hold Rowand, and then a brief conference on the mound with the pitching coach, and finally a pitch to Pierzynski, who looks at ball one outside.

The Angels crowd is anxious, but hopeful and supportive, and with Crede on deck and K-Rod warming up Escobar turns and fires to the plate, and Pierzynski bounces a comebacker at Escobar, and it bounces away from him and rolls towards the first base line, and now Escobar scoops it with his pitching hand and reaches to tag Pierzynski with his glove for the third out... *whoa! Wait a second!*

"Did you see that??!!!" I yell to no one. I laugh, nearly dumbfounded. "He tagged him with his empty glove!"

Pierzynski is initially called out by the first base umpire, who does not have a good sightline, but A.J. and Tim Raines argue, and Ozzie hauls ass out of the dugout to do likewise, and the umpires confer and overturn the call. The Angels fans are pissed, feeling betrayed — *Pierzynski again? I know what happened, but can't they just give it to us as a makeup?* — and Scioscia comes out to rage in vain. Poor Angels. You gotta feel for them.

No doubt about that one though, and there are runners at first and second with two outs. Rodriguez replaces Escobar and promptly stares down Crede. Ball, strike, strike, and then two more balls, and now the count is full, and it's the Angels' best reliever against the White Sox' best clutch hitter of the postseason with two outs and two on in a tie ball game...

…and BAM! Crede bounces one, hard up the middle past Rodriguez. Kennedy dives and stops it, but he's already in the outfield grass, and as he pops to his knee to throw home Rowand charges the plate and slides head first to score. *YES! YES!* 4-3 Sox in the eighth. More excited, audible cursing from Pierzynski, who is now standing at second, and once again it is the White Sox who prove that's it's not That Play that determines wins and losses, but rather what happens after That Play.

Rodriguez walks Uribe on four pitches to load the bases, and then in a tense at-bat that reaches a full count, K-Rod regains his control and K's Podsednik to end the chaos.

Despite having already thrown 95 pitches, Contreras remains in the game and works a perfect, eight-pitch eighth, retiring Cabrera in two pitches, Anderson in five, Guerrero on one. Vlad has been particularly absent during this series; before his at-bat FOX flashes a comparison graph of Vlad's '05 postseason against Dave Winfield's '81 postseason with the Yankees:

- WINFIELD '81: .086, 0 HR, 3 RBI
- VLAD '05: .053, 0 HR, 1 RBI

No sooner do they drop that stat does Vlad ground out to Iguchi. End of eight, Sox 4, Angels 3. *Don't say it, Jack. Don't say it.*

FOX goes to a shot of Reinsdorf in his box, and the two kids with him cheer madly. Joe Buck mentions that "his Chicago White Sox are three defensive outs away from their first pennant in 46 years." That stuff usually freaks me out, but I'm actually pretty cool right now. I know it's weird, and I'm kind of surprised about it, but this feels like a different team than we're used to.

Iguchi walks to start the inning. Then he swipes second. Top nine, runner in scoring position, nobody out, Dye at the plate, and Jermaine walks on a ball high. *Boy, K-Rod does not look like K-Rod. Now's the time…*

Konerko to the plate, the rain still coming. Ball low and away. 1-0. Ball up and in. 2-0. Crowd getting antsy. Rodriguez looks surprised, and now we have another mound visit, and Buck announces that the last time the White Sox put together four consecutive complete games was August of 1974. It feels so normal right now...

...and then, on a 2-0 pitch to Konerko, Paulie sends one over Vlad's head that bangs off the wall. Iguchi scores, and it's 5-3 Sox with runners at second and third. *Oh man! We're beating up their best pitcher!* Then Rowand hits one to right, and it's Vlad's Hall of Fame arm against Jermaine's less than swift feet... and he misses him! Guerrero makes an awful throw that Bengie Molina fields about four or five steps off the plate up the third base line allowing Dye to score easily. Molina fires to third, and Figgins makes the catch and the tag on the sliding Konerko to end the inning.

But the run counts, and now it's 6-3 Sox going into the bottom of the ninth, with the Sox now... *come on Jack, don't say it. Don't say it...*

When the ninth begins, Jenks and Cotts are warming up, with Contreras back on the mound. FOX gives us another grammatically-limited POSTSEASON FACT: **last time team had 4 consecutive complete games: 1956 W.S. (NYY)—5 consecutive (Games 3-7)**. I have a hunch, and I go online quickly to confirm, and sure enough I find that one of those complete games was Don Larsen's perfect game in Game 5, still the only perfect game pitched in the postseason... *Yogi Berra jumping into Larsen's arms after catching the final out...* and once again I am awed by the feeling of connection felt in baseball's steep history.

First up for the Angels: Darin Erstad. Strike looking, strike swinging, foul... *Sox fans wiping rain from their faces, waiting waiting...* and now Erstad chops one high to Uribe, who sits on it and then makes a quick throw to Konerko. One out.

Bengie Molina up, and as I try harder and harder to zone in on the at-bat and ignore the Big Picture, Joe Buck spells things out to a ridiculous level: "It has been 16,825 days since the White Sox last won a pennant. They clinched it in 1959, September 22nd"... (pause, as Contreras delivers strike one looking to Molina)... "against Cleveland."

A strike from Contreras, and Molina fouls it away. The rain pounds down. 0-2 to Molina, and Contreras misses away for ball one. Another foul tip, and a shot of Garcia in the dugout. 1-2 to Molina, and he shoots one into center that looks for a moment like it will drop in front of Rowand, but the Sox' ace of a defensive centerfielder has made the perfect jump on the ball. Two outs, and Buck says what I can't: "In the air to center... Rowand is there... one out away for the White Sox."

FOX cuts away to run clips from the Sox clincher on September 22, 1959, complete with "Go-Go White Sox!" playing on the soundtrack. My dad was nine... could he have appreciated that the Sox hadn't won a pennant since 1919? How could he know that they wouldn't win another until...

Not yet...Not yet...

...and now my head goes spinning back to Game 7, the Marlins celebrating on our field, and then to the pain and confusion of Game 6, and then back to Frank and Mags and Konerko swept by Seattle, and the Cubs being swept by Atlanta, and then back to the White Sox losing in six to Toronto, and then Will Clark pounding us in '89... my first real Cubs team... and then the Cubs in '84 and the Sox in '83, my brother's life beginning with back-to-back Chicago baseball playoff seasons, and now my parents are getting married after eight years of on-again/off-again dating/friendship, and now they're finishing college, and now the Mets have topped the Cubs and won the pennant and my mom is wondering if she'll ever be able to watch this team again, and now my dad is sorting his baseball card collection, and now it's Leo Durocher and Al Lopez, and now the Go-Go Sox are going to the World Series after a 40-year layoff, and surely it won't be another 40 years before they get there again...

Don't say it, Jack. Don't say it...

PART XVII: CLIMBING THE MOUNTAIN

...GROUND BALL TO FIRST! KONERKO STEPS ON THE BAG! SOX WIN! SOX WIN! SOX WIN! OH MY GOD THE WHITE SOX ARE GOING TO THE WORLD SERIES!

I am jumping up and down. I am shaking my head. There is a pure joy to this moment, and I feel a part of it, even though it is not a part of me. It's the release; the ball is a very hard chopper behind the bag, and Konerko gloves it calmly, steps on first, and then the release as he smiles and puts his arms out in celebration, running over to embrace Contreras, who is also smiling big now after a brilliant straight-faced performance. Everyone breathes, everyone cheers. The city is happy.

For 26 outs, nobody wanted to take any chances jinxing the Sox, and so they kept their mouths shut and their excitement bottled, and then the grounder to Paulie, and everything is fine. *Oh man! Oh my god! Holy shit! Holy cow!* I call Luke and then Sven, both of whom eventually answer the phone screaming, but I don't reach them immediately because they are on the phone with each other, and so I call my parents. Mom picks up:

"Wow." And then: "How great was that?"

Indeed. The story of the ALCS was three-fold:

1. **Four consecutive complete games** for Mark Buehrle, Jon Garland, Freddy Garcia, and Jose Contreras. Including Contreras' loss in 8 1/3 innings in Game 1, the Sox starters went 4-1 in 44 1/3 innings with a sparkling 2.23 ERA and a crippling 1.79 opponents batting average.

2. **The big bat of Joe Crede.** Paul Konerko somehow won the ALCS MVP, and though he played well (.286, 2 HR, 7 RBI), the Sox' best position player was easily Crede. He was the best batsman for either team, hitting .368 (next best average for a regular: Podsednik at .294 followed by Konerko and L.A.'s Kennedy at .286) with two home runs and seven knocked in. He also came through in the clutch, winning Game 2 with the walk-off double and producing three run-scoring AB's

in Game 5: the sac fly in the second to make it 1-0 Sox, the game-tying solo shot in the seventh, and the RBI single in the eighth that gave his team a lead they would never lose.

3. **Ozzie Ball.** Whatever it is, whatever it means, this team has played differently than have the power-Sox teams of recent years. The Sox outscored the Angels 7-0 in the first inning and 8-0 in the seventh inning and beyond. They also drew more walks (16 to 4), stole more bases (5 to 2), committed fewer errors (3 to 7), allowed zero unearned runs (6 for the Angels), and had an astounding edge in OBP (.315 to .196).

Put it all together and you get the White Sox going to the World Series.

And *thar* ya go.

Jan. 16, 2007, ReadJack.com
   Age 25

DA BEARS ARE GOOOOOOD

The following are perfectly acceptable storylines that could have easily been focused upon following the Bears' 27-24 overtime victory Sunday:

1. Thomas Jones looking like a Man On A Mission, dragging his teammates to the endzone twice and batting down a tipped ball to prevent an interception.
2. Robbie Gould drilling two kicks that, considering his NFL experience, may have been his version of Vinitieri's pair against the Raiders in the snow.
3. The Bears beating the Seattle Seahawks in the playoffs, a team that was one of only three NFL teams currently riding postseason streaks of four consecutive seasons or more, the other two being the AFC's two remaining clubs.

4. Rex Grossman playing a very strong game and leading our Bears—his Bears—to a postseason victory.
5. Briggs, Peanut, Berrian, and Rashied Davis all having big games, and Ricky Manning Jr., Hunter, Tank, Ced Benson, and Israel Idonije all making big plays.
6. The Bears advancing to the NFC title game for the first time in 18 years.

These are just some possibilities. There are others.

And yet we've been hammered with more negativity than I've cared to read, watch, or listen to. One gets a sense that this Bears team is, somehow, the most disappointing team in the postseason.

Of course, this is nothing new. The Bears have, apparently, been disappointing fans and critics all season long.

Well boo freakin' hoo.

Apparently it's not enough to win 13 games and your division, dominate on defense, produce a smothering and accurate and deadly special teams unit, and be the franchise's second highest scoring team since the season expanded to 16 games in 1978. Nope. You have to be flawless. Without flaw. Without peer. In fact, you have to be perfect. Beyond perfect, even. 1985-perfect, if there is such a thing.

Well, that's the thing. There isn't. Not even the '85 Bears were perfect...which, of course, is part of what made them so memorable. 15-1 isn't perfect, nor is a quarterback who moons cameramen, nor is a coach who flips off opposing fans, nor is a defense that barks at the opposition. That team wasn't perfect. They were unique. To duplicate them in personality is nearly impossible. To duplicate them in performance is to be one of the greatest teams of all-time.

OK, fine: the 2006 Bears have not been one of the greatest teams of all-time. They are not nearly as dominant, and certainly not as charismatic, as were the 1985 team. But name me a club since 1985 that has been? The closest thing we've gotten has been the '92-'95 Cowboys, but no single season stands out ahead of any other.

I struggle to think of another team in any sport as successful as the 2006 Bears that has been driven into the ground by the national and local media quite so much. Have they really been as disappointing as many have made them out to be? Or is it simply unfair and unreasonable to compare this club over the past two and a half months to the uninjured, relatively untested team of the first two and a half months? Of course it is, just as it was unfair to draw comparisons to the '85 team after this team's 7-0 start.

So what are the Bears? Well, to quote a former head coach who will remain nameless, the Bears are who we thought they were. Good. Damn good. The best team in the NFC all season, and arguably the best in the NFL. On a defense stocked full of wonderful players, three of them stand out as being "super important": Brian Urlacher, Mike Brown, and Tommie Harris. The Bears have lost two of those three guys and remained powerful. Their passing offense has been the best that it has been since 1999, yet this season it came under the guidance of one quarterback rather than three. And their rushing attack has improved all year: 98 yards a game in the season's first four games, 110.5 in Quarter Two, 131.8 in Quarter Three, and 139.3 in Quarter Four. How disappointing.

Whatever happened to appreciating a team that Finds A Way To Win? Isn't that what we always say about the great teams? Isn't that what we say is the difference between 11-5 and 5-11? Winning instead of losing: isn't that what matters most? I guess not. I guess what matters most are Super Bowl Shuffles and Punky QB's and obliterating teams 31.6 to 9.9 as the Bears did over their first seven games.

The 2005 White Sox made a habit of playing close games and giving their fans exciting wins, and they were loved for it. When Rex and Urlacher and TJ and co. do the same, they are booed and poo-poo'd, their will and skill questioned.

Ah well. You can't please everybody.

PART XVII: CLIMBING THE MOUNTAIN 403

Yes, the Bears are who we thought they were: an excellent football team that needs one more win to get to the Super Bowl. If you want to crown their asses, then crown them. If not, I guess they'll have to do it themselves.

Dec. 30, 2019, Twitter
Age 38

MY FIRST NIGHT IN THE BLEACHERS: THE CUBS REACH THE WORLD SERIES

I will never forget seeing Sammy Sosa hit his 500th career home run in 2003. I'll never forget Mark Grace's lead-off single in the 9th inning of Game 7 of the 2001 World Series, starting the rally that would end five batters later with a D-Backs championship. I'll never forget seeing Scottie Pippen sniff out Utah's inbound on the final play of the 1997 Finals and dive to deflect the pass and seal championship number five.

Those are massive moments of sports history. I watched them all.

On television.

But my memory of Sammy Sosa's 300th home run in 1999 is crisper. As is my memory of Mark Grace's 2000th career hit, also in 1999. As is my memory of Scottie Pippen blocking consecutive Knicks three-pointers as time ran out in overtime of a three-point Bulls win on Christmas 1994.

That's because I watched those too — in person.

While I do recall seeing Sammy's 500th home run, my memory is largely factual. I was visiting Sammy V at Mizzou. We were watching

TV in his apartment. Sammy hit a home run. It was #500. That's it. That's the whole memory. Sammy's 300th? That memory is infinitely richer. I was seated on the first-base side, second section. He launched the ball to center, giving me a profile view of the flight of the ball. I remember the warmth of a June day at Wrigley. We were playing the Phillies. We immediately looked at our ticket stubs as the Golden Ticket that proved our participation.

There is nothing like being there. There is also nothing like seeing your team make history. I never attended a Bulls playoff game during the dynasty days. I wasn't at either of our NFC championship games. I was in the house for the Seabrook goal to knock out Detroit, but the Hawks were never my team in the way the Bulls were, and I was there as a reporter, working in the press box. That creates distance.

October 22, 2016 was my day with no distance. Game 6, Cubs-Dodgers, NLCS. My team made history and I was there, incredibly for my first ever game in the famed Wrigley bleachers.

When I awoke that morning I did not know I would be hitting Wrigley. I'd had an incredible moment exactly a week earlier when Katie took me, Rose and Shawn to Wrigley for Game 1 of the NLCS. We were there for Miguel Montero's tiebreaking, 8th inning grand slam, giving the Cubs a 7-3 lead in an 8-4 win. We lost Games 2 and 3 and won Games 4 and 5, and on the morning of Game 6, the Cubs had their best chance to reach the World Series since the you-know-what game 13 years earlier. I was pumped to watch it, likely at home, possibly at a bar.

I already had my grandchildren story: "Gather round, kiddos, and let me tell you how your grandfather saw the Miggy Slam!" I had no idea that would be my second best moment of the series.

Indeed, just reaching the World Series in my life would have been enough. And then it happened: the call. I love getting the call. I got the call for the 2001 Bears-Eagles divisional game. I got the call for Game 1 of the 2005 Bulls-Wizards series. Just a year earlier, I got the call from Jimmy Greenfield, who invited me to Game 4 of the NLCS as the Cubs attempted to stave off elimination from the Mets on Back to the Future Day. It was not to be, as the Cubs lost 8-3. But that team was a year ahead of schedule, and after the final out, we all stayed at the ballpark to give our Cubbies a standing ovation.

Our generational refrain of "next year" was not said in jest.

Fast forward to another possible NLCS capper at Wrigley, this one in our favor, and I saw the name pop on my phone: Andy Shlensky, bringer of the magic words.

"Where are you watching tonight?"

"Don't know. You?"

"With you. There."

WHAT??? I was stunned. I was shaken. I needed answers. Andy provided them. Our dear friend Josh Frost worked for Major League Baseball, and his wife Jess had just given birth to their first, meaning their four tickets for Game 6 were up for grabs. He'd given them to Andy and I got the call. The quartet was set: Shlensky, Dan, me and another camp friend, Andy Rodheim. I told Rose the great news and threw on a gameday outfit: my new RIZZO 44 t-shirt jersey that I bought earlier in the playoffs, my Cubs winter cap, and my MY BLOCK MY HOOD MY CITY hoodie which would provide both warmth and Chicago spirit.

Not only was I suddenly headed to Wrigley to maybe see the Cubs advance to their first World Series since 1945, but we were sitting in the bleachers. The only time I'd ever sat in the bleachers was a 2012 screening of "The Blues Brothers." Here I was less than a month before my 35th birthday, finally doing what most Cubs fans knock out several times before they're teenagers.

The four of us met outside the ballpark and took a picture together at 6:28 p.m. First pitch was called for 7 p.m. It was time to enter.

I was filled with my standard Wrigley butterflies. More than any other stadium, even Soldier Field, I get goosebumps heading up the steps at Wrigley. I can't explain it, but I think it's the depth of the history of the park mixed with the fandom thrill of live sports mixed with the relaxation of the baseball mixed with the sport's smells, sights and sounds. Add to that the double newness of the event — me in the bleachers and the Cubs on the cusp of the Fall Classic — and I was tingling.

I bought a scorecard and pencil and we settled into our seats in left. Shlensky and I took a picture, and looking at it again, I can see that on a confidence scale of 1 to 10, 1 being watching the Bartman game when the Marlins tied us up but before they blew us out, 10 being watching MJ sizing up Bryon Russell, I was about a 3. Incredibly, Glick was a bit lower in the bleachers. We came together for a pregame camp picture then listened to John Vincent crush the national anthem, holding the "free" on "o'er the land of the free" for 22 seconds. Twenty two!

At 7:06 p.m., with the stadium P.A. blasting "Sweet Emotion" by Aerosmith, the Cubs took the field. Deep, dark emotion consumed me. As the Cubs ran out, I burst into tears and started giggling. The lineup:

1. Dexter Fowler, CF
2. Kris Bryant, 3B
3. Anthony Rizzo, 1B
4. Ben Zobrist, LF, offering a hat tip to us all
5. Javy Baez, 2B
6. Willson Contreras, C
7. Addison Russell, SS
8. Albert Almora, RF
9. Kyle Hendricks, P

The Cubs scored fast. After Hendricks allowed a single on the first pitch of the game but forced the next man into a double-play and then retired the side, Fowler led off with a ground-rule double against three-time Cy Young winner Clayton Kershaw, banging a ball into the right-field corner that bounced into the stands. In the two-hole, Bryant — who a month later would become the first Chicago player since Sammy to win MVP — poked a low-and-away 1-2 pitch into right, scoring Fowler. Rizzo reached on a bloop to deep left that the Dodgers' left fielder dropped, taking 2nd as Bryant reached 3rd. Zobrist hit a sac fly to center for the first out of the inning, scoring Bryant.

That was it, a 2-0 lead, and after Hendricks faced just four batters in the 2nd without a hit, Addison Russell doubled to left to open the 2nd. There's a jolt sitting in the bleachers that doesn't exist elsewhere, as you realize that a ball that gets out could be coming to you. It's different than being on alert for a foul ball, or even on high alert for a liner foul down the line, like when Ben, Ben, Tony the Packers fan and I sat on the Cubs dugout for, of all games, the Sammy Sosa cork game. It's like if every Jordan dunk was going to bounce off the floor and then change angles to launch into the stands.

Russell's hit stayed in the park, and after Kershaw retired Almora and Hendricks, Fowler ripped a shot down the 3rd base line to score Russell, getting caught in a rundown to end the inning. 3-0 Cubs, and my stupid sports brain had, naturally, only one thought: that was the score heading into the Bartman inning. We would need at least one more run to ease my mind...

...and in the 4th, we got it! Contreras lined a homer over the left-field wall, giving the Cubs a 4-0 lead. I was still hoping for a home run to come our way but mostly I was delighted to be comfortable with the score again, not just because four runs is better than three but because *anything* was better than leading 3-0 at Wrigley in Game 6 of the NLCS. I didn't need the fresh hell of entering the 8th with *that* score. Rizzo added a solo shot in the 5th, by which point I was absolutely annihilating my scorecard pencil. We're talking Jon Voight-level Costanza teeth marks. I knew I'd grind away at that pencil until we reached the second out of the 8th inning to reach a point I'd never seen: four outs away from a Cubs World Series.

Hendricks was dealing. And when he shut down L.A. 1-2-3 in the 7th we prepared for the greatest Seventh Inning Stretch of our lives. Kyle was posting one of those all-time October pitching performances: a one-hit shutout with six strikeouts against zero walks and just two baserunners, one on an error. As he walked off the mound, the announcement of our guest conductor arrived: Scottie Pippen! To use my own name in vain, I was jacked. My emotions were all over the place. The Cubs went down 1-2-3 in the 7th but that was fine by me. The sooner we got into, and out of, the 8th, the better.

And then, panic.

After getting Adrian Gonzalez to fly out, Hendricks allowed only his second hit of the game, a one-out single. For some reason, Joe Maddon went to the pen, summoning fireball-throwing closer Aroldis Chapman. I started hyperventilating. I'd been alternating throughout the game between my scorecard and my phone for photos and video, and I turned the camera on myself.

"Yo one out in the 8th, they just took Hendricks out after allowing his first hit after the first pitch of the game," I said while we all gave Kyle a standing ovation. "We're bringing in Chapman, and this is now uncharted territory if he gets this out."

While Chapman warmed up with one on and one out, my stupid brain kept replaying the Castillo at bat, again and again and again, the ball floating toward Alou, the fan's hands launching over Moises, Prior pointing hopelessly toward the crime. I couldn't stop seeing it. My brain would not let me escape. Hell, my *eyes* would not let me escape. We were in left, for goodness sake, and I kept staring over at the Bartman seat as if I was sitting in Dealy Plaza in 2016 for a presidential motorcade…

…and then, boom! Chapman gasses the count on Howie Kendrick to 0-2 on back-to-back 100+ MPH pitches and coaxes Kendrick into a scalding double-play ball to 2nd, the Cubbies turning the 4-6-3. In one pitch, we pass the Bartman out AND get out of the 8th.

I am Terrence Mann entering the cornfield. I am Jack and Rose facing the iceberg. I am shaking. I am shrieking. I am clutching Miggy's slogan deep in my heart: "We are good."

We are good.

We go 1-2-3 in the 8th, but all that means is that we are fast-tracking our way to destiny. At the gates. Knocking. Peering. Creeping toward 1945. Do I like the Eminem song "Lose Yourself"? It's okay. Was I rapping along with it before the 9th inning of the NLCS as it played on the P.A. WITH THE CUBS ABOUT TO REACH THE WORLD FREAKING SERIES??? Damn straight.

"We are in the 9th inning!" Shlensky shouts into my camera. "We're going to the World Series if we get three outs." "Three outs," I say, as I pan over to Dan, one of my holy trinity of Cubs fan friends, who silently holds up three fingers. "Three outs!" Shlensky says. "Aroldis Chapman is going to hit 100 on every pitch —"

"One," I say.

"...and pitch his way..."

"Two."

"...into the World Series."

"Three.

"Chicago Cubs, World Series. Here we go."

Andy is on it. Chapman hits 100+ on four straight pitches to strike out Kiké Hernandez. I look over at Dan, who just blows an exasperated blow, his eyes large and waiting. Then Chapman walks Carlos Ruiz and I have a decision to make. I've been running a balancing act, literally and figuratively, between scoring the game and filming the game. So with a runner on and one out, I take a chance.

I choose the camera.

And man oh man, my heart is flying. My eyes have tears on deck. Chapman delivers, Yasiel Puig swings, and I see it! A grounder to short! Russell! To Baez! To Rizzo!

THE CUBS ARE GOING TO THE WORLD SERIES!!!!!!

We are screaming. We are leaping. We are hugging. I'm filming the madness and I see the time: 9:45 p.m. I check the score around the stadium and see that all 27 outs have been recorded. Joy. Havoc. I was thrilled for the Sox in '05, thrilled for Luke and Sven and Josh, but this is unlike anything I've ever felt as a sports fan. My baseball team is playing in the World Series. *Mine.* I'm here. We're all here. I don't care where you were. *YOU* were here.

We're singing "Go Cubs Go!" We're calling our friends and family. We're screaming into our phones. The Cubs are marching around the field saluting the fans. It has happened. I'm flabbergasted. There's a woman to my right who was cursing at the Dodgers the entire game and now she's sobbing on the bleachers floor. *Sobbing.* This woman went from unleashing language unfit for a child to weeping like one. That's the vibe. Peak WTF.

The centerfield scoreboard is the newspaper of the moment. It's history locked in. "2016 NATIONAL LEAGUE CHAMPIONS." Glick hops up a few rows and joins us for a picture, the scoreboard behind us. The Wrigley sound system just starts repeating songs. We've got "Go Cubs Go" again, and I'm even more into it than before. Andy and I let it out.

They're back to "Sweet Home Chicago" and I am speechless.

At 10:44 p.m. we finally leave Wrigley. We won't be allowed back in and I take just a beat to enjoy one last moment in the ballpark on the night that the Cubs reached the World Series for the first time in my

PART XVII: CLIMBING THE MOUNTAIN

parents' LIFE. We walk out of the gate at Waveland and Sheffield. Someone has put a Cubs jersey on the Harry Caray statue with the number 16. There is a makeshift wall just outside the ballpark and fans are lined up on the outside of the wall, their backs to Sheffield, cheering Cubs fans as we leave. I run past them screaming as they scream back, waving their blue W towels.

I spot chalk on the exterior Wrigley wall. I hadn't noticed it on the way in four hours prior but I see it now, fan after fan adorning the wall with tributes to their fandom. We're all high-fiving strangers. I high-five and then pose for a photo with a guy carrying an enormous Adrian Gonzalez Crying Jordan poster.

We walk the streets of Wrigleyville, literally the streets, since CPD has shut down Sheffield. A man in a full-body Spiderman suit with mask is standing atop a mailbox as people cheer him. A band of drummers and a kazoo player are regaling walkers. Shlensky, Dan, Rodheim and I make our way to a small bar and duck inside for a drink. We're buzzing, and we're deeply grateful to the new Frost child, whose birth allowed us to be here for history. We were screaming his name in celebration throughout the game and now we start planning a series of onesies with phrases to special order and rush delivery to the Frosts for Game 1 of the World Series. We grab a pen from the bar and sketch out ideas on a napkin. We come up with four, and while I love them all I have a clear favorite:

"I waited 48 hours to see the Cubs in the World Series."

Nov. 1, 2016, Facebook
    Age 34

UNTITLED (A PUBLIC PLEA ON THE EVE OF GAME 6 OF THE WORLD SERIES)

This is for Cubs fans, and this is for Sox fans, and this is for Chicago fans.

To my White Sox friends, I'm sorry. Nationally and locally, you're an afterthought. It gets annoying, and it's getting particularly annoying with the Cubs in the Series. You don't want the bandwagon overflow. You just want acknowledgement and respect. You want a dynamic that does not result in reporters and fans claiming this is the first World Series in Chicago since 1945.

Nationally, that's gonna happen. Whatever. But locally, that mistake is inexcusable. And really, it only gets made if for some reason you didn't take advantage of having the Sox in your city in 2005.

To Cubs fans who missed out, I'm sorry too. The 2005 White Sox remain one of the greatest teams of my sports fan life. If you missed it, there's no going back.

Because here's the truth: No one who watched the Sox in '05 (to say nothing of the Go-Go Sox of '59) would mistakenly claim that the 2016 Cubs are the city's first series participant in 71 years. The memories of Paulie, Jermaine, Buehrle, Crede, Ozzie, A.J., Contreras, Scotty Pods and so many more are far too strong.

And if the Sox win their next pennant before the Cubs get back, no one who watched this merry band of Bryzzo and Maddon, of Dexter and Jake, of Lester and Rossy, of Javy and Russell and all the rest, would say that the, for instance, 2076 White Sox was the city's first World Series team in 71 years.

If you would say either — that is, if you refuse to watch the other team by instinct or dogma or familial stipulation — you've been brainwashed. Pure and simple.

I agree that claiming "I like both teams equally" is hogwash. That just means you're not a baseball fan. I get it.

But the notion that Cubs fans can't enjoy and even support the Sox, and Sox fans can't enjoy and support the Cubs is foolishness.

Admittedly, I have a tangled history with Chicago baseball. I discovered the sport through the '89 Cubs, became a hard core Sox fan because of 1993, and found my Cubs love again in 1998. I've stayed true to that fandom the past 18 years.

Thus I've never viewed the White Sox (or for five years, the Cubs) as rivals. I view them as another team in Chicago for whom my heart does not beat.

Like the Blackhawks.

That's the unspoken secret of Chicago fandom: yes, we are split down baseball lines, but MOST Chicago fans are also split down hoops/hockey lines. Fans my age and older have seen championship incarnations of both the Bulls and the Blackhawks, so we've honed our ability to watch and root for and discuss both.

But the makeup of probably at least 80% of Chicago sports fans is as follows:

Bears + one baseball team + one United Center team.

It's like what Tarantino wrote about the Beatles and Elvis: Bulls fans can like hockey and Hawks fans can like basketball, but somewhere in life, you draw the line.

Fortunately for us, the Bulls and Hawks aren't actual rivals. When the Bulls were peaking, hockey fans could increase their fandom. And in this era of Cup-winning hockey, hoops heads can break down Kane & Toews like they're Scottie & Mike.

Bandwagon Blackhawks fans have become a tolerated feature of this Coach Q era. Our residency bequeaths our teams, even when we only actively follow during the good times.

Tonight, the Cubs play Game 6 of the World Series. Tomorrow night, we play Game 7. Since 1906, 17 Chicago teams have played in the World Series. Only once has that series featured both. In all other instances, we've had one Chicago team on baseball's biggest stage. One.

The 2016 World Series should be a citywide celebration. It's not. And I get the feeling that it's not because Cubs fans did not turn the 2005 World Series into the citywide celebration it should have been. We all came together for the Bulls in '91 and the Hawks in 2010, but our silly baseball brains won't allow us to make the same leap.

As my friend and colleague Evan Moore pointed out in a new piece at Complex called "Cubs Fever and the Two Chicagos," part of the reason Sox fans aren't excited for this World Series is that Northsiders so rarely celebrate anything south of Roosevelt. I was living in Indianapolis in 2005, but judging by stories emanating from the city at the time, Cubs fans weren't cheering for their Sox fan friends.

Which is goofy, because it's really as simple as that. I don't cheer for the Sox, per se. I cheer for my friends who are Sox fans. I don't pretend to be a Blackhawks fan — I support the Hawks to support my hockey friends.

To my Sox fan friends, if you want to hop in here tonight and tomorrow, feel free! We're open. And when the Sox are back in the World Series, I hope my fellow Cubs fans do the same and cheer for their friends, the same people they high-five and hug at Soldier Field and the U.C. Perhaps then we'll realize all this city has to offer.

Andy Rodheim, Brian Glickman with flag, Andy Shlensky, me with scorebook and Dan Lichtenstein at Wrigley Field, Oct. 22, 2016, after the Cubs' 5-0 win over the Dodgers sends them to their first World Series since 1945.

PART XVIII:
THE BATTERY

Oct. 14, 2013, The Hoyne House
Age 31

"IT'S LIKE A FRICKIN' UNSOLVED MYSTERY." MARK PRIOR AND PAUL BAKO REFLECT ON THE BARTMAN INNING, 10 YEARS LATER

"It's like a frickin' unsolved mystery. An unexplained phenomenon. It's like Big Foot or the Loch Ness Monster. I've never looked at the box score like this. I'm looking at it right now, and it's just such an anomaly. It's such a crazy — you know, 0, 0, 0, 1, 0, 0, 0, 0, 0, 0, 0, 1, 0, 1, 8, 0, 0, 0. It doesn't even make sense, you know?"

— Paul Bako, Cubs catcher

******

The Cubs were a nightmare in 2013. But they weren't my nightmare. My nightmare was 2008. My nightmare was 2004. My nightmare, still, was 2003. So at the start of the year, I set out to face my fears. I would contact every member of the 2003 Cubs for a massive 10-years-later oral history on a magical season that devolved into historic demise.

My outreach was largely unsuccessful. Sammy Sosa's place of business did not return my calls. Eric Karros, then a broadcaster, didn't either. I couldn't get through to Moises Alou. I failed to find Alex Gonzalez. Tom Goodwin called me back but we never found time for the interview. Kenny Lofton said he wasn't that big a part of the team — "You were!" I told him. "You hit .327! You jump-started us!" — and said that he was happy to participate if Sammy did it, and if Dusty did it, and if Mo and Gonzo and a few others did it.

But my efforts weren't entirely for naught. I had an incredible interview with Shawn Estes, including a story he had never told publicly about a day when he was walking through his Lincoln Park neighborhood in 2003, depressed about his most recent outing and overall struggles, when who should he see in a parked car but Dusty Baker, who told Estes that management wanted to release Estes but that he, Dusty, wouldn't let him. The Hall of Fame skipper told his beloved pitcher that the run-in was a sign, and that he would give Estes one more start. Estes stayed on the roster and later came through with one of the biggest wins of the year.

I also had fun interviews with Kerry Wood and Pat Hughes. But the surprise goldmine was the one place where, later on, I realized my attention should have been from the start, the two guys who were actually making pitch-by-pitch decisions in the one inning of baseball that defined Cubs fandom for a generation: pitcher Mark Prior and catcher Paul Bako.

If I was going to face my fears, I had to realize that the so-called Bartman Game was not the act of a curse. It wasn't even the act of a fan. It was just baseball. Horrific, unlucky, historic baseball, yes, but just the game. Just a pitcher and a catcher making pitch choices to attack batters, and a lineup full of outstanding hitters fighting back.

And so, here is the story of the Bartman inning, as seen through the eyes and experiences of the only two men at Wrigley Field on October 14, 2003, who held control over these iconic at-bats.

******

MARK PRIOR, Cubs starting pitcher, Game 6 of the 2003 NLCS: We [Prior and Wood] definitely had confidence in ourselves and in our abilities. But it was never like, "We got it, no big deal." We knew we were in for a fight. We knew we needed to go out there and execute our pitches if we wanted to put ourselves in a position to win. The Marlins did what they did in the regular season by not giving up in battle till the end, so we knew we were still in a pretty intense dogfight.

PAUL BAKO, Cubs starting catcher, Game 6 of the 2003 NLCS: We had all the faith and confidence in the world in Mark. We *knew*, we all knew, and I bet you he knew as well, that without a doubt he was going to go out there and dominate. He was just on. He was in the zone. I don't know if there's ever been a pitcher in the zone for as long as he was coming down the stretch drive into the playoffs. We were looking forward to it. We couldn't wait for the game to start.

Heading into the 8th inning, the Cubs led 3-0 behind a brilliant Prior: 7 innings pitched, 3 hits, 2 walks, 6 strikeouts, no runs. Because of a double switch in the 7th, the Marlins led off the 8th inning with Mike Mordecai in the number 9 hole, followed by the top of the order.

MIKE MORDECAI, nobody on, nobody out, 3-0 Cubs.
4 pitches: Called strike (0-1). Ball (1-1). Ball (2-1). Flyout to LF.

> **PRIOR**: He flew out to left.
> **BAKO**: So there's one out, and we've got five outs to go.

JUAN PIERRE, nobody on, one out, 3-0 Cubs.
6 pitches: Ball (1-0). Ball (2-0). Called strike (2-1). Foul (2-2). Foul (2-2). Double to left.

> **PRIOR**: I don't know specifically what we talked about for that at bat, but I'm sure it was something along the lines of, "Let's try to get him out early in the count." For those types of guys, I'd rather get them out within the first two or three pitches. Because those guys get really dangerous when they see a bunch of pitches. That's when they can work the count, get on base by walking, or wait for the mistake.
>
> Double to left. I think it was down the line. That's what I'm saying: Pierre was a guy where you had to run it in on him so he couldn't get extended.

LUIS CASTILLO, runner at 2nd, one out, 3-0 Cubs.
9 pitches: Called strike (0-1). Ball (1-1). Called strike (1-2). Ball (2-2). Ball (3-2). Foul (3-2). Foul (3-2). Foul – BARTMAN. (3-2). Ball four, wild pitch, Pierre takes 3rd.

> **PRIOR:** Same situation [as Pierre]. I'd thrown a bunch of pitches to him and a lot of them were good pitches. They were right on the black, give or take, and I was trying to get him to put the ball on the ground. Early on you're trying to get him to put the ball up in the air, where it's just a fly ball and he can't use his speed, or put the ball on the ground so we have a shot at getting one out. He just kept working the count, working the count, and somehow it never got into our favor.
>
> Well, I should take that back. It was in my favor. But he kept fouling balls off. And then you take a pitch really close for a ball, and then he fouls the one ball off that led to the whole Bartman thing. But he was working the count. And it was frustrating. It was a frustrating at-bat.

After working the count full, Castillo fouled off three consecutive pitches, the last of which floated into the left field stands. Moises Alou, the Cubs left fielder, gave chase.

> **BAKO:** Castillo was just fouling off pitches, which he was tremendous at. Just staying alive with two strikes. Obviously there's no foul ground down there, and off the bat [the Bartman ball] looks like it's going to be a foul ball.
>
> But Mo's gonna catch it, because of the way Mo had a beat on it. He jumped after it like he was making a play. Mo is not one who was full of drama. If he was going to run after a ball and make a play on it, and jump like he did, he had a very good chance of making it. And that's what it looked like to me: that he was jumping up into the stands or jumping up against the wall to catch the ball.

PRIOR: Moises definitely had a play on the ball. He probably would have caught it. But it was a foul ball. I didn't think much of it, other than like, "He should have caught that. A fan got in the way." But I want to be perfectly clear: this issue obviously has been hyped and brought up and examined over and over, and I've said this before: 95% of anybody in that same situation as well as the three or four other people surrounding him would have probably – and they did – reach out and try to get that foul ball.

BAKO: My reaction was probably a little bit of a "Hey, fan interference" type thing. And then if not, immediately turn our attention to getting the hitter out and seeing what we could do there. Because that was either going to be turned into an out somehow, or we'll go back to square one [with] Castillo.

PRIOR: Do I think that Moises would have caught it? Yeah, probably. If he was in a position to catch balls, he caught balls. He wasn't somebody who dropped balls or made errors. He was there. It looked like he timed it perfectly and probably would have made the play. But at the point when it happened, for me, it was, "Whatever. It's a foul ball. Let's move onto the next pitch."

The next pitch was in the dirt for ball four, but it got past Bako and Pierre took 3rd.

BAKO: He just kept laying off pitches. He put up a helluva at-bat. And eventually you're just trying to get Castillo to put the ball in play somewhere, and hopefully it's at somebody, you know? He wasn't going to drive the ball. He's a singles hitter. So if we get him to put it in play there, we take our chances with it being a ground ball at somebody. And he ended up working a walk.

PRIOR: I know much has been played up and talked about, but honestly I was like, "Whatever. I walked a guy." I didn't think much of it. It was the 9th pitch in the at-bat. And then I probably would throw a fastball. Not because of what had just happened but because he kept fouling balls off and I felt like if I tried to put a little extra on it then maybe I would get the foul tip into Bako's glove. You put an extra mile or two on it, because obviously at that point he's got some pretty good timing on my pitches.

So that's kind of what happened – I think I just yanked it. That's how I walked him. That's more or less where the wild pitch/passed ball type thing came from. Not because we didn't catch a foul ball. I think it was a non-issue. It was a non-issue to most of us. And to be honest, nobody in the dugout even knew what happened because they can't see it. It wasn't until after the fact that we even knew anything about that situation.

SILVERSTEIN: Did you think Moises's reaction affected the team? I know it affected the fans.

BAKO: No. I don't think it could have or should have. He was acting in a fired-up, competitive way. If he'd reacted differently, that would have meant he didn't have a chance to catch the ball. I don't see how we could have taken that in any kind of negative situation. That's the way I look at it. Like, "Shit, it didn't work out. We gotta turn our attention and keep moving forward here."

IVAN 'PUDGE' RODRIGUEZ, runners at 1st and 3rd, one out, 3-0 Cubs.
3 pitches: Foul (0-1). Swinging strike (0-2). Single to left, Pierre scores, Castillo takes 2nd.

PRIOR: The Pudge at-bat. I had him 0-2. If I had anything to regret or be upset about it was that 0-2 pitch. Not the pitch itself. The execution of it. 0-2, it's got to be in the dirt no matter what. No questions asked. And I just spun it up there. Even if I had him fooled, he was a good enough hitter where he's going to throw his hands at the ball. It was sitting on a tee for him. That was a mental and physical mistake by me, and that cost us the first run, which probably led to the chain reaction.

BAKO: Prior tried to bury a curve ball, and he didn't quite get it as low as he had in previous at bats. He just left that one up. A lesser hitter, or maybe not quite as good of a bad-ball hitter as Pudge, probably wouldn't have gotten a base hit on it. But he was just a guy that with two strikes, especially, you have to go out of the zone and make him chase it. That pitch wasn't far enough out of the zone where he had to chase. It might have been a little low for another hitter, but the way [Pudge] could cover outside the strike zone, it wasn't a bad pitch for him.

PRIOR: I go back to Pudge. It starts with him, getting the out. You put that ball in the dirt – even if he takes it for a ball – I'm not saying he wouldn't have gotten a hit, but still, that's one of the first things you're taught: once you get to two strikes, you don't give him anything good to hit, and I gave him something good to hit. So he did what he was supposed to do with it.

SILVERSTEIN: How surprised were you that Pudge reached that pitch?

BAKO: Not as surprised as I was that Prior didn't get it where he wanted it. Not that it was a bad pitch from Mark. It wasn't quite as low or wide as I think he wanted it to be. I was more surprised by that. I was not surprised that Pudge got a hit off it. Because that's just how effective and how much in command Mark was. He could throw the ball anywhere at any time. He could do anything he wanted, you know?

Think about it man: that Pudge ball is a little lower, and then (pause) fuck. Again, like I said, the only thing I would have changed – obviously if I'd known the results I would have changed things up, but if I could have a walkie talkie or something to tell Mark, "Let's get in there again and let's make sure it's elevated at his hands," I'm pretty sure that's probably where Mark was trying to go with it anyway.

MIGUEL CABRERA, runners at 1st and 2nd, one out, 3-1 Cubs.
1 pitch: Ground ball to the shortstop, error on Alex Gonzalez, everybody safe.

SILVERSTEIN: And then the next pitch is the Gonzo play.

BAKO: Yeah, the very next pitch. Exactly.

The ball was a little bit to Gonzo's right. And watching Gonzo play all year, I knew that we had at least one out at second. Once I realized it wasn't going to the hole, I thought, "Well, there's at least one out." And then obviously it didn't work out. We didn't get him.

PRIOR: We got what we wanted. It wasn't a great pitch, but it was a pitch we were looking for. Off-speed pitch to start him in the count, he's either going to take a strike or have him looking for a fast ball which I think he was, based on his swing. And he hit a ground ball to short. It was exactly what we needed. We got what we needed. And, you know, he dropped the ball. So not only did we not get a double play, but we didn't get one out.

SILVERSTEIN: How big of a surprise was that error?

BAKO: Very big. Gonzo was as sure and steady as you possibly could get. He had 10 [errors] in the regular season. That's damn good for a big-league shortstop playing [152] games, you know? That's my point. That's how surprising it was. Gonzo just doesn't make errors.

PRIOR: Was I surprised looking back on it? Yeah. Alex – I don't know how many errors he made all year, but he was pretty sure-handed. I think everybody to a man, if you said, "Were you surprised he dropped it?" "Yeah," just because of how well he'd played defense.

But you gotta come from the mindset of, "They made an error, I'm going to pick them up." If I walk a guy, I love Alex making great plays and turning double plays. It's about picking up your guys. Like, "I'm going to make a pitch here and get the next guy out. We're going to get out of this."

DERREK LEE, bases loaded, one out, 3-1 Cubs.
1 pitch: Double to left, two runs score, Cabrera to 3rd.

> **BAKO**: We'd gotten into D-Lee's kitchen a lot with balls at his hands and belt-high and in, and that one was just a little lower than I believe Mark wanted. He definitely got it in there. It just wasn't quite as high as some of the other pitches we were beating D-Lee on the whole series.
>
> **PRIOR**: I threw a pretty good pitch to the next batter. And to this day I still think he – it was 95 on the inside part of the plate. He had to be looking for it because he turned on it and that's what scored the next run.

After Derrek Lee's run-scoring double, Dusty Baker made a pitching change, bringing in Kyle Farnsworth. The mood in the stadium continued to shift.

> **BAKO**: It was unbelievable. It was so loud when Mark was in the game, and even after the fly ball to left and after the ball Pudge hit and after the ball Cabrera put in play – all that stuff was fine and dandy. And then, you know, some of the energy definitely got lost when Prior came out and Farnsy came in.
>
> **PRIOR**: I was just sitting there [in the dugout] watching and hoping we get out of there sooner rather than later. It didn't happen. We got out of it later. (Laughs.) I don't remember having a whole lot of emotion one way or the other. I was

upset, but not down or depressed. Just a normal competitive madness kind of thing.

BAKO: I remember [Farnsworth] being pretty quiet and ready to go. I remember him being like, "Just get back there. I'm ready to pitch." Not verbalizing that, but he came to the mound ready for business, and was ready to take care of business.

Mike Lowell, runners at 2nd and 3rd, one out, 3-3 tie.
4 pitches: intentional walk.

Jeff Conine, bases loaded, one out, 3-3 tie.
1 pitch: sacrifice fly to left field, Cabrera scores, runners advance.

With runners at 2nd and 3rd, Farnsworth's first order of business was to intentionally walk Mike Lowell. On Farnsworth's first real pitch of the inning, Jeff Conine hit a sacrifice fly to left field to score Cabrera. The runners advanced to 2nd and 3rd, and the Marlins had their first lead of the game.

Todd Hollandsworth, runners at 2nd and 3rd, two outs, 4-3 Marlins.
4 pitches: intentional walk.

Mike Mordecai, bases loaded, two outs, 4-3 Marlins.
4 pitches: Ball (1-0). Called strike (1-1). Ball (2-1). Double to left, three runs score.

Todd Hollandworth pinch hit for the pitcher Chad Fox, and with 1st base open, Farnsworth intentionally walked Hollandsworth. This brought Mike Mordecai to the plate for the second time in the inning.

> **BAKO**: It's a tough position there for Farnsy to come in. He throws one pitch to Conine, right? And all of a sudden it's a 4-3 lead for the Marlins. And we walk Hollandsworth and bring up Mordecai.
>
> Mordecai was just a really good fastball hitter. We were trying to get ahead with something off-speed, and it didn't

work. He ended up getting a hitter's count with the bases loaded, where we had to come at him with a fastball, and he made us pay.

Mordecai hit a base-clearing double to boost the Florida lead to 7-3.

BAKO: After Mordecai hit that ball, that double, I remember standing at home plate and the only thing I could hear in the whole stadium was the Marlins' voices in their dugout celebrating. I'm not exaggerating. I couldn't hear anything else other than their voices. 12, 15 minutes before that, you couldn't hear yourself think, just because of the energy and enthusiasm. (Sighs.) It was the definition of a 180. It was just crazy, crazy eerily quiet after that hit.

Baker made one more pitching change, bringing in the left-hander Mike Remlinger to face the left-handed Pierre. Pierre singled to score Mordecai. The Cubs finally got out of the inning when Remlinger got Castillo to pop out to 2nd.

Juan Pierre, runner at 2nd, two outs, 7-3 Marlins.
1 pitch: single to right, Mordecai scores.

Luis Castillo, runner at 1st, two outs, 8-3 Marlins.
5 pitches: Foul (0-1). Ball (1-1). Ball (2-1). Swinging strike (2-2). Popout to 2nd.

BAKO: Man, [when the inning ended], I would say we were as shocked and awed as the crowd was. Obviously we're all professionals, but when you start that inning winning three to nothing and you come back in and you're down eight to three, that was definitely impossible to come back from that particular day. I mean Game 6, you know?

The competitor in you is like, "Let's go boys. We have six outs left to score. We can win this. We've done it before." But the reality is like, "Hopefully we can shake this off and come back tomorrow ready to play." As soon as the game's over, that's what we're thinking.

It was as bad a feeling as I've had from a game. The only time I ever had a comparable feeling was after losing the World Series [in 2009 with the Phillies]. It was very similar to the feeling of losing the World Series. The feeling in the stomach in both games was one and the same.

It's like a frickin' unsolved mystery. An unexplained phenomenon. It's like Big Foot or the Loch Ness Monster. I've never looked at the box score like this. I'm looking at it right now, and it's just such an anomaly. It's such a crazy – you know, 0, 0, 0, 1, 0, 0, 0, 0, 0, 0, 0, 1, 0, 1, 8, 0, 0, 0. It doesn't even make sense, you know? Almost like if you would take it to a statistician, he would say, "Is this a typo? What is this?" It doesn't make sense.

SILVERSTEIN: And it defies the rhythm of not just the game but almost of the series.

BAKO: Oh no doubt. Yes. Of the series. Of playoff baseball. It just defies everything.

SILVERSTEIN: So, final thoughts on 2003?

BAKO: The reality is that we were all completely disappointed. But from a whole body of work perspective, excluding the last two games of the season – which I know is hard to do – we were very tight. And I think we were proud of where we came from. From being in a brand new situation in spring training, to coming together so quickly and getting to the playoffs and the NLCS. As bittersweet as it was, I think it was a huge accomplishment.

The closeness and the chemistry and the camaraderie in the clubhouse was tremendous. And equal to that, or a very close second, was the turnaround. Turning it around from the season before. The worst-to-first. And how well we played. I think a lot of that was reflective of Dusty and how he got us all together and how tight of a group we were.

PRIOR: It was one of the better, if not the best team I was on as far as relationships and friendships. I think winning obviously helps, but I think winning was a byproduct of the way we all felt about each other. There weren't a lot of egos on that team. Everybody was pulling for each other.

Overall, it was just a lot of fun. It was a lot of fun playing the game and a lot of fun being in Chicago. I feel proud that we were part of maybe helping to nudge the culture of the organization and pushing for a championship. I think we did great things there, and I think we're all proud of the way we played together.

PART XIX: VICTORY!

June 14, 2022, readjack.substack.com
    Age 40

THE GREATEST.

"I could see every player and I remember exactly where they were as I came up the floor. Steve Kerr was in the corner. ... Dennis was curling underneath the post on the left. Scottie was on the bottom post on the right. I could hear sounds but it was like white noise. In that moment I couldn't distinguish one sound from another."

— Michael Jordan, recalling The Last Shot, Game 6, 1998 NBA Finals

******

Their heroes could not save them. Like Cassandra, they saw. Eyes pained. Souls scarred. Their dragon a knight. Their knights without steel. Their hands on their heads, on their cheeks, on their mouths. Their shrieks made no sound. Their prayers found no home. Before the ball reached the rim they knew. Before the ball left his hand they knew.

Michael Jordan had done it again.

He was there, same as them, yet not the same at all. He was making history. They were drowning in it. They are why I love Fernando Medina's iconic photo. That masterpiece that shows MJ's shot from behind and those Utah faces. That photo is history too, but it's more than history. It's the quicksand of fandom. The bad break of the wrong birth.

Two nights earlier, the Jazz had made it out of Chicago. Survived and alive. Now they had two games at home. That's what you play for over 82 — these two games right here.

And on the first play, a break. You don't like to say it that way, but after the historic dogfight of 1997 and the historic ass-whipping of Game 3, you take the breaks you can get. This break was Scottie Pippen injuring his back on the game's first points. A dunk, he landed, and a grimace. He would play only 26 minutes, the fewest he played in his 35 career Finals games. He scored just eight points, only two more than his career Finals low, which had come two days prior in Game 5.

But Pippen had 11 boards and 11 assists that game to go with his six points. This night, he had his career Finals low in rebounds, at three, and just four assists. He was playing hurt, and asked out of the game with just five minutes left in the 1st quarter. Ron Harper was playing sick. Toni Kukoc was playing tired: he missed his pre-game nap while watching soccer. Dennis Rodman was struggling in the Finals, averaging 8.4 rebounds per game with just three in Game 5.

"Are you ready to play 48 minutes?" Phil Jackson asked Jordan before the game began.

The GOAT had one answer.

"Whatever it takes."

******

I don't think any athlete in my life has as many signature moments as Michael Jordan. They started his rookie year and never stopped. Went into hyperdrive his second season. When he scored those 63 points in the playoffs against Boston, Larry Bird famously called him "God disguised as Michael Jordan."

Overshadowed is what Bird said about Jordan three days earlier:

"There is no question that Michael Jordan, healthy, is the best basketball player in the league."

This was Larry Bird talking, the man who by season's end would have his third ring, his second Finals MVP and would be the first player

PART XIX: VICTORY!

since Wilt Chamberlain to win three straight NBA MVP awards. Larry Bird, at the height of his powers, said that this 23-year-old was his, and everyone's, superior.

Hell, rewind to 1984, before Jordan had played even an NBA preseason game, and no less than Bob Knight called Jordan "the best basketball player that I've ever seen play." In his 13 Bulls seasons, Jordan did everything. He could do everything and he accomplished everything. He made you imagine everything and made you believe in everything. When he retired in 1993, he was merely 15th in NBA history in scoring, with "just" nine seasons under his belt, and was already getting GOAT love.

Five years later, when he set foot on the Delta Center court for Game 6, he had the most Finals MVPs in league history (5), the second most MVPs (5), the most scoring titles (10), the highest scoring average in a Finals series (41.0 in 1993) — so many "Mosts" it's silly to list them, so I'll just add one more that's unofficial yet I feel no harm in saying it:

Most signature moments.

The 63. The Free Throw Line. The Shot. The Layup. The Shrug. The Shot Part II. The Double-Nickel. The Flu Game. There are franchises that don't have that many The's.

So I don't know quite what I expected from Jordan in Game 6 of the '98 Finals. I just knew that to win the title, we would have to win this game, because a road Game 7 was too close to the flame. I knew that to win this game, we would need one of Jordan's all-time greats.

And I knew that a Michael Jordan all-time great was something no one but him could envision.

******

Michael Jordan's lowest scoring NBA Finals was 1996, in which he averaged 27.3 points. That was as bad as it got for MJ in the Finals, a series in which he averaged more points than a host of legendary Finals

MVPs. Kareem in '71. Hakeem in '94. Dirk in 2011. Moses in '83. LeBron in 2013. Duncan in '03. Bird in '86. "Here comes Willis" in 1970.

So when it came to wondering about an all-time MJ night in Utah, what that might look like was anyone's guess. I certainly did not know. After all, you don't want to be greedy. You just want to revel in brilliance.

He started slow. Eight points in the first quarter. But in the second, 15, with a half-court three that rimmed out.

In the third, slow again: six points on 2-6 shooting, the Jazz taking a five-point lead into the final quarter.

It was time.

In his final quarter as a Chicago Bull, Michael Jordan produced. Again. And again. Some from the floor, lots from the line. Dragging his body into the paint. Whistle. Foul shots. Swish swish swish. A perfect eight for eight from the stripe, half of his points that quarter.

And with a minute to go he seemed to have not done enough. John Stockton hit a three to give the Jazz a three-point lead: 86-83.

The final minute of this game would mirror my favorite Bulls game ever: Game 6, 1993 Finals. That one had an MJ layup, a 24-second violation for Phoenix and then the all-hands-on-deck final magic: MJ to BJ to MJ to Scottie to Horace to Paxson for three, sealed with Horace's block on Kevin Johnson.

That game celebrated the power of the team.

This game revealed the team within the man.

Because after Stockton's three with 41.9 seconds remaining, the only Bull to touch the ball on offense was Michael Jeffrey Jordan.

A fast layup. A remarkable steal on Karl Malone under the basket. And then, at a time when any other coach would have called timeout, a time when any other player would have been eyeing the sideline awaiting a timeout, Michael Jordan and Phil Jackson knew this moment was different. As they explained later:

> **JORDAN**: "I looked up and saw 18.5 seconds left."
>
> **JACKSON**: "At that moment, I think we were of one mind."
>
> **JORDAN**: "Crowd gets quiet. The moment starts to become The Moment for me. That's part of that Zen Buddhism stuff."
>
> **JACKSON**: "I was waving for him to go down court. I think he saw me out of the corner of his eye waving off a timeout."
>
> **JORDAN**: "I felt like we couldn't call timeout because it would give the defense an opportunity to set up."
>
> **JACKSON**: "The flow was the right thing at the moment, so we didn't want to stop."

You know what happened next. With his teammates fanned out, with Stockton unable to double because of Kerr's series-winner the year before, MJ dribbled the ball down with only Bryon Russell on him. Here's how Mike told it in "For the Love of the Game":

> "I had no intention of passing the ball under any circumstances. I figured I stole the ball and it was my opportunity to win or lose the game. I would have taken that shot with five people on me.
>
> "Ironically, I have problems going to my right for a stop, pull-up jumper because I have a tendency to come up short. I normally fade a little. But on this shot I didn't want to fade because all my jump shots had been short. Think about that.
>
> "I consciously extended my hand up and out toward the target because I had been coming up short. It looked like I was posing, but it was a fundamentally sound shot."

Moments later, Ron Harper's defense on Stockton gave the Bulls their sixth championship in eight years. Jordan held six fingers skyward. They had done it again. The hardest one. The greatest one. And he had done all he could: 43 minutes, 45 of the team's 87 points, one of the most iconic shots in NBA history.

"Once it went in, I knew we had been hanging around long enough," Jordan said later. "That was the game-winning basket."

Game 6 of the 1998 NBA Finals. That was June 14, 1998, 24 years ago today. Twenty-four years since MJ wore red. Twenty-four years since Scottie gutted it out. Twenty-four years since we silenced those fans. Twenty-four years since we said goodbye.

Michael Jordan gave us everything we could ever want. The good luck of the right birth. He was not the dragon. He was the knight.

What a night.

Oct. 27, 2005, "Bear Down and Get Some Runs"
    Age 23

REFLECTIONS ON THE IMPORTANCE OF SPORTS

It's 5:36 AM, Wednesday night/Thursday morning.

The White Sox are the 2005 World Series Champions.

Still.

Orlando Palmeiro bounced out to Juan Uribe five hours and thirty-five minutes ago to end the game, and it still counts. It's all Official. Chicagosports.com has it. ESPN.com has it. Whitesox.com has it. Luke, Sven, and my parents have all confirmed what I witnessed.

PART XIX: VICTORY!

It actually happened.

The White Sox are champs.

What do you do the day after your team wins the World Series?

I ask this not for myself but for my friends, as it was quite clear all the way through that the 2005 White Sox were never, at any point, close to becoming my team. Still, it was quite an exhilarating experience, watching this team play, watching them battle through each playoff game, watching them win Game 4. I was overjoyed for Luke and Sven and all the other Sox fans, happy for the city, excited to be watching such a historic moment in Chicago sports.

Nothing has changed for me personally, and yet I can feel the weight of what this means for so many people. Seeing replay after replay of that final out… Jenks leaping into the air… Jermaine dashing in from right… Carl Everett hoisting Willie Harris onto his shoulders in celebration: all amazing sights.

But for every hero there's a goat, and for every winner there's a loser. There were the Houston fans, sitting in their own park, watching another team celebrate a championship while their team sat dejectedly in the locker room. They had waited 44 years for a World Series appearance, and after that they still had to sit through two more games until they could watch one in their own hometown.

Those first two games took place in Chicago, the Sox winning both. Now their Astros were returning home, and the fans were there to greet them. When Houston fans got to Minute Maid Park Tuesday night, their ace Roy Oswalt was on the mound. Most people assumed Oswalt would lead Houston to the win that would get them back into the series, a pivotal Game 4 at home on the way. Instead, Oswalt lost a 4-0 lead and the Astros went to their pen. Houston fans, those who had waited 44 years for this World Series game, waited another 14 innings for its conclusion, a conclusion they were sure would be victory.

But no: 44 years, two games, and 14 innings brought not victory but rather defeat, defeat at the bat of White Sox' pinch hitter Geoff Blum, himself a former Astro.

Houston fans left Minute Maid Park early Wednesday morning, their team trailing three games to none, each knowing that only one team in the history of baseball had ever overcome a 3-0 deficit in a best of seven, and being that it was the 2004 Red Sox, the self-proclaimed "idiots" who overcame that deficit along with the Yankees and 86 years of frustrating history, it must have seemed unlikely that their Houston Astros, the team they loved so dear, would do the same. It must have seemed unlikely...

...yet there they were, those Astros fans, screaming and shouting all through Game 4, cheering on their team, trying to will them to victory. Even with each opportunity squandered by the Astros, the fans did not give up or give in, not even with two outs in the ninth inning. And then came the ground ball, the Uribe scoop and throw, the close play, the out recorded, the game, the series, the season, over...

But Houston's fans stayed on, and after the game the longest Astro of them all, Craig Biggio, sat for a postgame interview. Biggio has spent 17 years in the majors, every one with Houston. He came up as a catcher, a 22-year-old in 1988. He was an All-Star at that position in 1991, only to move to second base a year later. There he flourished, going to six more All-Star games and winning four Gold Gloves. Then, in 2003, the Astros had a chance to acquire All-Star second baseman Jeff Kent. *Not a problem*, said Biggio, who knew that Kent would be a good addition to the team, and so he, Biggio, he trotted out to play center field.

Then, in the middle of 2004, the Astros had a chance to acquire All-Star center fielder Carlos Beltran. *Not a problem*, said Biggio, and he trotted over to play left field.

And then, after last season, Beltran signed with the Mets while Kent left for the Dodgers... so Biggio went back to second base,

PART XIX: VICTORY!

and finally, with the help of longtime teammate Jeff Bagwell, led Houston to a World Series. After 17 seasons, Biggio was playing for a championship. Four games later, it was over. He had lost.

But the fans were out, and the press was curious, and so Biggio did what would make them both happy, and as he sat out there at Minute Maid Park answering questions while the White Sox deliriously sprayed champagne all over each other in celebration, the fans chanted his name — "B-G-O! B-G-O!" — over and over again.

White Sox fans have waited a long time for a title. They got one this year. Frank Thomas has waited a long time for his team to play in the World Series. He got there this year. Astros fans have waited a long time for an NL pennant. They got one this year. Craig Biggio and Jeff Bagwell have waited a long time to display their skills on a national stage. They got to this year. Of those four, only Sox fans got exactly what they wanted, but don't discount Frank's influence on this team, and don't discount Houston's joy of seeing their team in the Series or Biggio's and Bagwell's joy of getting there together. It was all there, for anyone to see, and even if this was the lowest-rated Series in baseball's history, all that means is that a bunch of lazy and careless baseball "fans" missed out on seeing what sports is all about.

******

"What are you getting so bent out of shape about? It's just a game."

I've heard it. You've heard it. We've all heard it, usually from people who don't like sports, who think that we place too much emphasis on them, who think that they are a waste of time, who think that they are "just a game."

"It's just a game," they tell us.

Well, the thing is, it is and it isn't.

You see, sports are life.

I know that sounds cliché, and absurd, and totally improper, but many truths do, and so I will say it again: Sports are life.

Sports are life, and if you are dedicated to either, your truest emotions will be brought to light at one point or another. We are born, and we die, and in the middle we behave as if neither were true, as if we are the most important beings ever created. In turn our actions and our decisions become the most important that anyone will ever have to do or make.

But all things must pass, and all that is new must grow old, and while the Earth remains, we do not. We know this. We deny it, but we live each day knowing it to be true. So we find ways to immortalize ourselves, to make meaning out of our actions, to hold onto something that will outlast us.

A baseball team, for example.

Because it is just a game, and for that we are grateful. Since these games "don't really matter," we can experience them fully as if they do. We can cry when the Cubs lose Game 7 while being strong for our families after a death. We can be overjoyed at the success of a home run or a touchdown while being level-headed about meeting our social and financial obligations. We can acknowledge that every at-bat must have a final pitch, that every game must have a final out, that every season must have an ending, be it happy or sad, all while striving for goals that suggest we will live forever.

The White Sox and the Astros showed us that this year. They played honorably and passionately, for themselves and for their fans. They played with talent, energy, and agility. They played with emotion, camaraderie, and desire. They played with professionalism and with exuberance. They played with brains and brawn. By giving their all, leaving everything on the field, and doing whatever it takes to win, they made every sportswriting cliché a reality. They competed, pure and simple.

In the end, the White Sox were the better team. There are many moments we can point to that illustrate where exactly the Astros messed things up and where the White Sox took control, but that would be pointless. The game must have two teams, and one will win while the other will lose. That is simply the nature of sport, and in a way, those details are incidental. Out on the field, two teams competed, and 25 men on each side showed us how to play.

That's why Craig Biggio could sit out on the field after the game and calmly answer questions. The game was over. He had played it as best he could. A noble and heroic performance, from start to finish, for him and everyone else involved.

Now try telling me that it's just a game.

Jan. 21, 2017, Windy City Gridiron
    Age 35

THE DAY THE BEARS BEAT THE SAINTS IN THE NFC CHAMPIONSHIP

For a second there it felt like we would never catch Reggie Bush. I mean ever. I mean, felt as if the Saints had cracked the seal and the offense that sportswriters couldn't stop slobbering over was awake and forever running. Points would flow. Our defense would whither. We were 13-3 and we couldn't win.

Few had picked us to. Adewale Ogunleye kept a list in his locker of media analysts who picked the Bears to lose. In Chicago, six of 16 writers in the *Tribune* and *Sun-Times* did too. The six writers who picked the Bears to lose were united in their reasoning: our defense — ranked 3rd in the NFL and 1st in takeaways — couldn't hang with the high-scoring Saints attack.

"We were kind of pissed off," Jason McKie told me in 2017. "I was pissed off. I know Olin was pissed off. The offensive line was pissed off. Thomas was pissed off. And the defense was really pissed off because all they kept talking about was Drew Brees and Reggie Bush and all the weapons they had and we've got the No. 1 defense in the league."

Compounding that challenge, the sportswriters said, was Rex Grossman's inability to, as Jay Mariotti of the *Sun-Times* put it, "survive a possible shootout." Three other *Sun-Times* writers picked the Saints to win, each riffing on these themes. Brad Biggs wondered if the Bears would get the "stout defensive effort" and "solid play from Rex" needed to beat the Saints. Carol Slezak said the D was vulnerable and inconsistent without the injured Tommie Harris. Greg Couch's assessment cut deepest: with a snowfall expected, the "small and quick" Bears defense was not "suited for Bear Weather."

That one stung. And the *Tribune* writers weren't much nicer. Melissa Isaacson praised New Orleans as "the best offense the Bears have faced" while Mike Downey noted his "dread" for Brees-to-Bush passes which would "drive Peanut Tillman nuts."

"Not one person picked the Bears to win," Ogunleye said after the game. He was referring to the predictions on whatever sheet of paper he was carrying, but the statement applied to the Chicago papers too. "Everybody said the reason why is the Saints offense. That kind of [ticked] us off a little bit, because we knew we had the No. 1 defense in the league, and we're getting no credit."

The "we get no respect" mantra may seem like boiler plate to fans or media, but when you're perceiving that treatment as a player, the feeling is real as it gets. When the Bears ran out of the Soldier Field tunnel for the NFC championship game, the expectations were stacked oddly against them. Their 14-3 record was apparently insufficient proof of their superiority against the 11-6 Saints. They were only 3-point favorites at kickoff.

They were also the less compelling national story, since the Saints were the ultimate feel-good success, winning 10 games after a 3-13

PART XIX: VICTORY!

2005 and doing so in the first season back in New Orleans after a year at LSU due to Hurricane Katrina.

"All week we kept hearing about the New Orleans Saints and the hurricane they went through and how they were America's team because they had to go through so much adversity," McKie said. "And we were like, 'We understand that and respect that,' but everybody's talking about them and we're like, 'We're the best team in the NFC. They have to come here to Soldier Field.'"

The key to the Saints' turnaround was the new coach — Bears alumnus Sean Payton — and new quarterback, Drew Brees. The final four quarterback quartet was the 2006 1st team All-Pro Brees, two-time NFL MVP Peyton Manning, three-time Super Bowl champion Tom Brady, and Rex Grossman, he of the 73.9 quarterback rating and 25 starts in four professional seasons.

So no, national folks were neither predicting nor rooting for a Bears victory.

That's what made the Bush touchdown a nervous moment. We'd started the game with three Robbie Gould field goals, forcing the Saints into four punts and two fumbles. After punt number four, Thomas Jones cracked off a magnificent drive: eight carries (every play of the drive) for 69 yards, including a 33-yarder on 2nd and 8 and a two-yard run to convert the drive's only 3rd down.

After Jones' two-yard touchdown, though, the Saints figured us out. Brees converted a pair of 3rd and 10's on pass plays, and then connected with Marques Colton for a 13-yard touchdown with less than a minute remaining in the half. The Bears received the football in the second half leading 16-7, punted, and two plays later Brees floated a beauty to Bush down the left sideline.

He caught the pass at the 26 ahead of Tillman, Chris Harris, and Lance Briggs, cut toward the middle of the field in front of a staggering Danieal Manning, and outran a gang of Bears to the endzone including a hard-charging Brian Urlacher.

His final 15 yards are, to this day, burned in the collective memory of Bears fans.

As he pulled away from the pack, Bush turned to look over his left shoulder, spotted the trailing Bears brigade in pursuit, and wagged his finger at them, or perhaps at Urlacher, who was a full 10 yards behind Bush when Bush made his cutback and finished about three steps from him and three steps ahead of his teammates.

Then Bush did a full front flip into the endzone.

Then Bush danced in the endzone.

Then Bears fans lost their minds.

Then the Bears said: enough.

"You're a rookie in this league, and you had a good play," Ogunleye said about Bush. "But to turn around and taunt Brian — taunt basically the whole team — was a slap in the face."

Whatever it takes though, right? Because the Bush touchdown caused the Bears to strike back, closing out the Saints with a 23-0 run to advance to the franchise's first Super Bowl in 21 years.

The Saints actually had a good shot at taking a lead, but missed a 47-yard field goal the drive after the Bush touchdown. That was as close as they would get. On the next drive, pinned at the 5, the allegedly undermanned, undersized, underskilled Bears defense forced Brees into intentional grounding in his own endzone. Safety. 18-14, good guys.

Two Bears drives later, Rex Grossman and Bernard Berrian connected on the instantly iconic slow down-dive-catch-flip-stand-run-celebrate touchdown. 25-14 Bears.

Two plays later, Ogunleye sacked Brees, drove him to the ground, landed on him, and came up with the football. It was snowing now — Bears Weather, as it were — and that was fine with us.

PART XIX: VICTORY!

"It kind of became a snowball effect," Ogunleye said after the game about the fumble. "It really dug them a hole, and they weren't able to climb out of it."

Five plays later, Cedric Benson banged home a 12-yard touchdown run. 32-14 Bears, and we could smell it now, taste it now, see ourselves in South Beach for Super Bowl XLI.

"That was an exciting moment," Benson told me in 2016. "I wanted to do really good in the game. Yet at the time I didn't realize the full spectrum of it. Some guys never make it to the Super Bowl. So yeah, I was really excited."

Two plays after Benson's touchdown, Nathan Vasher intercepted Brees, the fourth Bears takeaway against zero turnovers. The next Saints drive ended on a failed fourth down conversion. Four plays later, Thomas Jones gained four yards to reach 108, passing Walter Payton for the most rushing yards in a playoff game by a Bear. The next play he ran for a 15-yard TD, ending his day at 123 yards.

Bears 39, Saints 14, and a final fourth down stop plus a few more powerful Benson runs put the ball in Rex's hands for a quarterback's favorite play: the kneel down.

At this point the snow was heavy, reminding Bears fans everywhere of the magical NFC championship game victory 21 years earlier over the Rams, also at Soldier Field, also in the falling snow, also an ass-kicking. We saw visions of Wilber Marshall and the Fridge and looked back at the guys on this field and said, "We are with you. Let's make a memory."

For most Bears fans, I would guess that the Berrian catch is their favorite moment of this game, since it is spectacular on its own terms, game-changing in its position in the game, and spiritually the closest that game got to Wilber Marshall's fumble return. It's a great play, no doubt. But it's not my favorite moment.

No, my moment of that game came after the game was finished. Grossman rose from his kneel down, reared back, and heaved the football into the stands.

This was a moment of both defiance and celebration. Grossman was named the NFC's Offensive Player of the Month in September and was an early MVP candidate. Through five games, he had 10 touchdowns, three interceptions, and a 100.8 quarterback rating.

Then, after an early debut, the "Bad Rex" games started rolling in: six turnovers and a 10.2 rating in the legendary Cardinals comeback, three picks against Miami in the team's first loss, three more with no touchdowns in a loss to New England, and a 1.3 rating against Minnesota that was the closest he'd come all year to losing his job.

Grossman was seen from the outside as the team's weak link. Maybe he was. But among teammates he was a fearless, fiery leader who never lost his confidence or his team's respect.

Prior to the game, he and Jones talked about "what it would be like if we won, how cool that would be," Jones said. Together, Jones, Grossman, Urlacher — *everyone* created a moment bigger than any one man. In the AFC, the story was "Peyton Manning finally gets to the Super Bowl." In the NFC, it was "Bears somehow defeat Brees and weapons." Rex was at the center of that national reluctance.

And that to me was the beauty of Grossman's ball heave. It was a moment that said everything we presumed Rex wanted to say: "I don't need to save this ball because I'm going to get a better one in two weeks" plus "This one's for you, Chicago" plus "I'M THE QUARTERBACK AND LOOK HOW FAR I CAN THROW. UNLEASH THE F****** DRAGON."

"Going into that game we had a chip on our shoulder," McKie said. "We had just come off a close game with Seattle which we had barely won, so we wanted to make a statement to show them that we are the best team and we are going to the Super Bowl and we are going to win the Super Bowl. We came out and wanted to establish our physical presence. Our physical dominance. We wanted to come out there and hit them in the mouth and that's what we did — we knocked them out. And there was no question about who the best team in the NFC was after that game."

After the game, Rex told reporters that the team had "one more win before we can call ourselves 'World Champions.'" I loved that moment. It said to me, "All this crap I've been through? All this crap WE'VE been through? No one will remember it. The only thing they will remember is what we do in the Super Bowl."

On this day, the Bears won big. The 25-point victory was the biggest for any team in the playoffs that season. Up on the podium, Virginia McCaskey famously cheered and clapped and laughed while accepting the George Halas Trophy, named for her father.

Urlacher also celebrated with it on the podium, an image used prominently by both papers the next day. His statement echoed Grossman's: "This overshadows everything," he said, adding about Grossman: "I don't know what his career record is. I don't care what his stats are. He's a winner."

On the field, the players were ecstatic. Jones recalls seeing a choked up Desmond Clark exclaiming, "We did it. We did it," while Jones himself wondered, "Is this really happening?" Benson, Rashied Davis, and Jason McKie posed for a photo, their faces pure ebullience.

Benson has barely any happy memories from his Bears tenure, but he described going to the Super Bowl as "really exciting," while a giddy Tillman convened with his wife for some family planning.

"When the clock hit zero, the snow was coming down on the field," Tillman told me in 2016. "My wife made her way down, and I remember the first thing I yelled at her was, 'We're gonna have another baby!' I made a bet with her that if we went to the Super Bowl we would have three kids. At the time we only had one child. We probably planned on having two, and she said, 'If you go to the Super Bowl, we'll have three.' And that was the first thing I said to her. It was perfect."

"The emotions were running crazy," Berrian said after the game. "It has been our dream to be in the Super Bowl. Now we have to go down there and win it."

Through it all, the snow kept falling. The fans kept cheering. The players kept grinning. The city kept celebrating. The Halas Trophy was home. The Super Bowl was back. For one more night, our Bears were champions.

June 10, 2010, ReadJack.com
    Age 28

WHY WE ROOT.

What is the value of a championship?

I don't mean for the players. When you watched Patrick Kane whip around the net as, briefly, the only person on the planet who knew the 2010 Stanley Cup Finals were finished... when you witnessed Jonathan Toews hoist the Cup after declining to set fingers on the Campbell Trophy... when you saw Marian Hossa accept the Cup from Toews after watching from the losing side in 2008 and 2009... hot damn, how could you not know how important this was to those guys?

I'm talking about the fans.

I'm talking about the miles of fans who swarmed the streets of Wrigleyville, the Loop, and from my own eyes, Wicker Park.

Yes, let's talk about Wicker Park for a moment.

This was a great scene. We watched the game at Crust, a pizza joint at Division and Hoyne. Just after the game began, a puck-colored stretched Hummer pulled up on Division – out of the back emerged many Hawks fans, including a man carrying an enormous Hawks flag and wearing a Blackhawks goalie helmet and CHELIOS 7 jersey. The gathering around Small Bar and The Fifty/50 across the street was so large that from our seats in Crust, we heard those crowds reacting to goals before we realized the puck was in.

When the third period ended without a winner, Rob and I decided, yes yes, we'd better watch OT across the street, out on the walk.

We'd hardly toasted our beers when Kane took his man one-on-one and attacked like Derrick Rose. Chaos and confusion among everyone but Kane and his teammates. A trickle of celebration out on Division, nobody sure, nobody sure, but hey… if the Hawks are celebrating… holy crap, Kane just scored! This thing is over! HAWKS BABY! HAWKS!

Horns honking everywhere. Toasts and high-fives, everywhere. A Chicago Water Department truck driving past, flashing its lights. Police officers in the wagon leaning out of their windows to yell celebratory celebrations with people they may have soon been restraining. And of course that song, always that song, and you know what? I finally sang it. Louder and madder than I ever imagined.

Da, duh-da-da, duh-da-da, duh-da-da da-da-da!

We walked east on Division to Wood and hung a left to Milwaukee. Fans were blaring air horns, cheering through bullhorns, and exploding fireworks. The sound of The Song carried on a bullhorn loud as hell and getting closer, until the source passed behind us on Division and we saw it was a fireman on his fire truck.

On Milwaukee now, heading west toward the six corners, every car honking horns and always with at least one fan leaning out of the car… fans hoisting makeshift Cups… strangers high-fiving and posing for pictures… camera phones documenting with video clips…

As you got closer to North-Damen-Milwaukee, the celebration grew louder and happier and sillier still. Fans were singing and cheering, and drumming on newspaper dispensers for their percussion section. Drivers foolish or fearless enough to traverse the intersection found themselves recipients of high-fives from fans on the street. Police blocked off the area when fans overtook it anyhow in a leaping, cheering, champagne-spraying, hand-slapping and hugging Black Hawks hullabaloo, singing *We Are the Champions* and *Celebration* and chanting CHI-CA-GO! and DE-TROIT-SUCKS! and HAWKS! HAWKS! HAWKS! HAWKS!

This scene continued, in the streets and in the bars, long into the night. Rob and I went to Cans for a shot and a beer and toasted with many fans, including one guy with LARMER 28 on his back. Hadn't seen that one in a while, no sir.

******

During the many Hawks-related discussions I've had with friends this past month, there was plenty of talk about bandwagoners, and whether or not they were annoying beasts with no right to participate in Hawks celebrations.

My old friend Sammy V, however, wanted to debate the more universal topic of We.

As in, "Who are we playing tonight?" "We have to win this one!" "We've always had trouble against small point guards."

Said Sammy: "As someone who has no intrinsic (let's say emotional) nor extrinsic (let's say money) investment in professional sports, I can only enjoy the momentary pride in my city as someone on the outside looking in at players who achieved "their" goal and have excelled as professionals in "their" career. What have I really done to help the Hawks? I can't stand people that refer to sports teams as "we." NO, you are NOT part of the team. The Blackhawks need to win and it would be an amazing achievement for the Blackhawks."

It's a common argument. And it makes sense. I am not, nor have I ever been, a member of the Chicago Bulls, Chicago Bears, Chicago Cubs, or the Northwestern University football program. My days of extreme sports fandom and emotional drainage are behind me; what I enjoy now is the amazing physicality of these athletic feats, the

PART XIX: VICTORY!

natural drama of a game or a season, and the camaraderie that these games breed in their followers.

So why did I violate my personal rule to "Never enter a mosh pit if you are under 5'10"? Why was I leaping like an idiot in the six corners, happily soaking in the sweat and champagne, shouting into camera phones, allowing myself to be hoisted airward by strangers?

I guess for the same reason that a rocking concert, New Year's, a wedding, or a street fest can get me dancing. It's just too much fun! Just too much fun.

I was probably also releasing some of the tension that bottled up after the Bears lost the Super Bowl and the Cubs fell in '08.

And after being in Indianapolis when the Sox wrapped the Series, it felt good to be on the streets of Chicago for the next bit of sports-crazed madness.

It felt good to celebrate. To sing and cheer in the streets, to clasp hands with strangers, to text EVERYBODY, to gather together, to smile and laugh. Is it silly to personally identify with a sports team? I guess so, but no sillier than to personally identify with a nation or religion.

You settle on your sports team, embrace them, soar with them, crash with them. Ride or die, as the fellow says.

There are problems in professional sports. Of course there are. Too much money, too much hero-worship, too great an emphasis on events not totally worth it.

But these are problems of society, not sports. In the week the Hawks won the Cup, 40 people were killed in a suicide bombing at a wedding in Afghanistan… a 14-year-old Mexican boy was murdered by U.S. border patrolman… the UN placed a fourth round of sanctions on Iran… three World Cup reporters were robbed in South Africa… we added three more casualties to World War II… and Tony Hayward became the new Brownie as oil drowns the Gulf Coast…

All of these stories and many others are More Important than a handsomely paid collection of talented athletes winning an athletic tournament to gain temporary possession of a 34 and ½ pound cup.

And yet if all the world's unnecessary external problems were solved, we'd still have sports teams and postseasons, and teams would still win championships and fans would still gravitate toward one team over another and Sammy V would still think it silly to refer to someone else's job as "we."

We don't live in that world. There *is* physical warfare and class warfare and poverty and bombing and famine and Crime and crime and nasty feelings among us. *The Leaders* are guilty of most of it, and we are guilty for following the leaders.

In all that sadness, all that tragedy, all that impotence, weakness, cowardice, anger, injustice, brutality, and fear, it's nice to celebrate something once in a while. Like a birthday or Purim or a random date on the calendar like "January 1st."

Or, even better, charged up athletic events that we're already enjoying. And since we watch some teams more than others, we will align ourselves with those teams. It's a sort of penance, I suppose, and more satisfying than annual celebrations. One could cheer every Cup champ every season and applaud their excellence and teamwork, but where would be the fun? The heart? The spirit? The soul?

Most seasons don't end in victory. Sometimes you spend entire years watching the 2001 Bulls or the 1998 Bears or the 1999 Cubs or the 2004 Blackhawks.

In fact, sometimes you spend entire stretches of years watching the '99-'04 Bulls, or the '95-2000 Bears, or the '90-'97 Cubs or the '98-'08 Hawks.

That's why we have multiple teams in the same big cities: the people need release. The '85 Bears, '90s Bulls, '05 White Sox, and 2010 Blackhawks sure take the sting off those 102 years and counting at Clark and Addison.

And sometimes, when the wait is too long and you're missing that good 'ol fashion communal celebratin' feelin, you drive to Indianapolis and watch the Butler-Michigan State game at a Butler bar with Butler fans. Or you head to Division Street or the six corners to mosh with Hawks fans after the Hawks have won the god damn Stanley Cup. Sometimes, you just have to celebrate. In this world of ours, it makes no sense not to.

So kick your head back, fly your Hawks flag, grab a bullhorn, and sing it with me:

Da, duh-da-da, duh-da-da, duh-da-da da-da-da…

Dec. 31, 2013, ReadJack.com
    Age 32

MY FAVORITE TEAM OF 2013: THE CHICAGONOW DIRT ANGELS

For most Chicagoans, the city's list of biggest sports stories in 2013 looks approximately like this:

1. Blackhawks win their second Stanley Cup in four seasons
2. Derrick Rose misses the 2012-13 season, returns for the 2013-14 season, plays 10 games, injures other knee and is lost for another season
3. The Bears offense becomes historically good, the defense becomes historically bad, and the team loses a playoff spot at home to Green Bay

4. Cubs suck, White Sox suck, Jabari Parker soars, Northwestern football implodes, etc.

For me, however, no list is complete without mention of my favorite Chicago team of 2013:

The ChicagoNow Dirt Angels.

If you haven't heard of the Dirt Angels, that's because they are a relatively little-known 16-inch softball team that won the 2013 Kup Cup awarded to the champion of the Kup League, a Chicago media softball league in its third year.

The reason the Dirt Angels were my favorite team of 2013 is simple: I play for them.

And after disappointing finishes in our 2011 season (an upset at the hands of our soon-to-be archrival WBEZ in the semifinals) and our 2012 season (another semifinal loss to BEZ), finally hoisting the Kup in 2013 was a singular highlight of my year.

Our team was rather vocal about our Dirt Angels pride, perhaps to the consternation of our bewildered friends & family, who often could not understand why we placed so much pride in winning a softball championship.

My question to them: Wouldn't you?

I love Chicago sports. Always have, and despite my noticeably waning interest these past few years, always will.

Additionally, I fully understand why sports fans use the term "we" in relation to their favorite teams. I am and have always been a we-er.

As a sportswriter, I've spoken with many professional athletes about whether or not they find it odd that a bunch of people they don't know refer to their team as "we." To a man, nearly all of them understand

PART XIX: VICTORY!

why we do it, and think it's exciting and meaningful to play for a team with such passionate backing.

Some players — like Jerry Azumah and Kelvin Hayden, for instance — even grew up watching the teams that they eventually played for. They then had the double pride of rooting for a team and rooting for themselves.

That's how I felt with the Dirt Angels.

The team mattered to me because I played on it and wanted to win. But it also mattered because I enjoyed rooting for my teammates in the same way I enjoy rooting for any athlete I watch.

I loved watching Curtis leg out a triple, watching Joe paint corners, watching Jeremy crash into fences on flyouts, watching Andy cover himself in dirt as he goes to his knees to field a ground ball.

And I loved learning about personalities. Fist-pumping Brandi, no-nonsense John, affable Steph, dogged Joe Grace.

I'm a fan of Dan's versatility and Jimmy's passion and Scott's humor and clutch hitting. I'm a fan of Keith's gloves and Lauren's tenacity and Rick's team-first spirit.

And in becoming a fan of our team, I then became a fan of other players on other teams. I'm a fan of WBEZ's Hendersonian five-tool leadoff man Adam Peindl and their Albert Belle-esque first baseman and captain Justin Kaufmann.

I'm a fan of Gapers' Andrew Huff and his compact power swing, of the Reader's Kevin Warwick and his long-limbed inside-out-swing, of CHIRP's Dave Cohn and his high-arching pitches and plaid shorts, of the toughness of players like WBEZ's Lauren Chooljian and the Journal's Joe Barrett and *RedEye's* Brian Moore.

When we won the Kup, my teammates and I celebrated long into the night. And I gotta be real with you: It was the most fun I ever had celebrating a sports championship.

Granted, it's not the same as celebrating with strangers in the middle of the Six Corners after the Hawks' victories in 2010 and this past June, or honking car horns for the 90s Bulls or my mom telling me about people on her quiet suburban block lighting fireworks after the White Sox won the World Series.

Feeling the city cheer in unison is a thrill and, in its way, a blessing.

But hot damn – what a feeling to win your own championship! To hoist a trophy, to hug and congratulate teammates, to reflect upon the work and sacrifice needed to win it all.

Sports fans love any opportunity to shout "We did it!"

This time, I got to be "we."

Dedicated with friendship, respect and fandom to our teammate Lauren Neal.

The 2013 ChicagoNow Dirt Angels, Aug. 28, 2013, at Athletic Field Park following our 15-13 Kup League win over Gapers Block.
Top row: Lauren Neal, Stephanie Esposito, Keith Hoehne, Joe Grace, Joe Campagna, Dan Raspatello, Curtis Shaw Flagg, Jimmy Greenfield, John Chatz. Bottom row: Brandi Wall, Andy Kissko, me with ball, Scott King, Jeremy Berrington, Rick Lobes

Nov. 3, 2016, ReadJack.com
   Age 34

WE ARE THE CHAMPIONS. THE CUBS ARE THE CHAMPIONS.

To know why a Cubs win can elicit fireworks on a Wednesday night and grandparents giggling and strangers hugging on the moonlit streets of Chicago, Illinois, you have to first know what broke those people. Mine was Game 7, 2003. I couldn't drink after that game. I was in college and I was too sad to drink.

I called my parents on my walk home that night and kept muttering variations of "I thought they'd do it. I really thought they'd do it." My mother comforted me. Then my father took the phone, heard me out, and said:

"Just wait till it gets bad."

That was the hammer blow. As much as I knew about the Cubs by 2003, the true depths of that burden were obviously still a mystery. With that game and those six words, the mystery was solved. Not only was Pops not fazed, he viewed this catastrophe as typical. Your run-of-the-mill calamity. A "Cubbie occurrence," as Lou Piniella once said.

That's the baggage that saddled me until we cleared the 5-outs-away mark of this year's NLCS.

That's the baggage I released into the atmosphere like a billion balloons when Rizzo's glove clutched the final World Series out.

When it happened, I whipped screaming around the room, then ran to the door, then ran back inside and got my keys, then ran back to the door, then trucked outside and screamed "YEAAHHHHH!" at nobody and everybody, then went back inside to breathe and drink water.

I would wager every Cubs fan experienced a wave like that. We were calling and texting everyone we knew. Think about when people get engaged and then call everybody, and everybody's cheering and congratulating the newly engaged couple. Winning the first Cubs World Series in 108 years felt like all Cubs fans getting engaged simultaneously and calling each other to celebrate.

This time around, I just kept muttering, "We did it. We did it. Holy crap we did it." I went back outside and ran circles in the intersection and high-fived other people running circles in the intersection. I high-fived people lighting sparklers from the sidewalk and sent air high-fives to people lighting sparklers from 2nd- and 3rd-floor windows. I high-fived a guy in an Urlacher jersey. I high-fived a guy in a "WE AIN'T AFRAID OF NO GOAT" t-shirt. I went back inside for more water. I spoke with my parents and celebrated with them. I went back outside. A guy my age was now standing on the corner, just shaking his head and staring at nothing. He was wearing a Cubs hat. We looked at each other.

"We did it," I said, which was the only concrete concept I could articulate.

But he looked right back at me and his eyes widened and he nodded and said, "Dude." And we walked right up to each other and hugged and patted each other on the back. And he smiled and looked at me and said, "We did it."

In the locker room after the game, an inebriated Bill Murray interviewed an inebriated Theo Epstein in one of the great post-championship locker room interviews that's ever lived. Incredibly, Murray practiced solid journalism: when Epstein sprayed him in the face with champagne instead of answering his question, Murray refocused and asked again.

"Are there any relatives or any folks you haven't talked to this week who you want to say," he said, smiling, "you're sorry you didn't get them tickets for the game?"

"No," Epstein said into the camera. "I just want to thank everyone who's ever put on a Cubs uniform and anyone who's ever rooted for the Cubs. It's been 108 years of love, support, and patience, waiting for a team like this, to make it happen on a night like this. You guys are all world champs tonight. And I couldn't be happier for you."

That's the "we" in "we did it." Those two groups. Everyone who played for the team and everyone who rooted for the team. Sports fans debate "we" all the time, but we do so in terms of fans calling the team "we" as if we played, and whether it's appropriate to claim ownership of and participation on a team for which we never were employed. I get that "we" complaint. I disagree, but I get it.

This is a different "we." This is about those who endured.

Bill Murray understood that.

"Thank you," Bill told Theo immediately after Epstein said Cubs fans and ex-Cubs players were world champs. "My mother thanks you. My father thanks you. My sisters thank you. My brothers thank you. I thank you."

"We did it," the guy outside in the Cubs hat said to me a second time, after we hugged. We stood for a few seconds, looking at the sparklers on the other side of the street.

"Who gave you the Cubs?" I asked him. "Back in the day."

"My dad," he said. "And my grandparents."

"Same," I said. "Here's to them."

******

At 1:56 a.m., I heard a voicemail from a call I'd missed three minutes earlier from a Sox fan friend.

"Congratu-fucking-lations!" Nick shouted. "Hopefully when you get this message tomorrow you'll just start smiling dog. Literally, that shit was — I'm happy for you. As a Sox fan, to see my childhood team win a World Series, that shit was cool as hell. And that was the greatest Game 7 in baseball I've ever seen in my life."

I called him back soon after and opened with a wimpering, "We did it. We did it." This was still all I could say, which slayed him and left us both grinning and laughing. And then we talked about something that doesn't get discussed enough:

The unknown.

Sports share qualities with cinema, theater, and concerts. Among the key differences, though, is that there are no assurances of your preferred result. In sports, you don't necessarily get happy endings. You don't necessarily get an entertaining product. You don't necessarily cheer good people. You sometimes go decades without cheering a championship.

I'm a pretty calm sports fan at this point in my life. I've seen just about every template of Crazy Game possible. Yet every so often a game still has the power to surprise me. Watching the Indians score three runs in the eighth to tie the game six to six was a shocker. In fact, it was the exact sort of sequence that in years past would have barbecued my heart.

Instead I remained weirdly confident. I continued to openly predict victory. I relayed positive messages to friends. I was concerned in the way you're concerned about John McClane making it to the end of the movie: you don't know HOW he will defeat Team Gruber. You just know he WILL.

After Rajai Davis's game-tying home run in the eighth, I just kept telling people to be calm. That this was our final test. The final challenge to our faith. I told them we would overcome. I told them we were still on track.

What I learned was that the curse was not the same as the championship. We broke the curse when we believed it could and would be broken, when we believed we were McClane and anyone in front of us was Hans Gruber. The curse would have remained broken and obsolete even if we lost Game 7. Only the ring was waiting.

******

The moment I knew the Cubs would one day win the World Series (something I'd not long earlier convinced myself, for my own sanity, would never happen) was earlier this year when I saw Jake Arrieta in a t-shirt reading "108 YEARS. WE'RE READY."

That attitude, founded on organizational excellence, is how we broke the curse. From Ricketts on down, this team simply did not believe in anything but their own talent.

Previous teams may have acknowledged that they accepted the responsibility of breaking the curse. They may have even said they wanted that responsibility.

These Cubs took it one step further: they themselves were not cursed and instead wanted to lift OUR curse.

We, the lifelong fans and the former players, WE were cursed. We carried the mark. We felt the burden. We could not do it ourselves. Only they could bring us there. And they could do so because it wasn't on them. It was as if their responsibility was to remove our burden. They could lead us out because they were not afflicted.

Previous teams were. In spring training 2013, I began an interview series with members of the 2003 Cubs. One of the players I talked to was Paul Bako, a catcher who caught Mark Prior in Game 6 of the NLCS. In the midst of what was probably a two-hour phone call, Bako asked me a simple question:

"Do you think they'll have a rally for us, or invite us back to the park?" Bako asked. "Have you heard anything?"

"I hate to say this bro, but I don't think it's happening," I told him. "People are still pretty well shaken up. Maybe when they win, you know?"

He knew.

He's part of "we." The "we" is every Cubs player who wanted so badly to win one for the "we" — and didn't. The "we" is every player who donned the Cubbie blues, learned the history, and said, "I'm going to be a part of this. I'm going to do it."

The "we" is every Cubs fan who watched for decades not knowing if this day would ever come. The "we" is the bond forged by being there together, rooting your ass off on a random Tuesday in August in the midst of a lost season. The "we" is saying "Yeah, but next year," and knowing you'll have to say it again next year.

After the game, relief pitcher C.J. Edwards told a reporter that we don't have to hear anymore about curses or goats or "that fan and the foul ball."

"Steve Bartman," the interviewer said as champagne sprayed in the locker room all around them.

"Yeah, Steve Bartman," Edwards said. "He should throw out the first pitch next year."

Edwards smiled. I did too. He knew about "we." He did not need to explicitly state it. We could tell he understood. He saw the full picture. He saw the "we" out there that can finally be at peace. He saw how he helped make it happen.

******

I've only truly been broken once as a fan. After Alfonso Soriano struck out to end the 2008 season, my heart crumbled. In 2009 I didn't watch baseball until June. In 2010 I didn't watch until August. In 2011 I declared that the Cubs "should just take a year off and think things through." In 2012 I ended a Cubs essay with a line that, at the time, represented to me the peak of positivity:

"The Cubs will never win a World Series, and I can live with that."

The truth was, I couldn't live with that.

I couldn't live with the feeling that it might never happen.

I was at my lowest.

This team brought me back.

In doing so, they gave peace to every Cubs fan who died without seeing the mountaintop. They gave peace to every Cubs fan who thought it might never happen. They gave peace to every Cubs fan who thought it WOULD happen, "but not in my life."

Rooting for a team is frequently illogical. We pour ourselves into them, even during horrific seasons. We stay dedicated during the '97 Bears and the 2000 Bulls and the '06 Hawks and the '89 Sox. This is where "we" is forged. Where our mettle is tested. Where friendships are made.

Kris Bryant matters because we remember the years where we trotted out a new 3rd baseman every opening day. Anthony Rizzo's joy matters because we saw his loneliness in a 101-loss season. Addison Russell and Javy Baez and Kyle Schwarber and Kyle Hendricks and Albert Almora and Jorge Soler and Willson Contreras and Carl Edwards matter because we watched a million-and-one can't-miss kids become answers to trivia questions for the beer-soaked die hards. Dexter Fowler and Ben Zobrist and Jake Arrieta and Jon Lester and Jason Heyward and David Ross and Miguel Montero matter because we saw a million-and-one "this is it!" acquisitions disintegrate by the middle of May. Joe Maddon matters because we were there for every new manager who said "We're gonna do it!" at his introductory press conference and left the team in disarray, wondering if he'd ever work again.

I went to sleep last night and dreamed of joy. I awoke this morning and it's still here.

I promise you this from the bottom of my heart:

It will always, always, still be here.

HER FIRST CHAMPIONSHIP

HER FIRST CHAMPIONSHIP

"Who do we like?" the girl asked her father.

"The women in the light blue shirts," the father answered.

"Oh. Who are they?"

"The Sky."

"Oh. Who is that?"

"That's Candace Parker."

"Can-daaaaaace!"

She sang this with a fledgling pride, as well as an awareness that these games were the only time she saw her father rowdy. Rare, but it happened, like when the man kicked the football and it bounced the wrong way. She learned the names and the colors. She learned the songs and the chants. At thirteen months, her first time staying out until near sundown was a Saturday night at Wrigley. She sat with her mother and father and their friends. When they clapped, she clapped. When they cheered, she cheered. When they groaned, she giggled.

They held her between them, their new, little family. She nodded in line with her parents' best friends and a park full of strangers, all the grownups singing: "For it's root, root, root for the CUHHHH-BEEEES!" She had a Cubs jersey and a Cubs hat, and later a winter Bears hat with googly monster eyes.

The Sky were her first winner. Her father explained the stakes. If they keep winning, they will get a trophy. They will be our heroes.

Finally, October 17, 2021. A Sunday afternoon. The Sky up 2-1 in the best-of-five, within striking distance of the championship. Candace and Copper and Quigs and Sloot, Stevens and Dolson and Diamond DeShields. She stayed with her father, watching the game's swings. Her blue team was actually wearing black jerseys that day, and nearly as soon as the fourth quarter started, they were down 11, staring Game 5 in the face.

But then, Quigley for 3! And again! And again. And a two. Eleven of the Sky's 13 points, the lead down to five. The girl looked at her father. He was on his toes, his head bobbing. A layup for Copper. A three to tie from Candace... YES! And then two Phoenix misses and a layup for Dolson!

She was moving a bit around the house, working on an art project, when her father beckoned.

"Sweetie! The Sky are winning!"

"Our team?"

"Our team."

She began to sing. "Our team is winning! Our team is winning!"

Under a minute now. Another Dolson bucket. The home crowd at Wintrust Arena pulsing. They can feel it. Over a year of a pandemic, quarantining, our country fraying, crumbling, imploding. In Chicago, no all-city championship since the 2015 Stanley Cup Finals. And now, this team. This shot. Her father felt every bit of energy from Wintrust blasting into the living room. Bit by bit, so did she.

Diana Taurasi to the line after a missed three. She makes, she makes, she misses. Sky rebound, up two. Timeout. The camera right into James Wade's huddle. Candace Parker's huddle. The Sky take the floor, ready to take the trophy. The girl is watching now, closely. Not looking at her father. Looking at them. Looking at Courtney Vandersloot taking a Dolson screen on the right, cutting into the lane to her left, throwing a strong ball fake to her left and spinning back to her right. Turns. Jumps. Shoots. Hiiiiiigh ball. Floating. Bucket!

"Yay!" the girl shouts.

Phoenix drives the other way, desperation now, under 24 seconds, a two-possession game. A jumper – missed! Sky rebound! Wintrust erupting! Her father leaping. She can tell that at long last, this one has gone the right way. Another foul sends Vandersloot to the line. "Candace Parker starting to burst into tears!" the announcer calls, as the girl and her father and the whole sports-loving world of Chicago celebrated the hometown kid come home.

10.5 seconds left. Sloot hits both. Sky up six. Phoenix passes midcourt. Brittney Griner launches a three with six seconds left. Iron. Rebound. Parker. Dribbles it out and then boom! Bursts past midcourt as the girl watches. Her father cheering, Wintrust cheering, the clock to zero as Parker races to hug her family. The Sky players exalting. The girl smiling and shouting as her father picks her up in the air and shouts, "We did it! We won the championship!"

He sits her down and pulls out his phone. She loves it when he makes videos with her. He flips on the camera, faces it on them and hits record.

"TT, what happened?"

She grins so big. "Our team won! Yayayayayay!"

"Say 'Go Sky!'"

"Go Sky!"

Her father presses stop and turns off the camera. She hugs him, and smiles, says, "I'm going back to drawing" and walks to the activity table.

"Daddy!" she shouts, markers in hand, not looking up.

"Yes?"

"Tell me when they're on again."

ABOUT THIS BOOK

The articles in this book span my career, and I have placed different levels of edits on them for this publication. The pieces written more recently are largely untouched from how they ran online, typos aside. I've done a bit more editing and tightening on the older pieces, the kind of editing I probably needed in my 20s.

In short, consider this book the director's cut with, say, 25-year-old Jack receiving the editing ability of 42-year-old Jack. As I always say, everyone needs an editor, and a lot of the older pieces were ones I wrote independently. Please send any corrections to 6ringsbook@ gmail.com.

The source material for my articles:

- *New Trier News,* New Trier High School
- *Indiana Daily Student,* Indiana University
- *Bear Down and Get Some Runs,* my unpublished book on the Chicago sports year of 2005
- *ReadJack.com* aka *readjack.wordpress.com*
- *The Sports Blog Network*
- *Cubs Den* of my beloved ChicagoNow, RIP
- *Blog a Bull*
- *Windy City Gridiron,* home of my Bears work since 2015
- *16 Wins a Ring*
- *Bulls Confidential*
- *A Shot on Ehlo* aka *readjack.substack.com,* the newsletter for my 90s Bulls book "6 Rings"

Shoutout to The Hoyne House: Rob, Justin, New Jack, Ken, Burdo and Nick Chuck.

The following articles were originally published on Windy City Gridiron of SB Nation, and are reprinted here with permission from Vox Media LLC:

- See? THAT is why we want Jay Cutler back (Oct. 1, 2015)
- Damn it feels good to be a Bears fan (Dec. 3, 2015)
- A salute to Devin Hester's magical rookie year (Aug. 11, 2016)
- We need to talk about the Lions (Sep. 30, 2016)
- 6 questions about #6 (Dec. 3, 2016)
- Thomas Jones: pain, power, pride (Jan. 10, 2017)
- The day the Bears beat the Saints in the NFC championship (Jan. 21, 2017)
- How I grew to hate, then pity, the Vikings (Oct. 4, 2017)
- Tyji Armstrong, a mother's love, and the meaning of sports (Sep. 27, 2018)
- Barry Sanders once beat the Bears so badly on Thanksgiving, I felt nothing but awe (Nov. 22, 2018)
- Let's beat the Pack and clinch this damn division (Dec. 14, 2018)
- The premature pain of the double doink (Jan. 10, 2019)
- WCG 30-Day Challenge: My most painful Bears memory — Super Bowl XLI (June 27, 2021)
- She's seen a century: Reflections on Bears football on Virginia McCaskey's 100th birthday (Jan. 5, 2023)
- Goodbye to a great friend: a love letter to Soldier Field (Apr. 4, 2023)

ABOUT THE AUTHOR

Jack M Silverstein is Chicago's sports historian. He is the Chicago Bears historian for Windy City Gridiron, and a regular guest historian around the city, including 670 The Score, WGN-TV, and ESPN 1000. His sportswriting has appeared in numerous publications, including Chicago Magazine, Chicago Reader, NBC Sports Chicago, RedEye Chicago, Chicago Sun-Times, Chicago Tribune, his beloved ChicagoNow and the Barber's Chair Network. He was a featured historian on the 2022 Audible - History Channel podcast series "American Football," hosted by Michael Strahan.

Sportswriters have cited his work and interviewed him for stories in *Chicago Sun-Times, Chicago Tribune, The Athletic,* NBC Sports Chicago, SB Nation, Bleacher Report, *Forbes, Fast Company,* and for radio and television segments for ESPN Radio (national), Sports Illustrated, Fox Sports 1, BBC Radio, Keep Hope Alive with Jesse Jackson, The Santita Jackson Show, 670 The Score, ESPN 1000, NBC Sports Chicago, CHGO and The Ringer. His 2019 Windy City Gridiron story, "Throwback: The truth about George Halas and the NFL's ban on black players," caused Chicago Bears chairman and George Halas grandson George McCaskey to release a video in which he, along with five players, admitted the role that the Chicago Bears had played in banning Black players from the NFL in the 1930s and 1940s.

Silverstein is the author of *Our President* and *How the GOAT Was Built: 6 Life Lessons From the 1996 Chicago Bulls.* His next book, *6 Rings: The Bulls, The City, and the Dynasty that Changed the Game,* will be published by Keylog Media. To follow his work on that book, subscribe to his newsletter at readjack.substack.com.

DEDICATIONS

While this book is dedicated to all we've lost, four in particular cut me deep:

- Jason Shaw
- Dr. Victoria Shlensky
- David Silverstein
- Gail Wenk

May your memories be a blessing.

ACKNOWLEDGEMENTS

To many people not here, I appreciate you!

This book is about family, and I would not be in any position to write it without the 1232 Club: my parents, Mickey and Charlie Silverstein, who made me a fan, and my brother Mike, my partner in video games and pickup games. Family is Nana and Papa. Family is Danny Lorber, with whom I watched the first Bears game I remember. Family is Aunt Gail Wenk, who gave me my game.

We love you Gail and always will.

Thank you to friends, from Orrington to the Backlot to NSC, with whom I found these teams and myself. Thank you Luke Larmee for Sox fandom, Sven Stafford for Big Ten obsessions, Josh Phipps, who always hustled, Eric Sirota, from Peter Pan to EYBA to NSC to nice rappers, and Ben Schwartz, my original The Bulls Are Bad partner.

Thank you Julian Lapkus, for pickup to Tecmo to the Teddy Bear Club, Josh Engel, for teaching me to dribble, Donny Burba, my Dyche Stadium compadre, Aaron Wightman, our Detroit brother, Mitch Hubbarth and Gabe Mengin, for the neighborhood, Jenny Brodsky and Carrie Stern, and the great Avi Kulla. Thank you Sam Vangelovski, Jonny Corwin and Jake Bressler. And my goodness, look at us now, Tony Lonien.

Thank you to the editors whose offer of an opportunity, guiding hand, or both, helped craft the pieces in this book: the late John Lucadamo, and Tim Dohrer, *New Trier News*; J.P. Benitez, *IDS*; Chris Reed, *The Sports Blog Network*; Jimmy Greenfield and Mike Raspatello, *ChicagoNow*; Jonathan Eig, *ChicagoSide*; the late, great John Arguello, *Cubs Den*; Sandy Mui, *16 Wins a Ring*; Michael Walton, *Bulls Confidential*; Lester Wiltfong Jr. and Dane Noble, *Windy City Gridiron*. Thank you Brian Moore and Chris Sosa, two great editors.

Thank you to several other *IDS* editors whose names I've lost to the sands of time, and to my IU writing instructors, Loyal Miles, Manny Martinez, Alyce Miller, and a great Chicago fan himself, Tony Ardizzone, who taught us to sweep, then mop, then wax. To my editors of *Chicago Daily Law Bulletin*, Pat Milhizer and Josh Weinhold, who had a massive influence on my skills as a reporter and non-fiction storyteller. A big thank you to *CDLB* copy editor extraordinaire John Corcoran, along with my fellow reporters Marc Karlinsky, Jamie Loo, Andy Maloney, Pat Manson, Roy Strom and the legend John Flynn Rooney, dearly missed.

Thank you to these other editors who gave me a shot to write sports: Jim Poyser of *NUVO Newsweekly*, my first professional paycheck; Rick Telander and Chris DeLuca, *Chicago Sun-Times*; Tran Ha, *RedEye*; Bettina Chang and Whet Moser, *Chicago Magazine*; Jake Malooley, *Chicago Reader*; Scott Lewis, Joe Lewis, Pierce Roberson, *The Barber's Chair Network*; Mike Allardyce, *NBC Sports Chicago*.

Thank you to the team at Gatekeeper Press, especially Rob Price and Jen Spampinato. Thank you for your book-related guidance and assistance: Mary Anne Gerstner, Dan Ferri, Mike Breen, Scott Lewis, Blake Schuster. Thank you to Jonathan Eig: a book business guide who has gone above and beyond.

Thank you to so many Chicago athletes, especially: Michael Jordan, Walter Payton, Jerome Walton, Shawon Dunston, Lee Gissendaner, Lenny Williams, Cliff Levingston, Craig Hodges, Tom Waddle #87, Dante Jones, Maurice Douglass, John Mangum, Myron Baker, Scottie Pippen, Jeremy Roenick, Chris Chelios, Ed Belfour, Steve Larmer, One Dog, Rock Raines, Frank Thomas, Ozzie Guillen, Bo Jackson, D'Wayne Bates, Darnell Autry, Pat Fitzgerald, Hudhaifa Ismaeli, Chris Martin, the late Matt Hartl, Sammy Sosa, Mark Grace, Bernie Nicholls, Raymont Harris, Glenallen Hill, Kerry Wood, Neifi Perez, Jud Buechler, Dennis Rodman, Marcus Robinson, Magglio Ordonez, Tim Anderson — and a team not represented in this book but one we loved: the 1999/2000 Blue Demons of Quentin Richardson, Lance Williams, Bobby Simmons, Rashon Burno and Paul McPherson.

ACKNOWLEDGEMENTS

RIP to Ernie Banks, Ron Santo, Norm Van Lier, Jerry Sloan, Stan Mikita, Gale Sayers, Dick Butkus and the GOAT, Walter Payton.

Thank you to the Bears who have helped me better understand this game I love: Thomas Jones, Jason McKie, Charles Tillman, Rashied Davis, Pat Mannelly, Olin Kreutz, Mike Brown and Desmond Clark. Rest in peace and thank you to Cedric Benson.

Thank you to the Sportswriters on TV: Bill Gleason, Bill Jauss, Lester Munson, Ben Bentley and my main man Rick.

For the sports talk, debates, radio days and brainstorms, thank you to Chris Cason, Bryan Crawford, Jarrett Payton, Shaun Davis, Ernie Scatton, JR Bang, Lawrence Atkins, Camron Smith, Kyle Means, Tony Gill, and Nick Walcott.

Thank you to the whole Windy City Gridiron team, as talented and supportive a group of writers I've ever worked with: Lester Wiltfong, Robert Zeglinski, Sam Householder, Jeff Berckes, Erik Duerrwaechter, Ken Mitchell, E.J. Snyder, and Kev, Schweick, Robert S., Jacob, Patti, Josh, Will, Bill, Aaron and Dane. And to Jeanna Thomas for your tireless assistance.

Thank you to Laurence Holmes for lifting while you climb and meaning so much to so many. I feel fortunate to be in your orbit! Thank you to the reporters who welcomed me on the Bears beat — along with Laurence: Tom Musick, Adam Jahns, Sean Jensen, Rafer Weigel, Jon Greenberg. Thank you to the late Vaughn McClure for showing me how the job is done.

Thank you to the Chicagoans building their own path. I have drawn inspiration from all of you. DeAnna McLeary Sherman and Na-Tae' Thompson, True Star Foundation; Maggie Schutz, Learnapalooza; Jenn Gibbons, Row 4 Row; Jahmal Cole, My Block My Hood My City; Scott, Joe and Pierce; Geno McIntosh and Terrence Tomlin, The Bigs.

Thank you to a community of Chicago sportswriters, hosts and others from whom I learn every day, including Evan Moore, Exavier Pope, Pete Nickeas, Demonze Spruiel and Ken Davis, Dave Watson and Chris Jordan of Bawl!, See Red Fred, Shakeia Taylor, Ricky O'Donnell, my main man Blake Schuster, Kia Smith, Michael Walton, Steven Hall, Subria Whitaker, ThoughtPoet, Greg Braggs and Matt Lindner. To Jon Leong, a friend when I needed one most; Larry Hawley, a welcoming presence in Chicago sports who gave so many of us our first TV experience; Cheryl Raye-Stout, a legend; Dyce, for believing in me; Javin Foreman, for the U; Santita Jackson and Rev. Jesse Jackson for welcoming me; Shoeless Dan Wallach and Graig "Once ONI, Always ONI" Kreindler. And to guys whose non-Chicago status is irrelevant: the Not in the Hall of Fame crew (thanks Kirk and Vinny!), and the men, the myths, the legends, Bigger Than the Game with Deremy Dove and Jose Ruiz. Check the archives! (Check 'em.)

Thank you to Scott & Craig at Herm's. Thank you to Steve and Lonnie at Mustard's. Rest in peace to Keith Woods and Jerry Starkman. You each made Evanston a better place to live.

Thank you to John and George Yedinak, who built the incomparable Aging Media Network and gave me a place in it. Thank you to all of my AMN colleagues, especially Liz Bandy, Tim Mullaney, Tim Regan, Alex Spanko, Bob Holly, Jeff Cheatham, Andrew Donlan and Shawnna Gallagher. And to John for giving me a bold challenge that I have kept near.

Thank you to my mentors, now friends, and two of the greatest with the pen: Rick Telander and Scoop Jackson. My life would not be the same without you two. They said, "Never meet your heroes." They were wrong.

Thank you to the two-time champion ChicagoNow Dirt Angels! Along with everyone listed in my stories published here, and with a second fist bump to Jimmy, the Disco and Chatz, thank you to Tim and Jess Falletti, Tracy and Kevin Stanciel, Greg, Tyler, Rowan, Mike Raspatello, Vernell, Meehan, Ryan, Kaufmann, Peindl, and Ernest, Huff and Reedy for your Kup League stewardship. Chicago WHEN?

ACKNOWLEDGEMENTS

Thank you to the Pirates: Rob Watson, Jason Garcia, Lamont Holden, Jason Shaw, Ashley Good, Marcus Rezak and a cast of thousands — Marv, Sabbs, Louchi, C3PO, Illi, Blink, Fundis, Longbons, Lebo, Xack and so many more. From the booths at Debonair to the SubT green room, from the Ambulance Factory to the Attic, from the blaze sessions to the rap sessions, the talks, the smoothies, the cyphers. The best of times! Here's to jet packs. We love you Brother Gatz.

Thank you to Ben! (I told you we'd use it one day.)

Thank you to family: Mary Anne, John, Jack and Lauren. Dad, thank you for the scoops!

For keeping those fires burning, thank you to Lou and Renee, to Leb and Sue, to Andy and Vickie, and to Dan. We love you, Vick.

Slide 'em, Denny's Den! This keylog is for A.J. Bayard, Mike Blumberg, Michael Cousins, Josh Frost, Brian Glickman, Ari Goldberg, Aaron Hamer, Adam Heldman, Alexander W. Heldman Esq. III, Dan Lichtenstein, Jeff McCormack, Robby Rutkoff, Jake Segil, Andy Shlensky, Marc Siegel, Mandy Sullivan, Mike Swiryn, Jon Weiss, and the Ladies of the Lake.

To the B&V crew, a true home team: Bailey, Gary, Katie, Shawn.

To TT and Wolfie, who learned quickly how to play catch, how to kick, how to climb, how to race, how to love watching hoops, how to love being teammates, and how to realize it's not you, it's the Bears.

And forever, hineys only.

— JMS, January 2024

www.ingramcontent.com/pod-product-compliance
Lightning Source LLC
Chambersburg PA
CBHW052129070526
44585CB00017B/1759